The Old West's First

POWER COUPLES

The Frémonts, the Custers,
and Their Epic Quest *for* Manifest Destiny

William Nester

Rio Nuevo Publishers®
P. O. Box 5250
Tucson, AZ 85703-0250
(520) 623-9558, www.rionuevo.com

Managing Editor: Aaron Downey
Book design: David Jenney Design
Maps: Jason Petho
Back cover art: *The Oregon Trail* by Albert Bierstadt,
courtesy of Butler Art Museum, Youngstown, OH.

Printed in the United States of America.

10   9   8   7   6   5   4   3   2   1

Library of Congress Cataloging-in-Publication Data has been applied for

Contents

"I may lose everything yet there is a strange, indescribable something in me that would enable me to shape my course through life, cheerful, if not contented."
— GEORGE CUSTER

"I would not lose my individuality, but would be, as a wife should be, part of her husband, a life within a life."
— LIBBIE CUSTER

"I am…ready to take hold of Fortune's wheel and pull it to the place I would have it 'stick.' We shall get there….You know how glad I am to join in the lifting process, and to make the dry bones of history take on flesh and color and life—and shew them how after all, the conditions of humanity are all made from the same elements, and that pain and sorrow and certainly death come to all."
— JESSIE FRÉMONT

"How fate pursues a man!"
— JOHN FRÉMONT

Introduction

A NEW PHENOMENON CAN BE PUZZLING. Sometimes people marvel at it a long time before someone gets around to inventing a word that labels it. Take the term "power couple."[1] It did not join the lexicon for more than a century and a half after John and Jessie Frémont (1813–1890, 1824–1902), and George and Libbie Custer (1839–1876, 1842–1933), pioneered the concept.[2] The wives not only lived through the triumphs, scandals, and disasters of their husbands, they did whatever they could to promote their careers and popular images. Indeed, the women proved to be far more adept than their men in wielding the behind-the-scenes political skills vital to advancing their interests. One tactic exceeded all others in effectiveness. Each couple insisted that they deserved special treatment because they were standard bearers of America's "Manifest Destiny," or the nation's "God-given right" to spread across the continent to the Pacific. As power couples, the Frémonts and Custers were novelties not just for America but also for the rest of humanity. Until then, the divide was strict between the public realm where men ruled and their wives might be glimpsed but not heard, and the private realm where spouses cared for each other and their families as more or less equal partners.

What made the Frémonts and Custers so famous? In popular culture, John Charles Frémont and George Armstrong Custer became all-American, if tarnished, heroes. Frémont was renowned as "the Pathfinder" who mapped swaths of the west in five expeditions and helped lead America's conquest of California from Mexico. His fame and anti-slavery views got him nominated as the newborn Republican Party's presidential candidate in 1856. During the Civil War, Custer was celebrated as the "boy general" who led cavalry charges that routed rebel forces in a score or so combats. He achieved immortality for the "last stand" of him and 262 of his men against overwhelming numbers of Indian warriors during the battle of the Little Bighorn, an epic defeat nearly as culturally powerful as America's Thermopylae, "the Alamo." Frémont and Custer epitomized the themes and lived their own adventurous versions of the Odyssey and the Iliad, respectively.

Then there were their wives. Although little known today, Jessie Frémont and Libbie Custer were nearly as famous as their husbands. Jessie and Libbie hero-worshipped their husbands, basked in their fame, and spurred their ambitions. Each happily served in the mundane but essential roles of being their husband's secretaries, editors, accountants, and, most vitally, political advisors. Both women were scrupulously honest and struggled to provide their husbands the moral ballast that they often lacked. For their part, Frémont and Custer fell passionately in love with girls from families with wealth, power, and status far above their own humble beginnings. Jessie's father was a United States senator and Libbie's father was a judge. At first both potential fathers-in-law adamantly opposed the marriage of their daughters to young, nearly penniless army officers, but eventually each recognized the flawed brilliance in his son-in-law.

The Frémonts and Custers were eye-catching couples. In their younger years, Jessie and Libbie were beautiful, vivacious women with sexy hourglass figures. Both loved entertaining and being the center of attention. Each knew how to appropriately wield her charms so that she inspired admiration rather than unwanted advances from men or jealousy from women. Frémont and Custer were handsome, dashing, courageous men. Their personalities did differ. Frémont was Byronic, reserved, solitary, and brooding. Custer was Apollonian, boisterous, and outgoing; off duty he loved swapping tales and pulling pranks. Frémont sought power and fame but felt uncomfortable publicly displaying it. As a deep introvert, he disliked appearing let alone speaking before others. Custer was the opposite. He reveled at being in the spotlight.

Power couples are not always happily married. Like every marriage, a power couple faces challenges of compatibility, separation, tragedy, and temptation that might unravel it. That was certainly true of the Frémonts and Custers. Although madly passionate romantic love initially brought John and Jessie, and George and Libbie together, like most couples they struggled to sustain that for years and decades. Duty and business kept Frémont and Custer away from their wives for long stretches and at times each pursued the siren calls of beguiling other women. Although most likely Jessie and Libbie kept sexually faithful to their husbands, each enjoyed serious flirtations with attractive men that might otherwise have blossomed into genuine love.

The Frémonts and Custers exemplified two other American concepts, "self-made man" and "celebrity." Statesman Henry Clay coined the term "self-made man" to explain his own astonishing rise from obscurity to fame, wealth, and power. That notion aptly applied to countless Americans going back to the nation's earliest years, with Benjamin Franklin perhaps the most dazzling exemplar. Frémont and Custer each had his own "rags-to-riches" tale; they transformed themselves from humble economic and social beginnings into national heroes with their relentless efforts to excel and their ability to attract powerful mentors. Custer attributed his brilliance at war and rapid rise in rank to a virtuous cycle of skills, audacity, energy, courage, luck, and indefatigable faith in himself. Of those elements, he reckoned his positive outlook was the key: "I may lose everything yet there is a strange, indescribable something in me that would enable me to shape my course through life, cheerful, if not contented."[3] Frémont could have echoed those words.

American celebrity is the logical extension of American invention and reinvention of oneself. Celebrity proved to be a double-edged sword for each man and his wife. Being famous attracts opportunities that, if cleverly exploited, bring more fame along with wealth and power. Alas, celebrity can be at once a spur and a trap for personifying a popular, often contrived, even false image. Celebrity can imprison rather than liberate one's self when one becomes a shallow persona rather than a deep character. In her biography of Jessie Frémont, Pamela Herr offers this insight: "With Jessie's help, John had created an image that at times…seemed to control his actions. Made a hero by the reports, he felt obliged to live up to the image. Eventually some would charge that for both him and Jessie, reputation—'this eternal vanity of how we must look'—had become more important than truth."[4] That paradox of celebrity power was just as true for George and Libbie Custer.

Character is destiny for everyone in varying ways and degrees. One's deepest values and drives determine what one does with one's life and, as importantly, how one does it. The finest attributes of Frémont and Custer were endurance and courage. Both men sought exhilarating, death-defying adventures. Frémont felt most alive and fulfilled when he was exploring, Custer when he was warring.

Proudly backed by their wives, Frémont and Custer committed epic acts in epic times that brought them enormous fame. Yet, eventually each self-destructed, Frémont with an accumulating series of disastrous decisions as an explorer, general, politician, and businessman; Custer spectacularly at the Little Bighorn. The reason was simple—serious character flaws made each man his own worst enemy. Had Shakespeare been born three centuries later, his plays on the Frémonts and Custers would likely rank with Macbeth, Lear, Hamlet, Richard III, or Julius Caesar. Hubris was the Achilles heel of both men. Becoming adored heroes at an early age warped each to believe that he could get away with anything.

Frémont and Custer shared lesser, nonfatal flaws. Narcissists believe they can only do right and never wrong. They adamantly refuse to compromise or acknowledge their failings. They grab the credit for any successes. When things go wrong they sternly point the finger of fault to someone or something else. And because narcissists are often highly charismatic, their disciples zealously celebrate and defend them, and condemn any critics. As such, narcissists are arrested emotionally in their early childhoods. They behave like spoiled, deluded, self-centered children. Ample doses of narcissism infected the characters of Frémont and Custer.

An authoritarian personality is a critical component of being a military officer as long as the leadership is firm but adaptive. Bad leaders are martinets, refuse to admit mistakes, and persist on the same course despite mounting evidence that it will lead them and their men to disaster. Frémont and Custer seesawed between being inspiring leaders and loathed tyrants. At times each man bristled at being commanded by others, Frémont often, Custer less so. Each was court-martialed and found guilty on serious charges of disobeying orders, dereliction of duty, and, for Frémont, even mutiny.

Introverts and extroverts tend to handle criticism differently. Frémont weathered hostile fire with tight-lipped denials as he burrowed turtle-like deeper into his psychological shell. On exploration expeditions he withdrew to his Indian teepee and firmly closed the flaps. During his four months as commander of the Department of the West, he surrounded his headquarters with ever more guards who turned away anyone, including envoys from President Lincoln, with any contrary views. In contrast, Custer squared off with his accusers and hurled the same and worse charges against them.

Neither Frémont nor Custer was a model of probity. Each sought fortune as well as fame. Neither was good with money. Custer was addicted to gambling and quickly lost whatever money he somehow pocketed. Yet, to his credit, he appears to have sidestepped temptations for shady dealing to recoup his losses or gain more winnings. Frémont's gambling was on a vastly greater scale than Custer's and was far more ethically questionable. He embarked on a series of investments in mines and railroads that at first reaped incredible riches but sooner or later bankrupted him and countless other investors. And, unlike Custer, Frémont's name was repeatedly sullied with charges of claim jumping, fraud, and corruption.

Jessie and Libbie mostly lived vicariously through their husband's adventures, achievements, and fame, yet each had her own share of life and death experiences. They were courageous women who followed their husbands to war, the frontier, and even into the wilderness where they endured extremes of bone-numbing cold, stifling heat, deluges, and clouds of mosquitoes; resided in drafty tents or cabins; and at times feared being victims of violence.

What they enjoyed most was advising their husbands on politics and lobbying powerful men on their husbands' behalves. Indeed, each wife was the better half of her power couple as she displayed far more sophisticated political skills than her husband. When Frémont and Custer jeopardized their careers with blunders and hubris, their wives helped rehabilitate them by buttonholing key players behind the political scenes. Yet both women became increasingly ambitious and prideful. Having Thomas Benton for a father and John Charles Frémont for a husband swelled Jessie's pride and ego. Being married to dashing, fearless George Armstrong Custer boosted Libbie's ego nearly as much.

Politically, Jessie exceeded Libbie in one extraordinary way. Not only did Jessie's husband campaign to be president but she also literally stepped beside him in the political spotlight. Jessie was the first woman to appear with her husband at presidential campaign rallies where she received louder cheers than he did. "Frémont and Our Jessie" became his most powerful campaign slogan. That was the first and last time in American political history that a potential first lady got equal billing with a potential president.

Yet Jessie and Libbie were not feminists in the nineteenth century, let alone contemporary, meaning of that notion. Neither embraced the suffrage movement that began at Seneca Falls, New York in 1848, when Elizabeth Cady Stanton and Lucretia Mott organized a convention that called for equal legal and political rights. If anything, Jessie and Libbie reinforced the traditional ways that women participated in politics. A woman's political place was confined to speaking gently, reasonably, and firmly with her husband and other influential men behind closed doors. They did so more from wariness rather than conviction. Both women tried publicly to express their minds as freely as was acceptable in that era. Jessie was far more outspoken and endured blistering criticism the few times she took strong stands on controversial issues. She resented being the victim of a double standard: "Strange, isn't it, that when a man expresses a conviction fearlessly, he is reported as having made a trenchant and forceful statement, but when a woman speaks thus earnestly, she is reported as a lady who has lost her tongue."[5]

Jessie and Libbie benefited early in life by being adored by their fathers, who were powerful, successful, and moral men. That gave them the confidence and skills to handle their often volatile spouses. Nonetheless, each woman paid a heavy emotional cost for the fame, power, and status that came with her marriage. Both had to endure prolonged periods when their husbands were far away in the most dangerous of circumstances. Libbie suffered enough with her husband often gone for months at a time fighting rebels or Indians. But Jessie suffered far more as her husband was absent five of their first eight years of marriage and thereafter periodically for months. Not just the physical separation but also the possibility that they would never again see their husbands emotionally calloused Jessie and Libbie. Neither could have endured without developing a deeply fatalistic attitude toward marriage and life.

If asked to compare their lives, both women would have said the biggest gulf between them was children. Jessie had one girl and two boys who survived to adulthood; Libbie was childless. Without children as an object and source of affection, Libbie had to endure Custer's absences alone. Jessie had an outlet for her emotions with her children, but they too suffered from their father's absence. That was bad enough, but Frémont was an aloof father even when he was home. Jessie confided to her best friend that her husband lacked a "parental instinct" and when he was home was "only a guest—dearly & honored but not counted on for worse as well as better."[6]

Without children, Libbie's self-worth was doubly dependent on her husband's successful career. She strove to develop and retain her own self in a dynamic and inseparable balance with her role as wife. She explained that challenge in a letter to Custer: "I cannot love as I do without my life blending with yours. I would not lose my individuality, but would be, as a wife should be, part of her husband, a life within a life. I never was an admirer of a submissive wife, but I wish to look to my husband as a superior in judgment and experience and to be guided by him in all things."[7]

The Frémonts and Custers were powerhouses as literary as well as political couples. All four authored books and articles. Overall, the ladies were better writers. Jessie and Libbie edited and even co-wrote many of their husbands' reports. The Frémonts wrote official versions of his first and second expeditions in a novelistic style that made them bestsellers that were favorably compared to the works of James Fenimore Cooper and Washington Irving.[8] Unfortunately, Frémont's *Memoir of My Life* is a ponderous tome that dully details his adventures through California's conquest.[9] In contrast, Custer's *My Life on the Plains* is an excellent page-turner about his role in the Indian campaigns in the late 1860s, filled with vivid characters, adventures, and humor that recalls Mark Twain.[10] Libbie's three books—*Boots and Saddles, Tenting on the Plains*, and *Following the Guidon*—are wonderful if idealistic accounts of what it was like being married to a brilliant cavalry commander in often-dismal conditions.[11] Four of Jessie's five published books,

The Story of the Guard, A Year of American Travel, Souvenirs of My Time, and *Far West Sketches* colorfully depict some of her life's highlights, while her *The Will and the Way Stories* are sweet tales for children.[12]

Yet something vital was missing in all these writings. Although each author was bright, articulate, animated, and literate, one searches their countless words mostly in vain for deep insights into himself or herself or others. That is hardly surprising. Before Sigmund Freud, even questioning people like Henry David Thoreau and Ralph Waldo Emerson lacked the analytical tools to delve far beneath surfaces.

Literally and figuratively the Frémonts and Custers were flag-bearers for another all-American idea. "Manifest Destiny" is the belief that Americans are a chosen people with a God-given right and duty to multiply themselves and subdue and exploit the continent westward from the Atlantic to the Pacific Ocean, and to realms beyond.[13] Although the term was most likely not coined until 1845 in an editorial by John O'Sullivan in his newspaper *The Morning Sun*, Americans had believed and acted on the notion for 238 years since the first settlers stepped ashore at Jamestown in 1607. The essence of "Manifest Destiny" was first best articulated by John Winthrop with his "City on a Hill" sermon of 1630, followed much later by Thomas Jefferson's espousal of an "Empire of Liberty" in 1780.

The Frémonts and Custers simultaneously personified being power couples and championing Manifest Destiny. Indeed, there was a dynamic between the phenomena with each bolstering the other. That was doubly appealing for most nineteenth-century Americans, but ever since then the Manifest Destiny half of that equation has become ever more controversial. Once extolled as symbolizing America's greatest traits of courage, decisiveness, and ingenuity, with time John Frémont, George Custer, and, by extension their "enabling wives," have increasingly been reviled for representing imperialism, racism, and genocide.[14]

Their lives are long past due for a critical reappraisal. As usual, the truth shifts mostly far from the extremes. *The Old West's First Power Couples* neither celebrates nor demonizes John and Jessie Frémont, and George and Libbie Custer. Instead each is explored as an extraordinary, gifted, flawed, unique individual who was half of a unique couple that made history.

Jessie Frémont

PART ONE

The Frémonts

John Frémont

CHAPTER I

Ungovernable Passions

"I saw visions.... I would be traveling over a part of the world which still remained the New—the opening up of unknown lands; the making of unknown countries known; and the study without books— the learning at first hand from nature herself."
— JOHN FRÉMONT

"I came into my father's life like a breath of his own compelling nature, strong, resolute, but open to all tender and gracious influences and above all, loving him."
— JESSIE FRÉMONT

THE MAN WHO BECAME John Charles Frémont was born a bastard in Savannah, Georgia, on January 21, 1813.[15] Although modern readers might enjoy the romance behind his origins, that stigma scarred and haunted him all his life. When his mother, Anne Whiting, was seventeen years old, she was forced to marry Major John Pryor, a wealthy Richmond, Virginia, man forty-five years her senior. For fourteen years she endured a loveless and childless marriage until 1810, when Pryor rented a cottage to a music teacher named Jean Charles Fremon, who claimed to be a royalist exile from the French Revolution but was most likely a French Canadian. Anne and Jean soon became lovers. In July 1811, after Pryor found out and confronted them, they fled to Savannah. Jean and Anne had restless souls, a trait they passed to their first son, John Charles. They journeyed across the southern states, making do with fees from Fremon's French lessons and dancing lessons, with their longest sojourns in Savannah, Nashville, Norfolk, and the Dinwiddie Court House, Virginia. Along the way they had two more children, Frank and Elizabeth. After Fremon died in 1818, Anne and her children settled in Charleston, South Carolina, where she supported them by renting rooms to boarders.

Throughout his life, John Frémont sought fame and fortune to bury his childhood's illegitimacy and poverty. His first notable act of liberation was to add a "t"

II

and accent to his last name, thus distancing himself from his father, who he never mentioned in any of his subsequent writings. Naturally, he was drawn to prominent father figures who excelled in business, politics, science, or war. They in turn were happy to mentor the reserved but bright, brave, dutiful, and handsome young man as a surrogate son.

Frémont's first big break came when he was fourteen years old. John Mitchell, a lawyer he clerked for, saw enough promise in him to pay for his classes at Dr. John Robertson's school for two years. Robertson in turn got him enrolled at Charleston College in May 1829. Pressured by his mother, Frémont studied to be an Episcopal minister. Robertson was skeptical that Frémont had chosen the most appropriate future career, later recalling: "When I contemplated his bold, fearless disposition, his powerful inventive genius, his admiration of warlike exploits, and his love of heroic and adventurous deeds, I did not think it likely he would be a minister of the Gospel."[16]

Academically, Frémont did best at mathematics and French. But his heart was elsewhere. He neglected his studies after falling in love with a girl named Cecilia and spending as much possible time with her. He was expelled in February 1831 for "habitual irregularity and incorrigible negligence."[17] That filled him with an exhilarating sense of liberation rather than shame: "I smiled to myself when I listened to words about the disappointment of friends—and the broken career. I was living in a charmed atmosphere and their edict only gave me complete freedom."[18]

Once again, a father figure rescued Frémont from obscurity. Joel Poinsett had recently returned from serving as America's ambassador to Mexico and was now a trustee for Charleston College and a member of St. Philip's Episcopal Church, which Anne and her children attended. Impressed by Frémont's math skills, he secured him a post as a tutor on the naval sloop *Natchez* that, in May 1833, was bound for South America's waters to "show the flag" and chart the seas for the next two and a half years. After Frémont returned, Poinsett got him a job as an assistant engineer with two back-to-back surveys led by Captain William Williams, first for a possible railroad route from Charleston to Cincinnati, then of the Cherokee reservation in the southern Appalachian Mountains that together lasted from spring 1837 into early 1838. One participant recalled: "I am mystified with...the character of my companion Frémont. The most taciturn, modest man I ever met... not readily drawn into conversation, looking at times as if he were resolving some difficult problem in Euclid." Yet Frémont displayed "indomitable perseverance" with his "determination to surmount every obstacle" and so was "loved, respected, and admired by us all."[19]

Frémont accompanied Williams to Washington City in February 1838. While Williams submitted his expedition reports, Frémont applied for a second lieutenant's commission with a new military force to be formed later that year, the U.S. Army Corps of Topographical Engineers. Living in Washington, however, depressed him: "It was a lonesome place for a young man knowing but one person in the city, and there was no such attractive spot as the Battery by the sea at Charleston, where a stranger might go and feel the freedom of both eye and thought."[20]

Once again Frémont was in luck. Poinsett was now President Martin Van Buren's secretary of war. Poinsett approved Frémont's application and Van Buren issued him his commission on July 7, 1838, three days after the Corps of Topographical Engineers was inaugurated with Colonel John Abert its first commander. Poinsett then appointed Frémont the assistant to Joseph Nicollet, a brilliant French-born cartographer who had migrated to America six years earlier to conduct surveys of the Mississippi River from its headwaters to the Gulf of Mexico. Nicollet was just about to embark on an expedition to map the Minnesota River from its mouth on the Mississippi westward to its source on the Great Plains.[21] Frémont would earn good money for his efforts, four dollars a day and ten cents a mile. Most importantly, he would forge a deep bond with the fifty-two-year-old Nicollet. Anticipating that mission filled Frémont with near ecstasy. Decades later he recalled, "I was low in my mind and lonesome until I learned, with great relief, that I was to go upon a distant survey into the West."[22]

Nicollet and Frémont journeyed to St. Louis where they rounded up recruits and supplies, and met Indian Superintendent William Clark and Captain Robert E. Lee of the topographical engineers. Among the sixteen men in the party was Charles Geyer, a German-born botanist. On May 18, they boarded a steamboat bound for Fort Snelling far up the Mississippi River at the Minnesota River mouth. They bought supplies from Henry Sibling and hired Henry Laframboise as a guide from the American Fur Company trading post at St. Peter's across the river. The survey work began on June 9, when they headed up the Minnesota River valley, with the party split between men riding horses or paddling dugout canoes. The Dakota Sioux lived in a series of villages up that valley and welcomed the expedition. For Frémont, the journey's highlight was being among the first white men to visit the quarry where for centuries Indians had acquired the red stone that they carved into beautiful pipes. By mid-July the explorers reached Coteau des Prairies, a broad plateau that rose eight hundred feet above the plain and was the source for the Minnesota, Red, and Big Sioux Rivers. There they turned back, acquired more supplies at Fort Snelling, again ascended the Minnesota valley, then headed south over the divide to the Des Moines River headwaters and down to the Mississippi River, finally reaching St. Louis by mid-January 1838. Nicollet remained there while Frémont returned to Washington, where he submitted the expedition's documents to Colonel Abert and awaited orders.

After studying the documents, Abert summoned Frémont to chastise him for his sloppy accounting and urge him to avoid "similar difficulties hereafter, & impress upon your mind the necessity of bills in detail and receipts."[23] Among the paradoxes of Frémont's life is how someone so skilled at mathematics was so bad at bookkeeping throughout his professional career. Was it merely laziness, outright deceit to cover up unwarranted expenses and possibly outright thefts, or some pathological combination? Believing that the young lieutenant would mend his ways, Abert assigned Frémont to assist Nicollet on another expedition.

St. Louis was again where Nicollet and Frémont organized the expedition, which departed on April 4, 1839. This time the explorers journeyed by steamboat up the Missouri River to Fort Pierre, which they reached two months later. During their three-week sojourn at Fort Pierre, Frémont was mighty tempted to acquire a wife, "a pretty girl of about eighteen, handsomely dressed." Chief Sleepy Eyes of the nearby Sisseton Sioux village brought his daughter to camp and tried to sell her to Nicollet, who demurred, explaining that his existing wife might object. Sleepy Eyes then turned to Frémont, who expressed his great appreciation but "was going far away and not coming back and did not like to take the girl away from her people." He soothed any disappointment between the father and daughter by giving the girl "a package of scarlet and blue cloth, beads, a mirror, and other trifles."[24] This was Frémont's first recorded foray into Indian diplomacy. The expedition headed north to Devil's Lake and the Red River, then angled southeast to Coteau des Prairies to reach the westernmost point of their previous expedition, thus completing their survey of portions of lands between the Missouri and Mississippi Rivers. At one point along that long trek, Frémont got lost during a buffalo hunt and was only able to find the expedition after two lonely and disconcerting days and nights on the immense plains: "To be lost on the prairie in an Indian country is a serious accident, involving many chances and no one was disposed to treat it lightly."[25] They descended the Minnesota River valley to Fort Snelling, from there down to St. Louis, and finally east to Washington, which they reached in December 1839. By now Frémont was both an expert topographer and wilderness survivalist.

Nicollet and Frémont moved into quarters with Ferdinand Hassler, America's leading astronomer and the United States Coast and Geodetic Survey's director. There they began drafting the maps and writing the expedition's report. Frémont was excited to accompany Nicollet to the White House for a meeting with President Van Buren and War Secretary Poinsett. One day as they labored at their residence, the most prominent senator who advocated America's westward expansion paid them a visit to observe their progress and grill them about their experiences. Frémont later pronounced this meeting the most "pregnant of results and decisive of my life."[26]

Thomas Hart Benton was born on a plantation near Hillsborough, North Carolina, in 1782.[27] He was eight years old when tuberculosis killed his father—a land speculator, merchant, and lawyer—leaving his mother and her eight children exorbitant debts and questionable land claims. Fortunately, Ann, his mother, could maintain her family with stipends from her own wealthy parents and other relatives. Nonetheless, as the third child and first son, Thomas had to grow up quickly by earning money working various jobs. Ann nurtured his intelligence with tutors, and he eventually earned admission to the University of North Carolina at Chapel Hill when he was sixteen. He was a college student for only three months when he was expelled for stealing money from his roommates. He fled to Tennessee hoping to lose his disgrace behind him and find a profession. He settled on one of his father's land claims twenty-five miles south of Nashville and enticed the rest of his family to join him. He studied law and eventually became one of Andrew Jackson's protégées.

Then, once again, Benton squandered his latest opportunity for advancement. When Jackson mocked his younger brother, Jessie, for acting cowardly in a duel, honor demanded that both Jessie and Thomas seek vengeance. The result was a wild whip, gun, knife, and fist fight between the brothers and Jackson and his cronies at Clayton Talbot's Tavern in Nashville on September 14, 1813. Jessie fired a bullet that plowed into Jackson's shoulder, and nearly all the other participants received lacerations and bruises. In one of history's most startling coincidences, another shot that Thomas Benton fired came within inches of killing his future son-in-law, John Frémont, who was then a toddler with his parents in a nearby tavern room.

Tensions simmered between the Bentons and the Jackson factions for two more years until 1815, when Thomas headed to St. Louis to search for career opportunities that were denied him in Nashville. He found them, and developed related legal and political careers in St. Louis. Later, while visiting a friend in Richmond, Virginia, he was smitten with twenty-year-old Elizabeth McDowell, from a politically prominent piedmont family with a plantation at Cherry Grove. She rebuffed his repeated marriage proposals over the next seven years, finally succumbing in March 1821 when she was twenty-seven and he was forty and had recently been elected a United States senator. Elizabeth was bright but reclusive and sickly. Thereafter, their world revolved among Washington, Cherry Grove, and St. Louis.

Benton was a leading voice for America's expansion across the continent, inspired by Thomas Jefferson's notion of "an empire of liberty." He chaired the Senate Committee on Territories, whose duties included approving any exploration expeditions. He became Frémont's latest mentor, seeing in him a vigorous, courageous, talented, and ambitious young man who would explore the west for him. Frémont was ecstatic: "The thought of penetrating into the recesses of that wilderness region filled me with enthusiasm—I saw visions.... I would be traveling over a part of the world which still remained the New—the opening up of unknown lands; the making of unknown countries known; and the study without books— the learning at first hand from nature herself."[28] But before he could actually embark on those explorations, a complication arose. The then twenty-seven-year-old Frémont met and fell madly in love with Benton's fifteen-year-old daughter.

Jessie Ann Benton was the senator's second child and daughter.[29] Like countless fathers, with his first child a daughter, Benton wanted his next to be a son. His exuberance dampened when he learned that his wife had given birth to another girl on May 31, 1824. Benton insisted that they call her Jessie, a female version of Jesse, his father's name. She later reflected that "I came into my father's life like a breath of his own compelling nature, strong, resolute, but open to all tender and gracious influences and above all, loving him."[30] She grew up amply to fulfill her father's hopes in her. He reveled in her acute mind, free spirit, and sweet nature. She recalled that he "made me a companion and a friend from the time almost that I could begin to understand. We were a succession of girls at first with the boys coming last, and my father gave me early the place a son would have had."[31] The different characters of Benton's first two daughters was revealed by how they reacted to his anger when they chalked over a written speech he was going to deliver later that day before the Senate. When he demanded who ruined his speech, Elizabeth began sobbing but Jessie declared, "A little girl who cries 'Hurrah for Jackson!'" That instantly melted Benton's wrath into affection and he embraced both girls, but Jessie much more.[32]

Eventually, the Bentons had four daughters and two sons, but Jessie remained her father's favorite. From her early teenage years, she became his most trusted confidante, muse, hostess, and secretary. In doing so she displaced her reclusive mother, who never lived up to those roles, much to Benton's chagrin. In a time innocent of the discoveries of Sigmund Freud, Benton enticed a natural "Electra complex" in Jessie.

As for education, Benton provided tutors for Jessie and her siblings. Yet, here, too, he favored Jessie. He supplemented those lessons by spending hours with her in his library where he would pull books from the shelves and joyfully explain fascinating ideas and information that lay within. More critically, he exposed her to Washington's institutions of power. He would install her for an afternoon at the Library of Congress where the librarians kept an eye on her as she perused picture books. He had a servant accompany her to the Senate gallery where she could marvel as her father gave impassioned speeches that often lasted hours. In corridors, on the street, and in her family's parlor, he introduced her to that era's leading and minor politicians alike. He even proudly took her on visits to the White House.

Jessie later recalled President Andrew Jackson cuddling her and stroking her hair as he would a cat while he talked politics with her father. Unfortunately, when he got agitated, he would forget what he was doing and accidently pull her hair. Among other vital political lessons that would guide her life, she taught herself to endure the agony with stoic indifference: "Among my earliest memories of the White House is the impression that I was to keep still and not fidget, or show pain, even if General Jackson twisted his fingers a little too tightly in my curls; he liked my father to bring me when they had their talks, and would keep me by him, his hand on my head—forgetting me of course in the interest of discussion—so that sometimes his long, bony fingers took an unconscious grip that would make me look at my father but give no other sign."[33]

An array of controversial issues riled Jackson and other concerned Americans as two political parties and three political philosophies jostled for power.[34] The Whig Party emerged in 1832 as the belated successor to the Federalist Party, which had declined rapidly toward extinction after the 1800 election that brought Thomas Jefferson to the White House and the Democratic Party overwhelming majorities in both houses of Congress. Whigs championed the program of Alexander Hamilton, the Federalist Party's founder. That included a muscular, problem-solving national government that nurtured American entrepreneurship, inventions, and industries with infrastructure, education, and tariffs, and maintained a military strong enough to deter or defeat attacks by Indians within or the neighboring British and Spanish empires. The goal was to advance American wealth and power through a partnership between the public and private sectors that otherwise would have been delayed for decades if free markets prevailed with their myopic get-rich-quick psychoses. But few Americans were that farsighted. Jeffersonians demanded a bare-bones federal government, the bulk of political power in the state capitals, and markets left to themselves no matter what the outcome. During the 1820s, Jacksonians emerged to demand an ever more powerful army and navy while theoretically embracing the Jeffersonian notion of minimal national government; in practice, they carried federal and state corruption and cronyism to unprecedented heights.

No issue festered worse than slavery's future in America. In 1787, when the founders drafted the constitution, slavery existed in every state, although the portion of slaves to the total population varied considerably, with 2 percent in New

England, 15 percent in the mid-Atlantic states, and 40 percent in the southern states. One by one the northern states abolished slavery. As the number of free states swelled, "slavocrats" feared that one day abolitionists would dominate Congress and pass a law outlawing slavery. By 1820 most members of the House of Representatives came from free states, while the Senate was split evenly between slave and free states. A crisis erupted the previous year when Representative James Tallmadge of New York amended Missouri's statehood application to restrict slavery there. A deadlock arose over Missouri's application. Then in 1820, when Maine applied for statehood as a free state, the slave states blocked its admission to prevent the Senate's balance of power from tipping against them. Representative Henry Clay forged a compromise with two critical elements. Missouri and Maine were simultaneously admitted as slave and free states. A line was drawn westward from Missouri's southern border; thereafter any territories that became states north of that line would be free and those below would be slave states. That defused animosities between free and slave states for now, but they would steadily rise in the decades ahead.[35]

Jessie intimately understood slavery. The cook, maid, butler, and coachman were slaves in her own home. She and her family usually spent months each summer at Cherry Grove plantation, whose prosperity depended on the exploitation of forty or so field and house slaves. Despite her love for her grandparents, uncles, aunts, and cousins, she was always relieved to return to Washington. Her mother's family members upheld a strict propriety in all matters. They scolded and mocked her for reading too much and dressing too casually. Jessie increasingly identified more with the plight of the slaves than her own repressive relatives. She also observed slavery during visits to the Benton home in St. Louis and once during a steamboat trip down the Mississippi River to New Orleans where her father had business. Jessie's innate revulsion at slavery was bolstered by her parents' attitudes. Her mother loathed slavery despite or because of being its beneficiary; she emancipated the slaves she inherited from her father in 1855. Benton also despised slavery even as he refused to emancipate his own house slaves.

Meanwhile, Jessie experienced a trauma when, at age fourteen, Benton enrolled her in Miss English's Female Seminary, a boarding and finishing school in nearby Georgetown. She learned a lot there with its twenty-five instructors for forty-five students. Yet being exiled from her father and his fascinating world enraged and saddened her, and she vented her feelings by challenging her teachers. She received this evaluation: "Miss Jessie, although extremely intelligent, lacks the docility of a model student. Moreover, she has the objectionable manner of seeming to take our orders and assignments under consideration, to be accepted or disregarded by some standard of her own."[36]

Although Jessie remained defiantly passive-aggressive, she immersed herself in her studies and a friendship with Harriet Williams, an older, strikingly beautiful girl as worldly as herself. Another trauma engulfed Jessie when Harriet married Russian ambassador Alexander de Bodisco, a short, rotund, ugly but very rich man more than four decades her elder. Meanwhile, President Van Buren was courting Jessie, but she had no interest in being a First Lady in a loveless marriage with a grandfather figure forty-two years older than her. To protest the seeming loss of her friend and to ward off a similar fate, Jessie cut her hair and dressed in her brother's clothes. Her defiant appearance and attitude angered and saddened her father. Her determination to avoid an arranged marriage like Harriet made her eager to fall in love. She soon found her White Knight.

Thomas Benton asked John Frémont to escort his oldest daughter, Eliza, to attend a music recital by Jessie and the other girls at the school. Frémont was smitten at his first glimpse of Jessie: "She was then just in the bloom of her girlish beauty, and perfect health effervesced in bright talk.... Naturally I was attracted.... Months passed before...I saw her again, at her father's house.... She had inherited from her father his grasp of mind, comprehending with a tenacious memory, but with a quickness of perception and instant realization...and with these...a generous pity for human suffering.... There was a rare union of intelligence to feel the injury of events...and...a sweet, and happy, and forbearing temper which has remained proof against the wearing of time. Insensibly...in these meetings, there came a glow in my heart which changed the current and color of my daily life and gave beauty to common things. And so it came that there was no room for reason."[37]

A president's funeral, of all things, let Frémont carry their mutual attraction to a higher level. William Henry Harrison, the Whig Party candidate, beat Van Buren's attempt to win a second term in the 1840 election. Tragically, Harrison died on April 4, 1841, from enteric fever aggravated by pneumonia following his hour-long inauguration speech in bone-chilling rain a month earlier. Learning that the funeral procession would pass by his boardinghouse, Frémont invited the Benton family to watch from his balcony. Thomas and Elizabeth Benton had already accepted another viewing invitation but let Jessie attend, chaperoned by her Grandmother McDowell. Rather incongruously for a funeral march for a dead president, Frémont filled his rooms with roses and geraniums. While the grandmother was absorbed watching the parade, he beckoned Jessie aside, whispered his love to her, and asked her to marry him. She eagerly agreed. They would keep their engagement secret until the best time came to reveal it. The next morning, Frémont had all the flowers delivered to Jessie's mother. That gift did not have quite the effect that he wanted.

Jessie's parents grew alarmed at the obvious love swelling between their teenage daughter and the obscure lieutenant a dozen years her elder with tainted origins. Frémont recalled that the mother "was not friendly to my suit.… She thought her daughter much too young…and…that the unsettled life of an army officer was un-favorable to making such a home as she wished for her."[38] Benton sat Jessie down and sternly explained: "We all admire Lieutenant Frémont, but with no family, no money, and the prospect of slow promotion in the Army, we think him no proper match for you. And besides, you are too young to think of marriage in any case."[39]

Benton pulled political levers of power to dispatch Frémont with Nicollet to chart the Des Moines River across Iowa Territory and sent Jessie to pass the summer with her mother's relatives at Cherry Grove. That enforced absence only enflamed the love between Frémont and Jessie. Frémont dutifully journeyed with Nicollet to St. Louis where they recruited men and amassed supplies for their latest expedition. This one was relatively easy, safe, and swift, given Iowa's proximity, lack of hostile Indians, and 45,000 settlers across the territory. They departed St. Louis on June 27, 1842, and returned two months later.

Once Frémont was back in Washington, he sent Jessie secret messages via Maria Crittenden, the wife of Attorney General John Crittenden, and they covertly met several times in her parlor. With her parents still adamantly opposed to marriage between them, they felt that their only hope was to elope. The trouble was finding someone to perform the ceremony who was unafraid of provoking the wrath of one of Washington's most powerful men. Frémont failed to convince first a protestant minister and then Washington's mayor, William Seaton. Only Catholic priest Joseph Van Horseigh agreed to do so, marrying them on October 19, 1842, probably in the Crittenden parlor. The secret died the next day when they recorded the license at city hall.

Not surprisingly, the news incensed Thomas and Elizabeth Benton. When the newlyweds appeared nervously before them, Benton erupted in rage and yelled: "Get out of my house and never cross the door again! Jessie shall stay here!" To that, Jessie linked arms with Frémont and quoted the Bible's book of Ruth: "Whither thou goest I will go. Where thou lodgest I will lodge; thy people shall be my people, thy God my God."[40] With that they hurried out and fled to Baltimore for what must have been a tense honeymoon. After several days, Benton grudgingly accepted what he could not change and beckoned them back to live under his roof. He publicly accepted their marriage with an announcement in the *Washington*

Globe on November 27 but reversed the order of who married whom. When editor Francis Preston Blair pointed out what he thought was an error, Benton thundered: "Damn it sir! It will go in that way or not at all! John C. Frémont did not marry my daughter, she married him." In making that distinction, Benton at once expressed his feelings and legally shielded Frémont from any possible charges of marrying an underage girl. Upon hearing of the elopement, Jessie's cousin John McDowell, quipped: "I anticipated nothing else from her ungovernable passions."[41]

CHAPTER 2

A Second Mind

"I see the face of my second mind…. This invites discussion…with a mind and purpose in harmony with my own and on the same level… with Mrs. Frémont."

—JOHN FRÉMONT

"Every morning at nine I took my seat at the writing table and left it at one. Mr. Frémont had his notes all ready and dictated as he moved about the room."

—JESSIE FRÉMONT

NOW WITH A SON-IN-LAW AS WELL AS A PROTÉGÉE, Thomas Benton was doubly determined to make the most of the situation. Any successes that Frémont racked up as an explorer would at once advance Benton's political agenda and Jessie's economic and social status. And Jessie would be the confidante and secretary for both her husband and her father. She explained the synergy of love, interests, and actions among them: "I had grown up to and into my father's large purpose; and now that my husband could be of such aid to him in its accomplishments, I had no hesitation in risking for him all consequences. We three understood each other and acted together—then and later—without questions or delay."[42]

As the Senate Military Affairs Committee chair, Benton spearheaded a bill authorizing and funding a four-month expedition to map the Oregon Trail to the Rocky Mountain divide. But before Frémont could embark on that expedition, he had to finish his report on the Des Moines River expedition. This initiated Jessie's lifelong role as Frémont's assistant, editor, and, above all, muse. The report that he submitted in 1842 was in her handwriting. Now he could concentrate on preparing for his expedition. He ordered and forwarded many of the supplies to St. Louis, including an inflatable rubber boat, among the first of its kind. He hired only one man in Washington, Charles Preuss, a German-born mapmaker and artist.

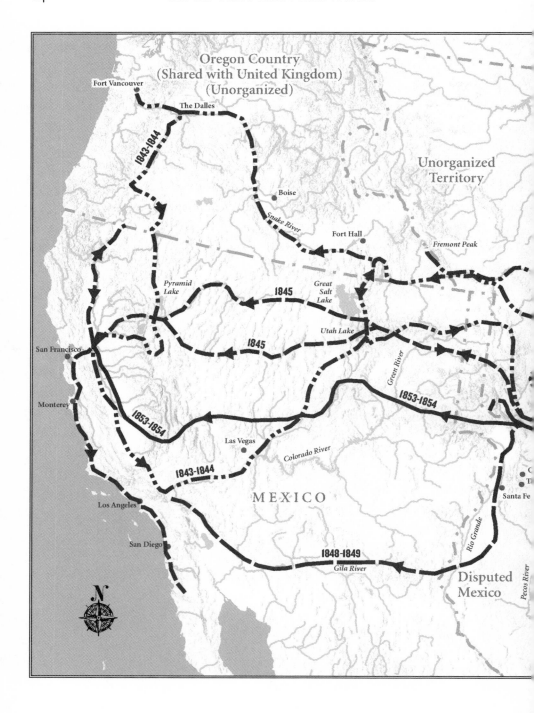

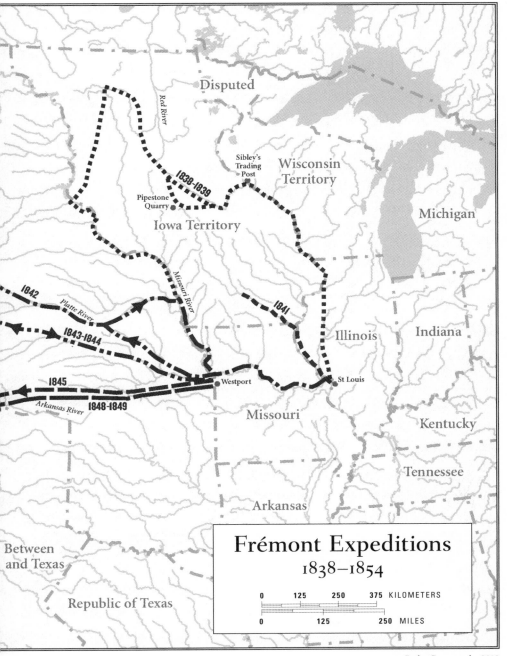

Frémont Expeditions
1838–1854

| 0 | 125 | 250 | 375 | KILOMETERS |
| 0 | | 125 | 250 | MILES |

Petho Cartography 2019

Jessie was pregnant when Frémont departed for St. Louis on May 2, 1842. For nearly half a year, the west swallowed up her husband like a black hole. The anxiety over when or even whether he would return left her morose and listless. Then a stroke left her mother speechless, paralyzed, and bedridden. Caring for her mother at once roused Jessie from her lethargy but exacerbated her worries. Her isolation worsened when her father left for St. Louis where he spent much of the summer tending political and business concerns. Then, on October 29, 1842, John burst into their home. He had extraordinary tales to tell.

Frémont spent two weeks recruiting men and organizing supplies in St. Louis, with his headquarters the mansion of Benton's niece, Sarah Benton Brant. Among his nineteen recruits were mountain men Basil Lajeunesse and Lucien Maxwell. Then on the steamboat from St. Louis to Westport, he met Christopher Carson, nicknamed Kit, who was not then the renowned American hero he subsequently became.[43] When Frémont informed him that he was looking for as many experienced guides as possible, Carson replied "that I had been some time in the mountains and thought I could guide him to any point he would wish to go."[44] After confirming Carson's claims with Maxwell and Lajeunesse, Frémont hired him for a hundred dollars a month. He described Carson as "a man of medium height, broad-shouldered and deep-chested, with a clear steady blue eye and frank speech and address: quiet and unassuming."[45] They soon became close friends. Carson would guide three of Frémont's expeditions and help rescue the fourth.[46] They met when Carson was returning to his home in Taos, New Mexico, after visiting St. Louis for the first time in twelve years; his Arapaho wife had died the previous year and he had just enrolled their daughter in a St. Louis boarding school. He had experienced extraordinary adventures since August 1826, when he ran away from his apprenticeship to a saddle-maker in Franklin, Missouri, and joined a party of traders bound for Santa Fe. Over the years he accompanied a succession of trapping and exploring parties that ranged through the Rocky Mountains, the Great Basin, and even California. Carson nicely captured the exhilarating "live for today, tomorrow ye shall die" mountain man spirit: "I would have to pass my life in labor that was distasteful to me, and being anxious to travel for the purpose of seeing different countries, I concluded to join the first party that started for the Rocky Mountains.... The amount due us was paid.... We spent the time gloriously, spending our lives freely, never thinking that our lives had been risked in gaining it. Our only idea had been risked in gaining it. Our only idea was to...have as much pleasure and enjoyment."[47]

Frémont and his men disembarked at Cyprian Chouteau's trading post, half a dozen miles up the Kansas River from its mouth on the Missouri River. There, Frémont bought enough horses to carry his men and a half dozen two-wheeled carts, each drawn by two mules, for his supplies. On June 10, they headed north-west across the plains. His orders from Colonel John Abert of the Topographical Corps were to map the Oregon Trail along the Platte River. Benton asked Abert to change the orders to let Frémont explore at least as far as South Pass, the broad plain on the Continental Divide. Believing that the assignment was already chal-lenging enough, Abert refused to change the written orders but did unofficially give him leeway to go farther "without hazarding the work committed to you."[48] This was Frémont's first experience of the tensions between military and political power, and the discrepancies between official and unofficial orders. Ultimately Benton got what he wanted for Frémont. Acting on this "lesson" would get Frémont in repeated and severe problems with various superiors over the coming decades.

Frémont's eventual report and memoir on this expedition and two subsequent ones are the most extensive accounts of them. Not surprisingly his versions gloss over, ignore, or exaggerate countless events and controversies that arose along those long trails. Fortunately, there are alternate views of which cartographer Charles Preuss's diary is the most insightful.[49] Preuss saw nothing heroic in Frémont or Carson. He dismissed Frémont as a "childishly passionate man" and Carson for exaggerating Indian threats "to make himself important."[50]

As the expedition rode up the Platte valley, they met Sioux and Cheyenne bands. At each village Frémont and his guides conducted standard Indian diplo-macy. They visited the chief, who had his wives serve them food. After his guests had eaten, the chief lit his pipe, presented it to the six directions, puffed deeply, and then passed it around the circle of guests and notable men of his village who showed up. Frémont gave the chief cloth, knives, beads, awls, and other eagerly sought items, and explained why he and his men were passing through. They swore eternal friendship and embraced before parting ways.

Frémont's party encountered a trapping party led by renowned mountain man Jim Bridger on July 8.[51] Bridger warned them that west of Fort Laramie and north of the Oregon Trail the Sioux, Cheyenne, and Gros Ventre bands "had broken out in open hostility" and were "scouring the upper country in war parties." That news made many of Frémont's men "dispirited and agitated by a variety of conflicting opinions" with most "strongly disposed to return" east to civilization. Frémont fi-nally talked them into continuing the expedition toward Fort Laramie and beyond at least as far as South Pass.[52]

At the forks of the Platte, Frémont split his party, leading half up the South Platte to Fort St. Vrain while the rest continued up the North Platte toward Fort Laramie. Frémont and his men reached Fort St. Vrain on July 10, spent the night, then three days later reunited with the other party at Fort Laramie. Frémont was greatly impressed by Fort Laramie with its fifteen-foot palisaded walls, "which surround a yard of about one hundred and thirty feet square…. There are two entrances opposite each other, one of which is a large and public entrance, the other smaller and more private…. Over the great entrance is a square tower with loopholes. At two of the angles, and diagonally across from each other, are large square bastions." As for trade, the Americans took buffalo robes in return for agreed upon measures of "blankets, calicoes, guns, powder, and lead…glass beads, looking glasses, rings, vermilion for painting, tobacco, and…in spite of the prohibitions… alcohol…diluted with water before sold." He contrasted long-term operators like the American Fur Company with smaller get-rich-quick competitors: "The regular trader looks ahead and has an interest in the preservation of the Indians and in the regular pursuit of their business, and the preservation of their arms, horse, and everything necessary to their future." In stark contrast, the fly-by-night operator "gets what he can and for what he can from every Indian he meets even at the risk of disabling him from doing anything more at hunting."[53]

Indian bands of various tribes were camped around Fort Laramie, and Frémont found himself in near incessant diplomacy with them: "These Indians had a confused idea of the number and power of our people, and dreaded to bring upon themselves the military force of the United States…. Some came for presents, and others for information of our object in coming to the country; now and then one would dart up to the tent on horseback, jerk the trappings from his horse, and stand silently at the door, holding him by the halter, signifying his desire to trade him. Occasionally a savage would stalk in with an invitation to a feast of honor—a dog feast—and deliberately sit down and wait quietly until I was ready to accompany him. I went to one; the women and children were sitting outside the lodge, and we took our seats on buffalo robes spread around. The dog was in a large pot over the fire in the middle of the lodge, and immediately on our arrival was dished up in large wooden bowls, one of which was handed to each…. Fortunately, I am not of delicate nerves and continued quietly to empty my platter…. My tent was the only place which they respected. Here only came the chiefs and men of distinction and generally one of them remained to drive away the women and children."[54]

Frémont convened a council among the Sioux chiefs where they passed a pipe and discussed the departure of many young warriors to attack the Oregon-bound immigrants traversing their country. Although the chiefs claimed to want peace with the Americans, they rejected his request that some of them accompany him to assure that none of their warriors raided the expedition. They explained that "they had no power over the young men and were afraid to interfere with them."[55]

That exacerbated the fears of most of Frémont's men. Fortunately, a wagon train bound for Oregon and guided by yet another renowned mountain man, Tom Fitzpatrick, rumbled up to Fort Laramie.[56] Frémont tried to shame his reluctant men by pointing to the hopeful settlers, including women and children, who were headed westward all the way to Oregon. He talked all but one man into staying with him when they proceeded on July 21. They left the North Platte where it bends from the Laramie Mountains southward and followed the Sweetwater River westward. Here the land grew more rugged and steep although the trail remained easy to follow. On August 7, they reached South Pass, a vast waterless plain with distant snowcapped mountain ranges northwest and southwest. The men were excited to learn that they had reached the Continental Divide where the waters behind them flowed toward the Atlantic Ocean and those before them flowed toward the Pacific Ocean.

Frémont was determined to reach the Wind River Mountains to their northwest and then climb the highest among them. Three days later, the expedition was camped in the foothills of those mountains. On the morning of August 12, Frémont got fifteen volunteers to join him in trying to reach the summit of what appeared to be the tallest mountain, which he now named Mount Snow but later named Mount Frémont. The three-day ascent was grueling; first they made their way through thick forests and boulders, then, as the trees thinned, they reached the snow line. At a certain point, altitude sickness afflicted Frémont and many others, provoking splitting headaches and vomiting. Most of the men gave up and camped near a lake. Frémont and several others struggled upward through deeper snow until they reached the 13,517-foot summit on August 15, 1842. That exhilarating feat diluted some of their nausea, exhaustion, and fear: "We looked down a thousand feet below, and, standing where no human foot had stood before, felt the exultation of first explorers. It was about two o'clock when we left the summit; and when we reached the bottom the sun had already sunk behind the wall.... We... lay down on the rock, and, in spite of the cold, slept soundly."[57]

Two days later all those who had attempted or succeeded in the ascent were reunited with the men in the base camp. They then retraced their steps eastward toward St. Louis more than a thousand miles away. At the confluence of the Sweetwater and the North Platte Rivers, Frémont unpacked the inflatable rubber raft to run the latter. With much of their equipment and supplies packed aboard, three men paddled down the swift stream, which soon transformed into raging rapids that capsized the boat: "For a hundred yards below, the current was covered with floating books and boxes, bales of blankets, and scattered articles of clothing; and so strong...was the current that even our heavy instruments, which were all in cases, kept on the surface....For a moment I felt somewhat disheartened. All

our books—almost every record of the journey—our journals and registers of as-
tronomical and barometrical observations—had been lost…. But it was no time
to indulge in regrets; and I…set about endeavoring to save something from the
wreck." Yet, despite this disaster, Frémont and his men remained enchanted by
their surroundings: "The scenery was extremely picturesque, and, notwithstanding our forlorn condition, we were frequently obliged to stop and admire it….
We had emerged from the water half naked, and, on arriving at the top of the
precipice, I found myself with only one moccasin. The fragments of rock made
walking painful, and I was frequently obliged to stop and pull out the thorns of the
cactus…with which a few minutes walk covered the bottom of my feet."[58]

Despite or, more likely, because of his disaster, Frémont was determined to
run the river. He had his men construct bullboats by stretching buffalo hides
over half a basket frame of interwoven willow boughs. Several of the men gingerly
settled into the boats and set off. This time the current swiftly carried rather than
capsized them and they made good time while the rest of the men on horseback
kept pace ashore. On August 31, they reached Fort Laramie, where they rested for
three days. Carson drew his pay and headed south for his home in Taos. Frémont
and the rest of the party resumed their journey eastward. They reached the confluence of the Platte and Missouri Rivers on October 1, three days later packed
aboard a passing keelboat heading downstream, and disembarked at St. Louis on
October 17. There Frémont discharged his men, sold his remaining equipment,
and caught a steamboat bound for Pittsburgh.

Frémont reached Washington City for a joyful reunion with Jessie and the rest of
the family on October 29. Jessie gave birth to a daughter, whom they named Lily,
on November 15. Fortunately, she had servants who helped care for her baby. She
may have derived as much or even more pleasure in resuming her role as her husband's secretary. She happily recalled, "Every morning at nine I took my seat at the
writing table and left it at one. Mr. Frémont had his notes all ready and dictated
as he moved about the room."[59] Certainly he was not just grateful but rejoiced in
their literary partnership that alleviated his chronic affliction of writer's block: "I
write more easily by dictation. Writing myself, I have too much time to think and
dwell upon words as well as ideas. In dictation there is not time for this and then,
too, I see the face of my second mind…. This invites discussion…with a mind and
purpose in harmony with my own and on the same level…with Mrs. Frémont."[60]

Frémont submitted his report to Colonel Abert on March 1, 1843. The following
day, Senator Lewis Linn, Benton's friend and fellow Missourian, made a speech
lauding the report and calling for a thousand copies to be printed and sold to the

public. The Senate and then the House approved that motion by acclamation. The report quickly sold out, spurred emigration to Oregon and California, and made Frémont a celebrity. Benton faced little opposition when he got Congress to authorize and President John Tyler to approve a second expedition. On March 10, Frémont received orders from Abert to map the Front Range of the central Rockies, then journey along the Oregon Trail as far as Fort Walla Walla on the Columbia River, where naval Captain Charles Wilkes had surveyed from the Pacific Ocean the previous year. Wilkes was a national naval hero for his five-year, round-the-world exploration voyage from 1838 to 1842.[61] Frémont would get in a nasty public dispute with Wilkes over whose maps were more accurate, as part of a broader rivalry over which man deserved greater fame.

Frémont initially recruited thirty-nine men at St. Louis, including Tom Fitzpatrick as a guide and Charles Preuss again as his cartographer. The expedition embarked on a steamboat to Westport, where Frémont bought enough horses to mount each man, while the supplies were packed in twelve carts drawn by two mules each. The cartography equipment included a telescope, two chronometers, two barometers, two sextants, six thermometers, and several compasses. Once again, he brought along an inflatable rubber boat.

In preparing for this expedition, Frémont made a decision that would impose unnecessary exertions among his men and controversy to the highest army and political levels. He requisitioned a 12-pounder mountain howitzer.[62] Colonel Stephen Watts Kearny, a Benton family friend, commanded the military department with its headquarters at St. Louis. He ordered Captain William Bell, who commanded the arsenal, to release the howitzer and a supply of ammunition without going through the usual War Department's Ordnance Office channels in Washington. Bell was astute enough to obey Kearny's order, while informing the Ordnance Office. The word that a howitzer had been released to Frémont without following standard procedures angered James Porter, then the acting but unconfirmed secretary of war. He fired off letters to Kearny and Bell, insisting that "order, regularity, and system must be preserved. I cannot sanction the proceeding."[63] Yet, rather than write Frémont directly, he had Abert send him a letter ordering him to return the howitzer to the arsenal and report to Washington to explain other questionable requisitions that violated his budget.

The letter arrived too late at the Benton mansion in St. Louis. Frémont had already departed for Westport. Before leaving, he had instructed Jessie, who would wait Penelope-like in St. Louis until his return, to open and act on any letters addressed to him. After reading Abert's letter, Jessie had Baptiste Derosier, who had

belatedly enrolled in the expedition and was about to hurry after it, carry a letter
to Frémont with this urgent message: "Only trust me and go." To that Frémont
scribbled this terse reply: "I trust, and go."[64] A few weeks later, Benton reached St.
Louis, where he approved his daughter's decisive act. He wrote Abert condemning
him for the letter he sent Frémont. He then returned to Washington where, as the
Military Affairs Committee chair, he blocked Porter's confirmation as war secretary. Porter resigned. Benton and Jessie were exultant, but the controversy would
not end there.[65]

Jessie once again spent month after month missing and worrying for her husband: "I shall feel like a sentinel on the lookout until Mr. Frémont returns."[66] At
one point Robert Campbell, learning of her distress, paid her a visit.[67] Campbell
had spent a decade as a mountain man before forming his own highly successful
mercantile business; he had sold Frémont many of his expedition's supplies. His
visit calmed Jessie, who wrote a friend that "last night Mr. Campbell, who has
been to Oregon himself twenty years ago nearly, when every difficulty was greater
than now, traced out on a map Mr. Frémont's route & gave me the date of his
probable arrival in each place.... As Mr. Campbell says, 'They may have a tedious
journey but I assure you not a dangerous one.' If you knew Mr. Campbell you
would feel as quiet as I do—for he is an honest man."[68]

Spurred by Jessie's letter, Frémont had his men break camp and hurry up the
Emigrant Trail. Two days later where the trail crossed the Kansas River and angled
northwest to the Platte River, Frémont led his men westward along the Kansas
River, then up the Republican River. Hard rains slowed their pace to a half dozen
or so miles per day as the wheels of the cannon and heavily laden carts sank in the
muck. Frémont split his command; he led fifteen men on horseback ahead while
Fitzpatrick followed with twenty-six men, the carts, and the cannon. On July 4,
Frémont and his advanced party reached the trading post of Fort St. Vrain on the
South Platte River. From there they headed south along the Rocky Mountain's
Front Range to the hamlet of Pueblo on the Arkansas River. Kit Carson was at
Bent's Fort when he learned that Frémont was at Pueblo and immediately rode up
the valley to join his expedition. Frémont led his men back north to Fort St. Vrain,
where Fitzpatrick's party was waiting, and he recruited mountain man Alexis
Godey as a guide. He sent Fitzpatrick north to the Emigrant Trail while he led
his men up Cache la Poudre River into the Rockies. The plan was to rendezvous
at Fort Hall, a Hudson's Bay Company trading post. Frémont's party crossed the
divide into the North Platte River's headwaters, then descended to the Sweetwater
River where they reached the Emigrant Trail. They headed west up the Sweetwater
to the Continental Divide at South Pass, then on to the Big Sandy and down it to
the Green River.

On their long journey, the expedition suffered the usual mishaps of encounters with grizzlies and rattlesnakes, broken axles and maimed mules. Near the Green River, a Cheyenne and Arapaho war party charged them, then pulled up before firing broke out after recognizing that they were Americans and not their Ute enemies. Frémont and his men suffered mixed feelings when they encountered wagon trains of emigrants. The sight stirred thoughts of home as "the women were occupied in preparing the evening meal, and the children playing in the grass and herds of cattle, grazing about in the bottom, had an air of quiet security and civilized comfort that made a rare sight for the traveler in such a remote wilderness."[69] The men may have also felt chagrined that they were accompanying rather than leading the nation's westward expansion.

Frémont was once again mapping paths trod by countless others, not just mountain men but ever more settlers. The number of recorded emigrants heading toward Oregon or California soared from 13 in 1840, to 71 in 1841, 196 in 1842, 1,109 in 1843, and reached 18,847 in 1848 even before word of the gold strike at Sutter's Mill, California.[70] Biographer Tom Chaffin noted the inescapable irony shadowing Frémont's expeditions: "Frémont would, in a sense, be locked into a race—trying to keep up with the very forces that he himself helped put in motion, forces which over the next few years seemed, at every bend, about to overtake him."[71]

Other powerful forces were transforming the west. As early as the 1840s, the voracious American and British demands for beaver furs and buffalo robes had decimated both animals and other species. Beavers had disappeared from most mountain streams while the buffalo were first encountered in a narrowing central plains zone ever farther west of the American settlements and ever farther east of the Rocky Mountains. Frémont conveyed the dismay of mountain men who had first gone west in the 1820s that the "buffalo had disappeared within a few years, and that now, as occasional buffalo skulls and a few wild antelope were all that remained of the abundance which had covered the country with animal life."[72]

Beyond Green River, Frémont and his men reached the Bear River, a horse-shoe-shaped stream that flows north and eventually arches west and then south to drain into the Great Salt Lake. When Bear River seemed deep and placid enough, Frémont had the rubber boat inflated. With four paddlers he set off downstream as the rest of the men rode along the shore. Bear River eventually shallowed out and the mariners had to drag the boat to Great Salt Lake. Along the way, the boat suffered a puncture, which they patched with resin. Air kept seeping out, which meant the men had to take turns laboriously pumping more air inside. Despite this handicap, Frémont insisted that they paddle to a distant island. He initially named the island Disappointment because he found no water, wood, or game on it, but later named it after himself. They returned to shore where the rest of the party waited, packed up the boat, and headed back up Bear River Valley to the Emigrant Trail.

There, Frémont and his men encountered yet another famed mountain man, Joseph Walker, who was on a long hunt with several men.[73] They journeyed together for several days to Fort Hall on the Snake River. To Frémont's relief, Fitzpatrick and his party were camped near the fort. Walker and his men departed with a wagon train that hired him to guide them to California. Frémont would engage Walker's wilderness expertise for his third expedition, but they would eventually have a bitter parting of ways.

A freak early snowstorm stalled Frémont four days at Fort Hall. This was not the only setback. Basil Lajeunesse and ten men informed Frémont that they were leaving the expedition and heading back east to St. Louis. On September 22, Frémont and his twenty-five remaining men left Fort Hall on the Oregon Trail. They reached Fort Boise, another Hudson Bay Company post, on October 10. Five days later, the trail passed over the 1,800-foot divide between the Snake and Columbia Rivers. An epiphany struck Frémont as he gazed south and imagined landscapes far beyond that horizon. He envisioned a vast stretch of the west that had no outlet to the sea and he named it "the Great Basin." That proved to be Frémont's greatest discovery from his expeditions.

They crossed over the Blue Mountains, where for the first time since the Rockies they enjoyed abundant game, water, grass, and towering Ponderosa Pines. On the western slopes they marveled at spectacular views of the Columbia River Valley and on the far horizon the Cascade Mountains studded by the snowcapped volcanic cones of Mount Hood and Mount St. Helens.

They reached the mission of Dr. Marcus Whitman, his wife Narcissa, and their followers with the Cayuse Indians on October 22.[74] He replenished his dwindling food supplies with potatoes rather than corn meal, the mill having recently burned. One of the emigrants who encountered Frémont was Peter Burnett, who later became California's governor. The young lieutenant impressed him: "He was then about thirty years old, modest in appearance, and calm and gentle in manner. His men all loved him. He gave his orders with great mildness and simplicity, but they had to be obeyed."[75]

Frémont and his men reached the Hudson Bay Company post of Fort Walla Walla on the Columbia River the next day. That evening Archibald Mckinlay, the commander, treated Frémont and his officers to a feast. The expedition descended the Columbia River Valley as snowcapped Cascade Mountains rose steadily before them. Upon reaching the Columbia River gorge on November 5, Frémont again split his party. He left five men to guard the carts and howitzer and with twenty men divided among three shallow-draft boats known as mackinaws, shot the rapids. Several days and ninety miles later, they beached their mackinaws before Fort Vancouver, the Hudson's Bay Company's regional headquarters, and enjoyed the hospitality of the director, Dr. John McLaughlin. Here Frémont faced a temptation: "It would have been very gratifying to have gone down to the Pacific and, solely in the interest and in the love of geography, to have seen the ocean on the western as well as on the eastern side of the continent, so as to give a satisfactory completeness to the geographical picture which had been formed in our minds." But time ticked on.

So, after purchasing supplies, Frémont and his men headed back upriver. At the gorge they attached long ropes to their boats and laboriously pulled them up the rapids. Once his two parties were reunited, they abandoned the carts, packed all their supplies on 104 mules and horses, and, on November 25, headed south along the stark eastern Cascade Mountain foothills. The broken terrain made dragging the howitzer even more onerous.

Although the small bands of mostly Paiutes that they encountered were friendly, they provoked contempt among Frémont and his men: "In comparison with the Indians of the Rocky Mountains and the great eastern plain, these are disagreeably dirty in their habits. Their huts were crowded with half naked women and children, and the atmosphere anything but pleasant to persons who had been riding in the fresh morning air."[76] The hand-to-mouth existence of those Indians was based mostly on rabbits, roots, and grubs, so Americans derided them as "diggers," a word that rhymed with the derogatory word for black people.

They learned of and followed a trail leading to a low pass over the mountains, then descended to the Upper Klamath River valley and Klamath Lake. This was a land of thick forests where the Klamath Indians had a well-deserved reputation for robbing and even murdering stray trespassers. Fortunately, none of their tense encounters with the Klamath turned deadly; they would not be so lucky the next time they passed through. From the Klamath valley, they followed a pass east over the Sierra Mountains and into the Great Basin. Frémont led his men southward along the Sierra foothills in search of the legendary Buenaventura River that supposedly flowed westward through the Sierras to the sea, just like the Columbia River did much farther north. In doing so, he rejected the discovery of expeditions led by Jedediah Smith in the late 1820s and Joseph Walker in the 1830s that the Buenaventura River was as much a fantasy of wishful thinking as the Northwest Passage.

Meanwhile the horses and mules weakened steadily and fifteen perished from the broken terrain and sparse grass and water. Washoe Indians trailed them, begging and looking for anything to steal. None agreed to guide them east across the Great Basin. One, however, promised to show them where a trail began that zigzagged west over the Sierras. Desperately short of supplies, Frémont reckoned they might well perish if they headed east, but beyond the Sierras lay California's settlements that could furnish all their needs. On January 16, 1844, they began ascending the Truckee River valley into the Sierras but within days encountered snow that eventually became a dozen or so feet deep. They abandoned the howitzer and took turns trampling down the snow into a firm path. One by one they killed their mules and horses for food. At one point, Preuss got lost and spent several miserable days trying to survive before rejoining the others. They marveled as they passed through groves of Sequoias and Redwoods soaring a hundred feet or higher above them. It took more than a month to struggle over the Sierras. Only thirty-three horses and mules survived. They lost a comrade when Baptiste Derosier went crazy, wandered away, and was never seen again. They spent several days grazing their animals and hunting deer in grassy meadows along the American River's South Fork.

Replenished, Frémont and his men followed the river west into Central Valley and, on March 8, 1844, reached Sutter's Fort. John Sutter had emigrated from Bern, Switzerland to California in 1839, and in 1841 received a 9,000-acre land grant in the Sierra foothills where he founded his fort and the town of New Helvetia.[77] Frémont recalled that Sutter "gave us a most frank and cordial reception—conducted immediately in his residence—and under his hospitable roof we had a night of rest, enjoyment, and refreshment.... The fort is a quadrangular adobe structure, mounting twelve pieces of artillery.... The whites in the employment of Captain Sutter, Americans, French, and German, amount to perhaps thirty men. The inner wall is formed into buildings comprising the common quarters, with a blacksmith and other work-shops; the dwelling-house, with a large distillery-house, and other buildings.... It is built upon a pond-like stream, at times a running creek communicating with the Rio de los Americanos which enters the Sacramento [River] about two miles below.... There were two vessels belonging to Captain Sutter at anchor near the landing," of which one "was shortly to proceed on a voyage to Fort Vancouver for a cargo of goods."[78]

At Sutter's Fort, Frémont discharged or lost to desertion six of his men, expanded his number of horses and mules to 130, and acquired thirty head of cattle, including five milk cows. On March 24, they headed south up the southern Central Valley then southeast over Oak Creek Pass in the Tehachapi Mountains. Only after traversing that pass and descending into the Mohave Desert did Frémont dismiss definitively the Buenaventura River as a myth: "No river from the interior does, or can, cross the Sierra Nevada.... There is no opening from the Bay of San Francisco into the interior of the continent. The two rivers which flow into it are comparatively short, and not perpendicular to the coast, but lateral to it, and having their heads toward Oregon and southern California. They open lines of communication north and south, and not eastwardly." Those geographical realities of California gave "great additional value to the Columbia, which stands alone as the only great river on the Pacific slope of our continent which leads from the ocean to the Rocky Mountains and opens a line of communication from the sea to the Valley of the Mississippi."[79]

That was the Frémont expedition's key discovery. For a generation the Buenaventura River myth had been a distraction not just for the handful of mountain men and explorers that fruitlessly searched for it but also for western expansionists in Congress as well. After Frémont returned with that knowledge, Benton and his colleagues who shared his vision of stretching the United States across the continent riveted their attention and efforts on taking the Oregon Territory with its strategic Columbia River watershed for America's exclusive ownership and exploitation. But that obsession lasted only a year or so before James Polk became president determined to take not just the Oregon Territory but New Mexico and California as well.

Frémont planned to follow the first half of the Old Spanish Trail, which linked Los Angeles with Santa Fe in a 700-mile arc that peaked north at the Sevier River, from where they would angle northeast to the Oregon Trail.[80] To blunt the Indian danger, he organized the daily march with military precision: "Scouts ahead and on the flanks; a front and rear division; the pack-animals, baggage, and horned cattle in the center; and the whole stretching a quarter of a mile along our dreary path."[81] Thirst for the men and beasts was nearly constant as some water holes were a day apart. Every day or so they butchered and devoured one of the cows.

One morning a terrified Mexican man and boy stumbled into their camp and blurted that Paiutes had attacked their camp, slaughtered their four companions, and stolen their horse herd. Carson and Godey heatedly explained to Frémont that the Indian raiders had to be caught and punished as severely as possible to deter further depredations. With Frémont's permission, they accompanied the man back down the trail to where the attack occurred, then, leaving him behind, followed the tracks of the herd several days further until they caught up with the raiders. Although outnumbered by at least ten to one, Carson and Godey screamed war cries and "charged into the camp…. The Indians received them with a flight of arrows shot from their long bows, one of which passed through Godey's shirt collar, barely missing his neck; our men fired their rifles upon aim…. Two Indians were stretched on the ground, fatally wounded; the rest fled, except a lad who was captured. The scalps of the fallen were instantly stripped off; but in the process one of them, who had two balls through his body, sprang to his feet, the blood streaming from his skinned head, and uttered a hideous howl. An old squaw, possibly his mother, stopped and looked back from the mountain side she was climbing, threatening and lamenting. The frightful spectacle appalled the stout hearts of our men, but they did what humanity required, and quickly terminated the agonies of the gory savage."[82] After reloading their rifles and pistols, Carson and Godey released the boy and searched the camp. They had surprised the Indians just as they were about to feast off several horses they had slaughtered and stewed in earthen pots over fires. They rounded up the surviving horses and drove them back toward the expedition far beyond the horizon.

Farther along the trail, Frémont and his men had a tense standoff with Paiutes who surrounded their camp and stole several of their horses. A chief approached and through sign language threatened to massacre them if they did not surrender the rest of their horses to him. Frémont had to restrain Carson and Godey from killing him. He tried to placate the chief by giving him an emaciated horse. That only briefly satiated the Paiutes, and they trailed the expedition for days waiting for any chance to pick off stray horses or men.

Despite Frémont's efforts to keep the expedition as tightly organized as possible, one of his guides, Baptiste Tabeau, fell behind to retrieve a lost mule. The Paiute murdered him, stole his mule, and vanished into nearby mountains. That enraged Frémont and his men, especially because they were incapable of retaliating. Frémont explained their churning emotions: "Men who have gone through such dangers and sufferings as we had seen become like brothers and feel each other's loss. To defend and avenge each other is the deep feeling of all. We wished to avenge his death but the condition of our horses languishing for grass and repose, forbade an expedition into unknown mountains."[83] Their mourning deepened when another man, Francois Badeau, went mad and blew out his brains with his gun. Frémont grimly noted "times were severe when stout men lost their minds from extremity of suffering."[84]

Their gloom lifted a few days later when they again crossed trails with Joe Walker and his men, who were driving a huge horse herd that they had stolen from California. Walker knew the most direct way through the Rocky Mountains to the high plains where they could follow the South Platte north to the Oregon Trail; he agreed to guide Frémont and his men there. Along the way they encountered the Ute band led by Walkara: "They were all mounted, armed with rifles, and use their rifles well…. They were journeying slowly to…levy their usual tribute upon the California caravan. They were robbers of a higher order than those of the desert. They conducted their depredations…under the color of trade and toll for passing through the country. Instead of attacking and killing, they affect to purchase—taking the horses they like and leaving something nominal in return. The chief was quite civil to me.... He knew of my expedition of 1842."[85] As a gesture of friendship, each gave his best blanket to the other.

Their next close call came as they ascended the Grand River's headwaters into Bayou Salade, a vast meadow high in the Rockies where a band of several hundred Arapahos and a score of Sioux were encamped. The women, children, and old men fled into the forest while the warriors grabbed their arms, mounted their horses, and raced toward the intruders. Frémont bought them off with presents from his dwindling supply of trade goods.

They crossed over a pass into the headwaters of the Arkansas River watershed and for days followed it downward, making wide detours as the river dropped into deep gorges. They reached a Ute village whose warriors had galloped off to fight a lurking Arapaho war party. The women urged Frémont to join his forces with their men, but he declined: "Neither party were our friends or under our protection, and each was ready to prey upon us that could. But we could not help feeling an unusual excitement at being within a few hundred yards of a fight in which five hundred men were closely engaged and hearing the sharp crack of their rifles. We were in a bad position and subject to be attacked in it. Either party which we might meet, victorious or defeated, was certain to fall upon us."[86]

Frémont pushed his men on to put as much distance between them and the warring parties rearward. With enormous relief they emerged from the mountains onto the high plains and followed the Arkansas downstream toward two outposts of American civilization.[87] That evening they reached Pueblo, a settlement of a dozen or so former mountain men and their Indian or Mexican wives and children. A few days later they camped for several days near Bent's Fort. Charles Bent told them to be on their guard, citing depredations by Arapaho, Comanche, and Kiowa war parties just weeks earlier.

At Bent's Fort the Frémont and Walker expeditions parted ways. Walker and his men, along with Carson, headed southwest to Taos, while Frémont and most of his men headed east on the Santa Fe Trail. That was not the last time they saw each other. Frémont would engage Carson and Walker on future expeditions. On the Smoky Hill River, they encountered a Pawnee village where they were treated with "rudeness" and "insolence" even after Frémont distributed most of his remaining goods. They rode joyfully into the trail's terminus at Westport, Missouri, on July 30. Fortunately, a steamboat was docked on the Missouri River below the town and could take on the expedition. The steamboat disgorged Frémont and his men at St. Louis after dark on August 6, 1844, nearly fourteen months after they had first set out.

During most of that time, Jessie waited at the Benton mansion in St. Louis. Her husband's expedition was only supposed to last eight months and that initial time was nerve-racking enough for her. But as the subsequent six months dragged on with no word of his fate, she seesawed emotionally between despair and fatalism. Frémont felt enormous guilt as he imagined what mingled pain, longing, and anger his prolonged absence inflamed in his wife. On the night of August 7, when he reached St. Louis, Jessie was staying at a cousin's house. Frémont approached the Benton mansion and roused the black coachman, Gabriel, by throwing pebbles at his window. Looking out, Gabriel recognized the emaciated figure in the moonlight as Frémont, but feared he was a ghost and at first refused to greet him. After Frémont finally convinced him that he was alive, Gabriel explained where Jessie was staying. Not wanting to cause a commotion in the middle of the night, Frémont did not immediately head to her cousin's house nor even stay at the Benton house. Instead, he passed much of the rest of the night in deep reflection on a park bench in front of the Barnum Hotel. Eventually the hotel clerk recognized Frémont and convinced him to accept a bed. Exhausted emotionally and physically, Frémont fell into a deep sleep. The next morning, Gabriel told Jessie of his mystifying encounter with Frémont the previous night. Jessie went in search of her husband. Her anxious inquiries finally led her to his room at the Barnum Hotel, where their reunion was likely as awkward as it was joyful.[88]

CHAPTER 3

Conquests

"I decided that it was for me rather to govern events than to be governed by them."

—JOHN FRÉMONT

"War with Mexico was inevitable; and a grand opportunity now presented itself to…make the Pacific Ocean the western boundary of the United States."

—JOHN FRÉMONT

THE JOY AT John Frémont's Odysseus-like adventures and homecoming was hardly confined to his family. Upon learning of the expedition's safe return after extensive explorations, newspapers across the country celebrated Frémont and his men. President John Tyler, Secretary of War William Wilkins, and General Winfield Scott agreed to award Frémont with two promotions, to first lieutenant and then brevet captain.

The Frémonts spent two weeks on a second honeymoon in St. Louis before heading to the Benton family mansion in Washington. Frémont was no sooner back than he and Benton began planning his next expedition. Newspaper accounts of his expedition made him a celebrity. The stream of adoring visitors to the Benton home made it difficult for Frémont to get any work done there so he rented a two-floor cottage a block away.

Once again Jessie served as his muse, secretary, and ghostwriter. They reserved the second floor solely for their own work together. There, for four hours each morning, she recorded his dictations, often asking for clarifications or expanded explanations. At one o'clock, a servant would bring lunch and their daughter Lily. Then each afternoon they opened the first floor to other collaborators. Charles Preuss, the expedition's cartographer, spent the most time, while occasionally other veterans would show up. Whenever Preuss or others were present, Jessie would guide discussions to draw out and accord their memories and perspectives. In drafting the map, they received assistance from Joseph Hubbard, a Yale University graduate. Of their collaboration, Frémont wrote: "Mrs. Frémont now worked with me daily at the little wooden house…. Talking incidents over made her familiar with the minute details of the journey, outside of those which we recorded, and gave her a realizing sense of the uncertainties and precarious chances that attend such travel…and it gave her for every day an object unusual in the life of a woman…. Mrs. Benton was alarmed by this pull on her daughter but Mr. Benton was delighted. He used sometimes to turn into our workroom to enjoy the pleasure he had in seeing the work grow."[89]

Frémont officially submitted his report on March 1, 1845. Both houses of Congress approved a motion to print and sell 5,000 copies. Eager readers snapped up that initial run and subsequent printings, making his report a bestseller and himself an all-American hero. The press dubbed him "the Pathfinder" even though Frémont always noted that others had blazed most of the routes that he and his men followed.

Meanwhile, the Benton family provided Frémont with a prosperous, respectable, loving home presided over by a strong father figure that was absent from his childhood. Each day's highlight was supper when the family joyfully gathered: "Mr. Benton held to some observances in family life which, though formal, were pleasant. He was fond of that degree of social decorum which respect for others' feelings should always exact and is grateful to every one…. With the dressing for dinner were laid aside any subjects not suited to general harmony. Mr. Benton always relaxed to the enjoyment of the interesting and cheerful dinner-table—himself contributing his large share and example; except when, on rare occasions, he came down from the Senate preoccupied."[90]

Yet the longer Frémont lingered in Washington, the more restless he became for adventures across the west, especially California: "I had returned inspired with California. Its delightful climate and uncommon beauty…and its grand commercial position took possession of my mind…. I determined to make a home there."[91] Frémont would eventually realize this dream as he became a key player in the latest stage of American Manifest Destiny.

In his last and most significant act as president, John Tyler signed a joint congressional resolution whereby the United States annexed Texas on March 3, 1845. For countless Americans, that act took place years after it should have happened; for countless others, it should never have happened. The reason was that Texas's admission as a slave state upset the Senate's power balance between slave and free states, especially if Texans exercised their state's constitutional right to break themselves up into as many as five states. Regardless, the annexation of Texas was not inevitable.

After Mexico won independence from Spain in 1821, the government opened the country to trade and immigration. Thousands of Americans and other foreigners settled in Texas, and hundreds in California and New Mexico. By 1835, the six thousand Americans in Texas outnumbered Mexicans by six to one, and petitioned Mexico City for autonomy. When dictator Antonio Lopez de Santa Anna rejected that appeal and led his army to repress the Texans, they declared independence on March 2, 1836. The Mexican army slaughtered two hundred Texan rebels at the Alamo on the edge of San Antonio on March 6, and four hundred more outside Goliad on March 27. Santa Anna then marched east across Texas, mopping up resistance as General Sam Houston withdrew with most remaining Texan troops. Houston and his men turned and attacked Santa Anna's army, routed it, and captured the dictator at San Jacinto on April 21. By signing the Treaty of Velasco on May 14, Santa Anna recognized Texan independence. A coup deposed Santa Anna and the new government repudiated the treaty.

Texans in a plebiscite and then Texas's congress voted to be annexed by the United States and sent their request to Washington in August 1837. That set off a debate in Congress and across the United States that took nearly eight years to resolve. Democratic Senator Thomas Benton and Whig Representative Melton Brown sponsored a bipartisan compromise annexation bill that passed the House of Representatives by 120 to 98 on January 25, 1845. The Senate passed an amended version by 27 to 25 on February 27, which the House approved the next day. Envoys of the United States and Texas signed the annexation treaty on April 12. Upon learning of the annexation, Mexico's government severed diplomatic relations with the United States.

James Polk had two highly ambitious foreign policy goals when he took the presidential oath on March 4, 1845.[92] He wanted to end the joint American-British occupation of the Oregon Territory, established by treaty in 1818, so that only the United States owned that region. And he wanted Mexico to both recognize America's acquisition of Texas and sell a Californian port and ideally that entire province along with New Mexico to the United States. He hoped to pressure both Britain and Mexico to yield those vast lands through diplomacy, but if that failed he was willing to fight for them. If war was inevitable, he sought to manipulate events so that the other side struck the first blow, thus making America the victim rather than the aggressor. Polk's strategy was extremely high risk. Although the United States could eventually mass enough military force to defeat either Britain or Mexico, it might well lose a war against those countries allied against a common enemy. Ideally, Polk's policies would extend American territory from the Rocky Mountain's

Continental Divide all the way to the Pacific Ocean without firing a shot. Yet if war came, Polk intended to have American military forces in place to act decisively, especially in California. And Frémont would command one of those forces.

Secretary of State John Buchanan and Navy Secretary George Bancroft frequently joined Benton, Frémont, and Jessie at the Benton home during which their wide-ranging discussions inevitably circled back to Polk's vision. Buchanan relied on Jessie to translate Mexican documents that had been gathered by diplomats, businessmen, and spies. Benton and Frémont met with Polk along with Buchanan and Bancroft at the White House, where they forged a consensus on how Frémont's next expedition might advance America's Manifest Destiny. Nothing was recorded that could jeopardize the president's "plausible deniability" if things somehow went horribly wrong.[93]

As a result, Frémont received conflicting official and unofficial instructions. Colonel John Abert of the Topographical Corps issued him written orders to map the headwaters of the Arkansas and Red Rivers.[94] His secret mission was to reach California and join forces with American warships and marines in the ports to conquer that land if war erupted between the United States and Mexico: "I was given discretion to act. The instructions early sent, and repeatedly insisted upon, to the officer commanding our Pacific squadron…to be strictly followed in the event of war. But these frequent discussions among the men who controlled the action of the Government, gave to me the advantage of knowing more thoroughly what were its present wishes, and its intentions." Although Polk apparently granted him great leeway with which to act, he always insisted that "I was but a pawn, and like a pawn I had been pushed forward to the front at the opening of the game."[95] Here Frémont engaged in his own "plausible deniability."

Practicality as well as secrecy prevented Polk from issuing specific orders. Any messages between the White House and commanders in California had to traverse thousands of miles and months of time. So, Frémont on the ground and naval officers off the coast only received broad, vague instructions that let them respond creatively and decisively to any opportunities or threats that affected American national interests. The critical instruction was to do whatever was appropriate to keep the British from seizing California and instead to seize California as soon as word arrived that war had begun. Just how either goal was reached was entirely up to the officers on the spot.[96]

Frémont left Washington on May 15, 1845. Once again, St. Louis was his head-quarters for organizing his expedition. Among his initial seventy-four men were Alexis Godey as a guide and a dozen Delaware Indians to act as scouts and hunters; each man was equipped with a Hawken rifle, two pistols, a knife, two blankets, a horse or mule, and a bridle and saddle. Notably absent was Charles Preuss, whom Frémont failed to talk into leaving his family to reprise his role as chief cartographer. He found a substitute in Edward Kern, an accomplished Philadelphia artist.

The expedition departed Westport on June 26 and reached Bent's Fort on August 2. There, Frémont learned that Kit Carson and Richard Owens had started a ranch on the Little Cimarron River a hundred or so miles south. Carson later explained that he and Owens "concluded that we had rambled enough and decided to settle down on some good stream." Their retirement proved to be premature: "The year before I had promised Frémont that I should join him in case he should return for…making any further exploration." After a messenger arrived with an invitation from the captain, "Owens and I sold our improvements for about half its worth and joined Frémont."[97] In assessing his three scouts, Frémont wrote: "Carson, of great courage; quick and complete perception; Godey, insensible to danger, of perfect coolness and stubborn resolution; Owens, equal in courage to the others, and in coolness equal to Godey, had the coup d'oeil of a chess-player, covering the whole field with a glance that sees the best move."[98]

Frémont and his men headed up the Arkansas River valley on August 16. For months they trod westward, first over the Rocky Mountains into the Great Basin where they angled northwest to hit the California Trail along the Humboldt River. Along the way Frémont once again crossed trails with Joe Walker and his men, who eagerly agreed to guide them to California. They reached Sierra Mountain foothills on December 1, 1845. There, the expedition split, with Frémont leading his men westward over the Truckee River route while Walker and his men headed south to a pass familiar to them. They would eventually reunite in the Central Valley. Fortunately, no snow lay on the trail ahead nor buried either party during the week or so needed to cross over. On December 9, Frémont's party entered Sutter's Fort, where "Sutter received me with the same friendly hospitality which had been so delightful to us the year before." Frémont learned that "our previous visit had created some excitement among the Mexican authorities. But to their inquiries he had said that I had been engaged in a geographical survey of the interior and had been driven to force my way through the snow of the mountains simply to obtain a refuge and food."[99]

California was ripe for takeover by a superior military force, domestic or foreign.[100] The Mexicans were split among factions that vied with each other to amass wealth and power. From 1822 to 1845, Mexico's government appointed a dozen governors to run that distant province, but California's elite thwarted them and forced nearly all of them to resign. Most recently, in March 1845, General José Castro and former governor Juan Alvarado deposed Governor Manuel Micheltorena and asserted control over northern California with their capital at Monterey. In southern California, the brothers Pío and Andrés Pico refused to recognize their rule and instead formed their own government at Los Angeles.

California's population then included around 150,000 Indians, 7,300 Mexicans, and 680 mostly American foreigners.[101] Although Americans were a minority, their numbers were growing, and they tended to be California's best-armed and most enterprising people. The American community initially included sailors who had jumped ship and mountain men who had retired to marry Mexican women and acquire ranches or start businesses. Starting in 1841, their ranks swelled with annual influxes of settlers who arrived via the Overland Trail. Although Mexican law required foreigners to take a loyalty oath to the government and convert to Catholicism, few Americans did so sincerely rather than cynically. Nearly all Americans hoped to do in California what Americans in Texas had done a decade earlier—foment a revolution that threw off Mexican rule and formed a government over California that the United States annexed.

During his previous visit, Frémont had avoided the populous coast with its pesky officials. This time he led his men directly toward them. Sutter, who was a Mexican magistrate, issued Frémont and his men passports, and lent Frémont his schooner to sail down the Sacramento River and across the bay to San Francisco, then called Yerba Buena. There, Frémont consulted with William Leidesdorff, the American vice consul. He envied the consul's idyllic lifestyle: "His house was one of the best among the few in Yerba Buena—a low bungalow sort of adobe house with a long piazza facing the bay for the sunny mornings, and a cheerful fire against the fog and chill of the afternoons. His wife, a handsome, girl-like woman, Russian from Sitka, gave the element of home that had been long missing to my experiences. He was a cheerful-natured man, and his garden and his wife spoke pleasantly for him."[102]

Frémont and Leidesdorff journeyed overland to Monterey, the province's official capital, arriving on January 27, 1846. There they first went to the home of Thomas Larkin, the American consul.[103] Larkin agreed to issue Frémont $1,800 in government credit with which to purchase supplies and would try to get official permission for all of Frémont's men to come to Monterey. The excuse for doing so was truthful enough: "in order to refit and obtain the supplies that had now become necessary" since "the camp equipment, the clothes of the men and their saddles and horse gear, were either used up or badly in want of repair."[104] The next morning, the three Americans met General Castro and former governor Alvarado. Frémont explained "that I was engaged in surveying the nearest route from the United States to the Pacific Ocean, being under the direction of the Bureau of Topographical Engineers…and that it was made in the interests of science and of commerce, and that the men composing the party were citizens and not soldiers."[105] Castro and Alvarado readily gave their consent. Frémont and his men would soon wear out their welcome.

Over the next two days, Frémont purchased and forwarded supplies to Rancho Laguna Seco, six miles south of San Jose, where he summoned his men. By mid-February his expedition was camped there. From there, Frémont and contingents of his men explored the surrounding region, including Santa Cruz and the mountains leading north to San Francisco Bay. On February 20, 1846, he received a complaint from San Jose's alcalde, or mayor, that some of his men had stolen livestock. Rather than investigate that charge and make restitution if it were true, Frémont angrily rejected the notion. Instead, he led his men twenty miles south to camp beside Monterey Bay. On March 5, a Mexican officer and two soldiers rode into camp. The officer disdainfully presented Frémont a letter from Castro ordering him to depart immediately from California. The reason Castro abruptly changed from hospitality to expulsion was receipt of orders from Mexico City not to let Frémont's expedition enter California.

Frémont defied the command. He led his men to Gavilan Peak, a low mountain that overlooked the crossroads between San Jose and the Salinas Valley, and Monterey and the San Joaquin Valley. He had his men built a log fort and display the American flag atop a tall pole. On March 9, he wrote Larkin that "I am making myself as strong as possible in the intention that if we are unjustly attacked we will fight to extremity…trusting to our country to avenge our death…. We have in no wise done wrong to the people or the authorities of the country, and if we are hemmed in and assaulted…we will die every man of us, under the Flag of our country."[106] Larkin tried mediating between the two forces. He expressed his fear to Castro that an attack on Frémont would immediately result in unnecessary loss of lives on both sides and provoke a disastrous war between Mexico and the United States. He assured Castro that Frémont would leave as soon as his horses were restored to health.

For three days Frémont and his men remained atop Gavilan Peak as Castro mustered as many armed men as possible. On March 9, Castro led sixty men to the peak but seeing how powerful the American position was, consulted with his officers. They chose to ride back to Monterey for reinforcements. Shortly after they left, the American flagpole toppled over. Frémont took that as an omen that the expedition should depart. He led his men over the low pass into the Central Valley and then north toward Oregon. Castro was relieved that the Americans had departed without a fight and lauded Frémont for having "conducted himself as a worthy gentleman and an honorable officer."[107] Frémont's decision, however, disgusted another key participant. Joe Walker was spoiling for a fight and abandoned the expedition with his men after Frémont chose to retreat.

Frémont and his men reached Peter Lassen's ranch in the northern Central Valley on March 30. There they tarried ten days, fattening their horses and debating what to do about Wintu Indian depredations against settlers in the region. Frémont finally agreed to ask his men for volunteers to join the local frontiersmen in a retaliatory campaign. Carson and several others joined the attack against the nearest Indian village and slaughtered as many as 175 men, women, and children.[108] Carson later admitted, "Although I do not know how many we killed, it was perfect butchery. The survivors fled in all directions and...having given the Indians such a chastisement...it would be long before they would again think of attacking the settlements."[109]

Frémont and his men slowly continued northward along the Sacramento River through the Central Valley's narrowing plain, then through rugged mountains and pine forests with stunningly beautiful snowcapped 14,162-foot Mount Shasta looming nearby. In early May the expedition crossed the divide into the Klamath River Valley. They left a trail of death behind them. Expedition member Thomas Breckenridge recalled Frémont's "orders while in camp or on the move to shoot Indians on sight."[110]

On the evening of May 8, two white men galloped into camp with word that a marine lieutenant named Archibald Gillespie was on his way with vital news from Washington and had sent them ahead fearing that hostile Klamath Indians would kill him before he got there. The next morning, Frémont and nine men rode with the two messengers to meet Gillespie, while the rest of the expedition slowly followed. Late that day, Frémont and his party encountered Gillespie and two companions along Klamath Lake's shore. Gillespie indeed had extraordinary news.

In late October 1845, President Polk tapped Gillespie to conduct a secret mission to California.[111] He was to carry official instructions to two key Americans in the theater, Commodore John Sloat, the Pacific fleet's commander, and John Larkin, the consul in Monterey, and letters from Thomas Benton and Jessie Frémont to John Frémont. The instructions and letters were written in ways to make them appear innocuous to any Mexican officials who might peruse them but contained coded language for action. Gillespie memorized secret instructions to whisper to each man. The essence was for each player to do whatever he could to foil a British takeover of California while fostering an American takeover if war broke out between Mexico and the United States.[112]

With a black servant, Gillespie sailed from New York to Vera Cruz, and then crossed Mexico to Mazatlán where most of Sloat's warships were anchored. After Gillespie explained his mission, Sloat detached the U.S.S. *Cyane* to convey him to Monterey; Sloat and his other warships would follow as soon as they had replenished their supplies. On April 17, 1846, Gillespie reached Monterey, where he shared the official and secret instructions with Larkin. Gillespie then journeyed to Sutter's Fort, where he hoped to find Frémont. Sutter explained that Frémont's expedition was far north heading to Oregon and supplied Gillespie with guides and horses to catch up. As if the 300-or-so-mile hard ride to reach Frémont were not punishing enough, Gillespie and his escort ran a gauntlet of hostile Indians in northern California and the Klamath River valley. Fearing the worst, he had dispatched those two riders to Frémont. Now Gillespie finally shared the instructions with Frémont who later recalled that they "absolved me from my duty as an explorer, and I was left to my duty as an officer of the American army with the... knowledge that the Government intended to take California.... War with Mexico was inevitable; and a grand opportunity now presented itself to...make the Pacific Ocean the western boundary of the United States."[113]

That night, following the meeting of Frémont and Gillespie, the Klamath Indians attacked. Frémont recalled the nightmarish way that he became aware of the danger: "I had barely fallen to sleep when I was awakened by the sound of Carson's voice calling to Basil to know 'what was the matter over there?' No reply came, and immediately the camp was roused by the cry from Kit and Owens who were lying together, 'Indians.' Basil and the half-breed, Denny, had been killed. It was the sound of an axe being driven into Basil's head that had awakened Carson. The half breed had been killed with arrows."[114] Carson shouted that Indians were attacking the camp. There was a mad scramble in the pitch dark as the Americans grabbed rifles or pistols and began firing at flitting shadows and sounds all around.

At dawn, the Americans discovered that the Klamath had killed three of them and wounded another while suffering the death of their chief. Carson was so enraged that he smashed the chief's head to pulp with his hatchet. Frémont ordered his men to pack up and head toward the main party, which they joined later that morning. The expedition then had to fight their way south for several days. All along, the Klamath swarmed just beyond rifle shot and prepared ambushes at narrow defiles. At one point a Delaware slipped away to run down and kill two Klamaths, then returned triumphantly with their scalps. The Klamaths tried to pin and overrun Frémont and his men with Klamath Lake behind them, but the Americans took cover, lowered their rifles, and killed at least fourteen attackers. Later that day, in separate fights along the trail, the Americans killed two more Klamaths.

The Klamaths had locked themselves in a vicious cycle of vengeance. The more they attacked, the more warriors they lost, which compelled the survivors to seek vengeance, which led to more deaths to avenge. Frémont vividly recalled their running fight through the gauntlet: "We were skirting…the wooded foot-hills…and had reached the head of a rocky, wooded ravine…when a strong party of Indians suddenly…commenced an attack. They were promptly driven into cover of the wood…with a number wounded. One brave refused to be dislodged from behind a rock…from which he kept up a dangerous flight of arrows. He had spread his arrows on the ground and drove back the men out of range…Carson crept around to where he could get a good view of him and shot him through the heart."[115] Carson recalled a near death experience: "When I got within ten feet of him my gun snapped and he drew his bow to fire on me. I threw myself on one side of my horse to save myself. Frémont saw the danger I was in, and ran his horse over the Indian, throwing him on the ground. Before he could recover he was shot…Frémont saved my life on this occasion."[116]

The Klamaths finally ended their pursuit and turned back after the expedition reached the Central Valley's broad rolling plain. Exhausted from the ordeal, Frémont and his men recuperated at Lassen's ranch. Frémont dispatched Gillespie with a supply requisition order to Captain John Montgomery, who commanded the war sloop U.S.S. *Portsmouth* anchored in San Francisco Bay off Sausalito; the list's most important items were three hundred pounds of lead, a gunpowder keg, and eight thousand percussion caps.[117]

Frémont received a letter from Sutter explaining that Castro had sent Indian runners to the foothill tribes with the promise of a great reward if they attacked the expedition and American settlements. Frémont and his men agreed that they had to inflict a devastating blow against the nearby Maidu Indians to preempt any pending attacks: "My movement was unexpected and riding rapidly up the river…without discovery…among the hostiles…. Intending to surprise and scatter them we rode directly upon them, and…several Indians were killed in the dispersion. In the panic made by the sudden charge the Indians jumped into and swam the river…. With scarcely a halt we rode on…but the news of our attack apparently reached them…for the Indians were escaping from their villages as we rode in among them…. We had surprised them assembled in the height of their war ceremonies. This put an end to the intended attack on the whites."[118]

Frémont and his men resumed their journey down the valley on June 8, and a week later reached Sutter's Landing. Waiting there were Gillespie and several sailors in a launch packed with supplies. The following day as Frémont distributed the supplies, thirty-two Americans led by Ezekiel Merritt from Sonoma appeared with stunning news. The previous day, June 15, they had declared California's independence and had come to ask Frémont to lead their revolt against Mexico. With them were four prisoners, including Mariano Vallejo, northern California's most powerful landowner. The rebels had even fashioned a flag with a brown grizzly bear and a red star against a white field and in black letters "California Republic."

Frémont mulled the choice before him. This was just what he had hoped either to find or provoke among the Americans in California: "Affairs had now assumed a critical aspect and I presently saw that the time had come when it was unsafe to leave events to mature under unfriendly or mistaken direction. I decided that it was for me rather to govern events than to be governed by them."[119] Yet there was a catch. As far as he knew, the United States and Mexico remained at peace. Leading the rebels as Captain John Frémont of the American army would be an act of war. So, to let the Polk administration disavow his action if need be, he wrote the War Department a letter of resignation that he sent to Captain Montgomery to forward to Washington.

Frémont's gesture was prudent but turned out to be unnecessary. Stunning events had occurred since he and his men had disappeared into the wilderness nearly a year earlier. Polk had engaged in the diplomatic equivalent of dual life and death poker games with Britain and Mexico, in which the former split the pot and the latter doubled down.

Polk informed Britain's government that on April 23, 1846, Congress had repudiated the joint-Oregon occupation treaties of 1818 and 1828. He not only asserted America's sole ownership for Oregon Territory but also insisted that the boundary stretched as far north as the latitude of 54-40 or Alaska's southern boundary. War Hawks in Congress and the press asserted the slogan "Fifty-Four Forty or Fight" to warn Britain either to yield or face war. The British had no choice but to give in. American settlers in Oregon outnumbered Britons by ten to one. The respective American and Canadian populations were 17 million and 1.1 million people. Britain's army and navy were stretched thin defending or expanding the far-flung colonies of its global empire. British statesmen recognized that the United States would not just steamroll Britain in any war but probably demand Canada as the spoil of victory. On June 15, 1846, diplomats signed a treaty that extended the existing boundary between the United States and Canada along the 49th parallel that ended at the Rocky Mountains westward to the Pacific, while leaving Vancouver Island to Britain. On June 18, the Senate ratified the treaty by 41 to 14.[120]

Meanwhile, Polk's diplomatic efforts to resolve outstanding territorial and financial disputes with Mexico failed. Washington and some prominent citizens had significant grievances with Mexico. Mexico's government and citizens currently owed American creditors $3,250,000 and refused to pay it back; that debt, however, was below its peak of $6,291,000 in 1837.[121] The Mexicans had rejected

President Andrew Jackson's offers to settle outstanding claims by buying Texas in 1829 and 1835. Mexico severed diplomatic relations with the United States after it annexed Texas on March 3, 1845. Polk dispatched William Parrott to Mexico City to restore relations, but the government rebuffed him.

Polk then sought to bolster his diplomatic hand with saber-rattling. On June 29, General Zachary Taylor received Polk's order to lead his 1,500 troops from Fort Jesup, Louisiana, to Corpus Christi, Texas, where the Nueces River flows into the Gulf of Mexico; Taylor proved to be the second best American general during the Mexico War.[122] In October Polk dispatched Lieutenant Gillespie with secret instructions to Commodore Sloat, Consul Larkin, and Captain John Frémont to seize California if war erupted and prevent Britain from taking it. In November, Polk sent John Slidell to Mexico City with authorization to offer up to $25 million for Mexico to recognize Texas's annexation and cede New Mexico and California to the United States. Mexico's government refused to meet Slidell, let alone negotiate with him.

Polk's frustration worsened as the deadlock persisted. Finally, he decided to back diplomacy with military might. On March 4, 1845, Taylor received orders to march his army, now with 3,500 troops, to the Rio Grande mouth and establish a fort on the north bank. In doing so, the president asserted the American claim that Texas's boundary was on the Rio Grande, whereas both the Spanish and Mexican government placed that boundary on the Nueces River that flowed into the sea 130 miles north. On March 24, Taylor's army reached the Rio Grande. On April 4, Mexican President Mariano Paredes issued a secret war declaration and orders for General Pedro Ampudia, who commanded six thousand Mexican troops across the river, to drive Taylor from the Rio Grande and back to the Nueces. On April 11, Ampudia issued Taylor an ultimatum that either he withdraw his army within twenty-four hours or war would result. Taylor and his men stayed put. Upon learning of Ampudia's ultimatum, Admiral Daniel Connor, who commanded the American fleet operating off the coast, blockaded Matamoras, Mexico. On April 23, General Mariano Arista replaced Ampudia and two days later led his army across the Rio Grande, with 1,600 cavalry spearheading the way. That cavalry overwhelmed an American patrol led by Captain Seth Thornton of 63 dragoons, killing or wounding sixteen and capturing the rest, an incident later known as the Thornton Affair. Taylor reported the attack to Washington and readied his army to fight the invaders.

Polk and his cabinet were in the White House debating how to craft a war declaration to Congress when Taylor's message arrived on the evening of May 9. That the Mexican army had attacked and "shed American blood upon American soil" became the core of Polk's lawyerly request that Congress recognize that a state of war existed and expand the army from 10,000 to 50,000 troops to defeat Mexican aggression. Congress overwhelming approved by 40 to 2 in the Senate and 172 to 14 in the House of Representatives.[123]

Although outnumbered nearly two to one, Taylor boldly led his men toward the enemy and routed the Mexican army at the battles of Palo Alto on May 8 and Resaca de la Palma on May 9, then crossed the river and captured Matamoros on June 5. He received orders and reinforcements to march to Monterrey and secure northeast Mexico as a diplomatic bargaining chip. The hope in Washington and beyond was that the swift succession of American victories would convince Mexico's political and military elite to end the war diplomatically. That hope proved to be a chimera.

Frémont's first act of war was to deprive John Sutter, a Mexican official, of his own fort, landing, and other holdings. That, however, was actually a political fiction to protect him from Mexican retaliation for collaborating with the Americans if the rebellion failed. Although Frémont put Edward Kern officially in charge, Sutter still managed his operations. A false rumor circulated that at Monterey, General Castro had issued a decree ordering all foreigners to leave California.[124] Most California immigrants had prudently perched on the political fence after learning about the revolt. Faced with losing their homes, businesses, and other property, they now had nothing to lose by joining the rebellion. Frémont ordered three captive Mexicans murdered in retaliation after Mexicans murdered two rebel captives.[125]

Frémont and his swelling "army" marched to Sonoma, where the rebellion had originated. After arriving on June 25, he organized a government, formed 224 volunteers into the "California Battalion," and amassed supplies for a campaign to capture the rest of California. He was disappointed when Captain Montgomery rejected his request to supply munitions to his rebel army. Montgomery explained that he was responsible for protecting "the commerce and citizens of the United States lawfully engaged in their pursuits, and have no right or authority to furnish munitions of war, or in any manner to take sides with any political party, or even indirectly to identify myself...with any popular movement (whether of foreign or native residents)."[126] Undoubtedly he was astonished that Frémont had done so, notwithstanding his transparent fig leaf of a resignation letter.

Captain Joaquín de la Torre gathered a hundred or so loyalists at Mission San Rafael. Frémont led the California Battalion against them, but Torre and his men withdrew toward Monterey. Off Sausalito was anchored an American merchant vessel, whose captain, William Phelps, was happy to sell Frémont all the supplies he needed with the promise that Washington would eventually reimburse him. Frémont borrowed a longboat from Phelps, packed it with his twelve best marksmen, then rowed across San Francisco Bay's entrance. They grounded the boat ashore near Fort Point, whose several defenders fled. After spiking the fourteen cannons, Frémont and his men rowed back to Sausalito.

The stunning vista of San Francisco Bay's entrance in the afternoon light inspired Frémont to call it "the Golden Gate." That sobriquet would prove to be appropriate for more than the stunning sunsets; little more than a year and a half later, gold would be discovered at Sutter's Mill, inspiring a rush of over a hundred thousand people in a couple of years. Frémont would join that rush, investing in gold mines that for a while made him fabulously rich.

Frémont returned to Sonoma where the rebels celebrated America's Fourth of July, gathered supplies and horses, and debated how to spread their revolution across California. A letter from Montgomery arrived on July 12 that seemed to vindicate all of Frémont's actions since he first invaded California five months earlier. Commodore John Sloat and his marines had seized Monterey on July 7, issued a proclamation that the United States now governed California, and requested that Frémont hurry with his army to join him. The California Battalion's march to Monterey was peaceful, as Castro had withdrawn with his loyalists to Los Angeles. The rebels bloodlessly captured an arsenal at San Juan Bautista with nine cannons, nineteen gunpowder kegs, and 150 muskets.

At Monterey, the Americans enjoyed overwhelming power when Frémont arrived with around 250 men to join forces with Sloat's flotilla of the 54-gun frigate *Savannah* and sloops *Cyane* and *Levant*, with twenty-four guns each. Also anchored in Monterey Bay was the 80-gun H.M.S. *Collingwood* whose commander, Admiral George Seymour, and crew could only witness with dismay America's conquest of California. Frémont and his fellow Americans gloated at having bested the British in that imperial contest.

A key justification for seizing California was that if the Americans failed to do so the British would. The Polk administration reasoned that London had ample strategic and financial reasons for conquest. California's somnolent ports and commerce would flourish as part of the British Empire. The justification for conquest would be compensation for the £15 million that Mexico's deadbeat government and merchants owed and refused to pay back to British creditors. That American fear, however, turned out to be baseless, although the Americans would not know that until years later. Britain's man in Monterey, Admiral Seymour, had neither the standing instructions nor the naval strength to takeover California in any circumstances. British naval and army power was hard-pressed and spread thin elsewhere either defending or expanding the empire. The last thing the British government wanted was a war with the United States over California. The proof was how swiftly the British yielded the Oregon Territory in the face of the Polk administration's saber-rattling. American ignorance of British intentions worked to the nation's advantage by giving Polk and Congress a bogeyman to preempt.[127]

Frémont initially found Sloat "glad to see me. He seemed excited over the gravity of the situation in which he was the chief figure, and now wholly responsible for its consequences." The commodore's anxiety worsened when Frémont "informed him that I had acted solely on my own responsibility, and without any expressed authority from the government to justify hostilities." Sloat had assumed that Frémont's actions in northern California came from specific orders. That in turn had inspired Sloat to follow suit at Monterey. Sloat was so upset that he had unwittingly committed an unauthorized act of war against Mexico that "the interview terminated abruptly" and "he did not ask me for another."[128]

Sloat's reaction is puzzling. He was under standing orders to help conquer California if war erupted. He was aware that a Mexican army had crossed the Rio Grande and attacked American troops, only to be routed twice by Taylor's American army back across the river. Yet he hesitated to act without confirmation of an official American war declaration against Mexico. Why Sloat thought Frémont would know is also puzzling given that his expedition had just arrived from northern California's wilderness. Sloat did have an embarrassing precedent that he wanted to avoid. In 1841, Commodore Thomas Jones had acted under standing instructions to seize California if war erupted. A rumor prompted Jones to force Governor Juan Alvarado to yield Monterey on October 19. Upon receiving definitive proof that peace prevailed, he then sheepishly apologized for his intrusion, lowered the American flag, and withdrew his marines from Monterey back to their vessels. Sloat did not want Jones's humiliating excursion to be the dress rehearsal for his own.[129]

Frémont chose not to try to sway Sloat by sharing the insider information he held about what the Polk administration was willing to do to realize America's manifest destiny: "I knew that the men who understood the future of our country, and who at this time ruled its destinies and were the government, regarded the California coast as the boundary fixed by nature to round off our national domain.... I had left Washington with full knowledge of their wishes." His feelings about Sloat's reaction swiftly turned from disbelief to relief. Now he could solely occupy the spotlight on this historical stage: "I was relied upon to do what should be in my power in the event of opportunity to further their designs. And now that the opportunity came I had entered among the surrounding circumstances with great joy.... I felt that the die was cast.... There lay the pieces on the great chessboard before me with which the game for an empire had been played"[130]

Another critical actor soon appeared beside Frémont. On July 15, Commodore Robert Stockton aboard the frigate U.S.S. *Congress* accompanied by the sloop *Erie* sailed into Monterey Bay with orders to relieve Sloat. On July 23, he commissioned Frémont a major and incorporated the California Battalion into America's military. He then explained his plan to take over California as swiftly as possible. Rather than journey overland, Frémont and his troops would sail with two warships to San Diego, capture that port, cut off any possible retreat of the Mexican forces, and then head north to Los Angeles. Meanwhile, Stockton would sail with the *Congress* and other warships to San Pedro, land the marines, and then capture Los Angeles twenty-five miles inland. That would secure southern California. Finally, the Americans would head north to mop up any remaining Mexican resistance on the way to Monterey.

And that is what happened. Frémont and his men sailed on July 26 and dropped anchor in San Diego three days later. They captured a Mexican brig in the harbor and secured the town without bloodshed. Frémont had his 120 men gather horses and supplies for the push north. On August 6, Stockton led the marines ashore at San Pedro, then sent a polite request for peace talks to General Castro and Governor Pico, who commanded several hundred men at Los Angeles. As Castro and Pico debated what to do, Frémont joined forces with Stockton on August 13. Castro and Pico fled to Mexico. That effectively ended resistance for the time being. On August 17, Stockton and Frémont marched at the head of their troops into Los Angeles, and had the demoralized Mexican troops disarmed, paroled, and sent home.

Acting as governor, Stockton issued decrees that established a civil government in which Americans and Mexicans served together. He sent Frémont and his troops north to secure the loyalty of the remaining towns. That done, the California Battalion would be split among fifty-man garrisons in San Francisco, Monterey, and Los Angeles, twenty-five man garrisons in Santa Barbara and San Diego, and a hundred man mobile reserve. As soon as he was satisfied that California was subdued, Stockton planned to sail with his flotilla to conduct operations against Mexico's Pacific ports. He appointed Frémont California's military commander on September 2 and promised to name him governor at San Francisco on October 25 before he sailed south.

Then complications arose. Gillespie, who Stockton had promoted to captain, commanded both Los Angeles's garrison and government. He alienated the Mexicans by insulting their honor, imposing a curfew, and confiscating their wealth. On September 23, local leader Jose Flores began a revolt that within a week captured Gillespie and his forty-eight men, escorted them to San Pedro, and then released them to an American merchant ship. The ship sailed to San Francisco, where

Gillespie reported to Stockton what happened. Stockton summoned Frémont, who was in Sonoma, to hurry with his troops to San Francisco. On October 14, they sailed to Monterey to subdue Mexicans who had revolted there.

Stockton's next plan was for Frémont to amass as many men as possible, then march south while Stockton sailed with the flotilla to San Pedro and awaited him there. Frémont needed far more time to realize his mission than Stockton had optimistically foreseen. He eventually expanded his force to 430 men, but they were short of horses and supplies. Then, although Frémont and his men encountered no significant resistance along the way, heavy rains slowed their march and broke down their horses. They did not reach Santa Barbara, more than a hundred miles short of San Pedro, until December 26. Tired of waiting, Stockton sailed with the flotilla to retake San Diego on October 30.

Meanwhile, the Americans received reinforcements from an unexpected direction. President Polk had assigned Brigadier General Stephen Kearny the mission of conquering New Mexico, then marching on to assist the conquest of California. Kearny certainly appeared to be an excellent choice for that mission.[131] He was an 1812 War veteran, had served for decades on the frontier, and commanded the 1st Dragoon Regiment. Also, he was a friend of Senator Benton and admirer of Jessie Benton. He had mixed feelings toward Frémont, lauding his explorations but dismissive of his lack of military bearing and surfeit of vainglorious ambition. Kearny still fumed for having let Frémont talk him into requisitioning a cannon outside of official channels for his second expedition, with injury imposed atop insult after the Pathfinder subsequently abandoned the cannon in the snow-buried Sierra Mountains.

Kearny marched at the head of 1,400 troops from Westport along the Santa Fe Trail to peacefully take over Santa Fe, New Mexico's capital, on August 18. After deploying garrisons in New Mexico's key towns, he led three hundred dragoons toward San Diego. On October 6, he and his men encountered Kit Carson leading eight men east with dispatches from Stockton. Having left before the revolt, Carson reported that California was secure. Kearny retained 121 dragoons and sent the rest of his men back to New Mexico; his guide Tom Fitzpatrick would carry dispatches all the way back to Washington. He had Carson lead him to California. On December 2, Kearny, Carson, and the dragoons were at Warner Springs, 65 miles from San Diego. An expatriate Englishman who owned a nearby ranch warned Kearny that the Mexicans had revolted but that Stockton held San Diego. Kearny had the man ride to San Diego with a letter to Stockton informing him of his presence and asking how he could best aid operations. Stockton dispatched

Gillespie with thirty-seven riflemen to Kearny. Gillespie informed Kearny that 160 Mexican lancers under Andrés Pico at nearby San Pasqual threatened their march to San Diego.

Kearny chose to attack them on December 6. That was a mistake. Rain had dampened the charges in the American rifles and the dragoon's sabers were no match for the Mexican tactic of lassoing and lancing them. At the cost of twelve wounded, the Mexicans killed twenty-two Americans and wounded seventeen, including Kearny, captured their cannon, and besieged them on Mule Hill. That night Kearny had Carson and another man slip through the enemy lines to seek help from Stockton in San Diego. Stockton sent eighty marines and 120 sailors to rescue Kearny, and the combined force reached San Diego on December 12. Stockton and Kearny then readied over six hundred marines, frontiersmen, sailors, and dragoons to advance against Los Angeles. Their march north began on December 29. The Americans defeated the Mexicans near Mission San Gabriel a dozen miles east of Los Angeles on January 8 and again at a mesa near the town the next day, then entered Los Angeles on January 10.

Meanwhile, Frémont resumed his own campaign after spending several weeks in Santa Barbara resting and resupplying his men. The coast road from Santa Barbara to San Pedro was spectacular with rugged mountains usually just a mile or so away. However, at Rincon Point, only fifty yards separated high tide from the cliffs for several miles. It was there that Flores chose to make a stand with his troops. When Frémont and his men approached on January 8, they stopped just beyond rifle shot of a barricade with a hundred or so armed Mexicans packed behind it. Frémont prudently sent scouts into the hills where they found a way around. He then sent eighty of his men on that route while the rest of his men pinned down the Mexicans with rifle fire. The Mexicans fled with the California Battalion in hot pursuit. Flores joined Pico and his men at Cahuenga Pass in the Santa Monica Mountains a dozen miles northwest of Los Angeles.

Frémont sent an envoy to Pico with an offer of an honorable surrender. Trapped between Frémont westward and Stockton eastward, Pico had no choice. On January 13, 1847, Frémont and Pico agreed that the Mexicans would cede California to the United States in return for equal civil rights and property protection with Americans. With the Treaty of Cahuenga, Mexican resistance ended, and America's conquest of California was essentially complete. Frémont was no more authorized to end the war for California than he was to begin it seven months earlier, yet he committed both acts confident that he would be vindicated.

CHAPTER 4

Tarnished Hero

"My acts in California have all been with high motives, and a desire for the public service. My scientific labors did something to open California to the knowledge of my countrymen; its geography had been a sealed book. My military operations were conquests without bloodshed; my civil administration was for the public good."
— JOHN FRÉMONT

"You have the power to do justice & I ask it of you that Mr. Frémont be permitted to make his accusers stand the trial as well as himself. Do not suppose Sir, that I lightly interfere in a matter properly belonging to men, but at the absence of Mr. Frémont I attend to his affairs at his request."
— JESSIE FRÉMONT

WHAT SHOULD HAVE BEEN a triumphant celebration among fellow American officers over California's conquest morphed into a bitter conflict over rank and power on January 16, 1847. Commodore Robert Stockton was about to sail south for naval operations off Mexico's coast, so he fulfilled his promise to appoint Frémont the governor of California atop his existing position as military commander. That enraged Kearny, who three days earlier had shown Stockton his orders dated June 3 and 18, 1846, from War Secretary William Marcy authorizing him to act as California's rightful governor and military leader. Stockton angrily rejected that notion, displayed his own authorization from Navy Secretary George Bancroft, and warned that if Kearny persisted he would have him recalled. Kearny sent orders to Frémont to relinquish his military command and governorship, but said he would eventually hand the governorship back after he asserted his authority. To Kearny's astonishment, Frémont replied that he wanted to ponder the situation before deciding what to do.

The following morning, Frémont delivered to Kearny a letter whereby he announced that he would retain his positions with the following logic: "I found Commodore Stockton in possession of the country, exercising the functions of military commandant and civil governor as early as July of last year…. I learned…that on the march from San Diego…to this place, you entered upon and discharged duties, implying an acknowledgement on your part, of supremacy to Commodore Stockton. I feel myself…with great deference to your professional and personal character, constrained to say, that, until you & Commodore Stockton adjust between yourselves the question of rank…I shall have to report and receive orders as heretofore from the Commodore."[132] Struggling to control his temper, the general explained that he was a friend of Frémont's father-in-law, admirer of his wife, and for their sake as well as his career, he strongly advised Frémont to take back and destroy the letter. Frémont refused and walked out. The following day Kearny departed for San Diego and eventually sailed north to San Francisco, while Frémont remained in Los Angeles where for nearly four months he asserted what he believed were his rightful duties and powers as California's governor and commander.

What explains Frémont's defiance? Three forces mingled in his mind. One was genuine ambiguity over just who had more authority to act in California, a naval commodore or an army general, given that each was empowered to do so by his respective department chief. It stood to reason that a general had more authority over land than a naval officer. Yet Stockton had been in the field months before Kearny's belated arrival, then had to rescue him from the brink of capitulating with his men to the Mexicans; he had issued Frémont a major's commission, command of the California Battalion, and the governorship. Then there was hubris. Frémont naturally felt that becoming California's governor was only right given his vital role in the American takeover. Frémont's pride in his own stunning achievements in comparison to Kearny's tardy and dismal performances overwhelmed in his mind his legal duty as an army officer. Finally, atop ambiguity and hubris, he counted on Benton's political power in Washington to resolve the dispute in his favor. At least one observer reckoned that that was Frémont's primary motive; Kearny's surgeon scoffed at "Frémont's thirst for glory" and quipped, "I only wish I could marry a Senator's daughter."[133]

Frémont was determined to be a popular leader. He wore Mexican clothes, including a serape and a sombrero, released all war prisoners, subjected the military to civil power, appointed Mexicans to many public positions, and mingled socially with California's elite. He also curried favor by freely spending Washington's credit with over $600,000 worth of various requisitions. By generously paying himself various salaries for various "services," he acquired at least $3,000 that he invested in real estate.[134] He dispatched Carson and fifteen men to Washington to get President Polk to approve his powers and policies. At some point he learned to his delight that in June 1846 he had been promoted to lieutenant colonel. He would have been on top of the world but for Kearny's long, ominous shadow over him.

Frémont's message going east to Washington at some point passed a message from Washington going west. In mid-February, Kearny received definitive presidential orders authorizing him to form a civil government over California, then turn over the governorship to Colonel Richard Mason. Kearny moved to Monterey to exercise his duties and summoned Frémont to transfer all public documents and funds to him. On March 26, with several armed bodyguards behind him, Frémont appeared before Kearny to once again assert his defiance. Kearny was determined to avenge himself against his subordinate's hubris but was careful not do so until he had removed the popular leader from his hundreds of adoring and well-armed followers. Meanwhile, Kearny himself disobeyed two orders concerning Frémont. One from General Winfield Scott was that he dispatch Frémont at the head of sixty men and 120 horses to join his army that would invade Mexico. The other, from Secretary of War William Marcy, was that he deploy Frémont in a way that "will render his services most available to the public interest."[135]

Kearny sent Mason to Los Angeles to take charge of the civil government and the California Battalion. During several meetings in mid-April, Frémont repeatedly rejected Mason's orders to him. Finally, an infuriated Mason warned: "None of your insolence or I will put you in irons."[136] That enraged Frémont, who challenged Mason to a duel. Mason accepted with shotguns as weapons. Upon hearing of the pending duel, Kearny ordered both officers to desist.

Kearny journeyed to Los Angeles and summoned Frémont on May 10. Only then did Frémont indirectly submit to his authority by asking permission to march with the California Battalion against Mexico. Kearny replied by ordering Frémont and his nineteen topographical engineers to Monterey, where he would hand all his documents to Mason, who Kearny had appointed California's governor. Frémont would then prepare his men to journey with Kearny and fifty-five dragoons overland to Fort Leavenworth. Kearny returned to Monterey by ship. When the column departed Monterey on May 31, Kearny ordered Frémont and his men to march at the rear. Over the next two and a half months, Kearny hinted but never revealed what lay ahead for Frémont.

Jessie had spent Frémont's third expedition in Washington, where she eagerly awaited any scrap of news of his adventures from the other side of the continent. In June 1846, she sent him congratulations on his promotion: "So your merit has advanced you in eight years from an unknown 2nd. Lieut. to the most talked of and admired Lieut. Col. in the army.... Dear, dear husband, you do not know how proud & grateful I am that you love me. We have found the fountain of eternal youth for love, &...I try very hard to be worthy of your love."[137]

Jessie first learned of the power dispute between Frémont and Kearny when their family friend navy Lieutenant Edward Beale along with Carson reached Washington on June 6, 1847, and visited her after delivering dispatches. She asked Beale and Carson to escort her the following day to the White House, so she could plead with President Polk to resolve the conflict in her husband's favor.

Polk had already determined who was right and wrong in the dispute. In his diary he confessed: "An unfortunate collision has occurred in California between General Kearny and Commodore Stockton, in regard to precedence in rank. I think General Kearny was right. It appears that Lieu. Col. Frémont refused to obey General Kearny and obeyed Commodore Stockton and in this he was wrong.... Indeed both...acted insubordinately and in a manner that is censurable." He did not reveal this to Jessie: "Mrs. Frémont seemed anxious to elicit from me some expression of approbation of her husband's conduct, but I evaded.... In truth I consider that Col. Frémont was greatly in the wrong when he refused to obey the orders issued by Gen'l. Kearny. I think Gen'l. Kearny was right also in his controversy with Com. Stockton. It was unnecessary, however, that I should say so to Col. Frémont's wife."[138] Polk uttered noncommittal courtesies and platitudes to Jessie, issued Carson a second lieutenant's commission, ordered Carson and Beale to head west to deliver dispatches to California, and ushered them to the door.

Polk's bland rebuff of Jessie's attempts to get him to exonerate Frémont filled her with dread. She hero-worshipped her husband and was devastated by the accusations of such serious crimes against him. Benton did what he could to comfort his daughter with her "heart bursting, the brain burning, the body shivering; and I, her father, often called, not to witness, but to calm this terrible agitation."[139] He expelled some of her agitation when he let her accompany him to St. Louis where he immersed himself in political and business concerns.

Jessie took the steamship to Westport, "a cluster of frame and log buildings on the bluff." After finding a room in a boardinghouse, she waited seemingly endless anguish-filled days and nights. One day "the rapid trampling of many horses announced the long waiting was over." Their reunion was as awkward as it was joyful. Frémont was astonished and perhaps ashamed to see her, while Jessie was stunned at the change in him with his "stern set look of endurance and self-control...a silent repressed storm of feeling.... He had not thought to meet me up there and could not recover himself instantly from the long indignation of the return journey and the crowning insult that morning at Fort Leavenworth."[140]

That morning, Kearny issued Frémont written orders to pay off and discharge his men, then "consider himself under arrest, and...repair to Washington City, and report himself to the adjutant general of the army."[141] The Frémonts hurried east to Washington. Benton was sanguine, assuring them that: "I have a full view of the whole case—Kearny's as well as yours—and am perfectly at ease. You will be justified and exalted; your persecutors will be covered with shame & confusion."[142] But at the White House, Polk rebuffed Benton when he implored him to drop the charges.

Exacerbating Frémont's distress, word came that his mother was seriously ill. He hurried to Aiken, South Carolina, to be with her. She died just hours before he arrived. He had her body conveyed by train to Charleston for her funeral and burial.

Meanwhile, Jessie helped organize Frémont's defense by collecting any relevant, available documents and soliciting potential witnesses to testify on his behalf. She once again appealed to Polk, this time by letter, urging him to "see the manifest injustice to Mr. Frémont of letting his accusers escape from the investigation of the charge they have made against him…. You have the power to do justice & I ask it of you that Mr. Frémont be permitted to make his accusers stand the trial as well as himself. Do not suppose Sir, that I lightly interfere in a matter properly belonging to men, but at the absence of Mr. Frémont I attend to his affairs at his request."[143] Polk remained as unyielding as ever to her pleas.

When Frémont returned from burying his mother in South Carolina, Jessie tried to divert his mind and rekindle their marriage with a second honeymoon. She sent Lily to stay with the Benton family and recalled: "For a week we lived alone together on a happy island surrounded by a sea of troubles. We arose late and had breakfast in our room before the fire. After the mail came, we went for a walk or a visit with friends. We even drove in the moonlight out to the school in Georgetown and looked up at the back window where the Colonel's first love letter had come up hidden in a basket of laundry."[144]

Although Frémont's legal prospects looked bleak, he did win a pre-trial victory that seemed critical at the time. Originally, the trial was to be held at remote Fort Monroe 130 miles by steamboat at the end of a Virginian peninsula in Chesapeake Bay. Benton was able to assert his political power as Military Affairs Committee chair to get the trial moved to Washington's arsenal. He then hoped to pressure the jury to exonerate his son-in-law through three related forces: Frémont's fame, the spotlight of sympathetic newspapers, and his own nearly daily glaring presence. That, however, proved to be a delusion. He and William Jones, who had married Jessie's older sister Eliza, would serve as Frémont's lawyers, although as civilians at a military trial they could only advise him, not speak for him or cross-examine witnesses.

The trial unfolded from November 2, 1847, to January 31, 1848, five hours a day except Sundays and holidays. Frémont battled three charges with twenty-three counts: mutiny, disobeying a superior officer, and conduct prejudicial to order and discipline. Kearny depicted himself as the epitome of professionalism and reason, in contrast to Frémont who was obsessed with amassing political power, wealth, and glory. He explained that Frémont "had asked me if I would appoint him governor. I told him…that as soon as the country was quieted I should, most probably organize a civil government and that I at the time, knew of no objection to my appointing him governor. He then stated to me that he would see Commodore Stockton, and that, unless he appointed him governor at once, he would not obey his orders."[145]

Although Benton rarely spoke during the trial, he was determined to undermine Kearny psychologically with the only means at his disposal. What ensued was the "adult" version of a boy stare down: "On or about the first day of General Kearny's examination before this court, he fixed his eyes on Colonel Frémont... and looked insultingly and fiendishly at him.... And I looked at him till his eyes... fell upon the floor."[146] After Benton publicly bragged about staring down Kearny, the general felt compelled to publish his denial in the *Intelligencer*. Those conflicting accounts of just whose "honor" was sullied or preserved might have led to a literally explosive encounter between them, but mutterings by each of a duel never led to a direct challenge by either.

Kearny proved to be more adept at politics than he was at war. He curried popular opinion through Rose Greenhow, the hostess of one of Washington's most powerful salons. Treason lurked beneath Greenhow's charms. She was currently spying for the British and during the Civil War would spy for the Confederacy. She disliked Benton and saw Jessie as a potential rival. She was happy to unleash a steady stream of gossip that denigrated Frémont and promoted Kearny.[147]

No witness was more potentially vital to Frémont than Commodore Robert Stockton, who had named Frémont California's military commander then governor. In a stunning turn of events, Kearny neutralized Stockton with a conciliatory letter. Stockton replied in kind. Having made that commitment, a twisted sort of "honor" now kept Stockton from giving more than a cursory defense of Frémont. When asked under what authority he had acted militarily and politically in California, Stockton admitted that he had no official instructions or authorization: "Well, I do not think I had any.... I formed the government under the law of nations."[148]

Frémont failed to muster the best argument for his defense, that he was genuinely confused over just who held the superior rank and authority for California's conquest. He had acted under Stockton's orders for six months before Kearny's belated arrival. Had Kearny immediately shown his orders giving him command, Frémont would have respectfully submitted. But Kearny chose not to do so for several months. When Kearny finally did, Frémont yielded. In his closing statement, he asked the jury to weigh his accomplishments in California against the charges against him: "My acts in California have all been with high motives, and a desire for the public service. My scientific labors did something to open California to the knowledge of my countrymen; its geography had been a sealed book. My military operations were conquests without bloodshed; my civil administration was for the public good. I offer California during my administration for comparison with the most tranquil portion of the United States; I offer it in contrast to the condition of New Mexico at the same time…. I am now ready to receive the sentence of this court."[149]

After deliberating three days, the thirteen jurors unanimously found Frémont guilty on all three charges, but seven amended the decision to recommend suspending him from the service for a year. That was a relative slap on the wrist. Those convicted of mutiny in wartime tend to be executed by firing squads. Polk promptly pardoned him from all three convictions: "Lieutenant Colonel Frémont will accordingly be released from arrest, and will resume his sword, and report for duty."[150] Lest he appear to have leaned politically too far in one direction, Polk tacked the other way by promoting Kearny to major general.

A pardon suspends any punishment from a conviction but does not overturn the verdict. In a rage, Frémont declared: "I want justice, not official clemency. There is but one honorable course to pursue in the face of this dishonorable verdict."[151] He rejected Polk's pardon and resigned from the army on February 19, 1848. Although President Polk, Secretary of State Buchanan, and Senator Benton all begged him to reconsider, Frémont stuck to his guns. With the trial's verdict and his resignation, Frémont's skyrocketing career came crashing down. Biographer Sally Denton offers this assessment: "It seemed the end of one of the more promising military careers in the history of the young republic. No officer had risen so far, so fast, from such humble beginnings. None had fallen so far, so fast, from such heights."[152]

The trial and conviction caved in Frémont's world. In his memoirs, he explained: "that part of my life which was of my own choosing, which was occupied in one kind of work and had one chief aim…in the gladness of living…I lived… an unreflecting life among chosen companions; all with the same object to enjoy the day as it came, without thought for the morrow that brought not reminders, but was all fresh with its own promise of enjoyment. Quickly as the years rolled on and life grew serious, the light pleasures took wing and the idling days became full of purpose; and, as always, obstacles rose up in the way of the fixed objects at which I had come to aim." He contrasted being trapped in the cruel maze of political, economic, and social forces with the unbridled freedom he enjoyed in the wilderness: "No treachery lurked behind the majesty of the mountain or lay hidden in the glare of the inhospitable plain. And though sometimes the struggle was hard, it was an honest and simple life, and I had my own free will how to combat it. There was always the excitement which is never without pleasure and it left no griefs behind…. Now this was to end. I was to begin anew, and what I have to say would be from a different frame of mind. I close the page because my path of life led out from among the grand and lovely features of nature, and its pure and wholesome air, into the poisoned atmosphere and jarring circumstances of conflict among men made subtle and malignant by clashing interests."[153] Frémont clearly idealized and romanticized his early years of wilderness exploration.

All along Jessie stood by her man but now shame mingled with pride. On July 28, 1848, she gave birth to a sickly son that they named Benton. The mother's stress probably harmed the child in the womb. He did not have long to live, and his death would deepen their sorrows and sense of doom. The loss of their baby atop Frémont's humiliating disgrace obscured and poisoned his genuine achievements before and during the Mexican War.

Frémont's expedition was essential for America's conquest of California when and how it historically happened. Yet in any scenario, America's takeover of California was inevitable. Nine of ten Mexicans in California lived within sight of the sea. That rendered them prostrate to overwhelming American naval power. Had Gillespie not reached Frémont, Stockton would have seized California without him by anchoring an American warship or two in each port, then marines would have joined forces with American settlers to take over interior regions. If so, the conquest probably would have taken longer and been bloodier, with more defeats along the way. Without Frémont's men, the Bear Flag rebellion at Sonoma might have been stillborn or decisively crushed by Castro's troops. Mexican authority and loyalties were weakest in the north but strengthened steadily the farther south one journeyed. Even if the Bear Flag rebellion had secured that region, the Mexicans might have contained it there. The most likely result would have been an American takeover of Monterey and the rest of northern California, while the Mexicans amassed considerable forces to defend southern California, especially the stretch from Santa Barbara to San Diego. Yet, sooner or later, the Americans would have sent enough troops to California to complete its conquest. Kearny would have arrived with three hundred dragoons rather than the 120 he brought after learning that California had been taken.

Thanks to Frémont, America's takeover of California was nearly bloodless. The only significant battle was the American defeat at San Pasqual when Pico's lancers devastated Kearny's dragoons. Casualties in the dozen or so skirmishes usually resulted in just a few dead and wounded for either side, if that. Frémont's decisive role in California's takeover was part of a war in which America's military won extraordinary laurels.

The Polk administration initially launched two major campaigns and one minor to capture swaths of northern Mexico and hopefully force Mexico's government to the negotiating table. General Zachary Taylor's army marched up the Rio Grande Valley to Camargo and then southwest to Monterey, capturing that fortified city after fierce fighting from September 19 to 24, 1846. General Kearny's 1,400-man army marched from Westport to Santa Fe, and bloodlessly captured New Mexico's capital on August 15. Kearny then led three hundred dragoons to assist the conquest of California. Later that year, General John Wool's 1,300-man army marched from Laredo to capture Monclova on November 3, and then joined forces with Taylor.

General Antonio López de Santa Anna became Mexico's dictator again when he and his cabal overthrew the government on December 6. In January 1847, he took command of the 15,000-man Mexican army at Saltillo and marched against Taylor's 4,700 troops at Buena Vista. In desperate fighting, Taylor's troops repelled repeated Mexican assaults on February 23 and 24. Meanwhile, in January 1847, General Alexander Doniphan's 950-man army headed from El Paso south into northern Mexico, routed three thousand Mexican troops at the Sacramento River on February 28, and captured Chihuahua on March 1.

The Polk administration recognized that the only way to decisively win the war was to capture Mexico City and destroy any army defending it. Fortuitously, Polk tapped General Winfield Scott to lead that campaign. Scott ranks among the greatest of American generals as a strategist, tactician, combat leader, logician, and administrator.[154] He performed brilliantly as colonel of his regiment during the 1812 War. Militarily, his 1847 campaign was virtually flawless. He landed his 6,700-man army at Vera Cruz on March 12, captured that key fortress port on March 29, marched over the mountains, defeated Santa Anna's numerically superior Mexican army at Cerro Gordo on April 17, and then captured Puebla. A three-month lull ensued as Scott sought peace talks while he resupplied and reinforced his army. He resumed the offensive in late summer. He led his army into the valley of Mexico City by an undefended pass and defeated Santa Anna at the battles of Contreras and Churubusco on August 20, Molino del Rey on September 8, and Chapultepec on September 13. American troops fought their way into Mexico City the next day but needed another month to crush guerrillas in and around the city.

Even then, Santa Anna refused to surrender. What followed was a five-month standoff as American and Mexican troops seesawed between truces broken by maneuvers and skirmishes across the valley. Scott proved to be as skilled at man-aging a government as he was an army. He organized an administration in which Americans oversaw Mexican officials to maintain order and collect revenues. De-termined that the occupation would pay for itself, Scott ensured that $3,046,498 was garnered with minimal corruption.[155]

Meanwhile, the president, his cabinet, Congress, and the press argued over what territory, if any, the United States should take from Mexico. One's position on slavery shaped one's position on spoils. The Whig Party mostly opposed, and the Democratic Party mostly favored the nation's expansion with land that, being south of the 1820 Missouri Compromise, would be free for slavery. In August 1846 David Wilmot of Pennsylvania amended a war appropriation bill with what became known as the Wilmot Proviso that prohibited slavery in any new territory taken from Mexico. Although the House approved the bill, the Senate's slavocrat majority stripped the proviso from it. Those who championed slavery's extension split over how far to spread it. Some demanded conquering all of Mexico and others just northern Mexico, while most reckoned that Polk's initial bid for New Mexico and California was good enough. Slavocrats faced a racist dilemma—they wanted to spread slavery but were baffled over what to do with the millions of "mongrel" and Indian races already living in the acquired lands.

Polk assigned state department official Nicholas Trist to negotiate a treaty. The peace talks deadlocked as Mexico's envoys refused to make any significant con-cessions. Polk was increasingly frustrated by Mexican stubbornness and Trist's conciliatory nature. He recalled Trist and set state department officials to work mapping how much of northern Mexico to take. Trist refused to step down and made a final appeal to Mexico's diplomats to grab the existing deal before a far worse one literally came over the horizon. This time pragmatism squeezed out pride, and the Mexican delegation grudgingly signed the Treaty of Guadalupe Hi-dalgo on February 2, 1848. Although angered by Trist's defiance and being denied northern Mexico, Polk submitted the treaty to the Senate, which approved it by 38 to 14 on March 10. Mexico's senate ratified the treaty on May 25.

In little more than two years, the Polk administration realized nearly all of America's continental Manifest Destiny dreams at a relatively low cost in treasure and blood. Britain's cession of its share of Oregon Territory did not cost the United States a dime. The war against Mexico cost $101 million to fight, including $74 million for army and $27 million for navy operations, with additional $64 million for veteran's benefits and $10 million for interest payments. The war cost $18.25 million diplomatically to settle. Under the Treaty of Guadalupe Hidalgo, Mexico recognized America's annexation of Texas with a boundary at the Rio Grande, and sold New Mexico and California for $15 million plus Washington's assumption of the $3.25 million that Mexico's government and people owed American credits. The United States now extended from the Atlantic Ocean to the Pacific Ocean across a vast swath of North America's continent. However, the territory that eventually would be composed of forty-eight states was not yet complete. That came in 1854, when the United States paid Mexico $10 million for a wedge of land below the Gila River, a deal known as the Gadsden Purchase. As for the human cost, 104,556 Americans men served, including 31,024 regulars and 73,532 volunteers. Of that number 13,768 died, including 994 regulars and 607 volunteers in battle and 5,821 regulars and 6,408 from disease. Mexico may have suffered as many as 25,000 dead. The $15 million payment from the United States would have covered a good share of the war's financial costs if it went to the treasury rather than corrupt officials.[156] Those were Manifest Destiny's initial financial and human costs. Tragically, America's territorial expansion would prove to be a double-edged sword that eviscerated the nation.

CHAPTER 5

Fool's Gold

"That part of my life which was of my own choosing...in the gladness of living...was to end...into the poisoned atmosphere and jarring circumstances of conflict among men made subtle and malignant by clashing interests."

—JOHN FRÉMONT

"I was to be launched literally on an unknown sea, travel toward an unknown country, everything absolutely new and strange about me, and undefined for the future."

—JESSIE FRÉMONT

JOHN AND JESSIE FRÉMONT decided to put a continent between themselves and their humiliation in Washington. Frémont would redeem himself with another transcontinental expedition that would terminate at San Francisco, where Jessie and Lily would join him after sailing to Panama, crossing the isthmus, and then sailing up the Pacific coast. Whether they stayed in San Francisco remained to be determined. Amidst the maelstrom of the trial, yet another problem plagued Frémont. Before leaving California, he had made an investment that had turned out completely different from what he intended.

Frémont had asked Thomas Larkin, the American consul at Monterey, to purchase a tract of land in San Francisco overlooking the magnificent bay. Larkin ignored his instruction and instead, on February 10, 1847, paid land baron Juan Alvarado $3,000 for Las Mariposas, a seventy-square mile patch of the Sierra Mountain foothills 170 miles east of San Francisco. For that, Larkin pocketed a 7.5 percent commission. Frémont was flabbergasted after learning what Larkin had done but amidst his tug-of-war with General Stephen Kearny over California's governorship let it stand. He reckoned that if he could not later sell Las Mariposas he could develop it into a thriving ranch like Sutter's vast holdings 120 miles northwest. To his eventual astonishment, like Sutter he would learn that his land could yield a far more lucrative product than livestock.

There was literally a pot of gold at the end of Frémont's rainbow. One of American history's most consequential discoveries happened at a sawmill being constructed on Sutter's ranch on January 24, 1848. Supervisor James Marshall spotted a glittering speck in water, reached down, plucked it out, and peered at it. "Boys," he announced laconically, "I believe I've found a gold mine."[157] Marshall took the speck to Sutter, who urged him and his other workers to keep the discovery secret while they extracted as much of it as possible. That proved to be impossible. Word swiftly spread to San Francisco and from there by ships to the ends of the earth. The California gold rush was on.[158]

Meanwhile, Thomas Benton talked three wealthy St. Louis businessmen—Robert Campbell, Thornton Grimsley, and Oliver Filley—into backing a grand scheme. He would assert his Senate powers to authorize a survey expedition for a transcontinental railroad from New York to San Francisco that would pass through St. Louis. That would enrich St. Louis and other depots across Missouri and bring vast wealth to the railroad's investors. The expedition would cross the Rocky Mountains in winter to prove that a railroad could follow.

The plan had a bizarre catch that would lead to disaster. Benton and Frémont seized on the 38th parallel as the railroad's route. In doing so, Frémont committed a stunning act of cognitive dissonance. After three expeditions across parts of the west, he should have understood better than anyone that any route would have to be flexible and sidestep insurmountable mountain ranges and canyons. Instead, he would stubbornly cling to the 38th parallel route in not one but two disastrous expeditions. Yet he had already mapped the best route to the Pacific, the mostly flat or slightly inclined Emigrant Trail west along the Platte River over South Pass and far beyond the Green River, where eventually it split into trails bound for Oregon and California, whose Cascade and Sierra Mountains posed the only truly daunting obstacles to any railroad beyond the Great Basin.

But the scheme of Frémont and Benton faced a more immediate roadblock. Although Benton talked most of his Senate colleagues into approving $30,000 for a railroad survey along the 38th parallel, the House of Representatives overwhelmingly killed the bill by 128 to 29 votes. Atop that rejection, the House even refused to underwrite Frémont's writing of a report about his third expedition that led to California's conquest. To his credit, Frémont, with Jessie his anamnesis, did produce a sixty-eight-page report called "Geographic Memoir upon Upper California in Illustration of His Map of Oregon and California." Hastily and dryly written, his Geographic Memoir failed to capture a wide audience even though the Senate had 20,000 copies printed for sale.

Dreading their latest prolonged separation, Jessie was determined to spend as much possible time with her husband before he left. With her new baby in her arms and Lily beside her, she accompanied him to New York, where he bought sawmill equipment for Las Mariposas and arranged to have it shipped there. They then journeyed to St. Louis, arriving on October 3, where they boarded a steamboat bound for Westport. Three days later the baby died, plunging Jessie into deep depression. The child was embalmed and placed in a coffin, but not buried in Westport. Jessie was determined that his final resting place would be the family plot at Bellefontaine Cemetery outside St. Louis.

Frémont diverted his grief by spending most of his waking hours mustering men, mules, and supplies for his expedition at an encampment a few miles beyond Westport. Somehow, he rounded up thirty-three recruits despite admitting that he had no money to pay their wages and claiming that Washington would eventually compensate them. Undoubtedly, most of the men joined as an adventurous yet well-armed way to get to California's goldfields. The most notable members were guide Alexis Godey and cartographer Charles Preuss, veterans of previous expeditions, along with artist brothers Edward and Richard Kern, and botanist Frederick Creutzfeldt, wilderness greenhorns.

Frémont led his fourth expedition from Westport on October 20, 1848. As Jessie watched them ride off, she struggled to keep composed but the grief from their son's death and her husband's departure left her inconsolable. That night she lay filled with sorrow and dread in bed in a boardinghouse. Suddenly she heard footsteps approaching her room and then entering. Frémont had ridden back through the night to bid her a final farewell. That helped turn her emotional tide: "Unexpected joy is always so keen that...it seems to hold enough to reconcile one to the inevitable."[159] But that joy was fleeting. After a bittersweet hour or so together, Frémont kissed her goodbye and disappeared into the dark to catch up to his men.

The expedition followed the Santa Fe Trail to Bent's Fort, arriving on November 16. There he received dark warnings not to attempt that 38th parallel crossing in any winter, especially this one whose snows and plummeting temperatures had begun weeks earlier than usual. That discouraged but did not deter Frémont who was dead set to redeem himself by proving his critics wrong. In a letter to Benton, he explained that "they have never known the snow so deep in the mountains so early, and...there is every prospect of a severe winter. But this does not deter us. I have my party well prepared, and...expect to overcome all obstacles." Yet he admitted: "I do not feel the same pleasure that I used to have in those labors, as they remain inseparably connected with painful circumstances." He intended this to be his last transcontinental crossing other than via Panama. In California "I will drop into a quiet life."[160]

The expedition headed up the Arkansas River and after several days rode into Hardscrabble, a hamlet of mountain men and their Indian or Mexican wives.[161] There he got an earful from nearly everyone of the same dire warnings not to proceed. Only one grizzled old-timer claimed that not only would Frémont's crossing be a cinch but also that he would be happy to guide the expedition across for a price. "Old Bill" Williams was a western legend.[162] He was then sixty-one years old and his once-carrot-colored hair and long scraggly beard had turned steel gray and deep wrinkles etched his gaunt face. He was tall, lean, and slightly stoop-shouldered. During his life he had been an itinerant evangelical preacher, trader with the Osage, and free trapper across most of the Rockies, although at times he joined parties if they were heading his way, and he had married and divorced Osage and Ute wives. Frémont hired Williams for a dollar a day.

What ensued was a catastrophe.[163] They struggled over the Wet Mountains and then the Sangre de Cristo Mountains before descending into the San Luis Valley. They could and should have followed the Rio Grande south until they found an easier route westward. But that would have taken them far from the 38th parallel, so Frémont insisted that Williams lead them due west along that line. As a result, they ascended into the maze of the La Garita Mountains where they bogged down in belly-deep snows, blinding storms, fierce winds, and subzero temperatures, sometimes plodding only a few hundred yards a day. They butchered and devoured their mules and horses, and then began boiling and chewing anything leather, including their moccasins. Starvation and frostbite began killing Frémont's men, one by one. He sent back Williams with three men to get help at Taos; when one of them died along the way, Williams and the two others cannibalized him. After sixteen days of waiting, Frémont correctly surmised that his messengers had not gotten through. He led five men back, promising those too weak to accompany him that he would send help. In the San Luis Valley, Frémont swapped his rifle to a Ute Indian for food and guidance to the first settlement. Along the way they found Williams and the two others, who were near death. Frémont and his men reached the Red River settlement on January 20. There, he and Godey got horses and rode twenty-five miles to Taos. While Frémont recovered at Kit Carson's home, Godey organized a relief party that eventually reached and extracted the survivors.

Frémont had led his expedition into a disaster in which starvation and freezing temperatures killed eleven of the thirty-three men. Yet, rather than admit that his own hubris caused that catastrophe, he scapegoated Williams, claiming he led them astray, perhaps deliberately, and hinted that he had cannibalized at least one of the dead. In a letter to Jessie, he expressed no remorse for what he had done to his men, only amazement at how swiftly his own fortunes could change: "I write to you from the house of our good friend Carson. This morning a cup of chocolate was brought to me while yet in bed."[164]

Frémont talked a rich Taos merchant, François X. Aubry, into lending him a thousand dollars and with it bought enough horses, mules, and supplies to get him and his remaining men to California as long as they sidestepped any other disasters. Each man was mounted and pulled along a pack animal. They headed down the Rio Grande Valley and then west where the Rockies descend into flat desert, following the well-established trail to Tucson and eventually San Diego. At the Colorado River crossing near the Gila River mouth, he and his men encountered a party of twenty-eight Sonoran miners bound for the Sierra Mountain's western foothills, where gold had been discovered on John Sutter's ranch.

That news electrified Frémont. If Sutter's land held gold, then quite possibly his Las Mariposas tract 120 miles southeast might be just as blessed. He hired the Sonoran miners with the promise that they could keep half of any gold they found while he took the other half. Alexis Godey agreed to be their manager. He dissolved the expedition at Los Angeles. He had no money to give his men but simply let each keep his riding and pack animals. He did give them the same offer that he had the Sonoran miners, but apparently few took it. Frémont then headed to San Francisco to join his wife and daughter.

The previous October, as Frémont led his men across the plains to what would be a disaster, his nemesis suffered his own agonies. General Stephen Watts Kearny was stricken with severe dysentery as he passed through St. Louis and his condition worsened no matter what cures Dr. William Beaumont attempted. Jessie had returned with her dead child to St. Louis, where, after his funeral and burial, she rested in the Benton family home. When Kearny learned of her presence, he sent Beaumont to invite her to visit him so that he could apologize and beg her forgiveness. She spurned his offer, explaining that: "There was a grave between us I could not cross."[165]

Jessie's long perilous roundabout journey to her husband nearly led to her own grave. Death by shipwreck from New York to Chagres, Panama, or from Panama City to San Francisco was possible but unlikely. The worst danger came in Panama where mosquitoes swarmed laden with yellow fever and malaria, while cholera and typhoid festered in the water. Back in Washington, as Jessie prepared herself and Lily for that journey, she struggled to reconcile "myself to the fact that in a few months I should be cut loose from everything that had made my previous life …. I had never lived out of my father's house…. Mr. Frémont's long journeys had taken him from home more than five years out of the eight since we were married. I had never been obliged to think for or to take care of myself, and now I was to be launched literally on an unknown sea, travel toward an unknown country, everything absolutely new and strange about me, and undefined for the future."[166]

Fortunately, her sister Sarah's husband, Richard Jacob, agreed to escort Jessie and Lily. They were lucky to rent a cabin on a steamboat bound for Panama. The vessel was packed with hundreds of men dreaming of striking it rich in California. They sailed from New York on March 15, 1849. The journey delighted Jessie: "I loved it at first look. I had never seen the sea, and in some odd way no one had ever told me of the wonderful new life it could bring. It stays with me in all its freshness...that grand solitude...from horizon to horizon.... It is only there that I feel completed by the exultant, abounding vitality and keen happiness which it alone brings me." The serenity she felt made her philosophical about all the tragedies afflicting her life: "Perhaps the sharpest lesson of life is that we outlast so much— even ourselves so that one, looking back, might say, 'when I died the first time.'"[167]

Nine days later they disembarked at Chagres. The ship captain pleaded with Jessie to return to New York, citing three compelling reasons for doing so. She and her daughter would likely be stranded in Panama City on the Pacific coast because ships sailed to San Francisco but did not return because the crews joined the passengers in the mad rush to the goldfields. The longer they lingered in Panama, the more likely some disease would kill them. Finally, she would be surrounded by desperate men capable of committing any number of outrages against her. Although disturbed by the warnings, a powerful force, pride, kept Jessie from turning back: "If it had not been for pure shame and unwillingness that my father should think badly of me, I would have returned to New York on the steamer, as the captain begged."[168]

Their journey's next stage involved first being conveyed by dugout canoe upriver and then by mule along the muddy trail to Panama City. For three days, they struggled along, sweat-drenched in the oven-like jungle heat, at night sleeping in mildewed tents, and dining on iguana and monkey. The sight of the baked monkey especially disgusted Jessie because it resembled "a little child that had been burned to death."[169] In Panama City, they were lucky to find lodging with a wealthy family. All along, her brother-in-law was more hindrance than help. Jessie spent much of her time nursing Jacob, who suffered motion sickness at sea and sun stroke in Panama. Along with thousands of men, they waited week after week for a cabin on a ship bound for San Francisco. She caught some disease that afflicted her lungs and caused her to cough blood.

Atop these miseries Jessie received horrible news. Lieutenant Edward Beale, a naval officer and family friend, stepped ashore at Panama City en route from San Francisco to New York. Learning of her presence, he hurried to inform her that her husband's expedition had become snowbound in the Rockies and had to be rescued. Starvation and subzero temperatures killed many of the men. Frémont had injured his leg, was recovering in Taos, and would probably return to Washington. San Francisco was chaotic, filthy, and violent, no place for a lady and her daughter. Beale urged Jessie to turn back and promised to escort her to Washington. They could leave for Chagres the next day.

Jessie agonized over what to do. When Beale appeared the next morning, she thanked him for the tempting offer, but she would fulfill her promise to her husband to meet him in San Francisco. Beale angrily tried to convince her to change her mind, but Jessie was unyielding. After he left, she found herself doing "no more deciding, but let myself go with the current."[170] Miraculously, a letter from her husband caught up with her. He wrote it while recovering at Carson's home in Taos. After recounting the disasters that afflicted his men, he expressed his longing to reunite with Jessie and Lily in California: "When I think of you all, I feel a warm glow at my heart, which renovates it…and I forget painful feelings in a strong hope for the future. We shall yet enjoy quiet and happiness together…I see our library with its bright fire in the rainy, stormy days, and the large window looking out upon the sea in the bright day. I have it all planned in my mind."[171]

She had spent over two months languishing in Panama when, on May 18, she was able to book a tiny cabin on a ship headed for San Francisco. Over four hundred, mostly men, squeezed onto that vessel with berths for only eighty. Food and water was rationed. After the ship ran out of coal, the captain had the deck chopped up and fed into the furnace. Jessie and Lily disembarked at San Francisco on June 4.

Someone awaited them, but it was not her husband. Frémont was busy managing his businesses, so he sent a request to William Howard, a prominent merchant, to take in his wife and daughter at his home. Frémont appeared ten days later. He had two investments that he was confident would make them rich, a sawmill in San Jose and gold mines at Las Mariposas. He took Jessie and Lily to Monterey where they lived in the wing of a hacienda owned by General José Castro, who had fled to Mexico; his wife still lived there and was willing to accommodate her husband's former enemy for a price.

The Frémonts moved to Las Mariposas in July. Working Frémont's holdings was his original team of twenty-eight Sonorans, with whom he split fifty-fifty the gold they extracted each month, which came to $25,000 the first month and rose steadily thereafter. He offered subsequent miners far tougher terms, six-month leases in which he took five-sixths of any gold. During the summer of 1849, seventeen parties signed those leases. Frémont had entered 1849 with literally the clothes on his back and ended that year fabulously rich.

California's richest men sought political power to bolster their swelling economic power. In August 1849, they organized an election for forty-eight delegates to hold a constitutional convention for statehood at Monterey the following month. Frémont was among the delegates that convened on September 1. One key question was whether California would be a free or slave state. For practical rather than moral reasons, the delegates voted unanimously to outlaw slavery in California. Hardscrabble miners did not want to compete with miners rich enough to employ slaves. The delegates agreed to establish a standard state government with an elected governor, two-house assembly, and court system. The delegates unanimously approved the constitution on October 12. In the plebiscite held on November 13, California's voters approved the constitution by 12,061 to 811.[172] The next vote was for a governor and assembly on December 10. When the legislature met at San Jose for the first time on December 17, 1849, electing two senators to Washington was the top priority. John Frémont and William Gwin, who ran as a Free State Democrat and Democrat, respectively, received the most votes. They then drew straws to determine who would serve the initial short two-year term or the standard long six-year term. Frémont drew short. Nonetheless, he could return triumphantly to Washington as a senator and rich man. And Jessie would bask in that triumph beside him.

It took two months for John, Jessie, and Lily Frémont to journey from San Francisco to New York via the Panama route. Traversing the isthmus extracted a harsh toll. Each got violently sick, and stormy seas in the Atlantic compounded their miseries. They finally disembarked in New York on March 8, 1850, and spent a few days recuperating at the luxurious Irving House Hotel before heading to the nation's capital.

Frémont returned to Washington amidst America's latest political crisis. Free-Soilers opposed the slavocrat demand that slavery be legal in all territory taken from Mexico. Texans insisted that their state's western border lay on the Rio Grande; New Mexicans declared the border hundreds of miles east of that. Abolitionists called for outlawing the slave trade and slavery in Washington City; slavocrats condemned that notion. Slavocrats demanded a law that forced free-state governments and citizens to help recapture escaped slaves; free-state representatives rejected that violation of their states' rights.

Two men, Henry Clay and Stephen Douglas, devised compromises that stitched up the nation's political fissures. On January 20, 1850, Clay proposed a package of eight resolutions that would partly satisfy the different interests. California would be a free state, and the inhabitants of all other territory taken from Mexico could determine whether freedom or slavery prevailed. The border between New Mexico and Texas would be moved two hundred or so miles east of the Rio Grande River, with Texas compensated by Washington's assumption of its state debt. The territories of New Mexico and Utah were created. The slave trade would be abolished but slavery would persist in Washington City. Federal officials would help slave owners to pursue and recapture their "property" when it escaped to free states. Senators heatedly debated those measures for the next seven months as Clay struggled to forge a coalition to pass his bill. It was Douglas who advocated breaking up the bill and voting on each part separately. Even that would not have been enough because President Zachary Taylor opposed slavery's extension to the Southwest and threatened to veto that measure. His death from stomach flu on July 9 brought a more pliant successor to the White House. Millard Fillmore signed every bill.

Congress approved California's application for statehood on September 9, 1850. The next day, Frémont took the oath as California's senator. He would serve only twenty-one days before the session ended and he could return to his constituents. His most significant contribution came on September 13, when he presented a map of proposed California mail routes and a package of eighteen bills whose highlights included establishing a public land recorder for titles; a surveyor general; land offices; courts for the adjudication of conflicting claims; the regulation of placer mining; sections of land for schools and government buildings; 600,000 acres of land for internal improvements; six sections for a university; the extinction of Indian land claims in mining territory; and a road across the Sierra Mountains along the American River and Carson River route.[173] Unfortunately, the Senate did not approve any of those issues while he was a senator.

Frémont joined those who favored limiting the spread of slavery. He voted for abolishing the slave trade in Washington and against tougher penalties for those who aided escaped slaves. That enraged conservatives who zealously opposed any limits on slavery. Frémont got entangled with a slavocrat in a dispute that might have ended tragically. After interpreting a speech by Senator Henry Foote of Mississippi as insulting to himself, Frémont asked him to step outside the chamber and explain himself. When they confronted each other, Foote threw a punch that grazed Frémont's cheek. Bystanders seized both men and escorted them in different directions to forestall a bare-knuckled fistfight between them. The following day, Frémont had a colleague "demand satisfaction" from Foote—that he should either apologize or explain himself. Unsaid but perfectly understood was that, without satisfaction, Frémont would call for a duel. Foote said that Frémont had misunderstood his words and had no reason to feel insulted. Frémont accepted that explanation. Fortunately, during his brief Senate career Frémont became noted for more than being overly sensitive to slights. After interviewing many of Frémont's colleagues, John Bigelow, his first biographer, noted these characteristics: "He never rose without having something to say and always sat down when he said it. He displayed great clearness and precision of statement in the few forensic efforts which are reported, and established a character for modesty, good sense, and integrity among his associates."[174]

The Frémonts had been east little more than seven months when they headed back to California. Once again, they ran that two month or so gauntlet of tempestuous seas and tropical miasmas that inflicted them with fevers and nausea. Jessie suffered more than anyone since she was again pregnant. They reached San Francisco on November 21, 1850.

After buying a house for Jessie and Lily on Stockton Street, Frémont headed to Las Mariposas. Thereafter he spent most of his time at the mine but returned periodically to San Francisco for a week or so to combine business and family matters. He lingered the longest for his reelection campaign in February 1851. The Senate voted 144 times between Frémont and William Gwin, before a vote shifted and the latter was elected. Frémont's outspoken opposition to slavery offended Californian leaders who considered the issue a distraction from advancing their state's concrete economic interests. Worse, Frémont had alienated southern slavocrats in the Senate who were critical for voting on California interests. Gwin, a southerner, would be better in wooing key senators from his native region.[175]

The Frémonts later learned that Benton lost his senate seat that he had held since 1821. Like Frémont's candidacy, legislators split evenly over Benton; the balance tipped after forty ballots. Benton lost what had previously been a bulletproof seat because of his recent outspoken opposition to slavery's extension to the new western territories. He sublimated his disappointment, intellect, and energy into writing his political memoir, *Thirty Years' View, or A History of the Working of the American Government for Thirty Years from 1820 to 1850.*[176]

The depression that the Frémonts felt from these twin political defeats lightened when Jessie gave birth to a healthy baby boy on April 19, 1851; the proud parents named him John Charles. Frémont did not tarry long with his son and soon headed back to Las Mariposas. In doing so he turned his back not just on his family but on a city plagued by worsening crime, with daily robberies, frequent murders and rapes, and periodic arsons that burned sections of the city. Vigilante groups formed to avenge the victims and deter crime by lynching any suspects they caught. Some criminals retaliated by starting fires that raged out of control. The worst arson occurred on June 22, 1851, when fire destroyed one quarter of San Francisco. Jessie escaped with her children to join hundreds of refugees atop a nearby hill from which she watched her house burn to the ground. She and the children stayed with friends while she waited for Frémont to hurry back to care for them.

Frémont found Las Mariposas increasingly unmanageable and unprofitable. His laborers and squatters had picked clean the surface gold. He needed expensive equipment and more men to mine and refine ore from ever deeper in the earth. He also needed to arm his men to back him as he evicted squatters. He was entangled with expensive lawsuits from parties with overlapping claims to his land. Although his mines yielded enormous amounts of gold, his expenses were greater. He garnered additional income from lumber, cattle, and his company store in Bear Valley, yet even that was not enough to pay his bills. He sank much money in shares of ranches and mines elsewhere in California but those cost him more than they paid back. He desperately tried to paper over the widening gap between his revenues and his debts by borrowing more money.

In frustration, Frémont wrote David Hoffman, his London agent, "I am certainly disposed to rid myself of the trouble of managing the property." Hoffman passed that message to Benton, to whom Frémont had given power of attorney. Benton was not surprised to learn about Frémont's festering problems. He considered his son-in-law "not adapted to such business and it interferes with his attention to other business to which he is adapted."[177] He found someone willing to buy Las Mariposas for $1 million dollars in October 1851. After receiving the contract, Frémont refused to sign it. The most important reason was that legally he could not sell the property until the final court decision over which among the conflicting claims was valid. But he also insisted that he would make millions more dollars from Las Mariposas. As a lawyer, Benton should have understood and accepted the first reason even if he snorted at the second. Instead, he was infuriated at what he believed was Frémont's obstinacy, incompetence, and irresponsibility, and that led to the first serious breech between them.

Despite or because of his deepening financial and legal problems, Frémont left his affairs in the hands of his foremen and headed back east with his family in February 1852. They stopped for a week in New York, where they stayed at the Irving House, and Frémont met with past or potential merchants and financiers. They then sailed to Liverpool, stepping ashore on March 22, and took the train to London, where Frémont hoped to mix business with pleasure by enticing rich men to invest in Las Mariposas. He actually hired a lecturer to give two daily talks for six months at the British Museum on his exploits and the expanding wealth of his holdings; 300,000 people attended and some bought shares in his various schemes.[178]

During their first two weeks in London, Frémont's wealth and fame opened prominent doors to the very pinnacle of British power. Frémont met Arthur Welles-ley, the Duke of Wellington, and the Royal Geographic Society honored him with a gold medal and membership. Jessie actually had an audience with Queen Victoria and Prince Albert. Such an honor with such exalted persons might have flustered most people, but not Jessie: "When I beheld the Queen and the Prince Consort… at her side, I felt myself not a Democrat bowing the knee to royalty but an Ameri-can paying homage to a figure of womanly goodness and power."[179]

Then, on those heady heights, Frémont's shady past caught up with him. On the morning of April 7, 1852, he stepped outside the Clarendon House where they were staying and was promptly arrested by four policemen who hustled him off to debtor's prison for refusing to redeem $50,000 worth of his signed vouchers in British hands. That sum, a fortune at the time, was just a sliver of the claims against him. He had racked up $1 million in expenses during California's con-quest, paid for with vouchers. Congress had not authorized those expenditures. The notes rapidly lost value as they changed hands. At least $50,000 worth of Frémont's promises ended up in the hands of British speculators, who seized this chance for compensation.

Jessie hurried to seek help from David Hoffman, Frémont's London agent. The trouble was that Hoffman felt that he was among the victims of Frémont's questionable business practices. He had thought that Frémont had given him an exclusive only to discover that he was competing with other agents hired by the American explorer. Atop that, Hoffman was sick in bed and it was past nine o'clock at night when Jessie insisted on seeing him. When Hoffman remonstrated, Jessie blurted, "No, I want no words. I have no time for that. I want £4,000 and must have it."[180] Hoffman protested that he had nowhere near so much money nor could raise it anytime soon. Jessie stormed out. Later that night she was finally able to get George Peabody, a rich American merchant, to pay the bail. Frémont walked out of debtor's prison the next morning. Infuriated at that humiliation, he vented his anger with a sarcastic letter to his father-in-law who he blamed for not getting Congress to pay for his California expenses: "If I was as great a patriot as you, I would go to jail and stay there until Congress paid these demands, now over a million, but my patriotism has been oozing out for the last five years."[181] Benton did hurry to the White House to show the letter to President Millard Fillmore and Secretary of State Daniel Webster, who eventually convinced Congress to pay off Frémont's court costs but not a dime to the myriad merchants, investors, and speculators holding his signed vouchers.

Meanwhile, the Frémonts fled London for the relative safety of Paris, where they tried to entice rich Frenchmen to purchase shares of Las Mariposas. Unfortunately, word of Frémont's incarceration and debts shadowed him to Paris, rendering Las Mariposas all the appeal of a financial quagmire to potential investors. Nonetheless, as they had in London, the Frémonts lived far beyond their means in Paris. They rented a townhouse filled with servants on the Champs-Élysées and entertained and shopped extravagantly. They attended an audience with Emperor Napoleon III and then his marriage to Eugénie de Montijo at Notre Dame Cathedral. But all their free-spending and spectacles at best distracted them from festering financial woes compounded by tragedies. Jessie learned that her brother Randolph, a dissipated twenty-two-year-old alcoholic, had died unexpectedly of some disease, perhaps delirium tremens, in St. Louis. Then, on February 1, 1853, Jessie gave birth to a sickly daughter they named Anne Beverly; the baby died on July 11, 1853, just a month after they finally returned to America after passing fourteen months overseas.

The Frémonts moved into a small house a few blocks from the Benton mansion in Washington. Frémont and Benton tried to cool the burning tensions between them by once again uniting in common purpose. They lobbied President Franklin Pierce's administration and Congress to pay off Frémont's California debts from the conquest and appoint him to head one of the railroad surveys that Congress had authorized and appropriated $150,000 for in March 1853. Despite his disastrous expedition of 1848, Frémont along with Benton still clung to the delusion that a route from St. Louis along the 38th parallel would best serve the nation, and that Frémont was the best man to lead that survey.

Secretary of War Jefferson Davis adamantly opposed either plea for related personal and political reasons. He disdained the bombastic Benton and vainglorious Frémont. More so, he had invested in a transcontinental railroad scheme to run through his home state of Mississippi, with major depots at Jackson and Vicksburg, and so favored surveys for the best southern route to Los Angeles or San Diego. Eventually four expeditions explored possible routes, that of Isaac Stevens and Captain George McClellan between the 47th and 49th parallels, Lieutenants John Gunnison and Edward Beckwith between the 37th and 39th parallels, Lieutenant Amiel Whipple along the 35th parallel, and Lieutenant Robert Williamson from San Diego to Seattle.[182]

Unable to get an official survey, Benton and Frémont again turned to private investors, mostly from St. Louis. Somehow, they scraped up enough money for a small expedition. Jessie and their three children accompanied Frémont to Independence, Missouri, where he mustered recruits, horses, mules, and supplies. Twenty-two men, including ten Delaware Indians, departed Westport on Septem-

ber 20, 1853. Alexis Godey once again happily accepted Frémont's request that
he serve as guide. This time the most important member proved to be Solomon
Carvalho, a Jew, photographer, and draftsman who wrote a fascinating book about
the expedition.[183] Frémont did not initially lead them. He was recovering from an
infection in the leg he had injured during his previous expedition and caught up
several days later on the Santa Fe Trail.

For Frémont, the fifth expedition was not about finding a viable railroad route
through the central Rockies. That was an excuse, not a reason. After all, his disastrous fourth expedition had already proven beyond a reasonable doubt that
the notion was a chimera. The real purpose was deeply personal. He was dead
set to triumph over the snowbound mountains that had devastated his previous
expedition. He would mostly follow the same route, but this time overcome rather
than succumb to the nearly two-mile-high Rocky Mountain passes in the dead of
winter. In doing so, hubris thoroughly trumped reason.

Frémont led his men along the Santa Fe Trail to Bent's Fort, where they tarried
several days buying more horses, then up the Arkansas River Valley, over the Wet
Mountains into the San Luis Valley, and, on December 14, 1853, over 10,160-foot
Cochetopa Pass in the San Juan Mountains. They suffered cruelly from frostbite
and starvation, but this time no one died let alone was cannibalized by his half-
crazed survivors. Carvalho lauded Frémont for his inspiring leadership. With calm
authority, he shared all the hardships with his men, although he did sleep apart
in his own Indian tepee: "That in all the varied scenes of vicissitude, of suffering
and excitement from various causes…when the natural character of a man is sure
to be developed, Col. Frémont never forgot that he was a gentleman; no oath,
no boisterous ebullitions of temper…from the continued blunders of his men.
Calmly and collectively, he gave his orders, and they were invariably fulfilled to the
utmost of the men's abilities." As their plight worsened, he gathered them and insisted "that we should not under any circumstances whatever, kill our comrades to
prey upon them. 'If we are to die, let us die together like men.' He then threatened
to shoot the first man that made or hinted at such a proposition."[184]

By the time Frémont and his men crossed the Continental Divide and descended into the Colorado River watershed, they had devoured all their horses and
mules, and were boiling and chewing anything leather, including their moccasins.
They eventually staggered into the Mormon settlement of Parowan on February 8,
1854, just days before they most likely would have starved to death.

During that time, Jessie was psychically in touch with her husband. A depression seized her and worsened over two weeks before suddenly transforming
into serenity as soon as he reached Parowan: "In midwinter without any reason,
I became possessed by the conviction that he was starving…. It fairly haunted

me...until...this weight of fear was suddenly lifted from me as suddenly as it had come.... A hand rested lightly on my left shoulder and Mr. Frémont's voice, pleased and laughing, whispered my name."[185] They later consulted their journals and delightfully discovered that he spoke to her just as he reached that outpost of civilization.

After recuperating and buying horses, Frémont and his men traversed the Great Basin, crossed Tejon Pass where the Sierra and Coastal Mountains met, headed north up Central Valley, and finally reached San Francisco on April 16, 1854. He lingered in California only long enough for his overseers to brief him on Las Mariposas and his other investments. He then embarked on the long sea journeys broken by a land crossing, this time in Nicaragua, that took him back to New York.

For his fifth and ultimately final expedition, Frémont wrote not a book but a long letter to *The National Intelligencer*, which other newspapers and journals copied. Although he related the highlights of his adventures and scientific findings, the thrust of his essay was to advocate a transcontinental railroad that would enrich and empower the United States. His most critical and farsighted lines were these: "It seems a treason against mankind and the spirit of progress which marks the age to refuse to put this one completing link to our national prosperity and the civilization of the world. Europe still lies between Asia and America; build this railroad and things will have revolved about. America will lie between Asia and Europe—the golden vein which runs through the history of the world will follow the iron track to San Francisco; and the Asiatic trade will finally fall into its last and permanent road."[186]

CHAPTER 6

Political Stars

"I am opposed to slavery in the abstract and upon principle"
—JOHN FRÉMONT

*"I was able to look into the political cauldron when it was boiling
without losing my head."*

—JESSIE FRÉMONT

RÉMONT'S HOMECOMING with Jessie and their children was fleeting. He spent most of his time buying and shipping equipment and other supplies in New York and Philadelphia for Las Mariposas before heading back there. Jessie stayed behind with the children and watched him board a steamship in New York. She later reflected on the cruel choices she and her husband had to make: "The affairs of his mining property required his own supervision, but for once I failed to go with him. It was one of the conflicting decisions women have sometimes to make, between their old life and the newer; but we were both in full strength and early life, and I could not turn from my failing patient Mother, and my Father's reliance on my cheerful companionship."[187]

That year and the next the Benton and Frémont clans suffered a series of calamities. Jessie's mother Elizabeth died on September 10, 1854. Benton lost his reelection bid for his House seat in November 1854 and would never again hold public office. The county sheriff seized Las Mariposas after a lower court struck down Frémont's ownership claim and rewarded the land to his latest creditor, Palmer, Cook, and Company; his lawyers appealed the case to the Supreme Courts of California and the United States. Atop these blows, Jessie was pregnant and suffering depression and morning sickness.

A fire broke out in the Benton home's chimney in February 1855, and soon

87

engulfed the house. The family escaped without injury and sent a message to Benton, then attending his last session in Congress. Benton hurried home to find it a smoldering ruin. His worst losses were irreplaceable—decades of letters, essays, speeches, and his memoirs' second volume. That loss emotionally devastated Jessie nearly as much as her father, but with time she became philosophical about it: "One outlives many things. The burning of our old house was the funeral pyre of home bonds and old ties."[188]

Jessie invited the refugees into her home. After years of emotional distance between them, Jessie and her father rekindled much of their former close relationship. With her help, he would rewrite his book and rebuild his home. On May 17, 1855, Jessie gave birth to a son who she named Francis Preston. She now had three living children. For their emotional and physical health, she and her children passed that summer at Siasconset on Nantucket Island. She also had to care for her stormy teenaged niece, Nina, the daughter of her husband's recently deceased brother Frank. Jessie's resumption of affectionate ties with her father did not last long. Politics soon bitterly divided them as it did the rest of the country.

The latest crisis over slavery came in 1854.[189] The 1820 Compromise permitted slavery in Missouri and in territories and states below a line west from that state's southern border. Slavocrats provoked the 1854 crisis by demanding that slavery be legal in the new territory of Kansas-Nebraska north of that 36°30' parallel line. Stephen Douglas authored a bill, the Kansas-Nebraska Act, that let the citizens of those territories determine whether they would be free or slave. That law's passage transformed Kansas into an increasingly violent battleground between Free-Soilers and slavocrats. Although Free-Soilers were far more numerous, slavocrats were better armed and organized, and far more ruthless. Hundreds of "border ruffians" from neighboring Missouri rode deep into Kansas to intimidate Free-Soilers and stuff ballot boxes. In 1855, slavocrats organized a state convention at Lecompton that made slavery's legality the constitution's core. Free-Soilers responded with their own convention at Topeka. To their outrage, the slavocrat-dominated United States Senate approved the Lecompton constitution and rejected their Topeka constitution. A coalition of northern Democrats, Free-Soilers, and members of the recently formed Republican Party blocked the bill that would have made Kansas a slave state. The result was an increasing deadlock between Free-Soilers and slavocrats in Kansas.

Having arisen Phoenix-like in 1854 from the Whig Party's wreckage, the Republican Party was the latest manifestation of Alexander Hamilton's concept of government as a muscular problem-solving institution that assists the private sector in developing the nation.[190] Hamiltonism's goal is a dynamic economic cycle of related financial, mercantile, industrial, technological, and intellectual advances that expands American wealth and power decades ahead of what might have happened if the private sector were left alone. The federal government provides the economy the strategic guidance and intervention lacking in a Darwinian marketplace with its "get rich quick," "anything for a buck," "boom and bust" mindset. Hamiltonism manifested through the Federalist Party of the 1790s, the Whig Party of the 1830s and 1840s, and now the Republican Party. Henry Clay and Abraham Lincoln exemplified the Whig and Republican Parties, respectively, as much as Hamilton had the Federalist Party. The Republican Party advocated passing bills that promoted economic and intellectual infrastructure like roads, canals, ports, lower schools and universities, and industries with protective tariffs; regulated financial markets with a United States Bank and currency; a homestead act that gave federal land to settlers five years after they began farming it; an education act that granted federal land to communities that founded colleges committed to promoting teaching, agrarian, and industrial skills; and a transcontinental railroad that Washington nurtured with land grants and army protection to the corporations that built it.[191]

The Democratic Party fiercely opposed all that and instead championed Thomas Jefferson's agenda of a weak national government, dominant state governments, unregulated markets, and agrarian society. Jefferson was Hamilton's ideological and political foil during the 1790s and founded the Republican Party to counter the Federalist Party.[192] Soon the party became known as Democratic Republican and eventually just the Democratic to market its conceit that it represented "the people," as opposed to the "elitist" Federalist Party. The Democratic Party's ideology expanded during the 1820s and 1830s to embrace Andrew Jackson's militant "might makes right" nationalism.[193]

Both parties courted John Frémont as their presidential candidate for 1856. The Democrats first approached him during a three-day meeting at the Nicholas Hotel in New York in August 1855. The nomination was his for the taking as long as he publicly embraced the Kansas-Nebraska and Fugitive Slave acts. The offer was enormously tempting. Becoming president would redeem half a dozen years of devastating failures. Fortunately, he asked his friend Congressman Nathaniel Banks of Massachusetts to accompany him to the conference. Banks was among the many progressives searching for a new party that best represented their views. He began as a Democrat but in recent years joined the American Party, then the Free-Soil Party, and finally the Republican Party. Backed by Jessie, he advised Frémont to spurn that Faustian deal that grossly violated his principles.

Then came the Republican Party's informal offer. Francis Blair had been a power broker for decades as the *Washington Globe*'s publisher.[194] Until recently he had been an unabashed Jeffersonian and Jacksonian but broke with the Democratic Party over the Mexican War, which he opposed. Now he was the Republican Party's most influential member. It was Jessie who convinced Blair to make Frémont the Republican Party's first presidential candidate. She informed him that the Democrats were considering him, but before he took "so important a step...he wishes for" your "advice and friendly counsel."[195] That came in the form of a pitch to Frémont by Blair at his Silver Spring, Maryland, plantation outside of Washington in December 1855. Along with him and Frémont were a dozen other Republican leaders, including Nathaniel Banks, Ohio Governor Salmon Chase, and Senator Charles Sumner of Massachusetts. Frémont said yes.[196]

Frémont's business prospects also received a decisive boost. For years, the case of just who owned Las Mariposas had made its way glacially through the legal systems of California and the United States. California's Land Commission confirmed Frémont's title in December 1852, Northern California's district court declared it invalid in January 1854, and the United States Supreme Court finally declared Las Mariposas Frémont's legal property on March 10, 1855, and then rejected an appeal by opposing claimants on February 17, 1856. Two days after the last ruling, President Franklin Pierce invited Frémont to the White House where he formally presented him his deed to Las Mariposas. That proved to be a partial victory. The Merced Mining Company and other squatters continued to dispute Frémont's claim solely to own that land's mineral rights; they formed a militia group they called the Hornitos League to bully Frémont into selling out. Frémont would eventually learn of these threats but for now he had good reason to stay east and let his managers and foremen counter the militants.

The Republican Party embraced Frémont as one of its leading standard bearers during a meeting in Pittsburgh on February 21 and 22, 1856. That embrace was immediately echoed by such powerful publications as Blair's *Globe*, Horace Greeley's *New York Tribune*, John Bigelow and William Cullen Bryant's *New York Evening Post*, and Gamaliel Bailey's *National Era*. Most of that era's leading creative writers like John Greenleaf Whittier, Henry Wadsworth Longfellow, Ralph Waldo Emerson, Washington Irving, Robert Lowell, Bayard Taylor, and Walt Whitman enthusiastically backed Frémont. His potential campaign received another boost that month when Nathaniel Banks was elected the House Speaker after a bitterly contested election in which not a single southerner voted for him. Banks could wield his power to schedule debates on issues that enhanced publicity for Republican Party positions and Frémont's accomplishments. For Greeley, Frémont's appeal was that he was a national hero with limited political experience and therefore few controversial acts, words, and thus enemies: "I felt that Colonel Frémont's adventurous, dashing career had given him popularity, with our young men especially."[197]

These developments prompted Frémont to cancel his pending return to California. Instead he moved his family to New York City, first into the Clarendon Hotel, then a brownstone townhouse at 176 Second Avenue, and finally a mansion at 56 West Ninth Street. New York was ideal for rounding up investors for both his business and political schemes. His most overt political move was publicly to express his beliefs on the most divisive national issues: "I heartily concur in all movements which have for their object to repair the mischiefs arising from the violation of good faith in the repeal of the Missouri Compromise. I am opposed to slavery in the abstract and upon principle...While I feel inflexible in the belief that it ought not to be interfered with where it exists, under that shield of state sovereignty, I am as inflexibly opposed to its extension on this continent beyond its present limits."[198]

Jessie played her role by socializing with the elite. She wrote her friend Elizabeth Blair Lee: "Just here & just now I am quite the fashion—5th Avenue asks itself, 'Have we a Presidentess among us—' and as I wear fine lace and purple I am in their eyes capable of filling the place. So I go out nightly—sometimes to dinner & a party both the same night and three times a week to the opera where I hold a levee in my box." The downsides were that "I am getting...artificial...for want of a heart warming such as you would give me. Mr. Frémont might as well go back to Washington for we only meet in company—and when we get home silence is a luxury."[199] She performed double duty as a socialite to make up for her shy husband. The pressure on Frémont to be confident, knowledgeable, witty, and wise soared after he became the Republican's presidential candidate, and he floundered dismally in that vital role. After one dinner party, Jessie revealed: "Mr. Frémont was even worse off for he was put up as a mark in the centre of the room and a number of authoresses fired at him with brilliant sentences.... He said as we drove home he would much rather have fought a duel than have gone through that evening."[200]

Much to her distress, Jessie's political skills failed her where they most mattered. Frémont's most formidable opponent was his father-in-law, who dismissed both the Republican Party's chances for success and Frémont's political savvy. Benton's opposition went deeper than that. He viewed Frémont's embrace of the Republican Party as a declaration of political war against both the Democratic Party and himself. And when Jessie stood by her man, Benton scorned her as a traitor. That deeply wounded Jessie who repeatedly reached out to him with her love: "I have written constantly to Father. I always tell him whatever I think may interest him—never saying politics—but for four months I have not had a line from him." For now, she saw no chance of reconciliation: "I know both my people too well ever to look for concession from either side. And with Father this is only the expression of years of distrust of Mr. Frémont's judgment. Since the revoked sale of Mariposas nearly five years ago, Father has put great constraints on his temper and now he has what he considers a fair occasion for an opposition.... Father chilled all my feelings when I looked to him for sympathy the winter Mr. Frémont was in the mountains. So I stand aloof." She ruled out directly pleading to her father and suffering a heartbreaking rejection from him: "I do not think I can go to Washington. I have made one thing a fixed resolve—not be hurt at heart any oftener than it is forced upon me—to go deliberately into agitation and pain is almost suicide." She believed that the path back to her father's heart lay through her husband winning the White House: "Success if it comes, gives a more graceful position to be friendly from and if it should be so I think Father cannot resist the influence of it. And, if not, it would be a mortifying thing to add to the other annoyances of a defeat, that of having appeared to conciliate for a purpose."[201]

Frémont asked Jessie if she and her friend Elizabeth Blair Lee could jointly act as a bridge between him and her father: "He wishes very much that I should go to Washington...he seems to think you & I could act as peace makers.... This is all a sore point to me. Mr. Frémont does not think how much I mind it and you must not tell him—but if I can help in any way I will swallow my pride and go."[202] To her relief a few days later, "I had a very kind letter from Father who asks me to 'come on and bring the whole'—Mr. Frémont & Nina will stay at home but all my blood I will take to him. It has been a sore thing to me to see Father and Mr. Frémont arraying themselves against each other & with Father's high sense of hospitality he would feel it a breach of honor to do anything against Mr. Frémont while under his roof—so I go to keep peace...I want to keep them on such terms that in any event neither will have to feel in a wrong position."[203]

Jessie's hopes for reconciliation proved to be a mirage. Benton got cold feet and left for St. Louis shortly before she and her children arrived, leaving them with her angry sister and brother-in-law: "That was a very bad visit...to Washington. The disappointment of missing Father, the want of hospitality in the house, and the fatigue were altogether too much.... I heard myself saying things I was not pleased with but had not the control of myself to restrain." The days of tension and disappointment provoked after she returned home "a violent attack of neuralgia—beginning...in cramping of the heart." She understood that her physical pain had emotional roots: "When I look at my strong frame & see how sound the covering is I cannot realize that it is all so at the mercy of every agitation that touches too keenly that one little organ."[204]

Over one thousand delegates packed the Republican Party convention at Philadelphia's Music Fund Hall on June 17, 1856. Frémont won overwhelming support on the first ballot. Abraham Lincoln was not only present but received 110 votes.

On the second ballot everyone voted for Frémont. For vice president, the delegates chose William Dayton of New Jersey over Lincoln and Simon Cameron of Pennsylvania. The formal campaign slogan was "Free Speech! Free Soil! Free Men! Frémont!" Then there was the informal one, "Frémont and Jessie!"

As was the custom for likely candidates, Frémont was at home when the vote took place. Upon hearing that he was the nominee, an enthusiastic crowd gathered outside his New York City mansion. He appeared at the balcony and thanked the crowd below. Someone called for Jessie to appear and others loudly echoed that demand. He beckoned her, and the crowd cheered wildly as Jessie appeared smiling beside her husband. That popular summons for a candidate's wife to appear was unprecedented in presidential history. Frémont and Jessie journeyed to Philadelphia where he formally accepted the Republican Party's nomination on June 19.

The "Frémont and Jessie" campaign excited mass appeal across swaths of the northern states. Tens of thousands of people attended rallies in cities like Cleveland, Indianapolis, Paterson, Buffalo, and Chicago, where local political leaders spoke on the candidate's behalf. Although mass rallies were as old as the republic, what was unprecedented was that many in the cheering, boisterous crowds were women. Of the array of constituencies backing the Frémont campaign, the most passionate and outspoken were abolitionists and feminists. Many leaders and followers in those groups overlapped. Women cut their political teeth in the abolitionist movement and then embraced the feminist movement following the Seneca Falls Convention in 1848. Lydia Maria Child, Elizabeth Cady Stanton, Lucretia Mott, and Clarina Howard Nichols were the most prominent abolitionist and feminist leaders that declared for Frémont. None was more devoted than Child, who wrote: "I would almost lay down my life to have him elected." Frémont, however, was her second choice: "What a shame women can't vote. We'd carry 'our Jessie' into the White House on our shoulders."[205] Nichols actually brought the three causes of abolition, feminism, and Frémont together in fifty or so public lectures to sympathetic audiences across the north from Kansas to Massachusetts; underwriting her effort was the most prominent free-soil group, the New England Emigrant Aid Society.

Yet some female abolitionists opposed feminism, of whom Julia Lovejoy, a Kansas minister's wife, was the leading voice. Lovejoy tended to be a killjoy when it came to public protests by women for women. She insisted that women should be read but not heard, at least publicly. In essays that appeared in several eastern newspapers, she encouraged women to devise creative ways to express themselves through traditional ways: "Let little Misses and young ladies in their ornamental work for the parlor, have the names of 'Frémont and Jessie' wrought in choicest colors; let the matrons in the dairy-room, make a mammoth 'Frémont cheese,' to be eaten with a zest, at their annual State or County Fair."[206]

Jessie was Frémont's campaign manager, as she advised strategy, answered letters, hosted teas for key supporters, met with supplicants, and penned missives for friendly newspapers. Her most critical role was trying to filter information. She insisted, "all mail should pass through me and the few friends qualified to decide what part of it needed to reach Mr. Frémont." She was much less thin-skinned than her easily depressed husband and did what she could to shield him from attacks and lampoons: "Enough for us to meet slanders and coarse attacks—they gave me all the pain intended.... I was able to look into the political cauldron when it was boiling without losing my head."[207]

Jessie worked closely with John Bigelow, who hastily wrote and mass printed a biography of Frémont. That project's most delicate issue was somehow refuting or diluting accusations that Frémont was a bastard. For that she journeyed to places in Virginia like Richmond and Norfolk where Frémont's parents, Charles and Ann, became lovers, got discovered by his mother's husband John Pryor, and ran off together. Although Pryor applied for a divorce, Virginia's legislature refused to grant it, and Frémont was indeed born out of wedlock. Those facts were indisputable. What Jessie did was dig up dirt on Pryor, depicting him as crude, bullying, four decades Ann's senior, incapable of producing a child, and thus the story's villain. Ann was the victim of a horrific marriage and Frémont was the innocent issue of romantic storybook love. But she lied shamelessly by claiming that Pryor had divorced Ann, who promptly married Charles.

Then there was the accusation that Frémont was a secret Catholic. Here Jessie was on solid factual ground. She explained that Ann was an Episcopal and that Frémont was confirmed an Episcopal when he was fourteen years old.

The biography first appeared as a series in Bigelow's *New York Evening Post* and then was printed as a book that eventually sold more than 40,000 copies for a dollar each. The Democratic newspapers, *Richmond Dispatch* and *Charleston Courier*, tried to blunt the book's appeal by revealing the truth about Frémont's parents. The Frémont campaign countered by cooperating with two other biographies that essentially summarized Bigelow's hefty tome, Charles Upham's *Life*, and Samuel Smucker's *The Life of Col. John Charles Frémont*.[208]

The campaign transformed the Frémont home into a horrid mix of political circus and fishbowl. The constant stress ground down Jessie, who confessed that "I am horribly tired & don't write sense I'm afraid."[209] In July, the Frémonts escaped to a rented farmhouse on Staten Island. Jessie's doctor issued her this prescription: "no newspapers, no ideas, no excitement of any kind & by way of forgetfulness I am to get well enough to go to town next week when the opera recommences & lead a life steadily devoted to amusement disconnected with politics."[210]

Meanwhile, the Democratic Party held their convention in Cincinnati and selected James Buchanan as the presidential candidate after seventeen ballots on June 2. Benton attended the convention, and then hurried back to Missouri to campaign for governor. The Buchanan campaign swiftly got tough by accusing Frémont of being corrupt, inept, tyrannical, callous, and immoral. The Democrats called for a congressional investigation of Frémont's financial dealings and spread rumors that he was a bastard, Catholic, adulterer, alcoholic, and corrupt.

Benton not only did nothing to counter these accusations, he publicly declared that "I cannot only not support him, but I must take ground against him."[211] Atop that, he spurned any contact not just with his son-in-law but with his daughter and grandchildren as well. That emotionally tore up Jessie: "Father's silence when he has always been so prompt to do battle for the right hurts me literally to the heart.... This shuts off all future relations between Mr. Frémont & himself. Mr. Frémont says he would not willingly see his children go where he has been so injured."[212]

Frémont himself refused publicly to refute the charges against him. He viewed those as private matters that should play no role in politics. That stance of ignoring rather than dignifying accusations with a response was risky. When documents prove something that a candidate denies, then they also prove that the candidate is a liar. But the Republican Party's leaders summoned Frémont to the Astor Hotel and exerted enormous pressure on him to publicly deny the accusations, especially the easily dismissed charge of being a secret Catholic. Frémont stubbornly kept silent. To escape the daily and nightly political clamor, he moved his family into a farmhouse on Staten Island.

Then, as now, most regions and states had clear political leanings, while a few were toss-ups. Frémont could rely on New England, New York, and most Midwest states. Slave states solidly backed Buchanan. The swing states were Pennsylvania and Indiana, which also held early elections in October. Pennsylvania was Buchanan's home state. Frémont could only diminish Buchanan's advantage in Pennsylvania if he and his wife campaigned there. His official campaign manager, Nathaniel Banks, urged them to do so, but Frémont refused to stir from his Staten Island retreat. In staying put, Frémont conformed to the prevailing political custom whereby a candidate's surrogates hit the campaign trail while he stayed serenely at home.

When the votes were counted, Buchanan carried both states by large margins. In Pennsylvania, Buchanan won 230,686 votes or 50.13 percent; Frémont 147,286 votes or 32.01 percent; and American Party candidate Millard Fillmore 82,189 votes or 17.86 percent. In Indiana, Frémont did slightly better, taking 94,375 votes or 40.09 percent of those recorded; while Buchanan won 118,670 votes or slightly more than half or 50.41 percent; and Fillmore got 9,669 votes or 10.47 percent. Those key states were bellwethers for the national vote. Jessie bitterly acknowledged that reality: "I heartily regret the defeat…and do not look for things to change for the better" in the general election.[213] Pennsylvania's outcome might have favored Frémont had native son Senator Simon Cameron been his running mate rather than Senator William Dayton of New Jersey.

Another vital factor helped determine the outcome. The election might have been a cliffhanger had just the Republican and Democratic Parties squared off against each other, because most American Party voters would have backed Frémont. But, in the end, the election was not even close. Buchanan won a landslide with 1,860,072 votes or 45.3 percent and 174 electoral votes of nineteen states; Frémont 1,342,345 votes or 33.1 percent and 114 electoral votes of eleven states; and Fillmore 873,083 votes or 21.5 percent and eight electoral votes of one state.[214] Frémont took Massachusetts, Maine, New Hampshire, Vermont, Rhode Island, Connecticut, New York, Ohio, Michigan, Wisconsin, and Iowa; he carried the Northeast but split the Midwest with Buchanan. He attracted only 18 percent of California's vote and only 6 percent of the mining counties of Mariposas, Tulare, and Stanislaus. Meanwhile, Republicans in Congress had mixed results. In the House of Representatives, the Republicans emerged with ninety seats, having lost eight; the Democrats gained forty-nine seats to take 133; and the Know Nothings lost thirty-eight seats and ended up with fourteen. In the Senate, the Republicans won fifteen seats, up from seven; the Democrats fell three seats to thirty-four; the Whigs lost five seats and ended up with three; the Free-Soilers lost one of their two seats and the Know Nothings gained a seat to have two.[215]

For America, in critical ways, Frémont's loss was a blessing in disguise. Had he won, the southern slave states would have seceded, and the Civil War would have begun four years earlier. Frémont would have undoubtedly proven to be as inept a president as Lincoln was brilliant in that role. Lincoln not only presided over the American victory that reunited the nation and abolished slavery but also got Congress to pass laws that promoted western homesteads, public schools, and a transcontinental railroad. Given Frémont's incompetence and corruption, he most likely would have presided over America's breakup into two weak, mutually antagonistic countries. And the history of not just the United States but the world would have been forever altered for the worse.

So, what then was Jessie's impact on the 1856 election and the issue of women in politics? The "Frémont and Jessie" campaign generated excitement but probably few extra votes. That, of course, was not immediately apparent. Three weeks after the election, the seventh annual Woman's Rights Convention took place in New York on November 25 and 26. Keynote speaker Lucy Stone was optimistic about the future: "The ballot has not yet been yielded; but it cannot be far off when, as in the last Presidential election, women were urged to attend political meetings, and a woman's name was made one of the rallying cries of the party of progress. The enthusiasm which everywhere greeted the name of Jessie was so far a recognition of woman's right to participate in politics."[216] Alas, the optimism of Stone and other feminists proved to be misplaced. It would be another sixty-four years before women received the right to vote, and a woman has yet to win the White House.

Frémont's loss hurt Jessie far more than her husband: "I am afraid I am not of the right stuff for a political woman....Mr. Frémont has everything else—health and youth and...a moderate man might be contented with the vote he had last fall. I want the party to prevail" and "for Mr. Frémont...to triumph over the enemies who made it a personal matter last year."[217] By winning the presidency, Frémont would have surpassed Benton in political achievement, at least symbolically. That would have been a key step in completing Jessie's transformation from daughter to wife as central to her identity. She also believed that with her husband in the White House, her father would come back to her. That was likely wishful thinking. Such a narcissist as Benton would not humbly yield to his former protégée and ongoing son-in-law. As it happened, both her husband and father lost their respective elections. Sharing the bitterness of defeat lessened some of the rancor between them, to Jessie's relief: "Father stayed a day & night with us—cheerful & quite himself again. We're all dead men in the political world so we have all our talents free for private life and the hatchet is buried and we are ourselves again."[218] Frémont helped ease tensions by going out of his way to please his father-in-law by deferring to him.

Frémont sought to put his defeat literally as far as possible behind him by hurrying back to California to defend Las Mariposas and other investments against worsening squatters and the "1857 Panic" financial collapse that set off a domino effect of bankruptcies. Rather than follow her husband, Jessie embarked with her children to Europe in June 1857. That had the powerful effect of making her long even more for him and to seek to recapture their once sizzling romance: She penned him these bittersweet words: "My darling I want to see you more than you can think...I want to be still beside you with nothing to think about or do but sit and wait for a little kind word from you.... I am trying to make the sun go from west to east—that is trying to look young and pretty.... I am becoming coquettish in my old age.... I love you and I want you."[219]

Lengthening time and distance only partly explain Jessie's eagerness to rekindle her husband's passion for her. John Bigelow, who hastily wrote Frémont's biography,

abruptly broke off relations with her husband and herself. At first she assumed that
she had offended him and his wife by being critical of her: "I was at first hurt at Mr.
Bigelow's defection, especially as so silly & untrue a ground.... I know I never said
anything to justify a change so complete in Mrs. Bigelow...even if I told it to him
point blank, is not reason for turning the cold shoulder immediately after the loss of
the election."[220] At some point she apparently learned the secret behind Bigelow's
puzzling behavior. He had uncovered hard evidence that Frémont had "debauched"
a maid and had other sexual affairs. That repulsed Bigelow for the man whose presidential candidacy he had championed. Of course, Jessie could only deny Bigelow's
discovery, while that heartbreaking knowledge animated her to entice rather than
abandon her husband.[221]

News from Benton in October forced Jessie to end her sojourn in Paris and
hurry back. He had not told her the real reason for his peace feeler earlier that
year. Stomach cancer was devouring him. By chance, Frémont had returned from
California an hour earlier and greeted her at her ship's gangplank in New York on
November 4. Jessie traveled alone to Washington to be with her father and was
relieved to find him in remission. After a week she was back in New York. She had
hoped that her husband would return with her to Paris, where she had left their
children with their nannies. He struggled to convince her to move back to California. The thought of abandoning sophisticated cities like New York, London,
Washington, and Paris for the wilds of California depressed her. She recalled that
"as usual after a brief rebellion I am led in docile & already making the most of
my coming position. I refused so flatly to hear even of going to California that I
suspected myself at the time & of course I am going."[222] They sent word for the
nannies to bring the children back to New York. Jessie and the children paid a last
visit to Benton in Washington to celebrate his seventy-sixth birthday on March
14, 1858. Unfortunately, Benton spoiled the occasion by one last grasp for power
over his daughter's life, insisting she leave her children with him while she was
with Frémont in California. Jessie rebuffed his demand as gently and firmly as was
necessary.

CHAPTER 7

California Dreams

*"I think I magnetized Mr. Frémont into home life.... Mr. Frémont
used to be only a guest—dearly loved & honored but not counted."*
—JESSIE FRÉMONT

*"You may come and kill us, we are but women and children, and it
will be easy—but you cannot kill the law."*
—JESSIE FRÉMONT

ALTHOUGH ALL TOO AWARE OF THE PERILS, John and Jessie
Frémont looked ahead to life in California with more hope than
trepidation. They squeezed themselves, their children, niece Nina,
two servants, and dozens of trunks among 772 passengers aboard the *Star of the
West* on March 22, 1858. The nine-day voyage from New York to Chagres was
a pleasure. As for crossing Panama, conditions had improved remarkably since
Jessie's first transit in 1849. What took several grueling days by canoe and mule
now took hours by train. They did not linger in Panama City. Porters lugged their
baggage from the train to the ship in less than an hour. Ten days later the vessel
steamed through the Golden Gate and docked at San Francisco on April 11. Their
journey was not yet done. They transferred to a riverboat that chugged across San
Francisco Bay, up the Sacramento River, and then up the San Joaquin River to
Stockton. And from there they rode a stagecoach the eighty miles to Las Mariposas, arriving on April 24.

The news eventually caught up to them that Thomas Benton died in his
seventy-sixth year on April 10, 1858. Although Jessie deeply mourned her father's
death, she could not help but also feel a sense of liberation. He had been an over-
bearing presence throughout her life, both during those times when they were
tightknit and when they were estranged. He had opposed her marriage, then

embraced her husband as a son-in-law and political tool, rejected him again after he refused to sell Las Mariposas, and broke completely when he ran as the Republican Party's presidential candidate. That ripped Jessie along a roller coaster of emotions. Although she always stood by her husband, she was consumed with guilt for defying her father. Benton's death freed her from her anguish but did not automatically better relations with her husband. Frémont was a passionate but not an affectionate or intimate man. His natural reserve and selfishness had always stunted the relationship between them. As biographer Pamela Herr explained, Jessie "had felt more loving than loved. It was she who yearned for closeness, John who resisted."[223]

The Frémonts' two-story frame house was in Bear Valley half a mile from the first mine shafts. A quarter mile away was Frémont's company town with the Oso Hotel, saloons, stores, workshops, houses for thriving businessmen, and shacks and tents for the miners, some with families. The kids ran free, admonished only to look out for clumps of poison oak and stray rattlesnakes and grizzlies. Indians were no longer a threat after having been either exterminated or expelled from the region in a merciless war in 1850 and 1851.[224] Although the summer heat was suffocating, the winters were mild, if rainy. The family passed leisurely Sundays with picnics on the grass beneath black oak trees atop appropriately named Mount Bullion, 2,152 feet high and a few miles away. For several days they enjoyed an exhilarating excursion in magnificent Yosemite Valley, just forty rugged miles northeast of their home.

Las Mariposas along with the rest of California may have looked idyllic, but figuratively and sometimes literally, it was a cutthroat place to do business.[225] Supply, demand, greed, fear, and guns shaped that Darwinian market. In a dispute, usually the business with more armed and ruthless men trumped the business with fewer, no matter how well-grounded the latter's legal claim. Political corruption exacerbated the economic anarchy. The votes of many, perhaps most, assemblymen, judges, and governors went to the highest bidder. That ill-disguised political marketplace multiplied the volatility of the economic marketplace. A law or court ruling that favored an interest group one day might be reversed to favor a rival the next day. That forced scrupulous men to set aside their ethics if they wanted their businesses to survive, let alone thrive.

Frémont did whatever he could get away with to make more money or lose less. At times he was able to sway key power holders in his favor, and at other times they turned to his rivals with deeper pockets who were determined to destroy him. For instance, although the United States Supreme Court had validated his title to Las Mariposas in 1855, that ruling was little more than a scrap of paper on the frontier. Then, in 1857, a California Supreme Court ruling that anyone could take over any unworked mine sparked countless violent confrontations.

Nonetheless, Frémont brought on many of his own problems. Although he was skilled at math, he was a lazy bookkeeper with erratic entries and calculations, and at times deliberately obscured losses and expenses that might stampede existing investors or repel potential ones. He was also skilled at surveying, but the boundaries of Las Mariposas that he drew in 1855 far exceeded his original survey in 1849; that discrepancy tangled him in endless disputes with his neighbors with overlapping claims, especially the Merced Mining Company. He paid his miners from $2.50 to $3.50 for ten hours of daily grueling work, then extracted fifty cents for that night's bed in the bunkhouse and much more for overpriced goods in the company store and overpriced grub in the company dining hall; his laborers grumbled that he was exploiting them.[226]

His monthly legal fees to Halleck, Peachy, and Billings soared steadily as he tried to stave off various lawsuits; he fell further behind until he paid them off with company shares. His tax bill also skyrocketed; he avoided having his land seized for back taxes with under-the-table payments to collectors. To his credit, he did try to boost his productivity by purchasing the most advanced machinery for his mining, milling, and lumbering operations; by grading the roads; and even by building a five-mile-long canal to supply water to his mines and town, and a railroad from the mines to the crushing mill. But those investments cost vast amounts of money that would take years to pay off, if ever.[227]

So, although his array of businesses earned him from $60,000 to $100,000 a month, his costs were usually far greater, and he filled that gap by borrowing more money at sky-high interest rates. Palmer, Cook, and Company of San Francisco was his biggest creditor. Like him, his bankers were trapped in a vicious cycle. The more money they lent him, the more vulnerable they were to him declaring bankruptcy. That spurred them to lend him more money when he asked, but at exorbitant rates that might reap some return at the risk of pushing him financially over the edge.[228]

Frémont tried to co-opt the biggest rival for his land, the Merced Mining Company, by getting the owners to pay him $12,000 a year to work their claims. Instead they exploited that toehold by trying to muscle him out of all his holdings. Their operatives organized the Hornitos League of their own miners and others that were squatting on and extracting gold from his property.[229]

A crisis erupted on July 9, 1858, when seventy or so Hornitos militants took over Frémont's Black Drift mine and besieged seven miners in the nearby Pine Tree mine just three miles from his home. Frémont gathered nineteen men, armed them, and rode out to confront the invaders. The Hornitos militants pointed their rifles at Frémont and asserted their ownership of both mines. Badly outgunned,

Frémont withdrew with his men to town. Jessie vividly recalled what happened next: "The deputy sheriff came promptly on Friday & read the riot act & then went for warrants to secure the rioters, as they refused to disperse. Then the sheriff took it up & executed no warrants until Monday—then only on three persons, leaving the rest armed and angered.... The arrested men soon returned & incited their camp by tipsy speeches. Our men were kept from retaliating with the greatest difficulty." Then the sheriff, apparently after pocketing a generous bribe, issued warrants and made arrests for Mariposas employees; he even had a warrant for Frémont's arrest but did not enforce it. Nonetheless, "the greater part of our men had to go 12 miles to Mariposa to be tried as rioters for taking up arms in self-defense & in defense of the property they were employed to work upon."[230]

Throughout the siege, Jessie proved that she truly was a steel magnolia. She resisted the temptation to flee with the children, especially after the Hornitos militants threatened to burn her home and murder her family: "Five nights we kept guard—Lea & Isaac—our trusty colored men, both mountain men & good shots—a fierce dog named Rowdy, & Mr. Frémont made the home force. With pistols & double barreled guns we had 32 shots."[231] In standing firm, Jessie hoped to act as an example for the wives of Frémont's employees to defy the bullies. One day she actually strode down to a saloon in Bear Valley where the militants were drinking and confronted them with these words: "You may come and kill us, we are but women and children, and it will be easy—but you cannot kill the law."[232]

Frémont appealed to Governor John Weller, who promised fairly to examine the claims of both sides; otherwise he would call out the state militia. The Hornitos League agreed to disperse and await Weller's opinion. That ended five days of a hair-triggered standoff that could easily have ended in mass death and maiming. Eventually, Weller announced that Frémont's claim was stronger. That, however, was not legally binding, so both Frémont and Merced asserted a new round of lawsuits against each other.

Although on paper Las Mariposas was worth more than $10 million to Frémont, it was increasingly a liability rather than an asset. The next crisis came in early 1859, when he ran out of money and stopped paying his bills. Investors back east would eventually learn of his default and demand compensation. Two local investors, Trenor Park and Joseph Palmer, insisted that he pay them with land. He yielded and signed over a valuable chunk of his holding to them. Frémont then held his nose and cut a similar deal with George Wright, the Merced Mining Company's president.

Jessie accepted rather than loved life at remote Bear Valley. Stir crazy for re-fined, creative, and challenging minds, she experienced enormous relief when one showed up for a few days but instantly felt the loss when he departed. Her most esteemed visitors were just as delighted to be with her. Among them was Richard

Henry Dana, who wrote the best-selling book *Two Years Before the Mast*, about his adventures at sea and along California's coast before the American takeover. He was smitten with Jessie, gushing that she "was a heroine equal...to the salons of Paris and the drawing rooms of New York and Washington, or the roughest life of the remote and wild...Mariposas."[233]

By 1860, Frémont had finally diversified Las Mariposas as a business realm so that it produced steady streams of revenue from his mining, milling, mercantile, real estate, lumbering, and ranching operations, while the value of the new loans that he took to paper over the value of his old ones diminished a bit. Sensitive to his wife's increasing restlessness at Las Mariposas, he paid $40,000 for a thirteen-acre estate with a mansion at Black Point on San Francisco Bay overlooking the Golden Gate, Alcatraz Island, and the distant coastal mountains. There, the Frémonts enjoyed the best of both worlds, a magnificent box seat at one of the world's most stunning panoramas and a half-hour carriage ride to San Francisco's increasingly sophisticated cultural world.

To Jessie, Black Point was heaven: "The sea is my life and my love. I love the light—& the sound and the smell of its water & here on this point of land we have it on three sides while the slope down to the very water's edge is covered with wild holly & laurel & other native trees & good taste and money have been for seven years adding all sorts of planted flowers & vines & shrubs...thorough country comfort with a city at our door."[234] Most vitally, her house had become a true home because she was finally able to entice her husband into being a genuine part of it: "When I knew I should never see Father again I turned my whole heart into this house and sometimes I think I magnetized Mr. Frémont into home life. He takes part in & likes all the details of our household—the children's plays & witticisms & lessons—he looks after our comforts & in fact is head of the house.... It's so easy to take care of children when two help. I feel now as if we were a complete & compact family.... Mr. Frémont used to be only a guest—dearly loved & honored but not counted on for worse as well as better."[235]

Jessie made Black Point into a salon for San Francisco's transplanted or transient essayists, poets, actors, singers, artists, photographers, editors, publishers, intellectuals, and wits. For her guests she was at once an enticing queen bee and inspiring muse. They went away aroused on many levels and sublimated their feelings with greater efforts to excel in their respective professions, so they could later bask in her praise.

Of her circle, Jessie was closest to Thomas Starr King. Inspired by Ralph Waldo Emerson and Henry David Thoreau, King was a transcendentalist who saw the divine in nature. He shared his visions as a minister at the Hollis Street Unitarian Church in Boston. After eleven years, he talked his wife Julia into starting a new church in San Francisco. King's brilliant and impassioned services attracted a huge following, including the Frémonts, who attended weekly services in a rented pew.

Thomas and Julia King were not happily married. Julia could not keep up with her husband's dazzling, roving mind, and hated having to follow him from her beloved staid Boston to garish, boisterous San Francisco. Jessie always invited her and their daughter to accompany her husband, but Julia rarely accepted the offer. Julia felt inadequate enough when alone with her husband and wilted completely when he was matching wits with his equals.

Jessie and her milieu enchanted Thomas King as it did all her guests. His diary entries captured his joyful experiences: "I rode to Mrs. Frémont's, two miles off, & sat in her lovely cottage, hearing her talk & enjoying it hugely.... Yesterday I dined with Mrs. Frémont & walked bareheaded among roses, geraniums, vines, & fuchsias in profuse bloom.... We have had a glorious talk & time."[236] King was not impressed by her husband, who he dismissed as her intellectual and moral inferior. After someone remarked that Frémont would make a fine ambassador to France, King quipped that Jessie "would have made a most brilliant and serviceable minister, & she can at least talk French."[237]

Jessie and King quite likely fantasized about swapping spouses, recognizing that they were far more compatible with each other than with whom they had married. Yet their love could never have been anything more than platonic. First, there was the insurmountable practical barrier that they were never alone in the same house together; servants and children were usually just a few footsteps away through open doors when they were not in the same room. Bolstering that was Victorian morality that straitjacketed behavior, although much less for men than for women. Any hint that Jessie was unfaithful would ruin her for life; Frémont, however, could get away with sexual affairs as long as he and his paramours remained discreet. Indeed, however much Jessie and King relished each other's company, that era's etiquette forced them to address each other formally by their last names.

Jessie had another platonic love affair. Among her frequent guests was Joseph Lawrence, who founded and edited San Francisco's first literary journal, appropriately named *Golden Era*. Through Lawrence, she met the writer Bret Harte, who earned a dollar for his weekly column in *Golden Era*. At first, she was probably more smitten with the handsome but bashful young man, twelve years her junior, than his writings. She saw promise in his poems, stories, and essays but encouraged him to abandon his florid style for leaner, sharper prose. She insisted that Harte dine with the Frémont family each Sunday after which she gently edited his latest submission. When Jessie felt Harte was ready, she got him a sinecure with her old friend Edward Beale, who was California's surveyor general. Harte's light office duties gave him plenty of time to write.

Jessie's efforts to lead a California cultural revolution were either behind the scenes at her rural salon or by attending the theater and opera in the city. She stepped into the political limelight only once, but it was highly controversial. A former black servant, Albert Lea, was arrested, tried, and convicted to hang for murdering his wife. In February 1861, Jessie wrote the editor of the newspaper *Alta California*, calling for the governor to commute his sentence to life in prison, citing his exemplary character when she knew him.[238] The victim's mother countered with an impassioned plea that the governor sustain the hanging of the man who had murdered her daughter. The governor sided with the victim rather than the murderer. On March 1, Lea was hanged, an event cheered by virtually everyone.

Having bruised herself in the public eye, Jessie suffered a serious neck injury when her carriage overturned while descending Telegraph Hill in April. She spent several weeks convalescing in bed. Jessie's halcyon days at Black Point were coming to a close. As the Frémonts enjoyed their delightful home overlooking San Francisco Bay, worsening political turmoil was engulfing the eastern United States.

A succession of controversial events in the late 1850s exacerbated animosities between Free-Soilers and slavocrats, northerners and southerners, and Republicans and Democrats. All along, violence, mostly by slavocrats against Free-Soilers, plagued Kansas. Slavocrats cheered and Free-Soilers condemned the Supreme Court's 1857 *Dred Scott* ruling, written by Chief Justice Roger Taney, that slaves could never be free and that blacks could never be citizens. National anxieties worsened with that year's "panic" or stock market collapse that precipitated an economic recession. Two years later, on October 16, 1859, terrorist leader John Brown and eighteen followers seized the federal arsenal at Harpers Ferry and called on slaves to revolt against their masters. President James Buchanan assigned Colonel Robert E. Lee to lead the marine detachment that retook the arsenal and killed or captured the terrorists. Brown was tried and hanged. While slavocrats reviled Brown as an evil manifestation of their worst nightmare, abolitionists celebrated him as a hero.

These issues came to a political boil during the presidential election year of 1860. Frémont's 1856 defeat gave other ambitious, powerful men within the Republican Party hope to be the presidential candidate. As for Frémont, virtually all Republican insiders dismissed him as a has-been and echoed Thurlow Weed's harsh view: "Four years ago we went to Philadelphia to name our candidate and we made one of the most inexcusable blunders.... We nominated a man who had no qualification for the position."[239]

The Republican Party's convention unfolded in Chicago from May 16 to 18,

1860. Illinois' favorite Republican son, Abraham Lincoln, made the most of his home court advantage and won the nomination, besting such formidable rivals as William Seward, Salmon Chase, and Edward Bates. Lincoln would sooth their disappointment by giving them cabinet posts. The Republican Party's platform advocated a protective tariff for industry, a homestead act, teacher's colleges, a transcontinental railroad, and, most controversially, preventing slavery's extension to the western territories. Meanwhile, the Democratic Party split into separate conventions, with one nominating Senator Stephen Douglas of Illinois, and the other Senator John Breckinridge of Kentucky. Dissidents formed the Constitutional Union Party and nominated Senator John Bell of Tennessee as its nominee. On November 6, Lincoln won a plurality with 39.8 percent of the popular vote and 180 electoral votes, Douglas 29.5 percent and 12 votes, Breckinridge 18.1 percent and 72 votes, and Bell 12.6 percent and 39 votes.[240]

That triggered the political equivalent among the southernmost slave states of lemmings jumping into the sea. South Carolina's government voted to secede from the United States on December 20, 1860, followed by Mississippi on January 9, 1861, Florida on January 10, Alabama on January 11, Georgia on January 19, Louisiana on January 26, and Texas on February 1. The secession statements by these states cited their fears that the pending Lincoln administration somehow threatened their sacred institution of slavery. Then, for six days starting on February 4, delegates from those states met at Montgomery, Alabama, declared the Confederate States of America, drafted a constitution, and elected Jefferson Davis their president.

What those states did violated the Constitution because nothing in it permits secession, let alone rebellion and treason. On March 4, 1861, Lincoln explained that in his inaugural address: "I hold that, in contemplation of universal law and of the Constitution, the Union of these States is perpetual.... It follows...that no State...can lawfully get out of the Union; that resolves and ordinances to that effect are legally void; and that acts of violence within any State or States, against the authority of the United States are insurrectionary or revolutionary.... I shall take care, as the Constitution itself expressly enjoins upon me, that the laws of the Union be faithfully executed in all the States." He then explained the core issue that divided the nation: "One section of our country believes slavery is right, and ought to be extended, while the other believes it is wrong and ought not to be extended.... In your hands, my dissatisfied fellow-countrymen...is the momentous issue of civil war.... You can have no conflict without being yourselves the aggressors." If the rebels attacked the United States, Lincoln would be forced to wield every legitimate power to "preserve, protect, and defend" the nation. He pleaded with the secessionists to rejoin the Union: "Though passion may have strained, it must not break our bonds of affection. The mystic cords of memory, stretching from every battlefield and patriot grave to every living heart…all over this broad land, will yet swell the chorus of Union when again touched…by the better angels of our nature."[241]

The rebels completed their treason and began the Civil War when their artillery batteries opened fire on Fort Sumter in the bay of Charleston, South Carolina, on April 12 and forced its commander to lower the American flag two days later.[242] On April 15, Lincoln called for 75,000 volunteers to serve for ninety days to crush the rebellion. A special session of Congress passed laws that empowered the president with vital legal, institutional, and financial means to repress the rebels. Davis called for 100,000 volunteers to fight for the Confederacy. More slave states joined the rebellion, with Virginia beginning a secession process on April 17, followed by Arkansas on May 6, North Carolina on May 20, and Tennessee on June 8. The border slave states of Missouri, Kentucky, Maryland, and Delaware remained in the United States, but contained varying portions of rebel sympathizers. On May 21, the Confederate Congress defiantly voted to move the capital from Montgomery, Alabama, to Richmond, Virginia, just a hundred miles south of Washington.

Ironically, the man whose election had provoked that wave of secessions was the only man capable of eventually restoring the United States. Lincoln's greatness was certainly not immediately apparent.[243] Few men had won the presidency with so little national or administrative experience. Lincoln served only one term in the House of Representatives from 1847 to 1849. He lost a bid to be a United States Senator from Illinois. He was a small-town lawyer and part-time state legislator. His only management experience was a few months serving as his militia company's elected captain.

What explains Lincoln's election and brilliance as president? It was Lincoln's oratory that made him famous, as his eloquent speeches were printed in newspapers across the nation. In 1856, backers actually promoted him as the newborn Republican Party's vice-presidential candidate, but William Dayton of New Jersey won it instead. Then came the debates between Lincoln and Stephen Douglas for the 1858 Senate race. The Democratic majority in Illinois's statehouse elected Douglas, but Lincoln's reputation soared on the wings of his profound rhetoric.

Lincoln excelled as president because of his intellect and character. His mind quickly sized up a threat or an opportunity from every possible angle and then seized the best way to deal with it. Just as swiftly, he could figure out a person's interests, aspirations, values, strengths, and weaknesses, and turn all that to his own advantage. With those skills he mastered the art of politics, the essence of which involves gaining the confidence of voters and politicians and then cutting deals with them. His law partner William Herndon marveled at his skill "at giving away six points and carrying the seventh with the whole case hanging on the seventh."[244] He had no military experience other than his short militia stint, but in the White House he constantly questioned generals, studied field reports, read books on military history, and pondered. No one during the Civil War exceeded Lincoln's ability to understand the war's colossal dimensions and devise winning grand strategies.

Among his toughest challenges was finding cabinet members and generals as talented and wise as he was. Through much of the war he had to endure with much less. Of his cabinet, Secretary of State William Seward and Secretary of War Edwin Stanton matured to become first-rate leaders, while Ulysses Grant, William Sherman, and Phil Sheridan became brilliant generals.

Lincoln enjoyed two great advantages in getting his policies passed and implemented. The rebellion's only positive result was the mass resignation of southern conservatives from Congress, leaving that body dominated by progressive Republicans. Atop that he took full advantage of the spoils system by replacing 1,195 of 1,520 appointed federal jobs with men who backed him and the Republican Party. The federal bureaucracy expanded from 40,651 to 195,000 employees during the war, and nearly all those jobs went to party loyalists.[245]

Of course, Lincoln's most critical decisions involved just how to crush the rebellion and restore the Union during four years of war. The northern states had clear advantages in hard power over the rebel states. The North's 22,339,989 people were two and a half times more numerous than the South's 9,103,332 people, of whom 3,521,110 were slaves and 132,760 were free blacks. The North's 1,300,000 workers in 110,000 factories dwarfed the South's 110,000 workers in 18,000 factories. The North's 21,973 miles of train track was two and a half times greater than the South's 9,283 miles. There were 800,000 draft animals in the North and only 300,000 in the South. The American army numbered only 1,105 officers and 15,239 men when the southern states began seceding. One of four, or 296, officers resigned as their states rebelled against the United States. The North's navy numbered nine thousand sailors in ninety ships; the South had no warships.[246] But all that was just potential power. It would take vast reserves of soft power—strategy, tactics, organizational ability, morale, and will—to mobilize and assert all the hard power vital to winning the war. And it was soft power where the South had the edge at first. The American cause depended on Union armies invading the South to destroy Confederate armies and occupy major cities as a tightening naval blockade starved the rebels of critical foreign supplies that they could not themselves manufacture. Ultimately, the North had to decimate the rebel will as well as ability to fight. As commander-in-chief, Lincoln eventually mastered the art of smart power, of mustering and asserting the appropriate mix of hard and soft power resources to crush the rebellion, reunite the nation, and abolish slavery.

As if those achievements were not extraordinary enough, Lincoln also spearheaded a Hamiltonian economic revolution. With Lincoln's advice and consent, Congressional leaders drafted and passed a series of laws that transformed America's economy, including the Legal Tender Act of February 1862, which created "greenback" paper money; the Internal Revenue Act of July 1862, which raised taxes on the incomes of the rich and luxury goods; the Homestead Act of May 1862, which promised 160 acres of free western land to anyone who farmed it for five years; the Morrill Act of July 1862, which established colleges that trained teachers; the Pacific Railroad Act of July 1862, which granted land and money for any company dedicated to building a line across the country; and the National Banking Act of February 1863, which granted federal charters to banks that held at least a third of their assets in government bonds. But all that lay ahead. For now the nation was torn asunder into warring camps with no conceivable way to reunite it.

Although Jessie followed the news from back east with worsening fears, disunity in her marriage was her greatest concern. Her belief that she had finally domesticated her husband proved to be a delusion. On January 1, 1861, Frémont departed on a business trip that would take him first to America's east coast and then on to Europe. He was accompanied by his attorney Frederick Billings, Mariposa Mining Company trustee George Wright, key shareholder Trenor Park, and, secretly, his mistress Margaret Corbett and her child. Whether rumors reached Jessie that her husband was traveling with his lover is unknown. What did happen was that the four men secured more than $2 million for Las Mariposas from investors in London and Paris, enough either to capitalize a business renaissance or further swell the soaring mountain of debt that could never be repaid. Frémont racked up debts not just for his own business but also for the United States. Without authorization, he purchased an array of military weapons worth $125,000 in Paris and $75,000 in London, and had them shipped to Washington; somehow, he sincerely believed that Congress would automatically approve and appropriate money for the sale.[247] Wright, Billings, and Park returned to California to try to save Las Mariposas and other businesses from years of Frémont's mismanagement and dubious financial dealings. Frémont headed to Washington where he hoped to engineer his latest reinvention, this time as a victorious general that saved America from itself.

CHAPTER 8

Misfires

★

"For it is a very risky thing to tell the whole truth. Especially if people are displeased with themselves."
—JESSIE FRÉMONT

"In respect to Mr. Lincoln, I continue to hold...his administration has been politically, militarily, and financially a failure, and that its necessary continuance is a cause of regret for the country."
—JOHN FRÉMONT

JOHN FRÉMONT COUNTED ON the patronage of Washington's most powerful political clan to realize his dreams of saving America as a victorious general. Francis Blair was the *Washington Globe*'s publisher and a long-standing political ally of now deceased Thomas Benton and his son-in-law. Blair's power expanded through his two sons, Frank Blair, who chaired the House of Representatives Military Affairs Committee, and Montgomery Blair, the Postmaster General. Worried that President Abraham Lincoln would soon run out of generalships to hand out, Frémont penned on May 6, 1861, his latest plea to Francis Blair: "I trust that you have already offered my services to the President.... My great desire is to serve my country in the most direct and effective way that I possibly can."[248]

Abraham Lincoln can be forgiven for not making John Frémont's ambitions his immediate priority. Like nearly everyone, Lincoln expected a short war, which was why initially he summoned only 75,000 volunteers for a mere three month's service. That belief would seem to defy anyone who knew anything about equipping and training soldiers, then marching them against the enemy, in this case eleven rebel states with nine million people spread across a vast territory. The administration's only Cassandra had impeccable credentials for making his case, Lieutenant General Winfield Scott, the army commander. In America's Valhalla of great generals, Scott is in the inner circle.[249] He fought brilliantly at his regiment's head during the 1812 War and at his army's head during the Mexican War. He tersely explained that it would take the combined relentless efforts of hundreds of thousands of troops, hundreds of warships, and tens of billions of dollars and many years to crush the rebellion. The first stage demanded amassing vast armies as the navy steadily blockaded more stretches of the rebel coast. Only when the blockade began to throttle the South's economy, would the armies march against the rebel armies and destroy them. Eventually Scott's "Anaconda Plan" became the American blueprint for victory. But the president and his cabinet initially rejected it as politically unpalatable and militarily unnecessary. It took a crushing defeat nearly at Washington's front door to begin to change that mindset.

By mid-July General Irwin McDowell commanded 34,000 blue-coated men gathered at Centreville, Virginia, just twenty miles south of the capital. Half a dozen miles southwest around Manassas Junction, General Pierre Beauregard's rebel army numbered 24,000. Lincoln urged McDowell to attack, parrying his objection that his men were not ready with this argument: "You are green, it is true, but they are green, also; you are all green alike."[250] On July 21, McDowell sent his men into battle along Bull Run creek just days before many of their enlistments would expire. Initially, the Confederates retreated before the Union onslaught, but 11,000 fresh troops under General Joe Johnston arrived to smash McDowell's right flank. That panicked the entire Union army into fleeing toward Washington. The casualty figures of 2,800 Union and 1,750 Confederates appalled all Americans but were merely a harbinger of the horrors that lay ahead.[251] The humiliating rout prompted Lincoln to accept Scott's formula for victory. During a special session, Congress passed, and Lincoln signed, two bills with each authorizing the enlistment of five hundred thousand troops for three years, or a million altogether.

The excitement that preceded the battle of Bull Run and the gloom that followed obscured promising news for the American cause coming from Missouri.[252] That state's Governor Claiborne Jackson was a slavocrat zealot determined to lead Missouri into the Confederacy. At Jefferson City, he tapped General Sterling Price to command an army of regiments being mustered across Missouri, including seven hundred troops at Camp Jackson in St. Louis.

At this critical point the concerted efforts of two men, Congressman Frank Blair of St. Louis and Captain Nathaniel Lyon, led the effort to prevent the rebel takeover of Missouri.[253] Blair organized four regiments of volunteers to reinforce Lyon, who commanded the small contingent of Federal troops defending the United States arsenal at St. Louis. Lyon, Blair, and their troops transferred the arsenal's arms and munitions to safety in Illinois. Then, on May 11, they surrounded Camp Jackson and forced the rebels to surrender. Although they did so without a shot being fired, a riot erupted as they conducted the prisoners through the city and twenty-eight civilians and two soldiers died in the fighting. Blair returned to Washington to brief the president on Missouri's dire situation and resume his congressional seat.

Lincoln rewarded Lyon's decisive actions by promoting him to brigadier general and sending him reinforcements and authority to secure Missouri for the Union. Lyon led his small army up the Missouri River valley. As Lyon's triumphant force neared Jefferson City, Jackson, Price, and their troops withdrew to Springfield in southwestern Missouri. A pro-American convention formed a provisional government and elected Hamilton Gamble the governor. Missouri seemed secure for now. Then Lincoln made a decision that nearly lost Missouri to the Confederacy. Lyon had proved to be a dynamic, far-sighted, courageous leader. Yet, rather than promote him to major general and give him the region to command, Lincoln put politics before sound military judgment.

Frémont's anxious wait for a key role in the war ended on July 3, 1861. That day Lincoln established the Department of the West with its headquarters at St. Louis, named Frémont its commander, and commissioned him a major general. At the White House, Lincoln briefed Frémont on his duties and strategy. Of the meeting, Frémont wrote: The president had gone carefully over with me the subject of my intended campaign…. This he did in the unpretentious and kindly manner which invited suggestion, and which with him was characteristic. When I took leave of him…I asked him if…there was anything further…that he wished to say…'No,' he replied, 'I have given you carte blanche; you must use your own judgment and do the best you can. I doubt if the States will ever come back.'"[254]

That was an extraordinary promotion and conferral of trust to a man who had never commanded more than a few hundred armed men. Tragically, Lincoln's hopes for Frémont were misplaced. Frémont served as the Department of the West's commander for about four months. During that time, he made an utter mess of things, strategically, organizationally, ethically, and politically. The power entrusted to Frémont warped him. He had risen to his highest level of incompetence. He was incapable of running anything larger than a hundred or so troops or employees and now he oversaw an army and a vast expanse of territory. The result was a vicious psychological cycle whereby the more overwhelmed he became, the more he ignored critical problems of administration, training, supply, and strategy, and the more he focused on minutia and personalities, which exacerbated the critical problems and thus caused him to burrow deeper into the trivial. But that lay ahead.

Frémont met his family at New York's wharf on July 13, and proudly informed them of his promotion and command. He, his family, and his entourage arrived in St. Louis on July 25. There he sought the same grandeur as a general as he was accustomed to enjoying as a millionaire, but at the taxpayer's expense. For his headquarters he rented the stunning mansion on Chouteau Avenue owned by Jessie's cousin, Sarah Benton Brant, and charged the $6,000 monthly rent to Washington. He moved his family into the third floor, his staff occupied the second floor, low-ranking personnel and guards filled the first floor, and the basement became an arsenal.

Jessie served as Frémont's unofficial chief of staff. She read all his correspondence, penned replies, and actually attended his meetings with officers, merchants, and politicians. Many men resented what they called her meddling; others lauded her efforts to bring some order and reason to her husband's erratic decisions, management, and bookkeeping. She was soon known as "General Jessie" either in scorn or relief. One of her female friends during this time described Jessie's attributes and challenges: "She had a man's power, a man's education, and she did a man's work in the world, but her wonderful charm was purely feminine."[255]

When Frémont took command, he had only about 16,000 troops scattered at nine positions across Missouri. His men lacked virtually everything they needed to be soldiers, both the hard power of rifles, cannons, munitions, uniforms, food, blankets, tents, medicine, and horses, and the soft power of leadership, training, and morale. Frémont could not provide either. He knew nothing of substance in how to nurture and wield soft power, while his supply requisition orders to Washington were shuffled to the bottom of a steadily rising pile. The White House's priority was the rebel army just twenty miles south of Washington. Many shipments that did trickle to St. Louis were cast-off rifles and shoes that fell apart after a day on the parade ground. Jessie conceived a way to cut through the bureaucracy's Gordian knot: "The President is a western man and not grown in red tape. If he knew the true defenseless condition of the west it would not remain so. I have begged Mr. Frémont to let me go on & tell him how things are here. But he says…that I shan't expose my health and more & that he can't do without me."[256]

Frémont was well aware of the contempt that most West Point graduates had for him. So rather than employ them as his officers, he chose European military veterans from Prussia, Hungary, France, and elsewhere. He formed an elite corps of three hundred cavalrymen led by Colonel Charles Zagonyi, a Hungarian; those troops wore blue uniforms and white plumed hats, carried German made pistols and sabers, and rode chestnut-colored horses. Rather than dispatch that cavalry to scout and raid the enemy, he deployed them around him as his bodyguard day and night.

Frémont made only one indisputably positive decision for the American cause, but it decisively determined how and when Washington crushed the rebellion. On August 27, he appointed Brigadier General Ulysses Grant to command a subdistrict with a 3,000-man brigade at Cairo, Illinois, the critical juncture where the Ohio and Mississippi Rivers joined. Years later he explained why he did so after briefly meeting Grant: "I believed him to be a man of great activity and promptness in obeying orders without question or hesitation.... I did not consider him then a great general, for the qualities that led him to success had not had the opportunity for their development. I selected him for the qualities I could not then find combined in any other officer, for General Grant was a man of unassuming character, not given to self-elation, of dogged persistence, and of iron will."[257] Grant was at once grateful for the mission and puzzled by Frémont: "He sat in a room in full uniform, with his maps before him. When you went in he would point to one line or another in a mysterious manner, never asking you to take a seat. You left without the least idea of what he meant or what he wanted you to do."[258] This was actually an advantage for a decisive leader like Grant who took advantage of the ambiguity to do what he thought was best.

After receiving myriad complaints from different sources about corruption, incompetence, timidity, and favoritism emanating from Frémont's headquarters, Lincoln sent his aide John Hay to St. Louis to investigate in mid-August. Although Hay was very bright and perceptive, he was just twenty-two years old and had no military experience. He reported that all seemed right but did note that Jessie seemed inappropriately omnipresent at headquarters. Lincoln sent Frank and Montgomery Blair to take a closer look. After several days, Frank wrote Montgomery, "I am beginning to lose my confidence in Frémont. He seems to occupy himself with trifles and does not grasp the great points of the business. Men come with affairs of regiments and go away without seeing him or without an answer."[259]

Then Frémont committed an act on August 30, 1861, that provoked a political crisis that potentially threatened the American cause. He issued a proclamation that declared martial law, confiscated the property and freed the slaves of rebels, and threatened summarily to execute any rebel guerrillas caught behind American lines. He did so not after consulting the president, the secretary of war, or even his own staff officers. Indeed, he ignored them. Instead, on August 28, he informed Jessie, knowing that she would immediately and unconditionally embrace the proclamation, along with two fervent abolitionists, Owen Lovejoy and John Gurley. Hundreds of copies of the proclamation were printed and nailed in public places across Missouri under Union control. Abolitionists across the northern states wildly cheered his emancipation proclamation. *Uncle Tom's Cabin* author Harriet Stowe was among those who sent him congratulatory letters for his bold act.

There was no celebrating in the White House. Word of Frémont's act exasperated Lincoln. Frémont's actions threatened to destroy the president's very sophisticated diplomacy designed to keep the border slave states of Missouri, Kentucky, Maryland, and Delaware in the United States. Typically, he concealed his anguish in the two letters that he wrote Frémont over his policy's potentially disastrous results. On September 2, he raised two serious concerns. First, summarily shooting captured rebels would provoke retaliation against captured federal troops and result in an endless escalation of mass executions. Second, confiscating rebel property and freeing slaves would incense slave owners in the still loyal Border States and push them into the rebel ranks. He ordered Frémont to rescind both of these measures. Always sensitive to the easily bruised pride of others, Lincoln offered these conciliatory words: "This letter is written in a spirit of caution, and not of censure. I send it by special messenger, in order that it may certainly and speedily reach you."[260]

Lincoln's instructions prompted rage rather than contrition in Frémont. For days he steamed over his presidential orders. Then, on September 8, Frémont fired back his refusal to comply, arguing that: "If I were to retract of my own accord, it would imply that I myself thought it wrong.... I acted with full deliberation and upon the certain conviction that it was a measure right and necessary; and I think so still." He insisted that if the president opposed his proclamation then he should publicly renounce it himself.[261] That same day, Jessie boarded a train bound for Washington to present that letter to the president.

After checking into the Willard Hotel on September 10, Jessie dispatched a note to Lincoln requesting a meeting.[262] While she awaited a reply, she was joined by Judge Edward Coles, a family friend and abolitionist from New York. She soon received an invitation from Lincoln to meet him that evening. Jessie and Coles hurried to the White House just half a dozen blocks away. An usher led them to the Red Room. Soon Lincoln strode into the room, bowed, and without speaking stared hard at Jessie. She introduced Coles, who excused himself to wait in the hall while they spoke. Jessie handed Lincoln the letter. He frowned as he read it. Looking down at her, he curtly stated: "I have written to the General and he knows what I want done." Jessie then launched into a defense of her husband's motives. He cut her short with these damning words: "You are quite the female politician."[263] He then criticized Frémont for not following the advice of the Blair brothers, whom he had sent to investigate and resolve a list of serious charges of incompetence and corruption against him. That enraged rather than shamed Jessie. She vented a tirade of pent-up frustrations that she and her husband believed that they had suffered at the hands of the White House and Washington. Lincoln later complained that Jessie "taxed me so violently with so many things that I had to exercise all the awkward tact I have to avoid quarreling with her."[264] Instead, he walked her to the door and bid her good night.

The following morning, Lincoln wrote Frémont a second letter, this one released to the newspapers. Despite his anger, he once again restrained his response, reiterating his earlier lawyer-like arguments behind his decision to Frémont. The president even bowed to the general's request "that I should make an open order for the modification, which I very cheerfully do." He then ordered Frémont to alter his proclamation to comply strictly with a congressional act of August 6 that established clear rules for confiscating rebel property that did not include liberating slaves.[265]

That same morning, Francis Blair confronted Jessie at the Willard Hotel, castigating Frémont for disobeying the president and her for defending him: "Well, who would have expected you to do such a thing as this, to come here and find fault with the President.... Look what Frémont has done; made the President his enemy!"[266] Jessie was defiant rather than contrite. They argued for two hours with neither yielding to the other's position until Blair angrily departed.

The next day, Jessie sent Lincoln a letter curtly demanding that he give her copies of his instructions for the Blair brothers to investigate Frémont and his command in St. Louis.[267] When she did not receive a reply, she fired off a second letter, this time insisting on receiving those documents "without much further delay" as she "is anxious to return to her family."[268] Lincoln was a model of diplomacy in his reply. He acknowledged receipt of her two notes, explained that he sent a new order to Frémont reiterating his previous order, and deferred sending her copies of his instructions to the Blairs without their permission. He ended by trying to reassure her with these words: "No impression has been made on my mind against the honor or integrity of Gen. Frémont and I now enter my protest against being understood as acting in any hostility toward him."[269]

Jessie's mission turned out to be the political equivalent of the proverbial bull in the china shop. She had infuriated and alienated the President of the United States and America's most powerful political clan. This was Jessie at her absolute worst—arrogant, condescending, insensitive, uncompromising, paranoid, overflowing with hubris, and zealous in her loyalty to her husband. Despite her keen intellect and years of observing firsthand and even occasionally participating in politics, she had grossly violated the fundamental rules of the game. If she ever rued the results of her behavior, no extant letter, essay, or book records it. But undoubtedly, she was deeply aggrieved that her intransigence had alienated her best friend and confidant, Elizabeth Blair Lee, the sister of Frank and Montgomery.

Amidst these histrionics in Washington, word arrived of a critical Union defeat in Missouri. Lyon and 5,400 troops occupied Springfield. Scouts brought word that Price and 12,000 rebels were approaching. Rather than withdraw, Lyon chose to attack the enemy at Wilson Creek half a dozen miles south of Springfield on September 10. He divided his force in two to hit Price's army from different directions. Although the Union attacks initially pushed back the enemy, the rebels rallied and drove the bluecoats from the field. The North and South suffered 1,300 and 1,200 casualties; Lyon was among the dead. That was truly a tragic loss for the American cause. Had Lyon lived, he might well have ranked with Grant, Sherman, and Sheridan as among the best generals. The remnants of the Union army retreated to St. Louis. Price led his army north to reoccupy Jefferson City, then on to capture Lexington with its 2,800 defenders and $900,000 of gold on September 20.

Ironically, that crisis saved Frémont. Lincoln did not fire him but encouraged him to do everything possible to repel the rebel invasions. He did dispatch Montgomery Blair and Army Quartermaster General Montgomery Meigs for the latest investigation. He also sent to St. Louis General David Hunter with these insightful instructions to aid and possibly replace him in command: "Gen. Frémont needs assistance which is difficult to give him. He is losing the confidence of men near him, whose support any many in his position must have to be successful. His cardinal mistake is that he isolates himself, and allows nobody to see him; and by which he does not know what is going on in the very matter he is dealing with. He needs to have at his side a man of large experience. Will you not, for me, take that place?"[270]

Frémont was evasive to Blair, Meigs, and Hunter, but became enraged after Lincoln had Frank Blair inform him that he had better chalk up some victories against the rebels or else. Frémont responded on September 18 by having Blair arrested and jailed on charges of "insidious and dishonorable efforts to bring my authority into contempt with the government."[271] Blair was so incensed that at first he refused to leave his cell after Frémont ordered him released, then finally left swearing that he would seek vengeance. Within days, Blair filed multiple charges of dereliction of duty and corruption against Frémont. Nonplussed by the political and legal opposition swelling against him, on September 23, Frémont had the *Saint Louis Evening Post*'s editor arrested and shut down the newspaper for criticizing him for failing to prevent Price's rebel army from overrunning central Missouri.

Frémont's utterly bizarre and tyrannical act of imprisoning Frank Blair destroyed forever his relations with the Blairs, then America's most powerful political clan. For decades, the Blairs had staunchly backed the Manifest Destiny schemes of Benton and Frémont, and in 1856 championed the Pathfinder's presidential campaign. They proudly lived up to their family motto: "When the Blairs go in for a fight, they go in for a funeral."[272] That is the kind of clan with whom those who are both ambitious and wise curry favor and avoid any dispute. In this case, Frémont displayed a surfeit of blind ambition and void of wisdom. His hubris, ineptness, timidity, and paranoia transformed the Blair clan from a faithful ally into an implacable enemy.

Yet even after Frémont's series of gross military, political, legal, and constitutional offenses, Lincoln did not cashier him. Instead, he continued to bend over backwards trying to avoid humiliating the Republican Party's first presidential candidate and a national hero. He sent Secretary of War Simon Cameron to St. Louis with written standing orders to relieve Frémont of command if the offensive that he had been promising failed. In doing so, he hoped but could not be certain that the erratic Frémont would not dare to have the secretary of war arrested on trumped-up charges. To the president's relief, Frémont did receive Cameron and, after being shown the orders, promised to begin his campaign in just a few days. Cameron returned with the unissued order to Washington.

Frémont endured blistering criticism for failing to concentrate enough troops first to support Lyon at Springfield then to attack Price as he occupied Jefferson City and besieged Lexington. Price withdrew his triumphant army to Springfield. Only then did Frémont advance at the head of 38,000 troops up the Missouri River valley. His troops reoccupied Jefferson City on September 30, Lexington on October 16, and then headed south to march into Springfield on November 2. Price's 20,000-man army was deployed just a few miles south of Springfield. Frémont readied his army to attack the next day. Then a twist of fate intervened. On the evening of November 2, a messenger from Lincoln somehow managed to talk his way through a series of guards all the way to Frémont's headquarters and appear before the general. "Sir, how did you get admission into my lines," Frémont asked in mingled wonder and indignation as the messenger saluted and handed him the president's orders.[273] Once again, one of Lincoln's subordinates had failed to follow his instructions. The president had told the messenger to withhold the orders if Frémont's army was on the eve of battle.

Frémont responded by immediately convening his generals to inform them that he had been relieved of command and so was canceling the battle. The army's morale plummeted. Price withdrew his army from Springfield into northwestern Arkansas. After Hunter arrived a couple of days later, he led the army into Springfield but did not pursue Price.

Frémont hurried to his family in St. Louis, where they tarried for a couple of weeks before heading for a prolonged stay at the Astor House Hotel in New York. There, they immersed themselves in comforting abolitionist circles that blamed their woes on everyone but themselves. At times the praise could be embarrassing, at least for Frémont. He was at the Cooper Institute attending a lecture by abolitionist Wendell Phillips when the speaker pointed to Frémont as an exemplar of acting on principle. The audience cheered wildly as Frémont slunk red-faced in his chair.

Frémont's actions as the Department of the West's commander were eventually vindicated by the most authoritative source, the Joint Committee on the Conduct of the War. He was lucky that three key abolitionists dominated that committee, including its chairman Benjamin Wade of Ohio, along with Zachariah Chandler of Michigan and George Julian of Indiana. Critics blasted the committee's report as a whitewash of Frémont's appalling behavior.

All along abolitionists cheered Frémont as a hero. John Greenleaf Whittier captured the essence of their adulation for Frémont's emancipation proclamation with this poem:

> "The error, Frémont, simply was to act
> A brave man's part, without the statesman's tact.
> It had been safer, doubtless for a time,
> To flatter treason, and avoid offense…
> Still take thou courage! God has spoken through thee.
> Irrevocable the might words, Be Free!"[274]

Lincoln held an olive branch of sorts to the Frémonts by inviting them to a White House party for five hundred guests on February 5, 1862. The driving force behind the party was First Lady Mary Todd Lincoln. She endured withering criticism for throwing an extravaganza when the nation was being torn apart by a war in which well over a hundred thousand men had already been killed, wounded, or captured. Compounding the absurdity was that the Lincolns' third son, Willie, was dying of typhoid upstairs. Mary Todd's only grudging concession was to agree that dancing would be inappropriate. At first, the Frémonts demurred from attending but succumbed when the president made a personal appeal. Then, when they tried to leave early, Lincoln recalled them to meet General George McClellan and his wife. It was a ghastly night of feigned jollity and deep sorrow for nearly everyone.

Lincoln gave Frémont a second chance to redeem himself. Political expediency rather than military necessity motivated his decision. Frémont was such a loose cannon and radical Republican leader that trying to co-opt him seemed better than trying to exile him. The challenge was finding him a post where he could inflict the least harm to the Union cause. In March 1862, Lincoln assigned him the Mountain Department that was headquartered at Wheeling, Virginia, and extended over the Appalachian region dividing the Virginia and Tennessee fronts. Tragically, Frémont proved to be no fitter for that command than his previous one. He recalled many of his staff from his Missouri sojourn, most notably Charles Zagonyi. Although this time he did not establish an elite bodyguard, he was just as inept at organizing, supplying, and leading his army into the field. The campaign opened in May 1862.

Lincoln conceived a plan for converging three armies—John Frémont's 15,000 troops from Wheeling, Nathaniel Banks's 18,000 troops from Winchester, and James Shields's 17,000 troops from Centreville—against General Thomas "Stonewall" Jackson's 17,000 rebel troops in the Shenandoah Valley. It was an ingenious plan that might well have destroyed Jackson's army if competent rather than inept generals carried it out. Although outnumbered more than three to one, Jackson launched a whirlwind campaign of quick-marching his men to defeat each enemy army in turn and prevent them from uniting. After each victory, his men replenished their haversacks and cartridge boxes from captured supply wagons before racing off to the next battle. Jackson's men repelled Frémont's advanced guard at McDowell on May 8, defeated Shields at Front Royal on May 23, Banks at Winchester on May 25, Frémont at Cross Keys on June 8, and finally Shields again at Port Republic on June 9. Jackson then withdrew over the Blue Ridge Mountains to Charlottesville, where his corps boarded trains bound for Richmond's defense against General McClellan's 100,000 troops slowly moving up the Peninsula. None of the three defeated Union generals dared follow Jackson.[275]

The northern press and most congressmen condemned the incompetence of Frémont and his two colleagues. Jessie burned with anger but restrained herself from publicly expressing herself, knowing that politically it would provoke more harm than good: "I could speak out but…I must do it through friends who will not misunderstand & who know the beauty as well as the utility of silent activity."[276]

Once again Frémont proved to be his own worst enemy. He resigned his command on June 26 after Lincoln converted his army into a corps in the Army of Virginia commanded by General John Pope. Frémont hated Pope for being one of General Stephen Kearny's officers that humiliated him after California's conquest. Even then, Lincoln was willing to throw Frémont a bone by offering him a future command of black troops. Instead Frémont drew pay as a major general until August 12, 1863, when he finally resigned his commission. Jessie justified her husband's act with convoluted, paranoid sentiments: "It was only a question of time, the resigning. It would have been so contrived that the General would have been forced to do so, but if he had stayed they would have prepared defeats & destroyed his reputation."[277] As always, her husband was blameless, and their enemies were omnipotent.

Meanwhile, Jessie and her children and servants abandoned Washington to stay at Little Neck, New York, on Long Island, where she hobnobbed on weekends with such literary luminaries as William Cullen Bryant and Horace Greeley, who had country mansions nearby. They encouraged her to write a book, her first. After twelve frenzied days, she finished *The Story of the Guard*, about her husband's 300-man bodyguard, and sent the manuscript to James Fields, who published the *Atlantic Monthly* and co-owned the Boston publishing firm of Ticknor and Fields. Of the many reasons behind her book, one dominated—justice. She felt that her husband and his bodyguard had been grossly maligned. Her husband's enemies in Congress and the press had claimed that he was hiding behind his mostly foreign-born guard. She wanted to reveal the valor with which those men fought and the injustice of their disbandment after her husband was dismissed from the Missouri command. She pledged to donate her royalties to the families of the guard who lost their lives. Finishing a book in such a short time was not just an extraordinary intellectual feat. Far more daunting was overcoming two related emotional constraints, setting aside her privacy and entering a realm dominated by men: "It has been a real sacrifice for me to lay open even so small a part of my life…. The restraints of ordinary times do not apply now."[278] Jessie's book appeared before Christmas 1862 and became a best seller.

The Frémonts passed the summer of 1863 at the beachside writer's colony at Nahant, Massachusetts, with such distinguished neighbors as Henry Wadsworth Longfellow and John Greenleaf Whittier. Jessie swiftly established a salon in which those poets and an array of other creative people gathered for stimulating fellowship. As the summer waned, the Frémonts moved into a brownstone mansion at 21 West Nineteenth Street in New York City. Jessie got involved in volunteer work and fund-raising for the Sanitary Commission dedicated to providing medical care for wounded soldiers. By the war's end, the New York committee alone raised over a million dollars.

Jessie plunged into deep grief when she learned that diphtheria and pneumonia had killed her dear friend Thomas Starr King in San Francisco on March 2, 1864. That was not the only bad news from California. The federal government had seized their Black Point estate on San Francisco Bay to make a fort but refused to pay for it; Frémont would fight Washington for compensation the rest of his life. Adding insult to injury, the government renamed the land Fort Mason to honor Colonel Richard Mason, General Stephen Kearny's second in command with whom Frémont had nearly gotten in a duel. Even worse, Las Mariposas was $2 million in debt to an array of creditors and investors, with $13,000 in monthly interest payments, and $600,000 in snowballing legal fees. Frémont kept judges from confiscating his entire tract by selling off pieces of it to the most powerful claimants. In 1863, he found enough gullible buyers to sell the rest of his holdings for $1.5 million, a vast fortune in those days but far below the $10 million that Las Mariposas was once worth to him. Yet he sidestepped a worse loss by selling when he did. When the new owners listed Las Mariposas on the stock market in October 1863, the initial price of $30 a share plummeted to $19 within days.[279] Frederick Olmsted, who later designed New York's Central Park, was among a managerial team hired to revive Las Mariposas. He penned this exasperated account of Frémont's business legacy: "He seems to have worn out the patience, after draining the purses, of all his friends in California. I am overrun with visits from his creditors."[280]

Frémont could have deployed his golden parachute from California in safe real estate investments that sustained opulence for his family for generations. Instead, he made a series of high-risk rolls with his fortune that eventually exhausted it. He bought the Leavenworth, Pawnee, and Western Railroad and the Southwest Pacific Railroad, and then combined them into the Atlantic and Pacific Railroad. He sold that and bought the Memphis and El Paso Railroad with dreams of making it the centerpiece of a line running from Norfolk, Virginia, to San Diego, California. The trouble was that exactly zero miles of track for his grandiose vision then existed west of the Mississippi. He paid fire sale prices for these various railroads because rebel raiders had devastated them. He would be unable to make any significant upgrades let alone expansions until the war was over, if the maintenance costs had not financially crippled him before then. The 1864 presidential election briefly diverted him from these investments.

John Frémont's most critical contribution to America may have been what he almost did but finally agreed not to do. Abraham Lincoln was up for reelection in November 1864 and throughout most of that year appeared to be heading for a stunning loss.[281] The American people were exhausted and exasperated by three years of a seemingly endless bloodbath. The Republican Party was split between conservatives and radicals, each harshly critical of Lincoln. The conservatives sought to crush the rebellion and reunite the nation; the radicals insisted that abolition must accompany reunification. In contrast, the northern Democratic Party was committed to peace at any price with the rebels.

A rump group of 350 breakaway Radical Republicans held a convention at Cleveland on May 31, called themselves the Radical Democracy Party and in a resounding acclamation nominated John Frémont as their presidential candidate. Frémont reached the convention and formally accepted the nomination on June 4. The Republicans met at Baltimore on June 7, renamed themselves the National Union Party, and renominated Abraham Lincoln. During the Democratic Party convention in Cleveland on August 29, the delegates chose General George McClellan as their presidential candidate. McClellan promised that if elected he would accept peace on rebel terms. Ironically, Frémont and McClellan, two militarily inept generals, were heroes to broad parts of the northern population, while Lincoln, a brilliant political and military leader, feared that he was doomed to defeat in the election. In a three-way race, Lincoln's pessimism was well founded.

Had Frémont persisted in his candidacy, he would have been the spoiler that brought McClellan to the White House and a rebel victory with America split between weak northern and southern halves. Senator Zachariah Chandler of Michigan spearheaded the Republican Party's effort to convince Frémont to drop out. If appeals to Frémont's patriotism and morality did not suffice, Lincoln authorized Chandler to promise that he would find him an ambassadorship and fire Montgomery Blair as postmaster general.

Frémont issued a public letter on September 22 that renounced his candidacy and attacked the president: "In respect to Mr. Lincoln, I continue to hold...his administration has been politically, militarily, and financially a failure, and that its necessary continuance is a cause of regret for the country." He insisted that he was "not in favor of Abraham Lincoln, but in order to preserve the Union, and keep the administration of its affairs in the hands of the party which had forced the emancipation of the slaves and was slowly forcing the war to a termination."[282] Lincoln's sole response came the next day when he dismissed Blair.

Frémont's blistering critique of Lincoln was a classic example of projection. People afflicted with festering pathologies and accumulated humiliating failures tend to deny them and instead project their vilest characteristics onto some hated other. That was exactly what Frémont did with his renunciation statement. It was Frémont who had repeatedly proven to be "politically, militarily, and financially a failure," but he could never admit that to himself let alone the world.

Jessie offered a partial insight into this phenomenon although she was talking about a completely different subject when she did so: "For it is a very risky thing to tell the whole truth. Especially if people are displeased with themselves."[283]

Here she argued that it was better to bolster people with delusions rather than expose them. Certainly, that was what she spent decades doing not just with her husband's delusions but when doubts began to emerge, with herself.

CHAPTER 9

Downfalls

*"I am only a ghost of the past and my place now is not to work or help
in great things, but to...confine myself to putting money in my purse."*
— JESSIE FRÉMONT

*"The buoyant hopes and busy life
Have ended all in hateful strife
And baffled aim.
False Roads to Fame."*
— JOHN FRÉMONT

AS A POWER COUPLE, the Frémonts peaked politically in 1856 and financially around 1870. Only a series of astonishingly lucky breaks brought John Frémont success in either realm, although to his credit he did capitalize on the opportunities. He married the daughter of the most powerful senator who championed western expansion and subsequently wrangled five exploration expeditions for him to lead across the west. His broker bought what appeared to be a worthless tract of land in the Sierra Mountain foothills rather than in San Francisco as Frémont requested; Frémont was about to sell that land when gold was discovered on it. His national fame as "the Pathfinder" got the newborn Republican Party to nominate him as their presidential candidate in 1856. His popularity with Radical Republicans pressured Lincoln to appoint him to two successive army commands. Yet Frémont proceeded to squander each success because he was an inept and dishonest politician, businessman, and general.

And all along Jessie did what she could to bolster her husband's sagging political, military, and financial fortunes. The trouble was that she was straightjacketed from doing more than lobby influential men behind the scenes. She could not openly manage his political campaigns, military commands, or business investments. Had she been able to do so, she could have brought the discipline, wisdom, and panache that might have led to the White House, military victories, or unending riches. Instead she had to watch helplessly first as her husband went from being a dazzling political, military, and business star to a derided has-been, and then as the family downsized their homes from opulent mansions to middle class abodes to cramped apartments.

By the time that Jessie reached her fiftieth birthday her once lush black hair had become white and her once svelte figure had fattened to near corpulence. Her mind, however, remained as sharp as ever. And her love for Frémont remained as powerful as ever despite decades of bankruptcies, sexual affairs, and prolonged absences. To friends deeply concerned that Jessie was locked in an abusive, degrading relationship, she insisted that they had nothing to worry about. To the poet John Greenleaf Whittier, she tried to explain what she loved about her husband: "But his is the most reserved and shy nature I ever met. Not that nor any other beautiful evidence of his inner life would ever be known but to those of us who have been his inner life."[284]

The same month that the Civil War ended in April 1865, John Frémont bought a magnificent mansion, built in 1847, on a hundred acres along the Hudson River at Tarrytown, twenty-five miles north of New York City. The Frémonts called their estate Pocaho. They split their time between their mansion on Nineteenth Street in Manhattan during much of the year and Pocaho during much of the summer, with prolonged excursions to playgrounds of the rich and famous at Saratoga Springs, New York; Newport, Rhode Island; and Bar Harbor, Maine. At Pocaho, French chefs cooked their meals, nannies cared for their children, maids cleaned up after them, and workers trimmed hedges, planted flowers, raked leaves, and drove carriages.

An especially gratifying moment came in May 1868, when the Frémonts journeyed to St. Louis to attend the unveiling of a magnificent bronze statue of Thomas Hart Benton in the center of Lafayette Park. The sculptor, Harriet Hosmer, captured Benton's essence as he stands, map in hand, atop a tall marble statue, and glares westward. Forty thousand other people attended the ceremony along with President Andrew Johnson and local dignitaries who made speeches lauding Benton's achievements. Bands played military tunes, and a thirty-gun salute marked each year that Benton had served in the Senate. For the Frémonts, the only sour note was that their once dear friend and political ally turned enemy, Frank Blair, was among the orators, while Francis and Montgomery Blair were among the special guests.

Shortly thereafter the Frémonts were saddened to learn that Kit Carson died at Fort Lyon on May 23. Frémont and Carson had forged a deep friendship during three expeditions across the west culminating with California's conquest, and Jessie had grown fond of him during his sojourns in Washington and New York. Like Frémont, Carson had become a national hero. Unlike the Frémonts, painfully shy Carson squirmed at being a celebrity. He especially resented the pulp novels that exploited his fame with stories of deeds, mostly heroic, some dastardly, that he had never done. One such tale appeared several years after his death, a poem by Joaquin Miller that had Carson abducting a Comanche girl then cowardly abandoning her to save himself from a prairie fire. That prompted indignation by the Frémonts, who were hypersensitive to how journalists, poets, novelists, historians, and politicians depicted themselves, their friends, and their allies. In a letter to General William Sherman, Jessie asked him to join them in publicly defending their friend's honor and place in history: "Mr. Frémont and myself loved and valued Carson…. All we can do to prove our love for our friend is to keep his name as he kept it clean and honored…. Those who knew Carson will join us in overthrowing this shameful likeness of our modest brave unselfish friend."[285]

The effort to save a dear friend's reputation from a false, malicious portrayal is certainly laudatory. The trouble with the Frémonts was that throughout their lives they often sought to counter truthful as well as exaggerated or manufactured negative stories about themselves with their own carefully contrived versions. The easiest tactic was to attack the mass media, as Jessie did in his missive to the family lawyer: "as usual our name is put out to bear the brunt of a mingling of true & false which is not fair and which we only submit to because there is so much else demanding our attention and work. And because the truth would not be published even if it were given to those papers."[286]

The late nineteenth century was an age where "caveat emptor," or "buyer beware," characterized America's economy. The onus of blame was on the victims rather than the perpetrators of swindles. Frémont was a businessman of his time. He was both a victim and perpetrator of fraud schemes that often involved millions of dollars.

Frémont suffered a blow to his fortune on June 7, 1867, when Missouri's government seized his Atlantic and Pacific Railroad to pay for back taxes that he and other investors owed. The blow could have been worse had Frémont actually made a serious attempt to develop the railroad rather than milked his fellow investors for as much as he could. Only twelve miles of track were laid during his four years of ownership. He insisted that he could not afford to pay taxes or lay track because the federal government failed to give him public lands westward to finance his railroad.

Frémont then changed tracks by pouring much of his wealth into the Memphis, El Paso, and Pacific Railroad that would have angled southwest through Arkansas and Texas and then westward through southern New Mexico, Arizona, and California. Certainly, that route made geographic sense because the terrain was largely flat all the way. The engineering challenge was financial and political rather than physical. For that, Frémont faced a conundrum that proved to be insurmountable. He could not rustle up enough big-money investors unless he received congressional permission for a right-of-way and enveloping land grant, and Congress would not hand him that vast corporate welfare unless he proved that he had lined up enough backers to capitalize on it. So, he and his railroad remained mired in the political and financial muck.

He conceived two ways to outflank that gridlock. One was to lobby the Texas government for an 18,200,000-acre land grant across the state that he would sell off for $10 million in railroad company bonds. Meanwhile, his junior partner and brother-in-law Baron Gauldree Boilleau, who had married Jessie's younger sister Susan, would sell those bonds to rich Europeans, especially in Paris. Boilleau blatantly lied that Washington had granted the company 8,000,000 acres along the right of way that could be developed or sold to finance construction and guaranteed the principal and interest on the company's bonds. Eventually the company sold $5,343,000 worth of bonds to Europeans, with Frenchmen taking the lion's share. Of that, Frémont pocketed more than $1 million and Boilleau $150,000 in "commissions" and "business expenses."[287]

The Frémonts spent six months in Europe in 1869, after reaching France in June. While Frémont conducted business mostly in Paris, Jessie and her children took prolonged trips to other cities and countries. In Paris, he got to know an extraordinary young woman. Vinnie Ream was then a twenty-two-year-old prodigy of a sculptress.[288] Five years earlier she had actually spent a half hour daily for five months with Abraham Lincoln in the White House sculpting his bust. Her beauty and sexual allure matched her artistic talent. She was petite but curved with shoulder-length thick curly brown hair and a heart-shaped face with large chestnut-colored eyes, a button-nose, and pouty lips. Naturally, men went wild over her. Whether Frémont counted Vinnie among his lovers is unknown. What is known is that he introduced his family to her and had Vinnie sculpt a bust of Jessie. What is also known is that he visited her almost daily during September when Jessie and the children were traveling in Germany. Although Vinnie lived with her parents, she sculpted alone in her studio. Although Frémont was then fifty-six and grey-haired, he was still handsome, vigorous, and rich—irresistibly alluring for most women. The Frémonts sailed from Liverpool bound for New York on November 13, 1869. In doing so, Frémont unwittingly sidestepped a cataclysm.

The Frémont-Boilleau multi-million-dollar fraud scheme was exposed in March 1870. Although Frémont was then safely in New York, Boilleau lingered in Paris where he was arrested, tried, and convicted of fraud, then sentenced to three years in prison. Although Frémont insisted that he knew nothing of Boilleau's stunningly false claims, he dared not return to Paris to make his case. A court tried and found Frémont guilty *in absentia* and sentenced him to five years. He never served a day because he never set foot in France again and there was no extradition treaty between the United States and France. However, American ambassador Elihu Washburne was so appalled by the scale of the blatant fraud and its damage to America's relations with France that he asked Congress to investigate. Luck again favored Frémont when Congress failed to do so. Yet, although he evaded prison, his reputation was shattered.

Frémont could not escape the scandal's business impact. All along he refused to let increasingly nervous investors examine his company's account books. He had plenty to hide. His latest business nosedived into bankruptcy in January 1871, when investors finally learned that the millions of dollars they had invested in the Memphis and El Paso Railroad had resulted in a grand total of three miles of track laid and twenty-five miles graded. Yet, once again, Frémont escaped with a golden parachute by selling his shares before the news got out as nearly all other shareholders financially crashed and burned. Rather than retire into opulence, Frémont poured his millions of dollars into the Texas and Pacific Railroad. This time he did not get out in time but lost virtually all his money when the company went bankrupt in the spring of 1873.

The *coup de grâce* to Frémont's fortune came half a year later, on September 13, 1873, when banking giant Jay Cooke and Company collapsed. The resulting "panic" or financial domino effect wiped out the wealth of the Frémonts and countless other Americans. At fire-sale prices, the Frémonts had to sell their beloved Pocaho along with most of their paintings, books, and furniture. Jessie bitterly resented receiving "notice that the mortgage on my home will be foreclosed.... This place is worth three hundred thousand but for want of six thousand I shall lose it."[289] That was just the beginning. Frémont liquidated their Manhattan mansion and moved into a humble apartment at 924 Madison Avenue near Seventy-Seventh Street, then amidst a vast tenement district.

The Frémonts were so poor that Jessie had to support them by penning newspaper articles for the *New York Ledger*. She received a hundred dollars for each of her series entitled "Distinguished Persons I Have Known," which included most prominently Kit Carson, Andrew Jackson, Martin Van Buren, and Thomas Starr King. That must have been a bittersweet experience, as the memories of past glories that she conjured up clashed so starkly with her family's recent plummet into poverty. She admitted to Nathaniel Banks, then a Massachusetts congressman, that "I am only a ghost of the past and my place now is not to work or help in great things, but to...confine myself to putting money in my purse."[290]

The stress of losing their fortune devastated each member of the family in varying degrees and ways. They spent the first months of 1874 recovering their minds and bodies on Nassau in the Bahama Islands. In 1875, Frémont made a business trip to San Francisco on the transcontinental railroad, which had been completed in 1869. It was a melancholy journey as he recognized many sites along the way that he had passed during his expeditions decades earlier. He penned a mournful poem that reflected opaquely on his lifetime of soaring successes and devastating defeats. These lines were especially poignant:

> "Long years ago I wandered here
> In the midsummer of the year
> Life's summer too...
> These dreary wastes of frozen plain
> Reflect my bosom's life again
> Now lonesome gloom.
> The buoyant hopes and busy life
> Have ended all in hateful strife
> And baffled aim...
> False Roads to fame."[291]

The Frémonts were eking out an existence in a small rented cottage on Staten Island in 1878, when, once again a powerful patron saved Frémont from himself. Desperate at their worsening plight, Jessie committed an act that her husband would have forbidden if he knew she was going to do it. She wrote Senator Zachariah Chandler of Michigan imploring him to give her husband some government post. Her key argument was that the Republican Party still owed Frémont for dropping out of the presidential race against Lincoln in 1864. Chandler shared the plea with President Rutherford Hayes. As a young lawyer, Hayes had campaigned for Frémont for president in 1856 and later served under his command in Missouri in 1861. Saddened to learn of Frémont's descent into obscure poverty, Hayes offered him the governorship of Idaho Territory on June 8, 1878. The offer startled Frémont but in turning it down, he cited reasons of health rather than pride. He worried that serving in such a freezing winter post might endanger his family's medical problems. Hayes then offered him Arizona Territory's governorship, explaining that the hot dry climate might be perfect for his family. Frémont accepted the post, which would uplift his family with prestige, a $2,600 annual salary, and, most alluringly, a chance to invest in various mining schemes across that mineral strewn land.

The Frémont family headed west on the transcontinental railroad, arriving in San Francisco on September 12, 1878. To their delight, a delegation from the Society of California Pioneers met them at the station, treated Frémont like a returning hero, installed them at the Palace Hotel, and feted them for several days before they resumed their journey. They took the train to San Diego, then hopped another bound for Fort Yuma on the Colorado River. There, General Sherman assigned them three mule-drawn army ambulances for the eight-day 230 mile journey north to Prescott, the territory's capital.

Prescott was hardly a plum post. It was a small town built around a large dusty square. More than a mile high at 5,366 feet above sea level, the winters were dry and cool, but the summers were blistering. Prices for most goods were sky-high given the remote location and steady stream of gold, silver, and other minerals that miners brought into town from surrounding sites. There was no governor's quarters, let alone mansion. Each governor had to find a dwelling to rent or buy. The previous governor, John Hoyt, was eager to yield the office to Frémont and hurry to serve as governor of Idaho Territory, which Frémont had spurned.

Frémont needed four days in bed to recover from the rigors of the long round-about journey from New York, capped by that grueling desert trek. His exhaustion was probably more emotional than physical. Although he remained tight-lipped, guilt at subjecting his family to years of plummeting fortunes followed by perhaps years in this bleak outpost of civilization undoubtedly ate away at him.

Jessie typically made the most of her experience. As always, she served as her husband's key advisor, secretary, and accountant. She found them a large adobe house, although the ninety-dollar monthly rent consumed much of her husband's salary. She hired a Chinese couple, with the wife to serve as the housekeeper and the husband as the cook. She presided over the "high society" of wealthy inhabitants and officers from nearby Fort Whipple. She organized knitting and reading circles among the wives. Each Friday she lectured on history at the local school. She reveled in exploring ancient Indian ruins and gazing at stunning sunsets. This recent comeback for her and her family swelled her confidence to seek more: "I am just splendidly well and ready to take hold of Fortune's wheel and pull it to the place I would have it stick."[292]

Once Frémont was on his feet, he devoted his efforts not to governance, whose duties were fairly light, but to prospecting for mines that could make his family fabulously rich again. He partnered with Charles Silent, the territory's judge, and they explored various possibilities, but none ever struck pay dirt. The legislature did appropriate Frémont $2,000 with which to pay off key senators and representatives in Congress to transfer to Arizona potentially mineral rich lands that by treaty were granted to various Indian tribes. In February 1879, Frémont and Silent began the long trip back east. Frémont took along Frank, leaving behind Jessie and Lily.

Frémont spent most of the money entrusted him to promote his own interests rather than those of the territory. He and Silent stayed at swanky hotels in New York, Washington, and elsewhere, and nurtured potential investors with fine dining and other enticements. The most important person who expressed an interest was Charles Rogers, a friend and secretary to President Hayes. The partners spent six months back east before returning to Prescott. With them were two mining experts that they dispatched to promising sites. Many Arizonans condemned Frémont for being away so long and neglecting his official duties. Jessie hastily wrote most of his annual territorial report for him. Frémont and Silent stayed in Prescott for several months over the winter while the legislature and court were in session. They agreed to send Jessie east to set up a company with the investors that they had nurtured earlier that year.

That was an extraordinary task for a woman at that time. What her husband asked her to do was perhaps unprecedented. So, Jessie returned to New York in November 1879, doubly excited to be back in that dynamic city and to prove herself as a businesswoman. With the Everett Hotel as her headquarters, she began a series of meetings with potential investors. In December she founded the Silver Prince Mining Company, in which Frémont and Silent each owned a quarter share and the rest bought up by Rogers and numerous other investors. Through Rogers she was able to get leave for Frémont to return east in March 1880. Reunited, Frémont and Jessie solidified the mining venture and promoted ranching and railroad schemes. In October Frémont had to return to Prescott when the legislature reconvened, but Jessie stayed to manage the various businesses. In March, Frémont provoked the latest eruption of criticism when he moved his residence 220 miles from Prescott to Tucson, a much larger town on the main east-west transcontinental route.

Frémont managed to cling to his sinecure as Arizona governor until October 11, 1881, when he finally succumbed to worsening pressure to resign. Complaints about his incompetence and corruption as governor piled up at the White House over the years but was ignored amidst varying complaints about countless other federal officials. Using public resources for private gain was ingrained in America's political culture at that time. As long as a fellow Republican was in the White House, Frémont could count on staying put in Arizona unless extraordinary circumstances arose. That happened. Hayes declined to run for a second term in 1880, and Republican Party presidential candidate James Garfield won the election in November. After being inaugurated on March 4, 1881, Garfield served little more than half a year as president. On September 19, 1881, a lawyer named Charles Guiteau, enraged that his repeated attempts to obtain a federal job had been rebuffed, shot Garfield to death. Three days later Vice President Chester Arthur took the oath to become president. It was Arthur, eager to put one of his cronies in the post, who forced out Frémont.

Once again Frémont was jobless and near penniless. His latest round of investments in mining, ranching, and railroads had hemorrhaged money and he was drowning in debt. Frémont, Jessie, and Lily returned to New York, where they rented an apartment at 218 West Fifty-Ninth Street but soon fell behind in their payments and moved to New Brighton on Staten Island. Having destroyed his public and business careers through incompetence and corruption, Frémont was forced into retirement. With nothing but dwindling time, he sank deep into morose reflections on seven decades of triumphs and debacles. The three of them scraped by on money Jessie earned by writing stories for *Wide Awake*, a children's magazine. Over the next decade she penned fifty stories and three books, *Souvenirs of My Time* in 1887, *Far West Sketches* in 1890, and *The Will and the Way Stories* in 1891, all of which reviewers generally lauded.[293] The royalties let them move back to New York into an apartment at 130 East Sixty-Sixth Street. Nonetheless, they remained mired in genteel poverty.

Jessie and John Frémont could at least take pride in how their sons turned out. John and Frank graduated from the naval and military academies, respectively, and embarked on respectable if undistinguished military careers. Lily, however, never married, and outlived them both. John and Jessie Frémont each died worrying about their daughter's fate, since they had virtually no wealth to leave her for whatever decades lay before her.

Jessie's friends felt mingled sorrow and anger that she had fallen so low. Although they mostly blamed Frémont's irresponsibility, venality, and incompetence for ruining their lives, they partly blamed her for falling for his Byronic charms in the first place. Her sister Elizabeth lamented "Jessie's infatuation about Frémont" and "his power over her," while her old friend Elizabeth Blair Lee condemned Jessie's "insanity" that let Frémont "gamble away his own & her children's bread over & over again…and he is too faithless even to pretend to live with her."[294]

The Frémonts received what proved to be a delusional emotional boost when Josiah Royce, a twenty-nine-year-old Harvard philosophy professor, asked to interview the general for a book he was writing on California's conquest. Royce was a protégée of California historian Hubert Bancroft who was amassing tens of thousands of documents on the state's history and, with a team of assistants, was writing his own multivolume history. By opening up to Royce, Frémont hoped to get his version of events adopted as the "real" history. In this, the Frémonts suffered their latest disappointment. Royce saw through Frémont's blatant scheme masked behind a gentleman's demeanor: "cordial he still was, dignified and charming as ever, and the good Jessie sat calm and sunny and benevolent in her easy chair; but alas, he lied, lied unmistakably, unmitigatedly, hopelessly.... The more you consulted him the fonder you were of him, and the less you were convinced by what he said.... One may say that General Frémont possessed all the qualities of genius except ability."[295] Royce's subsequent book, *California from the Conquest in 1846 to the Second Vigilance Committee in San Francisco: A Study of American Character*, published in 1886, unsparingly exposed Frémont's hubris, delusions, and blunders. Yet Royce was grossly unfair when he scapegoated Frémont for subsequent animosities between Americans and Mexicans in California.[296]

That did spur Frémont finally to do what Jessie had been urging him to do for decades. With Jessie acting as his muse, interviewer, editor, and scribe, Frémont dictated his memoirs. To access government archives, they moved to an apartment at 1320 Nineteenth Street in Washington. Frémont's *Memoir of My Life* appeared in 1887. Unfortunately, it was a ponderous, cut-and-paste tome that sold few copies and lost money for the publisher.[297] Unable to afford living in Washington, they moved to Point Pleasant on the New Jersey shore. Frémont's health deteriorated with chronic bronchitis. Jessie feared that her husband would die unless they got to a drier climate.

Jessie once again rescued them from their latest poverty-stricken dead end. Without telling her husband, she paid a call on railroad magnate Collis Huntington when he was visiting New York. They had first met on a steamship bound for California in 1849, and Jessie had beguiled him with her courage, beauty, charm, and intelligence. Now she was sixty-three years old, white-haired and stout, but still as animated and bright as ever. She implored Huntington to help transport them to a new life in Los Angeles, California. Although normally his fist was as tightly closed as his heart, Huntington was happy to oblige. He not only got them free railroad passes to carry them to Los Angeles but ensured that they stayed free in the finest hotels at cities wherever they had to change trains. When Frémont expressed his gratitude, Huntington replied: "You forget our road goes over your buried campfires and climbs many a grade you jogged over on a mule; I think we rather owe you this."[298]

They reached Los Angeles on Christmas Eve, 1888, and moved into the Marlborough Hotel. Frémont had hoped to capitalize on the city's building boom, but it collapsed shortly after they arrived. In 1889, Frémont returned to Washington to lobby Congress for a pension. Meanwhile, Jessie created a circle of progressive, wealthy friends of whom her closest was Caroline Severance, a suffragette leader. She also found a brilliant young artist to mentor, John Gutzon de la Mothe Borglum, who three decades later would sculpt the busts of Washington, Jefferson, Lincoln, and Roosevelt on Mount Rushmore. All along she wrote her stories and books. In March 1890, Frémont sent word that he had finally secured an annual $6,000 pension. He would receive only two payments.

Food poisoning and a burst appendix killed John Charles Frémont on July 13, 1890. His son Charles was with him when he died. Appropriately, his last words were "California of course."[299] Jessie and Lily could not afford to journey across the country to attend his burial at Rockland Cemetery across the Hudson River from their former estate Pocaho. Jessie would survive her husband for another dozen years.

Libbie Custer

PART TWO

The Custers

George Custer

CHAPTER 10

Growing Pains

"My career as a cadet had but little to commend it to the study of those who came after me, unless as an example to be carefully avoided."
— GEORGE CUSTER

"We all have our battles in the march of life."
— LIBBIE BACON

GEORGE ARMSTRONG CUSTER, nicknamed Autie, was born on December 5, 1839.[300] His birthplace was the remote village of New Rumley in Ohio's rural east. It was a second marriage for his father Emanuel and his mother Maria, each a widower with two children from the previous marriage. George Custer was the first of five children born to his parents who reached adulthood, followed by Nevin, Thomas, Boston, and Margaret.

Emanuel was a blacksmith, farmer, and justice of the peace for livelihood and an evangelical Methodist and Jacksonian Democrat for conviction. He thumped the Bible to demand a stern morality, while embracing the Jacksonian creed of every man for himself, buyer beware, and survival of the fittest. Looking back at his long life, he boasted: "My first vote was cast for Andrew Jackson, my last vote for Grover Cleveland."[301] Emanuel was an authoritarian, or, to use a modern notion, a control freak. His son George was a free spirit. Authoritarians and free spirits have trouble getting along. Authoritarian fathers end up stunting the emotional growth of free-spirited sons. That was true not just for Custer but his younger brothers Thomas and Boston; Nevin was a mama's boy. Although Custer lived to be thirty-six years old, he never grew up emotionally. He remained a teenage boy of authority defying, daredevil, boisterous energy and shape-shifting enthusiasms. That was at once part of his charm and notoriety; it propelled him to dazzling feats of combat along with hundreds of demerits at West Point and two courts-martial.

Yet, although Custer instinctively rebelled against authority figures, he was a mostly dutiful son at home. Indeed, he later wrote these words of gratitude that any parents would be delighted to receive from their child: "I never wanted for anything necessary. You and Mother instilled into me principles of industry, self-reliance, honesty. You taught me the value of temperate habits, the difference between right and wrong. I look back on the days spent under the home roof as a period of pure happiness, and I feel thankful for such noble parents." To that, Custer's mother replied: "When you speak about your boyhood...I had to weep for joy.... I was not fortunate to have wealth to make home beautiful.... So I tried to fill the empty spaces with little acts of kindness.... It is sweet to toil for those we love."[302]

Custer's mother was probably far more influential than his father in restraining his behavior at home. Custer naturally had a very affectionate, considerate, generous side to his character. He deeply loved each member of his family but was especially close to his mother. His wife Libbie described how each time he was about to leave home to return to a military campaign, he would "follow his mother about, whispering some comforting word to her; or, opening the closed door of her own room, where, womanlike, she fought out her grief alone, sit beside her as long as he could endure it." Then, when he had to go, Custer "would rush out of the house, sobbing like a child, and then throw himself into the carriage beside me, completely unnerved."[303]

His mother was not the only affectionate woman in Custer's life. His stepsister Lydia Ann was just as sweet and nurturing. Custer's narcissism was bolstered by the unconditional love showered on him by his mother and stepsister. After she married David Reed of Monroe, Michigan, Custer stayed with them and attended acclaimed Stebbins Academy from 1852 to 1855. Indeed, that institution's reputation was so stellar that an indifferent student like Custer was hired at age sixteen to teach at Beech Point School in Hopedale, Ohio. For that he earned $28 a month. But he had no intention of pursuing an education career. He dreamed of living a life of adventure and glory as a great military commander. And for that he sought entrance to the United States Military Academy at West Point.[304]

Custer applied to local Congressman John Bingham for an appointment in 1856. He reckoned it was a long shot since Bingham was a Republican and he had adopted his father's allegiance to the Democratic Party. He was clever enough candidly to say so in his letter: "I am told that you can send boys to West Point. I want to go there and I hear that you don't care whether a boy is a Democrat or Republican. I am a Democrat and I hope that you can send me to West Point for I want to be a soldier."[305] Bingham saw promise in the lad: "I received a letter...that captivated me.... Struck by its originality, its honesty, I replied at once."[306] Custer shared his excitement at his appointment with Lydia Ann, noting that the family was divided: "Mother is much opposed to me going there but father and David [his older half brother] are in favor of it very much. I think it is the best place that I could go."[307]

Custer was truly lucky. He would not just get a free college education but be paid a monthly salary of $28 as well. Higher education in nineteenth-century America was reserved only for the very rich or very bright who could win scholarships. Only one of one hundred men could boast a college degree. In 1860, there were 209 colleges with an average hundred students each in a nation with 31 million people.[308]

Custer was enchanted by the military academy's setting: "I think it is the most romantic spot I ever saw."[309] West Point is indeed set within a stunning landscape, on a flat promontory five hundred or so feet above the Hudson River, which curls around its base with the Hudson Highlands soaring on both sides of the river. The routine of academy life immediately engulfs new starry-eyed cadets. The "education" is as much psychological as academic. Reveille is at five-thirty daily and taps at ten nightly. In between, cadets spend six hours in the classroom and three hours in military training and duties. Ideally each cadet's individuality is demolished and replaced with unquestioning obedience to and limitless pride in one's duty to one's superiors, the army, and the nation. First year cadets or plebes are subjected to near-constant hazing by upper classmen to emotionally test and toughen them. Cadets earn demerits for any breach of discipline or decorum. Anyone with more than one hundred demerits within any half-year was expelled.

At West Point, Custer revealed little aptitude for being either a soldier or scholar. Looking back years later, he sardonically admitted that: "My career as a cadet had but little to commend it to the study of those who came after me, unless as an example to be carefully avoided."[310] Over his four years he racked up 726 demerits, far more than any of his classmates. His roommate found Custer a "whole-souled generous friend, and a mighty good fellow, and I like him." The trouble was "that he is too clever for his own good. He is always connected with all the mischief that is going on and never studies any more than he can possibly help.... I admired Custer's free and careless way and the perfect indifference he had for everything. It was all right with him whether he knew his lesson or not; he did not allow it to trouble him."[311] He violated at least one of the oaths that West Point cadets take: "I will not lie, cheat, or steal." He slipped into an instructor's office, stole his test questions, and studied them. The instructor changed the questions and Custer, along with thirty other boys, flunked. They were all expelled but he was the only one recalled.[312] He liked sneaking out after taps to visit Benny Haven's Tavern a mile south of the academy. Some summer nights he swam across the Hudson to another tavern; just crossing over and back several hundred yards each way was quite a feat given the river's powerful tides and currents. One Thanksgiving he snuck out to escort a girl to a dance and did not get back till four in the morning. He later ruefully expressed the mixed feelings of countless college boys with similar experiences: "I was in poor humor for hard study during the next day...and under the circumstances I was almost (but not quite) sorry I had gone to the ball."[313]

Custer loved pretty girls and they loved him, given his good looks, confidence, powerful build, hypersexuality, and ability to sweet-talk them. His roommate recalled: "He is a handsome fellow, and a very successful ladies' man" who does not "care an iota how many of the fair ones break their hearts for him."[314] To one girlfriend named Molly, he penned these lines: "I've seen and kissed that crimson lip, With honied smiles o'rflowing, Enchanted watched the opening rose." He then expressed his eagerness to "see you next at the trundle bed."[315] Most "nice girls" did not go near as far as Custer desired, so he occasionally resorted to "professional girls" for fleeting relief of his passions. Of course, the danger with cavorting with prostitutes is an unwanted disease, rather than pregnancy with one's sweethearts. Custer was treated for gonorrhea in August 1859 after a prolonged furlough in New York. That treatment likely rendered him sterile because he was never able to conceive a child with his future wife Libbie, nor apparently with any of his other lovers.[316]

As graduation neared, Custer expressed a common feeling among anyone about to leave the security and fun of a university for "the real world": "We were happy then because our minds were free and had no care for the future, but now it is different.... Our dependence must be on our own abilities and on these we must rely for all we expect to be or have in future."[317] He graduated from West Point last in his class of thirty-four cadets on June 24, 1861. That is not as dismal as it appears. His class began four years earlier with 68 cadets and 34 had subsequently dropped out for various reasons. Regardless, a few days later he did something that nearly got him kicked out of the army. He was officer of the day on June 29, when two cadets squared off for a fight: "I should have arrested the two combatants.... But the instincts of the boy prevailed over the obligation of the officer.... I pushed my way through the surrounding line of cadets...and called out loudly, "Stand back, boys; let's have a fair fight."[318] Alas, First Lieutenant William Hazen saw what was happening, stopped the fight, and arrested Custer.

Custer's court martial began on July 5, 1861. He faced two charges, "neglect of duty" and "conduct to the prejudice of good order and military discipline." Custer pleaded guilty to both charges but asked for mercy both for himself and the nation—he had graduated after four years at West Point and there was an ongoing war. He received a reprimand. He hurried off to join his classmates, who remained loyal Americans, and to fight those who betrayed and rebelled against their country.[319]

Unbeknownst to Custer, a parallel life in Monroe would eventually merge with his own. Elizabeth Bacon, nicknamed Libbie, was born in Monroe on April 8, 1842.[320] Her father Daniel Bacon personified the American self-made man. He was born on a Connecticut farm but as a young man moved to Monroe, Michigan, to seek his fortune. He began his career as a school teacher and real estate developer, and then expanded into legal, business, and political pursuits as a lawyer, county supervisor, school superintendent, member of Michigan's territorial and later state assembly, associate judge, probate judge, president of the Merchant and Mechanics Bank, and fervent member of the Whig Party and then the Republican Party. He was forty years old when he got around to marrying. His bride, Eleanor Sophia Page, was seventeen years younger, very bright, well schooled, and a fervent evangelical Christian with stern notions of right and wrong.

Their daughter Libbie was also very bright, yet, like her mother, accepted rather than questioned, let alone defied, those with more power. That included her parents and society when she was a girl and spread to include her husband, the army, and the government when she was a woman. She best expressed her natural equanimity and adaptability when, at eight years old, she was naughty, and her mother locked her in a closet. Rather than protest or plead, she fell asleep there until her mother finally released her. Biographer Shirley Leckie attributed those characteristics to Libbie's fear of punishment and being the middle child, although genetics surely played a role as well. Then, as a teenager, she was an avid reader of Fanny Fern's two volumes of *Fern Leaves from Fanny's Portfolio*, with heroines who dutifully upheld filial, marital, societal, or governmental power, but were resourceful in evading or resisting those who committed evil acts or personified evil values like lust, greed, impiety, or hubris. Above all, one must defend the virtue and reputation of oneself and one's loved ones.[321]

Libbie suffered four tragic losses during her childhood that she was indoctrinated fatalistically to accept as God's will. She was three years old when one sister died, six when her brother died, seven when her other sister died, and twelve when her mother died. Of her mother's death, Libbie expressed these heartbreaking words through her diary: "My mother is laid in the cold ground, never to rise again until the Last Day. Oh, why did they put her in that black coffin and screw the lid down so tight? The last thing she looked at was my portrait.... I hope the Lord will spare me to my father for I am his only comfort left."[322]

As Eleanor lay dying, she told her husband, "I want you to be a mother as well as a father to Elizabeth." Bacon promised his wife to do so but thereafter was haunted: "I have ever felt the force of these words.... I feel the responsibility beyond anything in my life before or since." He did his best but finally recognized that he was incapable of providing the sort of intimacies and insights for his daughter that a woman could. He had relatives in Auburn, New York, and sent Libbie to attend the Young Ladies' Institute there. The transition from her father's indulgence to the strict school upset her. She wrote her father: "You want me to become womanly do you not. I don't want to though—I like being a little girl. I dread being a young lady so much.... I like acting free and girl like. Not being so prim and particular about what I say and do."[323]

Libbie received her latest jolt when she was eighteen years old and her father married a widow, Rhoda Wells Pitts. Bacon recalled his daughter to Monroe. To her relief, Libbie found Rhoda to be a loving and supportive stepmother. Libbie entered the four-year Young Ladies Seminary and Collegiate Institute. Her father loosened his reins a bit over her and her friends: "I have told the girls that they may play and laugh to their hearts' content, promenade, and walk in good weather. But must not ride fast horses, and no boat rides, and have as little to do with fast young men as is consistent."[324] In June 1862, Libbie graduated as Valedictorian, and the *Detroit Free Press* lauded her speech. Elizabeth had mixed feelings about finishing school. Tongue in cheek, she wrote an aunt that "We all have our battles in the march of life. Do you realize that I shall soon bid adieu to the teens and enter on my august twenties."[325]

Men may have admired Libbie's intelligence and grace, but probably most were more attracted sexually. She had a pretty heart-shaped face with high-cheekbones, blue-gray eyes, thick chestnut hair that curled past her shoulders, and pouty lips that spread in beguiling smiles. Although she was petite, she had an hourglass figure that she displayed in tight-fitting dresses. She had a powerful latent sexuality that Custer would breach and nurture to their mutual delight. Not surprisingly, she often received unwanted attention from men, starting with a doctor who tried to kiss her when she was just thirteen. Yet she naturally loved being courted by gentlemen. With time she learned how to exude that delicate balance between being coquettish and reserved that at once enticed eager suitors yet kept them respectfully at arm's length.

Libbie had conflicting desires. She wanted a handsome, successful, loving husband, but not too soon. In nineteenth-century America, she was free only to chat, stroll, and dance with suitors before settling on the best choice. She was determined to make the most of those fleeting years between being a young woman in her prime and an old maid. And then a storybook hero came into her life and began courting her.

CHAPTER II

Rising Stars

"And Monroe people will please mind their own business, and let me alone.... I wish the gossipers sunk in the sea."
— LIBBIE BACON

"I believe more than ever in Destiny."
— GEORGE CUSTER

GEORGE CUSTER REACHED WASHINGTON on July 20 and dropped off his bag at the Ebbitt House Hotel where his former West Point roommate James Parker was staying. He then hurried to report for duty at the headquarters of General Winfield Scott, America's commanding general. What ensued was the first instance of what became renowned as "Custer's luck." As a just-minted second lieutenant last in his class, Custer was the Union army's lowest ranking officer. He expected to receive his regimental assignment from some staff officer, which is what happened. But after handing Custer his orders to report for duty to Company C of the 2nd Cavalry, the officer ushered Custer before the general himself.[326]

Scott greeted Custer as if he owed him a great favor: "Well, my young friend, I am glad to welcome you in the service at this critical time.... Now what can I do for you?"[327] When Custer replied that he wanted to serve at the front, Scott praised him. He asked Custer to carry dispatches to General Irwin McDowell, who commanded the Union army that had advanced twenty miles south of Washington. McDowell was planning to attack the rebel army before him the next morning. And that was how Custer participated in the Civil War's first major battle.

The assignment, however, did have a catch. Astonishingly, Scott's headquarters had no spare horses. Custer had to find one and then report back to headquarters for the dispatches. Custer hurried out in a desperate search for a horse that could carry him to a pending glory. Fortunately, he ran into a West Point acquaintance who was a member of Captain Charles Griffin's artillery battery, was heading to the front, and had a spare horse. After retrieving the dispatches, Custer rejoined his friend for an all-night ride to the Union army.

Shortly after dawn, Custer reached McDowell's headquarters, handed over his dispatches, and then joined his regiment. The 2nd Cavalry was positioned just behind Griffin's battery atop Henry House Hill, a key position in the Union line. Although the cavalry remained in reserve, they could at least partly view the battle. They had to sit stoically atop their horses as stray rifle shots zipped past and cannon shells screamed overhead. This was first time that Custer came under fire and he thrilled at "the strange hissing sound of the first cannon shot that I heard" and observed that "a man listens with changed interest when the direction of the balls is toward instead of away from him."[328] To their horror, Custer and his comrades watched as rebel troops decimated and overran Griffin's battery. They waited in vain for an order to charge and retake the battery. Instead they were ordered to cover the army's retreat. Custer rode behind his own men "to show them that he would not expose them to any danger that he was not willing to participate in himself."[329]

As part of the cavalry's reorganization on August 2, Custer's 2nd regiment was redesignated the 5th and attached to General Philip Kearny's brigade.[330] Kearny tapped Custer to join his staff. Custer did not last long. A mysterious illness afflicted him and on October 3 he received leave to go home to recover.

Custer had not visited his parents for two years. Although he was happy to be with them, they had moved to a farm in Wood County Ohio, so he missed being with old friends in New Rumley. Also, he missed seeing his brother Tom, who, although just sixteen, had joined the army. He then journeyed to Monroe, Michigan, to visit his half-sister Lydia Ann and her husband David Reed. Having spent years in Monroe, he felt at home there. One night he celebrated with some friends in a drunken debauch. The next morning as Lydia helped him nurse his splitting hangover, she made him promise never to drink alcohol again. He would be faithful to that oath his life's remainder. He indulged his insatiable desire to be with pretty women by attending every dance that was held. As a young officer in uniform, he was doubly welcomed by the local ladies. Reluctantly, he headed back to the army in February 1862.

During Custer's prolonged absence, the Union army in northern Virginia underwent some critical changes. On November 1, Lincoln replaced General Winfield Scott as general-in-chief with General George McClellan, who had presided over a minor victory in western Virginia. Lincoln would soon rue the day he had ever heard of his new commander.

McClellan ranks among the very worst generals in American history.[331] He fancied and promoted himself as "the young Napoleon," but he was as timid, indecisive, and inept as the real Napoleon was truly a military genius. Time after time he had the opportunity to crush the rebel army, especially at Richmond in May 1862 and at Antietam in September 1862, yet failed to do so. What McClellan excelled at was self-promotion driven by deep-rooted narcissism and delusions of grandeur. Indeed, he even believed that God had handpicked him to save America: "I can almost think of myself as a chosen instrument to carry out his schemes."[332] He was intelligent but not enough to know his limits. He was a mean-spirited know-it-all who elevated himself by nastily putting down others. He was especially cruel to Lincoln, calling him "a gorilla," an "idiot," and a "well-meaning baboon." He kept the commander-in-chief waiting or at times refused to see him. Yet Lincoln retained his patience, once remarking that he would hold McClellan's horse if the general was victorious.[333]

In all, McClellan was the triumph of style over substance. He was only thirty-five years old, short and stocky, but fit and handsome. Most importantly, he oozed self-confidence and charisma. With carefully studied melodrama, he played the role of great general to an unsophisticated mass audience of mostly young men desperately seeking a storybook leader. McClellan created a personality cult of worship among his staff officers and attached journalists. Historian Richard Slotkin explained: "McClellan's headquarters was a closed echo chamber filled with followers and acolytes who praised his every decision as masterful."[334] Custer was among the countless people who fell under McClellan's spell, at one point declaring: "I have more confidence in General McClellan than in any man living. I would forsake everything and follow him to the ends of the earth. I would lay down my life for him…. Every officer and private worships him. I would fight anyone who would say a word against him."[335] He wrote those astonishing words in mid-March 1862 after having gotten only distant glimpses of the object of his worship in the camps around Washington. Such is the power of men of rare charisma to bamboozle others. Not everyone was so enamored. General Kearny was among countless officers beyond McClellan's inner circle who were contemptuous rather than fawning toward that master poseur: "McClellan or the few with him are devising a game of politics rather than war."[336]

McClellan was hardly the only man during the Civil War who rose to his highest level of ineptness. McClellan's worst enabler was Allan Pinkerton, a successful Chicago detective that McClellan tapped to be his intelligence chief. Pinkerton may have been good at tailing adulterers and solving murders but knew nothing about genuine espionage. He consistently doubled or tripled the rebel army's size by assuming regiments were at full strength when they were often seriously depleted by casualties, desertions, disease, detachments, and lack of new enlistments. That gave McClellan endless excuses not to advance let alone attack.[337]

Yet McClellan was not completely inept. He entered West Point when he was only fifteen years old and graduated second in the class of 1846. He was gifted in math and engineering. He was a veteran of two wars, although via the relative safety of headquarters rather than the front lines. During the Mexican War, he marched with General Scott's army from Vera Cruz to Mexico City. He was America's military observer in the allied British and French army fighting Russia during the Crimea War. He might have made a first-rate chief-of-staff to a general gifted at strategy and tactics who knew how to harness his bloated ego. During the Civil War, his sole accomplishment was to reorganize what he called the Army of the Potomac and give the troops a sense of esprit de corps. Ideally, each regiment had one thousand troops with ten companies of one hundred men each. Three regiments made a brigade, three brigades a division, three divisions a corps, and two or more corps an army. That aside, all else he did undermined America's cause.

After Custer reported for duty to Lieutenant Colonel William Grier, the Fifth Michigan's new leader, he made up for his absence. On March 9, General Johnston withdrew his army from Centreville south of the easily defended Rappahannock and Rapidan Rivers about midway between Washington and Richmond. McClellan ordered General George Stoneman, the Union cavalry commander, to trail the rebel army and determine its position. When the 5th encountered a rebel force on March 16, Grier asked for an officer to lead his company to attack the rear guard. Custer volunteered. In the first charge of his military career, "I took my position in front at a slow trot, so as not to tire horses and men. About halfway I bade the men fire their revolvers. We then took the gallop and the bullets rattled like hail." He and his men scattered the pickets but then pulled up before three hundred rebels deployed behind Cedar Run. Rebel bullets wounded three of his men before Custer led them from rifle range. Afterward, Stoneman summoned Custer "and seemed pleased with the manner in which I had performed my duty. I have not had my clothes off for a week."[338]

McClellan conceived a campaign plan that might have worked had a competent general implemented it.[339] Rather than directly attack Johnston's army, he decided to go around it. While keeping General McDowell's 35,000-man corps in northern Virginia to defend the capital, he embarked 121,500 troops, 1,592 cavalry horses and draft animals, 1,224 wagons, 44 batteries of cannons, and hundreds of tons of supplies on 113 steamboats and 270 sailing vessels. The flotilla descended the Potomac River and Chesapeake Bay to anchor off Fort Monroe at the peninsula's tip between the James and York Rivers. It took three weeks to disgorge all those men, animals, ordnance, wagons, and supplies onto shore.

From Fort Monroe it is eighty miles or an easy four-day stroll over mostly flat ground to Richmond. The rebels had limited forces on the peninsula, with the largest 13,000 troops under General John Magruder at Yorktown. A vigorous advance along the multiple parallel roads would have overwhelmed the enemy and swiftly brought the Army of the Potomac to Richmond, whose defenses were lightly manned. Tragically, McClellan was in charge of carrying out his own plan. He advanced the Army of the Potomac at a snail's pace up the peninsula with prolonged halts everyplace the rebels took a stand.

Custer was detached to the topographical engineer corps where he received thrilling assignments. He was to scout ahead of the army to discern the rebel army's positions, strengths, and weaknesses. His most spectacular experiences, however, were his four ascents a thousand feet in a hot air balloon at the end of a cable anchored to the ground. There he marveled eagle-eyed at the vista. With him was Chief Aeronaut Thaddeus Lowe, who headed the newly inaugurated Union Army Balloon Corps, a civilian organization attached to the army. During his first ascent, Custer sketched what he could see of enemy forces deployed across the terrain westward. Lowe took Custer's suggestion that better intelligence would be yielded at night because the campfires would reveal the enemy positions and number. The trouble with that was determining just where those troops were in the dark. Finally, he convinced Lowe that ascending just before dawn was the best time since smoke from the breakfast fires would be easily seen along with the exact locations. Thus, Custer made key contributions to Balloon Corps operations. With that done, he was eager to get his feet back on the ground before mounting nothing higher than a horse.

Custer experienced his first sustained combat on May 5, during the battle of Williamsburg, where General James Longstreet commanded 20,000 rebel troops. He was scouting for General Winfield Hancock's 3,400-man brigade, whose mission was to outflank the enemy. Custer rode up to Skiffe's Creek, with the bridge on fire and several rebel horsemen on the far side. He pulled his pistol and exchanged shots with the rebels until more Union cavalry rode up and the enemy fled. He and the other men then extinguished the flames on the bridge. Custer rode out again until he reached a position beyond the rebel left flank and waited as Hancock arrived and deployed his men and eighteen cannons. Magruder sent a reserve brigade to drive off Hancock. The Union gunners opened fire with shells then canister, killing and wounding hundreds of rebels. Hancock then ordered his brigade to charge. Custer galloped forward and captured a captain, five privates, and a rebel flag, the first ever taken by the Army of the Potomac. In all, the rebels suffered more than five hundred casualties and the Americans around a hundred.

Among the wounded was Custer's former West Point friend John Lea, a captain from a Mississippi regiment, who was shot in the leg. The two were startled to see each other. Lea wept with relief as Custer promised to take care of him. He got Lea's leg sewn up and installed him in a nearby house with a sympathetic family. Custer recalled, "We talked over old times and asked each other hundreds of questions concerning our classmates who were on opposite sides of the contest."[340] Custer gave him money before bidding him goodbye. Later that summer, he visited his friend to discover Lea and the daughter of the house were engaged. Custer served as Lea's best man in his marriage.

Custer explained the Civil War's curious nature, whereby the soldiers tried to kill each other by day but then often fraternized by night: "Scarcely a ten minutes interval during the day that the rebels and our men do not fire at each other.... At night, when it is too dark to shoot or be shot at, both come out of hiding places, holler at each other, calling names, and bragging what they intend to do. Then, when daylight appears, the party which sees the other first, fires, and that puts a stop till night comes, when the same thing is repeated."[341] Like all soldiers, he struggled to inure himself to the gruesome deaths and maiming of others, along with the ceaseless awareness that that could be his own fate at virtually any second. Burying the dead haunted him: "Some were quite young and boyish, and, looking at their faces, I could not but think of my own younger brother."[342] Contemplating his own mortality, he asked his half-sister Lydia to ensure that her children "if they never see me again...must never forget me." Yet he assured his parents that they had no reason to worry about him: "I think and feel confident that I will go through this war...safely...and that at its close I will return to you all."[343] It is impossible to determine how much of that Custer actually believed and how much was simply the comforting bromide that any soldier tells his loved ones.

Custer enjoyed his latest bout of extraordinary luck during a reconnaissance on May 24. He was with a force of cavalry and infantry led by Colonel Dwight Woodbury that reached the Chickahominy River, four hundred yards below New Bridge and guarded by rebel troops. Accompanying Woodbury was General John Barnard, McClellan's chief engineer. As Woodbury and Barnard debated whether the river was fordable, Custer proved it was by riding his horse across to the far bank. That encouraged Woodbury to split his force in two and send half to join Custer on the far bank. The Union forces advanced along each bank toward New Bridge, drove off the defenders, and repelled a counterattack. They then received orders to withdraw back to the army. A fellow officer described Custer's conduct that day as "the first to cross the stream, the first to open fire upon the enemy, and one of the last to leave the field."[344]

Barnard informed McClellan of Custer's courageous feats. To his delight, Custer soon learned that McClellan had praised him in a report to Secretary of War Edwin Stanton: "A very gallant reconnaissance made by Lieutenant Bowen and Custer came upon the Louisiana Tigers, handled them terribly, taking some 50 prisoners and killing and wounding very large numbers."[345] On May 28, McClellan summoned Custer to his headquarters, promoted him to captain, and asked him to join his staff. Custer was thrilled to accept that great honor.

Then a controversy arose, although Custer himself was not to blame. McClellan had a false story spread through the newspapers. He was beside the Chickahominy River contemplating its depth and asked whether anyone was willing to test its waters. Custer immediately plunged his horse into the river, rode over and up the far bank, then returned and saluted. McClellan promoted him on the spot. That fable was deeply revealing of McClellan's egomania and mendacity. He obscured Custer's genuine heroic feat of leading an attack that routed the enemy with a lie about how his staff members displayed undying loyalty to himself. To bolster his image as the "young Napoleon," McClellan stole that story from a similar true incident during one of Napoleon's campaigns.

Custer's devotion to McClellan largely reflected the general's confidence in making him his chief messenger and scout. Custer could gallop with orders to various generals or even roam within or far beyond the army's front lines, at times with an escort, at times alone. For Custer the only downside was that he missed most of the skirmishes of his regiment, the 5th Cavalry. Scouts are supposed to flee rather than fight any enemy troops they encounter as the need for information trumps gunfire. Custer's first impulse on seeing rebels was to charge them. McClellan praised his young captain: "In those days Custer was simply a reckless, gallant boy, undeterred by fatigue, unconscious of fear; but his head was always clear in danger, and he always brought me clear and intelligible reports of what he saw when under the heaviest fire."[346]

Custer's exploits dazzled his comrades but were a tiny part of a vast campaign involving hundreds of thousands of troops across swaths of Virginia. By late May,

McClellan's army finally neared Richmond, with General Erasmus Keyes' corps west of the Chickahominy River and the other four corps east. General Joe Johnston commanded the 75,000 troops defending the rebel capital. On May 31, he launched his army against Keyes' isolated corps at Fair Oaks or Seven Pines. In desperate fighting, Keyes' men, reinforced by two other corps, staved off the attack. Johnston was among the wounded. President Davis replaced him with General Robert E. Lee.[347]

Lee summoned General Thomas "Stonewall" Jackson from the Shenandoah Valley as soon as he finished trouncing armies led by Generals John Frémont, Nathaniel Banks, and James Shields in a whirlwind series of battles. Meanwhile, to distract McClellan, Lee sent General J.E.B. Stuart and his cavalry corps in a raid clockwise around the Union army to destroy supply depots and wagon trains, and defeat isolated regiments of Union infantry and cavalry. Then, on June 25, Lee opened what became known as the Seven Days' Campaign with a diversionary attack against McClellan's left flank at Oak Grove. With the hapless Union commander's attention riveted there, Lee hurled the corps of James Longstreet and Ambrose Hill against General David Porter's corps north of the Chickahominy River while Jackson's men hit Porter's flank at Beaver Dam Creek, a battle known as Mechanicsville, on June 26. Porter's troops withdrew in good order to Gaines' Mill, where Lee attacked him again on June 27. Rather than reinforce Porter while assaulting Richmond's thinly held defenses with the rest of his army, McClellan ordered all his troops to retreat. Lee's army struck McClellan at Savage Station on June 29, Glendale on June 30, and Malvern Hill on July 1. McClellan withdrew his army to Harrison Landing on the James River and had his men construct breastworks. In a week of relentless fighting, Lee had driven McClellan thirty miles from Richmond, demoralized him and his army, and inflicted 16,000 casualties while suffering 20,000. Lee then followed up his Seven Days' Campaign victory with a brilliant move. He knew that McClellan was too cowed to resume an advance against Richmond no matter how few troops stood in the way. So, Lee left a skeleton force of 20,000 men to screen and intimidate McClellan while he led 55,000 troops north toward Washington.

McClellan reacted exactly as Lee expected. He did nothing but preen at his headquarters, protected by his army. One of his adoring staff officers, however, seized any chance for action. Indeed, Custer's lust for combat overwhelmed his duty to avoid it. On August 5, he joined a raid by Colonel William Averell and four hundred troopers of the 3rd Pennsylvania south of the James River. Custer led a charge against the 3rd Virginia cavalry's advanced guard and captured a soldier. Then twenty or so rebel horsemen appeared from the rear and galloped through the Union ranks toward safety. Custer spurred his horse after the rebel captain and after twice hollering for him to surrender, shot him. By now Custer was far beyond his comrades and close to the enemy cavalry. He grabbed the reins of the horse of the man he had just killed and triumphantly rejoined his comrades. Although Custer had exchanged gunfire with the enemy before, this was the first man he knew he had killed. There was little glory in this act. He had fatally shot in the back a man who posed no threat to him but was merely trying to escape. He eased his conscience with this argument: "It was the officer's own fault. I called on him twice to surrender."[348]

Meanwhile, upon learning of Lee's approach, Lincoln unified the scattered troops in northern Virginia under General John Pope's command and, on August 3, recalled McClellan's Army of the Potomac from its vast encampment at Harrison Landing on the James River back to defend Washington. That meant shipping over 100,000 troops, 25,000 horses and mules, 300 cannons, and thousands of tons of supplies by steamboat. McClellan typically dawdled. The first regiments did not embark until August 14. Just as typically, Lincoln dealt with McClellan's mingled cowardice and insubordination as he did all absurdities or setbacks beyond his control, with humor rather than anger or despair. At one point he quipped, "If General McClellan did not want to use the army, he would like to borrow it." Another time he referred to the Army of the Potomac as "General McClellan's bodyguard."[349]

Heading the rebel army's advance, Jackson repelled an attack by General Nathaniel Banks's corps at Cedar Mountain on August 9. Then, rather than shadow the retreating Union army north, Lee quick-marched his army in a huge westward curl to try to cut it off. He nearly succeeded. Pope managed to mass his forces at Manassas, where Lee sent Jackson around Pope's right flank and routed him on August 29. Then Lee did something even more stunning; he led his army northwest to the Shenandoah Valley, detached Jackson to besiege the 12,500-man garrison at Harpers Ferry, and crossed the Potomac River with the rest of his troops. He gambled on winning the war with a decisive victory on northern soil.

By now, most of McClellan's army had disembarked in Washington. Lincoln urged him to find and destroy Lee's army. Typically, McClellan saw the Lincoln administration rather than Lee as his primary enemy. On the evening of September 11, he and his inner circle discussed committing treason. Although just what was said and who said it remains hazy through secondhand accounts, apparently McClellan and his disciples contemplated marching to Washington, deposing Lincoln, and imposing a military dictatorship. Although no plot jelled, the fact that McClellan actually mulled destroying American democracy rather than the rebel army reveals the depths of his depravity. Custer was probably not present, having been detached to the staff of General Alfred Pleasanton, the First Cavalry Division commander.

Two days later, the American cause received a stunning stroke of good luck. Some rebel officer had rolled cigars in a sheet of paper on which was printed Lee's campaign plan. A Union soldier found the packet, understood the significance of the orders, and hurried with it to his commanding officer. The "Lost Order" passed up the command chain to McClellan's headquarters. Then something astonishing happened—McClellan acted decisively. The orders revealed that Lee's army was scattered beyond South Mountain, a thirty-mile-long range of hills that ran north-south between Frederick eastward and Hagerstown westward. A rapid Union advance could destroy Lee's army piecemeal. On September 14, McClellan ordered his corps to march on a broad front west toward South Mountain.

Learning of McClellan's advance, Lee sent troops to guard South Mountain's passes. At the head of the 8th Illinois Cavalry, Pleasanton and Custer spearheaded the prong aimed toward Boonsboro. General Fitzhugh Lee's rebel cavalry defended that town. Custer helped lead the charge that routed them and secured Boonsboro. Elsewhere, Union forces drove the rebels from the passes.

General Robert E. Lee ordered his scattered divisions to reunite at Sharpsburg on Antietam Creek with the rain-swollen Potomac River just a few miles behind. Custer was with the army's advanced guard that found the rebels deployed there. Quickly assessing the situation, he had a courier gallop this message to McClellan: "The enemy is drawn up in line on a ridge...about a mile and a half long. We can have equally good position as they now occupy.... We are lacking in artillery.... Longstreet is in command and has forty cannons that we know of. We can employ all the troops you can send us."[350]

When Custer sent his message, only Longstreet's 15,000-man corps was at Sharpsburg. Most of Jackson's corps was still at Harper's Ferry, having just captured the 12,500-man garrison. Tragically, McClellan again hesitated, letting Lee mass most of his troops there by the morning of September 17. The battle of Sharpsburg or Antietam was the first and, mercifully, the last that McClellan actually directed. Predictably, he squandered a golden chance to win a decisive victory. The Army of the Potomac's 60,000 troops outgunned the Army of Virginia's 30,000 troops by two to one. The Potomac River arched behind Sharpsburg. The enemy left flank was anchored on the Potomac River, but the right flank was on Antietam Creek with two miles of undefended farmland leading to the Potomac. The obvious strategy would have been to pin down Lee's front with a massive artillery barrage while hooking two corps around the enemy's right flank. A rapid advance could have cut off the rebel army from the pontoon bridges over the river and forced it to surrender.

Of course, McClellan failed to do that. Instead, he launched his army in a series of uncoordinated assaults through the woods on the rebel army's strong left flank, then directly across Antietam Creek against the rebel center deployed behind rail fences and a sunken road. The result was slaughter, the deadliest day in American history, with 13,500 American and 11,500 rebel casualties. And by that day's end, Lee's army stood its ground, battered but defiant.

Lee waited the entire next day for McClellan to renew his attack. McClellan had a fresh corps that he could have curled around the enemy's right flank while massed cavalry arced wider to capture the pontoon bridges over the Potomac. Instead, McClellan simply waited for Lee to withdraw. He revealed his mindset in a letter to his wife in which he pledged "to do my best to hit upon some plan of campaign that will enable me to drive the rebels entirely away from this part of the country forever."[351] McClellan lacked the essential attributes of generalship. He sought to wait rather than search for the enemy, to avoid rather than fight battles, to let the enemy escape rather than destroy him. Lee obliged McClellan by crossing the Potomac with his army on the night of September 18. The Army of the Potomac would not follow for another six weeks.

Given how McClellan's and Custer's characters were fundamentally not just different but opposed, the latter's devotion to the former is nearly inexplicable. Custer was a fierce warrior with a killer instinct for decimating the enemy. McClellan was an engineer who loved the pomp and power of being a general but was terrified of war itself. Custer knew as well as anyone that Lee's battered army was on the ropes and a decisive push would have forced the rebels to surrender. Yet he cast blame for the failure of the Antietam campaign like the preceding Peninsula campaign not on McClellan's utter incompetence and cowardice, but on the imagined political machinations of others. After the war he insisted that McClellan possessed "all the natural and acquired endowments sought for in a great leader" and ascribed "the defeat of McClellan" not "to combinations made either in the Confederate capital or in the camp of the Confederate army, but in Washington. It was the result of an opposition whose birth and outgrowth could be traced to the dominating spirits who at that time were largely in control of the federal government."[352] For completely opposite reasons, Lee quipped that "I hate to see McClellan go. He and I had grown to understand each other so well."[353] McClellan was the best northern ally the south had, although how deliberate that was has been fiercely debated ever since.

Tragically, Custer's utterly baseless conspiracy theory was hardly the first nor the last in American history, just the latest in a putrid unceasing current.[354] Psychology helps explain that paranoid strain in American politics. The more pathological an individual or group, the more likely that person or those people will deny their own vilest characteristics and instead project them onto some hated other. Rather than admit their own timidity and incompetence, McClellan and his coterie continually hurled those charges along with treason against Lincoln and his administration. And if Lincoln's "regime" was treasonous, then the patriotic act was to overthrow it. Given his paranoid beliefs about the president, Custer's feelings can only be imagined as he joined McClellan and his staff to host Lincoln and conduct him on various tours of the peacefully encamped Army of the Potomac from October 2 to 4.

Custer had become a lifelong McClellan fan, inspired by his charisma and style. Not everyone was so enamored. McClellan's failure to destroy Lee's army enraged Lincoln. Nonetheless, the president capitalized on the "victory" at Antietam to issue on September 22, 1862, his Emancipation Proclamation that from January 1, 1863, all slaves in rebel hands, then 82 percent in the Confederate states and 74 percent of all slaves, were free.[355] The catch was that slaves had to liberate themselves, although every one that did denied the Confederacy a laborer. He justified his act under the constitutional guise that as commander-in-chief he was empowered to confiscate enemy property. He had no power to end slavery elsewhere in Border States loyal to the Union or occupied rebel territory. Only a constitutional amendment could abolish slavery but politically the time was not yet ripe to advocate that. Instead, he called for buying and freeing slaves from their masters during his annual address to Congress on December 1, 1862. He also tried to play off southerners against each other by promising the restoration of a state to the Union when ten percent of its citizens signed a loyalty oath and drafted a constitution that abolished slavery. Finally, he supported enlisting black soldiers in the army in separate regiments with white officers. By the war's end, one of ten Union soldiers was black.

McClellan supported slavery and hated Lincoln's Emancipation Proclamation. He wrote his wife that "I cannot make up my mind to fight for such an accursed doctrine as that of a servile insurrection—it is too infamous."[356] Lincoln spared McClellan that agony by finally cashiering him on November 7 and replacing him as the Army of the Potomac's commander with General Ambrose Burnside.

Tragically, Burnside soon proved to be as awful a general as McClellan, but reckless and callous rather than indecisive and timid. On December 13, he ordered the army to cross the Rappahannock River at Fredericksburg, Virginia, and attack Lee's army deployed along the low ridge behind the town. The result was slaughter, with 12,600 Union to 5,300 rebel casualties.

The bloodbath at Fredericksburg was a dismal end to what was a mostly victorious year for the American cause. The Union disasters and disappointments in the eastern theater overshadowed genuine progress elsewhere in 1862. Down the Mississippi River, Commodore Andrew Foote's Union flotilla of gunboats and steamboats packed with troops led by General John Pope captured Island Number 10 with 7,000 rebel defenders on April 8, and occupied Memphis on June 6. A flotilla whose vessels were led by Commodore David Farragut and troops by General Ben Butler sailed from the Gulf of Mexico up the Mississippi River, fought its way past two forts, and occupied New Orleans on April 29. After resupplying, Foote's flotilla steamed further upriver to capture Baton Rouge, Louisiana, and Natchez, Mississippi.

A lull settled over southwest Missouri after Lincoln recalled John Frémont as the commander at Springfield in November 1861, and the rebel army withdrew to Fayetteville, Arkansas. The Union army's latest leader, General Samuel Curtis, spent the winter reinforcing, supplying, and training his troops before leading them into northwest Arkansas in March 1862. Curtis's army defeated General Earl Van Dorn's rebels at Pea Ridge on March 7 and 8, and then marched into Fayetteville, securing northwest Arkansas and by extension Missouri for the foreseeable future.

General Ulysses Grant scored the most spectacular and decisive victories in the western theater. He began with 15,000 troops at Cairo, Illinois, a strategic juncture where the Ohio and Mississippi Rivers mingle. General Leonidas Polk's 18,000-man rebel army was just twenty miles south at Columbus, Kentucky, on the Mississippi River. Rather than go straight against Polk, Grant went around him. In February, he packed his troops in steamboats and, preceded by gunboats, headed up the Tennessee River to capture Fort Henry on February 6; its 3,400-man garrison escaped to Fort Donelson a dozen miles east on the Cumberland River. Grant led his troops to besiege Fort Donelson while the gunboats and steamboats journeyed there by river. General Simon Buckner surrendered Fort Donelson with its 14,000 defenders on February 16. When Buckner asked for terms, Grant's reply to his former West Point roommate exemplified his bulldog tenacity: "No terms except an unconditional and immediate surrender can be accepted. I purpose to move immediately upon your works."[357]

Those victories won Grant a major-general's commission and reinforcements from a grateful president. Grant led his now 42,000 troops back to the Tennessee River and up the valley, reaching a hamlet on the west bank called Shiloh by April's first week. That forced two rebel armies to withdraw, Polk's from Columbus all the way to Corinth, Mississippi, and General Albert Johnston's from Bowling Green, Kentucky, to join forces with Polk. President Davis had Johnston command that joint army of 44,000 troops. Starting in Louisville, Kentucky, General Carlos Buell's 20,000-man Union army cautiously followed Johnston, occupied Nashville, Tennessee, on February 25, and then marched to join Grant. Aware of that pending junction, Johnston launched his army at Grant's on April 6. That surprise assault routed the Federal troops until Grant rallied the men on a new line. Buell's army began arriving that night. The next day, Grant ordered an attack that drove the enemy from the field. The battle of Shiloh was the war's bloodiest to date, with Federal and Confederate casualties of 13,000 and 10,600, exceeding the combined losses for all battles leading up to it; Johnston was among the dead.

Grant was determined to follow up his victory with a rapid march south against Corinth, where the rebel army had withdrawn, but was stopped in his tracks. Unfortunately, Lincoln placed General Henry Halleck in direct command of the armies of Grant and Buell. Halleck was as timid as Grant was bold. He took a month to move his vast combined army of 110,000 troops the twenty miles to Corinth. Once there, he rejected Grant's plan to encircle and destroy the enemy. That allowed the rebel army, now led by General Pierre Beauregard, to withdraw to Tupelo and then east toward Chattanooga. Grant later wrote that "Corinth could have been captured in a two days' campaign commenced promptly on the arrival of reinforcements after the battle of Shiloh."[358] Tragically for the American cause, Halleck proved to be the McClellan of the west.

Halleck split his forces. He had Grant hold western Tennessee and northern Mississippi while Don Carlos Buell pursued the main rebel army, now led by Braxton Bragg. The war's history would read quite differently if Halleck had reversed the direction of the two armies. Grant's army repelled attacks by General Sterling Price at Iuka on September 13 and at Corinth on October 3. Meanwhile, Bragg sidestepped Buell and led his army north into Kentucky. Buell pursued and repelled Bragg at the battle of Perrysville on October 7. After Buell failed to follow up his victory, Lincoln replaced him with William Rosecrans, one of Grant's corps commanders. Rosecrans was just as cautious, slowly advancing to Nashville then sitting tight. Prodded repeatedly by Lincoln, Rosecrans finally marched against Bragg's army at Murfreesboro on the Stone River. The three-day battle that began on December 31 finally resulted in a rebel retreat, but Rosecrans's army was too battered to follow.

Grant's Mississippi campaign ground to a halt at Tupelo by late 1862. In mid-December, raids by Generals Bedford Forrest and John Morgan destroyed wagons, trains, tracks, warehouses, bridges, and small garrisons across western Tennessee, and then General Earl Van Dorn's army captured and burned Grant's supply depot at Honey Springs on December 20. Grant dispatched Sherman's corps down the Mississippi River to take Vicksburg, but General John Pemberton's army repelled his assault at Chickasaw Bluffs on December 31.

Custer went home to Monroe for an extended leave that would last from mid November 1862 to early April 1863. He joyfully immersed himself in a series of dances and parties where he flirted with all the pretty girls. One especially caught his fancy. George Custer and Libbie Bacon met for the first time at a Thanksgiving Day party. He was instantly smitten. For the rest of his leave he used every excuse to be with her. He loitered outside her home and when she appeared he escorted her to stroll, shop, or go to church. She could not help being attracted to him. He was about five feet ten inches tall, lean but muscular, had shoulder-length if thinning blond hair, and regaled her with tales of his death-defying adventures.

Her father, Judge Daniel Bacon, thoroughly disapproved of Custer's courtship. He sought a future husband for his daughter with far more wealth, status, and security than some penniless army captain from a humble family. But he was especially contemptuous of Custer. As bad luck would have it, Bacon had witnessed the one time that Custer had gotten drunk in Monroe and had lurched loudly home through the streets. Bacon was not yet aware that Custer's sister Lydia had convinced her brother to swear an oath to uphold temperance the rest of his life, and that, astonishingly, Custer would never break that promise.

Libbie obeyed her father's wishes. She tried to dissuade Custer from his courtship and gently rebuffed him when he confessed his love and asked her to marry him. She later wrote that he had come on far too strong: "The General's proposal was as much a cavalry charge as any he ever took in the field. First on the astonished me who knew that in books lovers led up to proposals by slow careful approaches and chosen language.... But this vehement, stammery disclose...I had not breath to protest. (Sometimes when greatly excited he had a slight hesitation in speech then out poured a torrent of words.)"[359]

With his direct assault repulsed, Custer shifted tactics. He tried to make Libbie jealous by courting her friend Fanny Fifield who was more outgoing and coquettish. Nonetheless, when he heard she was going to visit friends in Toledo, he appeared at the station to see her off. That proved to be awkward since Judge Bacon was there for the same purpose. Bacon fumed but said nothing. Libbie was red-faced, both flattered and irritated by Custer's persistence. Bacon wrote her a letter, warning her that she risked her reputation in Monroe by associating with Custer. Libbie replied with three strong points. First, although "I like him very much," she had insisted that they stop seeing each other for now. Second, her father just did not understand what she was experiencing and so should withhold his judgment: "You have never been a girl, Father, and you cannot tell how hard a trial this was for me." Finally, she was contemptuous of the town's busybodies who had nothing better to do than contrive mean-spirited rumors: "And Monroe people will please mind their own business and let me alone.... I wish the gossipers sunk in the sea."[360]

To Custer's chagrin, his nearly four-month campaign to win Libbie's hand had suffered a seemingly total defeat. Later that spring, he tried emotionally to distance himself from his loss by writing Lydia that "Libbie is the most devoted daughter.... There are not a dozen young ladies in Monroe of whom I think so highly."[361] Most likely he was as facetious as he was earnest when he penned these words. He also tried being philosophical about his seeming defeat: "When the time comes for me to give Her up I hope it will find me the same soldier I now try to be—capable of meeting the reverses of life as those of war."[362]

Custer finally reported for duty in Washington on April 10, 1863. He tarried at the War Department long enough to learn that he was unassigned and should await his orders. Instead he spent the rest of the day visiting McClellan at his home. He was angered to learn that his mentor was shunned by the Lincoln administration and most of Washington's political elite, and so could not help him get a plum assignment. Custer checked into the Metropolitan Hotel where he waited day after day as his money dwindled. Finally, on April 22, he received orders to report for duty with his former regiment, the 5th Cavalry, deployed with the Army of the Potomac at Fredericksburg.

The army had a new commander. Lincoln replaced Burnside with Joseph Hooker on January 26, 1863. As a general, Hooker appeared to be somewhere between the extremes of his predecessors. He was known as "fighting Joe" but emphasized maneuvers rather than direct attacks. He had 110,000 troops to Lee's 60,000. His plan was to leave 40,000 north of the Rappahannock at Fredericksburg to distract Lee across the river, while he led 70,000 troops upriver and crossed over to hit Lee from behind, as the three cavalry divisions united into a corps led by General George Stoneman, screened his advance. The offensive would kick off on April 29.

That was a great plan that would have worked had each commander been decisive and skilled rather than plodding and inept. Stuart's corps repelled Stoneman's corps. Hooker led his army to Chancellorsville but then stopped in bewilderment rather than marched on to assault Fredericksburg from the rear. Lee split his army in three. He left 10,000 troops at Fredericksburg, marched with 20,000 troops directly at Hooker, and curled Jackson's 30,000-man corps around Hooker's right flank. The fighting at Chancellorsville lasted from May 2 to 4 and ended with Hooker withdrawing his army back across the Rappahannock. General John Sedgwick drove General Jubal Early's division from Fredericksburg on May 4, only to retreat across the river when Lee united his army against him. The Union and rebel armies suffered 17,200 and 12,700 casualties; unluckily for the rebel cause, Stonewall Jackson was among the dead. Custer wrote McClellan words he knew would provoke mixed feelings: "My dear General, I know you must be anxious to know how your army is, and has been, doing. We are defeated, driven back…with a loss which I suppose will exceed our entire loss during the seven days battles…. You will not be surprised when I inform you that the universal cry is 'Give us McClellan.'"[363] The campaign was personally inglorious for Custer as his regiment played only a rear guard role.

Hooker replaced Stoneman with General Alfred Pleasanton at the cavalry corps' head on May 22. Pleasanton had Custer join his staff. That did not stop Custer from slipping away from headquarters to get into the thick of fighting. With his chief's blessing, he joined the 3rd Indiana Cavalry for a raid behind enemy lines. He also found time for politicking. In an astonishing act of chutzpah, he made the rounds of officers and men of the 5th Michigan Cavalry to get them to petition Governor Austin Blair to appoint him to the vacant colonel's position. He got no takers because, as one of them put it: "We all declined to sign such a petition as we considered him too young."[364] What that regiment's existing lieutenant colonel and majors thought of Custer's campaign to supersede them can easily be imagined. Undoubtedly, he exacerbated their ire when he outflanked them by getting Generals Hooker, Burnside, Stoneman, and Pleasanton to write letters of recommendation on his behalf to the governor.

Hooker received intelligence that J.E.B. Stuart was massing his cavalry corps near Culpeper Court House and ordered Pleasanton to attack him. The Union cavalry crossed several Rappahannock River fords on the morning of June 9. The resulting cavalry battle at Brandy Station was the war's largest.[365] Custer helped lead the charge of General Benjamin Davis' brigade, which overran and captured a rebel battery defending Beverly Ford, and then repulsed the 6th Virginia Cavalry, before withdrawing across the river. Pleasanton lauded Custer in his afteraction report and gave him the honor of carrying the captured 12th Virginia's flag to Hooker's headquarters.

Lee followed up his victory with another invasion of the north, determined to end the war with a decisive victory. Hooker had no idea where the rebels were. He ordered Pleasanton to slice through the enemy cavalry screen and find Lee's army. Pleasanton and his corps headed west toward the Bull Run Mountains. Custer was with General Judson Kilpatrick's brigade when they encountered rebel cavalry near Audie Gap on June 17. Custer led the charge. During the swirling melee of horsemen, he got in a saber duel with a rebel and killed him with a slashing blow to his skull. He then looked around to find himself surrounded by rebel cavalry who stared at him in awe. He wheeled his horse, cut down a rebel in his way, and galloped to safety.

Pleasanton was so impressed by Custer's feat that on June 28, he recommended his promotion to brigadier general, along with two other outstanding officers, Wesley Merritt and Elon Farnsworth. Upon hearing what Pleasanton did, Custer would have preferred a delayed timing: "I almost wished the General had not informed me of the recommendation, as I felt it would excite hopes and aspirations which, to say the least, could not be realized at present." He had been disappointed in his previous attempts to win a promotion and wanted to avoid another letdown. Then came word that he would indeed receive a star: "To say I was elated would hardly express my feelings. I well knew that I had reason to congratulate myself." For weeks he had lobbied to be named a colonel and head of a regiment, only to be rebuffed. Now he had been leapfrogged to become a brigadier general and head of a brigade. He could not help gloating, "I rather outwitted the Governor who did not see fit to give it to me."[366]

Pleasanton asked Custer to name his command. Custer promptly requested and received the Michigan Brigade composed of the 5th, 6th, and 7th Cavalry, to which the 1st would be added. War Secretary Edwin Stanton approved Custer's promotion and command of the Michigan Brigade on June 29. Custer's 2,300 or so troops would enjoy an enormous edge in any subsequent firefight with rebel cavalry; they had recently received seven-shot Spencer carbines to supplement their six-shot Colts. But Custer's brigade had an Achilles heel. Along with General Henry Davies' brigade, it was part of General Kilpatrick's division. Kilpatrick was among the war's worst generals. His troops scornfully called him "Kill-Cavalry" because he launched them in suicidal charges and drove them until their horses dropped dead beneath them.[367]

The Army of the Potomac's most important change came on June 27, when Lincoln replaced Hooker with General George Meade. Switching a commanding general amidst a campaign was certainly risky, but the president was fed up with Hooker's mix of bluster and cluelessness. In contrast, Meade was reserved and proficient if unimaginative and plodding.

Meade ordered Pleasanton to screen the army as it marched parallel to the enemy. By June 30, Lee's three infantry corps were north or west, while Meade's seven infantry corps were south or east of the crossroads town of Gettysburg. General John Buford's Union cavalry division was in Gettysburg. J.E.B. Stuart's cavalry corps was completing a counterclockwise circle of the Union army. Neither Lee

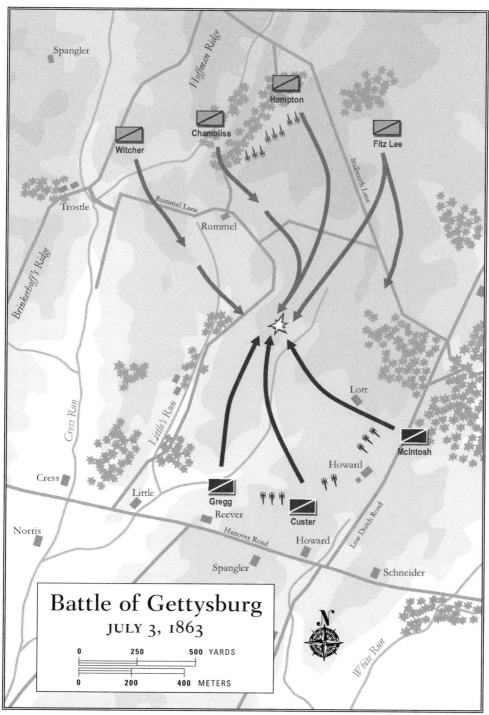

Battle of Gettysburg

JULY 3, 1863

Petho Cartography 2019

nor Meade knew where the other's corps were deployed. Rebel General Ambrose Hill sent one of his divisions to capture that strategic crossroads. On the morning of July 1, when his pickets brought word of the rebel advance, Buford deployed his cavalry on foot west of town and galloped a courier to seek help from General John Reynolds' nearby corps. The Confederate infantry drove back the Union cavalry, and Reynolds' troops appeared to repulse the rebels.

Upon learning of the fighting at Gettysburg, Lee and Meade ordered their corps commanders to converge there. Eventually 104,000 Federal and 75,000 Confederate troops fought in parallel fish hook lines with the shaft from south to north then curling eastward. From July 1 to 3, Lee launched a series of attacks along the Union line, culminating on the third afternoon with an artillery barrage of seventy cannons followed by the assault of General George Pickett's 12,000-man division against the center. Meade fed each corps as it arrived into his line's most vulnerable part and the Union troops repulsed every attack.

Meade split his cavalry corps to guard each flank, with Kilpatrick's division on the right flank.[368] On July 2, Meade had Kilpatrick probe around the enemy's left flank. Rebel cavalry was deployed at Hunterstown. Kilpatrick instructed Custer to sweep them away. Custer charged with around forty men. The rebel horsemen screened infantry hidden in nearby woods. The rebels opened fire as Custer and his men galloped up, killing or wounding twenty-seven. A bullet killed Custer's horse. He grabbed and mounted a rider-less horse and galloped to safety.

On the afternoon of July 3, Stuart and his horsemen were completing their seven-day circuit around Meade's army and were returning to their own army. They were exhausted but elated, having destroyed supply wagon trains and railroad trestles, and killed lots of Union troops along the way. Custer's brigade, then attached to General William Gregg's division, was posted at the crossroads where General Wade Hampton's division had to ride through to reach Lee's army. Although out-numbered three to one, Custer asked Gregg's permission to attack. Gregg nodded and assigned one of his brigades to support him. Custer's charge scattered the rebels but cost his brigade 29 killed, 123 wounded, and 67 captured, or 219 of 254 Union casualties, while the rebels suffered 181 dead, wounded, and captured.[369] As usual Custer emerged without a scratch.

As Custer was winning his latest laurels, the Union army repulsed Pickett's charge. Meade did not counterattack. That night Lee withdrew his army west and then south toward Virginia. In all, the Federal and Confederate armies suffered 23,000 and 28,000 casualties at Gettysburg. Much like McClellan after Antietam, Meade made no attempt to sidestep and cut off Lee. He simply ordered the cavalry corps to follow the defeated rebel army to ensure that their retreat continued beyond the Potomac.[370]

Custer was not content merely to trail Lee's army. On the night of July 4, he attacked the enemy's rear guard near South Mountain's Monterey Pass, where his troops captured a supply wagon train and 1,360 wounded soldiers. For another week, his brigade skirmished with the slowly withdrawing rebels. Rain fell nearly incessantly and turned the roads and fields into quagmires. The Potomac River rose to flood levels and swept away several rebel pontoon bridges at various crossing points.

On the morning of July 11, Custer led his brigade just beyond rifle shot of a couple hundred rebels in breastworks defending the village of Falling Water and a pontoon bridge across the Potomac River. As Custer scanned the rebel lines with his binoculars, Kilpatrick rode up and bolstered his "Kill-Cavalry" nickname by ordering Custer to charge the enemy defenses. Custer knew that to do so on horseback would result in mass killing and maiming for his men and likely death for himself. The boggy ground would slow his horses to a canter or even trot as the rebels unleashed a storm of lead at them from behind their barricade. Custer ordered two companies to dismount for an assault on foot. Kilpatrick ordered him to charge mounted. Grim-faced, Custer obeyed. The rebels easily repulsed the attack, killing 29 and wounding or capturing 40 more of Custer's men; Custer somehow evaded getting shot even though he cantered within pistol shot of the rebel defense. Custer then deployed his troops on foot, with every fourth man holding the horse of the other three who advanced against the enemy. This time the Union troops overran the position, killed or captured 52 rebels, took three battle flags, and freed their own comrades who had been captured.

The hatred against Kilpatrick at all levels soared as word spread of the latest mass killing and maiming of his men. On July 15, Meade granted Kilpatrick's medical leave request for his painful kidney disease and appointed Custer to replace him as the 3rd Cavalry division's commander. Looking back at his stunning series of wartime feats and promotions culminating with this latest, Custer wrote: "I believe more than ever in Destiny."[371]

Meanwhile, Meade finally caught up to Lee and most of his army at Williamsport with the Potomac behind them on July 12. Once again Meade did not attack but simply waited as Lee's engineers rebuilt the broken pontoon bridges and the rebel army withdrew into Virginia. Meade did not order his own army to begin crossing the Potomac until July 17. Custer's division was among the first across. On July 24, he was spearheading his division with just three regiments and a battery when he collided with what he thought was the rebel rear guard at Newby Crossroads. Actually, General Richard Ewell's corps was deployed nearby. Ewell ordered several brigades to surge against Custer, who hastily withdrew his men all the way back to Amissville, where Union troops were massing.

Kilpatrick returned from leave on August 4 and retook command of the division. He was jealous of Custer for his flamboyant courage, combat prowess, and popularity. Worried that Custer was too close personally and politically with Pleasanton, Kilpatrick ordered him to submit any communication with the cavalry corps commander through his own headquarters. Then Kilpatrick rebuked Custer for holding a parley with rebel Colonel Robert Hill.

American patriots celebrated twin victories on July 4, 1863—Lee's retreat from Gettysburg, Pennsylvania, and Grant's capture of Vicksburg, Mississippi, along with 29,400 rebel troops and 172 cannons. Vicksburg's surrender culminated a brilliant campaign. During the first phase, Grant marched his 35,000 troops down the Mississippi's west bank and steamed his gunboats past Vicksburg to Bruinsburg, Mississippi, where he ferried his army to the east bank. He faced two enemy armies, John Pemberton's 35,000 men at Vicksburg and Joe Johnston's 12,000 men at Jackson. He marched toward Johnston, scattering rebel troops at Port Gibson on May 1, Raymond on May 12, and Jackson on May 14. With Johnston in retreat, Grant headed west, trounced Pemberton at Champion Hill on May 16 and Big Black River on May 17, and then deployed his army around Vicksburg for what became a six-week siege. Meanwhile, General Nathaniel Banks led a 20,000-man army from Baton Rouge up the Mississippi River to besiege Port Hudson with its 7,000 defenders. Word of Port Hudson surrender on July 13 inspired Lincoln's poetic remark: "The father of waters again goes unvexed to the sea."[372]

As a general, Custer now enjoyed the power and income to provide himself with certain comforts denied those of lesser ranks. In doing so, he also satisfied a deep humanitarian impulse within himself. Strays, both human and lesser species, attracted him. He rescued a homeless twelve-year-old white orphan named Johnny Cisco, and gave him food, shelter, and an army uniform in return for acting as his servant. He hired a runaway eighteen-year-old slave girl named Eliza Brown to serve as his cook. He spotted her among a group of refugees. She later recalled that he walked over, beckoned, asked her name and if she could cook, then said, "Well Eliza, would you like to come and live with me?" She replied, "I reckon I would as long as you'll be good to me then I'll be good to you."[373] Whether their relationship was purely professional or something more can never be known. She would have at least two children but apparently neither resembled Custer. He loved animals, especially large hunting dogs, and adopted any lacking a master. Somehow, he got away with keeping his menagerie at his various encampments despite the noise, mess, and diversion of orderlies to care for them.

Meanwhile, a severe obstacle arose to the Senate's conferral of a brigadier gen-eralship on Custer. Jealousy drove Brigadier General Joseph Copeland, the Mich-igan cavalry brigade's first commander, to mobilize his influential political allies against the nomination. Custer pleaded his case in letters to Michigan's United States senators, Zachariah Chandler and Jacob Howard, and his district's con-gressman Francis Kellogg, all Republicans and Lincoln supporters. His key argu-ment was that his brilliant war record should trump any objections that he was too young and had served too briefly to merit such a high rank. Howard raised serious concerns that Custer was a Copperhead Democrat who, like his hero George Mc-Clellan, favored a negotiated peace with the rebels and accepted slavery's contin-uation. Custer replied by claiming to be apolitical as his profession demanded: "I have undertaken to be a soldier, and not a politician. So far has this sentiment con-trolled me that, at the last presidential election…I never expressed nor entertained a preference." Having said that, he expressed, "my most hearty, earnest, and cordial approval" for all of President Lincoln's "acts, proclamations, and decisions…. I for one was opposed to peace on any terms. And to show that my acts agree with my words, I can boast of having liberated more slaves from their masters than any oth-er general." As for McClellan, "I have never allowed my personal obligation to him for his kindness and favor toward me to interfere with my duty." Unfortunately, Custer did not confine his defense to these sensible, reassuring words. He then took a stunning, disturbing leap: "I would and do favor a war of extermination. I would hang every human being possessing a drop of rebel blood in their veins whether they be men, women or children. Then, after having freed the country from the presence of every rebel, I would settle the whole country with a popula-tion of loyal and patriotic who would not forget their obligations to the country…. I think the more rebels we kill the fewer will be to pardon and the better for us."[374]

What was Custer thinking? The character that he revealed in his letter was schizophrenic, with one side of him an outstanding professional and the other half an unhinged fanatic. Actually, both characters were false. Custer was indeed a Copperhead Democrat, who voted against and despised Lincoln, adored McClel-lan, and favored a peace that not only accepted slavery where it currently existed but also its extension to the western territories. Nonetheless, that letter did the trick. Howard along with Chandler voted for the brigadier general's commission. And becoming a general gave Custer the confidence to resume his campaign on a front vital to his heart.

CHAPTER 12

End Games

"If we begin by regulating our actions by the opinions of others we shall never have any of our own."
— LIBBIE CUSTER

"During the past six months, although in most instances confronted by superior numbers, you have captured from the enemy in open battle, one hundred and eleven pieces of field artillery, sixty-five battle flags, and upwards of ten thousand prisoners, including seven general officers.... You have never lost a gun, never lost a color, never lost a battle."
— GEORGE CUSTER
TO HIS 3RD CAVALRY DIVISION

BRIGADIER GENERAL GEORGE CUSTER resumed his courtship of Libbie, although for now from a distance. Artist Alfred Waud had sketched a scene of Custer leading the charge at the battle of Audie Gap. After receiving a copy, Custer forwarded it to his sister Ann in Monroe, and asked her to get her husband David Reed to show the sketch to Custer's two love interests, Libbie Bacon and Fannie Fifield, but deliver a letter only to Libbie. Reed accomplished his mission and reported that both young ladies were thrilled. Custer then made inquiries through a mutual Monroe friend, Nettie Humphreys, to see if Judge Bacon had softened his opposition. He was disappointed to learn that her father was as adamant as ever that his daughter have nothing to do with him. Custer reckoned his only remaining chance was a direct approach. In September, he wrangled a twenty-day leave and was about to leave for Monroe but had to postpone it.

Meade ordered Pleasanton to probe the enemy with his cavalry to confirm reports that Lee had sent Longstreet's corps to Tennessee and was withdrawing his army to a better defensive position. By early afternoon on September 12, the Union cavalry had crossed the Rappahannock River at Kelly's Ford and advanced within a mile of Culpeper Court House when the advanced guard reported a rebel brigade deployed behind a stream blocking the way. Pleasanton ordered Kilpatrick

to attack. Kilpatrick had the New York brigade charge while Custer's brigade outflanked the Confederates. The Union cavalry routed the rebel defenders. During
the fighting, Custer suffered his first and only serious wound when a bullet cut
through one of his calves but fortunately missed any bone or artery.

Now Custer had a guilt-free excuse for a prolonged leave to Monroe. He returned as a wounded hero and the army's youngest general. Libbie was not there
when he arrived, having taken an excursion with her parents to Traverse City on
Lake Michigan. Custer arranged for Nettie to invite Libbie to her home after she
returned. Libbie was stunned to see Custer waiting for her with Nettie in the
Humphrey parlor.

With a career as a businessman, lawyer, and judge, Daniel Bacon understood
human nature and psychology. Not surprisingly, he harbored severe doubts about
Custer, who was then just twenty-three years old and as cocky as he was brave.
Atop that were disturbing rumors that Custer womanized, gambled, and critically
questioned the Christian faith. Finally, there was the likelihood that the "boy general" who led from the front would be killed or maimed. At the very least, Libbie
should wait for the war to end before even considering marriage to such a man.
Meanwhile, Bacon sent letters to several influential military and civilian leaders
who were acquainted with Custer and asked them to assess his character. What
he learned surprised him. For everyone that Bacon queried, the young's man's
attributes far outweighed his faults. That shifted Bacon's view. He wrote Custer
a friendly, encouraging letter, although he did not go so far as to permit him to
resume his courtship.

Custer would not receive that letter until after his latest round of long hard rides
broken by fierce combats. He returned to his brigade on October 8, just in time to
join the latest campaign. Lee tried to slip around Meade's right flank and cut off
his retreat. It was a typically brilliant and audacious move for Lee, given that the
85,000 American troops far outnumbered his 48,000 men. A key reason for Lee's
military genius was his ability to assess his enemy commanders. He counted on
Meade to avoid rather than engage in combat. And Meade did exactly that. He
ordered the cavalry to cover his army's withdrawal to à better defensive position at
Bull Run. On October 11, Stuart's cavalry cut off Custer's brigade at Bristoe Station. Custer had two horses shot out from beneath him as he led several charges
that sliced through the rebel cavalry to safety.

Lee withdrew to his former position. Meade had the cavalry corps follow the
rebels. Custer's brigade led Kilpatrick's division. On October 19, rebels blocked the
way at Buckland Mills on Broad Run. Custer split his brigade, with one regiment

diverting the rebels and the other regiments outflanking them. Custer then deployed his regiments in a defensive cordon and let his troopers rest, unsaddle, and graze their horses. Kilpatrick arrived and ordered Custer to continue the advance. Custer refused, citing the exhaustion of his men and horses. Kilpatrick angrily led General Henry Davies' brigade through Custer's and rode toward Warrenton. There, Stuart hit Kilpatrick from three sides while racing General Fitzhugh Lee's division to Buckland Mills to cut off his retreat. Hearing the distant firing, Custer ordered his men quickly to resaddle and mount. Just then Lee's division charged Custer's brigade. The Americans repelled the rebel cavalry. Meanwhile Stuart's cavalry routed Kilpatrick's at Warrenton. Kilpatrick withdrew his battered division to the Army of the Potomac. From October 11 to 19, Custer's brigade suffered 214 casualties. Adding insult to injury, to Custer's mortification, Fitzhugh Lee's cavalry captured his wagon with all his personal effects including bundles of letters from Libbie and other girls he courted. Custer rightly condemned Kilpatrick's inept, reckless decisions for the debacle. Fortunately, Pleasanton backed Custer over Kilpatrick.

Elsewhere in autumn 1863, the American cause suffered a terrible defeat when Bragg's army routed Rosencrans's during the three-day battle of Chickamauga beginning on September 18, and then besieged Chattanooga. Lincoln ordered Grant to hurry there with most of his own army, take command, and expel the rebels. Grant's first step was to reestablish the supply line to Chattanooga and mass troops there. Starting on November 23, he launched a series of attacks that drove the rebels from key positions around the city, climaxing with the assault that overran Missionary Ridge two days later. Meanwhile, in Knoxville, General Ambrose Burnside's army repelled a series of attacks by General James Longstreet.

After Meade finally mustered the gumption for an offensive, the weather allied with the rebels to slow the Union army to a crawl. In what became known as the Mine Run Campaign, the Army of the Potomac crossed the Rappahannock on November 24, passed a week groping for the enemy, and withdrew on December 1. During that time, Custer commanded the division while Kilpatrick was on leave. His lead horsemen clashed in minor skirmishes with the rebel cavalry. After Kilpatrick returned on December 21, Custer headed to Monroe for an extensive leave.

At some point during the autumn of 1863, Custer received that encouraging if noncommittal letter from the man he hoped to make his father-in-law. These words undoubtedly stroked Custer's ego: "Your ability, energy, and force of character I have always admired, and no one can feel more gratified than myself at your well-earned reputation and your high & honorable position." Yet the judge needed weeks and probably months before he could decide Custer's case.[375]

But even before reading Bacon's letter, word undoubtedly got back to Custer that the judge was investigating his character. He must have composed his response countless times in his head before putting it in a letter to Bacon: "I had hoped for a personal interview.... It is true that I have often committed errors of judgment, but as I grew older I learned the necessity of propriety. I am aware of your fear of intemperance but surely my conduct for the past two years—during which I have not violated the solemn promise I made my sister, will God to witness, should dispel that.... I left home when but sixteen, and have been surrounded with temptation, but I always had a purpose in life."[376] He addressed all of Bacon's concerns about his character and his commitment to family, emotional development, temperance, God, and, above all, Libbie.

To Custer's joy, Bacon finally granted him permission to resume his epistolary courtship of Libbie. Custer promptly fired off a letter to her in which he expressed his eternal love and then asked her to return his love and marry him. Her feelings toward him had gone through convulsions over the preceding year, as she confessed to a friend: "He proposed to me last winter, but I refused him more than once, on account of Father's apparently unconquerable prejudice. I never even thought of marrying him. Indeed I did not know I loved him so until he left Monroe in the spring."[377] Now Custer seemed like something out of a fairy tale: "I read him in all my books. When I take in the book heroes there comes dashing in with them my life hero my dear boy general.... Every other man seems so ordinary beside my own particular star."[378] Yet his ardor at once excited and worried her. She made clear her mixed feelings: "If I am worth having am I not worth waiting for? The very thought of marriage makes me tremble. Girls have so much fun. Marriage means trouble.... The very thought of leaving my home, my family is painful to me. I implore you not even to mention it for at least a year." She wanted to savor being herself for as long as she could before immersing herself in someone else's identity: "How I love my Libbie BACON. Libbie B-A-C-O-N. Bacon. Libbie Bacon."[379] She confessed to Custer that: "My own faults are legion. I am susceptible to admiration. In church I saw a handsome young man looking at me, and I blushed furiously. Mother says I am the most sarcastic girl, and say the most withering things."[380] She worried that she would be unable to fulfill all his dreams and the duties of matrimony: "Oh Autie I tremble at the responsibility. I am but a little girl—not of course, in years, but being an only child.... It is a solemn thought to become a wife."[381] But one fear overshadowed all others: "The worst about loving a soldier is that he is as likely to die as to live...and how should I feel if my soldier should die before I have gratified his heart's desire?"[382]

Libbie attributed Custer's persistence in courting her to her own persistence in playing hard to get: "I know the reason he loved me [was] because I wouldn't let him kiss me and treat me as if we were engaged."[383] That is a high-risk strategy for even as lovely a young woman as Libbie to play to entice a young man as popular with the fair sex as Custer. Men react differently to rejection by women they love. Most soothe their sorrow by reasoning that there are plenty of easier fish in the sea and then they start casting elsewhere. Custer was one of those rare men who, when rebuffed, is stimulated to redouble his efforts to take home a rare trophy. With her ego boosted by his devotion, she rewarded him by secretly defying her father with not just three daily visits but attending a costume ball with Custer. She eagerly agreed to become his fiancée: "If loving with one's whole soul is insanity I am ripe for the asylum."[384] She now faced the daunting task of convincing her father and stepmother to accept Custer as their son-in-law. Both parents rejected the notion of marriage; her mother urged her to sever contact with him, but her father let them continue to exchange letters.

Custer then took a chance that might win over Bacon completely or repel him to his previous repugnance. During a brief leave in Washington, he had a hand-colored photograph of himself taken, then sent it to Bacon with a letter asking him to give it to Libbie for Christmas. In that same letter he asked Bacon's permission to marry his daughter. He was exhilarated to receive Bacon's reply accepting his proposal. The judge explained, "I feel...that I have no right to impose terms over my daughter...or to make choices for her." Atop that Custer's "explanatory and excellent letter" and "the wishes of my daughter perfectly reconcile me to yield my hearty assent to the contemplated union."[385] Custer shot back a letter with this promise: "I will endeavor throughout my future life to so shape my course, guided and activated by the principles of right, as will not only secure and promote the happiness of her who soon will become my wife, but I will also make it an aim of my life to make myself deserving of the high and sacred trust you have reposed in me, and I hope no act of mine will ever afford you the faintest foundation for supposing your confidence in my worth and integrity has been misplaced."[386]

Rounds of letters and delicate negotiations among Custer, Libbie, and her parents led them to plan for a wedding in February 1864. To a friend, Libbie expressed her enormous relief: "I no longer walk in the shadow but in bright sunshine. Father says he did not really know him or he never would have let himself be influenced against him. Mother also is happy in my choice."[387] She made these requests to Custer: "I want you to wear your full-dress uniform. I have changed my mind about not wanting ostentation. If we begin by regulating our actions by the opinions of others we shall never have any of our own."[388]

Custer and Libbie were married at Monroe's Presbyterian Church followed by a reception for three hundred guests at the Bacon home on February 9, 1864. Libbie triumphantly informed her father: "I have proved my admiration for your belief in self-made men by marrying one."[389] The next morning the Custers embarked on their honeymoon, although not alone. The groomsmen and bridesmaids accompanied them to Cleveland, where they checked into the Waddell House Hotel and attended a reception hosted by Libbie's relatives and friends in that city. They did not shed their celebrants until they boarded a train bound for Buffalo, New York, where they spent a night, then traveled onward with overnight stops at Rochester and West Point, and finally spent several days in New York where they stayed at the Metropolitan Hotel. Custer loved New York and reveled in showing his wife all the sights and dining with her in the finest restaurants. For him, their New York highlight was visiting McClellan and his wife Ellen. Libbie later wrote: "At that time General McClellan ran through our lives. We talked of him incessantly.... Autie adored General McClellan."[390]

They then traveled to Washington, where they tarried several days before heading to the Michigan Cavalry Brigade's headquarters at Stevensburg, Virginia. There Libbie experienced the culture shock of army life and being near the front lines of a horrendous war that frequently took her husband to the brink of destruction: "I was completely overwhelmed with intense anxiety for my husband, bewildered over the strange situation, and terror of the desolate place."[391] She had to form proper relations with Custer's higher, fellow, and subordinate officers along with his two servants, the young black woman Eliza Brown and teenager Johnny Cisco. She was happy to preside over the servants since "I felt no aspirations for housekeeping...and I knew that I was not foisted upon anyone without a perfect understanding of my ignorance of housework."[392] Although both women were about the same age, Eliza became like a mother to Libbie: "It was protecting and enveloping and for years when I was left alone, she seemed to stand between me and care, or responsibility, or danger. Sometimes for months on campaign I had no woman to speak with but Eliza, and even now I find that I unconsciously acquired her expression and accent."[393] With time, Libbie became an outstanding officer's wife, supporting Custer cheerfully and only releasing her fears and sorrows when he was gone. She confessed this after he embarked on campaign: "After you went I watched you admiringly as you rode along, then I went up to my room to cry."[394]

After that visit near the front, Custer found Libbie a room at a boardinghouse in Washington and handed over most of his salary for her expenses. In doing so he asked her to "practice economy and avoid extravagance. I do not wish to deny you anything needful for your comfort or happiness. Only bear in mind that we are just entering on life's journey with all its cares, and, I hope, in a short time, its responsibilities."[395] Libbie was even more eager to enter life's "responsibilities": "I think of the days of peace when little children's voices will call to us. I can hardly wait for my little boy and girl."[396] Alas, Custer's $125 monthly salary fell far short of paying even for Libbie's shelter, room, and other basic needs, let alone children, in a city racked by wartime inflation. Desperate, she betrayed both her pride and her husband with these words to her parents: "If Autie had not made me promise not to do so I should ask you for money. Money simply melts away here. After all, I am still your daughter."[397]

Libbie quickly fell in love with the capital's bustle, glamour, and diversity: "Washington begins to seem home-like. I have made so many friends." It certainly helped that she was married to a famous general: "I can't tell you what a place Autie has here in public opinion.... It astonishes me to see the attention with which he is treated everywhere.... I wonder his head is not turned. Tho not disposed to put on airs I find it very agreeable to be the wife of a man so generally known and respected."[398] As she explored more of the capital she discovered its dark side: "This is the saddest city, with maimed and bandaged soldiers in the streets, and the slow moving government hearses."[399]

Being Custer's wife opened prominent doors of power to her, including the White House. Libbie left some fascinating glimpses of Abraham Lincoln. Although "I am no abolitionist," she felt sorry for him because he was "the gloomiest, most painfully careworn looking man I ever saw." She saw him several times at the theater as he and his wife Mary sat in the presidential box seats. She then met him during a White House reception and was thrilled when Lincoln said: "So this is the young woman whose husband goes into a charge with a whoop and a shout." That praise for her husband transformed her view of the president: "Was I not honored? I am quite a Lincoln girl now. Afterward meeting one of his Secretaries, I bade him tell Mr. Lincoln he would have gained a vote if soldiers' wives were allowed one." Mary did not impress Libbie, who found her "short, squatty, and plain."[400]

It was difficult for a bright, informed young woman like Libbie not to express her views on the issues, especially those that affected her husband. She could only safely vent her views behind closed doors or in letters with her family and closest friends. In April 1864, she reassured her father that she had not forgotten one key duty: "You and Autie have cautioned me about holding my tongue on army and political matters." Having said that, she complained that army life was a "Sodom and Gomorrah" where "everybody drinks."[401]

One issue that mildly divided the couple was religion. Libbie was a devout believer and churchgoer. Custer rarely attended services and his views were nuanced. He believed in a supreme being, prayed whenever he felt the need, and was confident "that my destiny is in the hands of God." Indeed, his faith that he was among God's favorites "more than any other fact or reason, makes me brave and fearless as I am."[402]

At times each tried sexually to arouse the other through jealousy by alluding to forsaken possibilities. For instance, in a letter describing the capital's social whirl, Libbie at once confessed, reassured, and goaded him with these words: "If I were a young unmarried lady here I would flirt...but I have no desire to do so. Tho still enjoying gentlemen's society nobody could misconstrue my laughing and talking as flirting. I know, my dear, that tho I have a pretty face it is my husband's reputation that brings me so much attention.... I see so many wives in name only idling around with other men, for I feel how much better it is to be a correct wife."[403] To that Custer replied: "You know what ample cause I have to be suspicious or doubtful in regard to the conduct of women. One would naturally suppose my youthful experience would make me ever watchful. But I would as soon harbor a doubt of my Creator as I of my darling little wife."[404] Libbie reassured Custer that being with him was all she really wanted: "I love luxury, dress, comfort. But, Oh, how gladly I will give them up. I can be ready in a day or two. I can hardly wait."[405]

General Kilpatrick, Custer's division commander, also recently took an extended leave from which he returned a changed man, but not for the better. In November 1863, he went home to be with his wife when she gave birth. Tragically, both his wife and baby died during the delivery. That exacerbated his already volatile, callous, and aggressive nature. More than ever, he was driven to vent his volcanic rage and sorrow with an extraordinary military feat. He concocted the idea of a cavalry raid that galloped all the way to Richmond and liberated the American war prisoners held in horrendous conditions, destroyed the Tredegar Iron Works, and along the way nailed up copies of the Emancipation Proclamation. Lincoln approved the plan.

To hog as much possible glory for himself, Kilpatrick took direct command of Custer's Michigan Brigade and temporarily handed Custer the other, less acclaimed brigade whose general was on leave. Custer was to lead that brigade westward to divert the rebels. Custer made the most of his mission and men. On February 28 and March 1, 1865, his brigade destroyed warehouses, wagon supply trains, and flour mills, took fifty prisoners and five hundred horses, and liberated several hundred slaves. With rebel cavalry in hot pursuit, they withdrew toward the Union lines. Then Custer sent ahead his booty and prepared an ambush that the pursuers rode into. The Americans opened fire then charged, scattering the rebels. Custer triumphantly led his men back to the Army of the Potomac. Astonishingly, none of his men were killed. Meanwhile, Kilpatrick's raid was a debacle. Although he and his men got within sight of Richmond's church steeples, overwhelming numbers of rebel cavalry repelled and harassed him back to Union lines. Along the way he lost

340 men, including 176 from Custer's brigade, and five hundred horses.[406]

Pleasanton granted Custer an extended leave to reward his latest stunning feat. Custer and Libbie spent several weeks together, at first rapturously and then agonizingly. On March 14, he suffered a severe concussion when he was thrown from a carriage whose horses had spooked. Libbie wrote that her husband "does not remember anything about the accident or subsequent delirium and I suppose he never will."[407] Then Pleasanton ordered him to respond to accusations from a woman named Annie Jones who Kilpatrick had ordered arrested on spying charges; Jones claimed that she had been Custer's "friend and companion" during the summer of 1863, and that a jealous Kilpatrick had trumped up the espionage accusation against her. Custer replied that she had claimed to be a nurse, so he had kept her at his headquarters for a week, and then dismissed her, telling her not to return. He denied that he had vied with Kilpatrick for her favors. He also dismissed the notion that she was a rebel spy. She was instead an unstable woman who liked various kinds of adventures. The revelation of Custer's liaison with Annie must have provoked some awkward explanations and time with his wife.[408]

A critical turning point in the Civil War came on February 29, 1864, when President Lincoln promoted Ulysses Grant to lieutenant general and three days later gave him command of all American troops. Grant was the best general on either side during the Civil War.[409] He relentlessly battered into surrender three rebel armies, capturing 14,000 troops at Fort Donelson in 1862, 29,000 at Vicksburg in 1863, and 27,000 at Appomattox in 1865. His Vicksburg campaign brilliantly mixed rapid maneuvers and flank attacks that compared to the best of Napoleon's campaigns. He explained his strategy: "The art of war is simple enough. Find out where your enemy is. Get at him as soon as you can. Strike him as hard as you can and as often as you can and keep moving on."[410] If he failed, he tried something different. Yet his mistakes haunted him. A rebel army surprised him at Shiloh in 1862, although his troops eventually repelled the enemy after two days of hard fighting. To his dying day he lamented ordering the assault at Cold Harbor in May 1864, during which his army suffered 7,000 casualties. Nonetheless, his battle casualty ratios were actually lower than Lee's.[411] He was then forty-two years old, short statured, lean, rumpled, and taciturn, and chain-smoked cigars. Yet a highly thoughtful and intelligent man lurked below his unprepossessing personality and appearance. One of his aides lauded Grant "as a remarkable man. He handles those around him so quietly and well, he so evidently has the faculty of disposing of work and managing men, he is cool and quiet.... He is a man of the most exquisite judgment and tact."[412]

Custer and Libbie met Grant on a train bound for Washington on March 24. Probably most women reacted like Libbie to Grant: "He was no show off but quite unassuming. Tho disappointed in Grant's looks, I like him." Grant may have favorably impressed her because he was the opposite of her "show off" husband. Although Libbie adored Custer, his relentless egotism and energy could be draining. Grant's low-key, humble demeanor was the antidote to Custer's vanity. Whether Custer was genuinely awed by Grant, jealous of his successes, or simply had the good sense to sit down and shut up for a change is unclear. Jessie was astonished to see her husband subdued: "Instead of speaking with men who could do so much for him, Autie sat by me and only spoke when necessary."[413]

Grant shook up the cavalry. On March 25, he replaced Pleasanton with Philip Sheridan to head the corps. On April 7, he sent Kilpatrick west to join Sherman's army and replaced him with James Wilson. Both changes rankled Custer. He had lost his friend and mentor Pleasanton. He was relieved that his nemesis Kilpatrick was gone but rightfully thought that he should have taken his place to command the division rather than Wilson, a staff rather than combat general. Custer made his displeasure known. Sheridan transferred Custer's Michigan Brigade to General Alfred Torbert's 1st Division. Custer and Sheridan swiftly hit it off, with each admiring the other's ruthless aggressiveness. Sheridan was unequivocal in his praise: "Custer is the ablest man in the Cavalry Corps."[414]

Custer admired Sheridan as well and had good reason to do so, unlike his worship of the pseudo-hero McClellan. Sheridan ranks with Grant and Sherman as a brilliant general.[415] Earlier in the war, he achieved renown for his valor, initiative, and tactics at the battles of Perryville and Stone's River with the Army of the Ohio, and at the battle of Missionary Ridge under Grant's command. Indeed, Grant was so impressed that he insisted that Sheridan be transferred to the Army of the Potomac. Sheridan was a short, lean man, then thirty-three years old. He soon tangled with Meade over the cavalry's proper strategic role. Meade insisted that cavalry should simply protect the army's flanks and rear from enemy cavalry while scouting the enemy army's deployments. Sheridan argued that Union cavalry should emulate rebel cavalry with massive raids against the enemy's rear to destroy its supply lines. Grant resolved that dispute in Sheridan's favor.

Grant's orders to the army commanders were simple. Each would lead his men against the nearest rebel army or strategic position and not stop fighting until he destroyed that army or captured that position. Meade's army would attack Lee's army. Benjamin Butler's army would take Richmond. Franz Sigel's corps would clear rebels from the Shenandoah Valley. Nathaniel Banks's army would capture Mobile. Sherman's army would attack Johnston's army in northern Georgia. Lincoln made one change in that plan. He had Banks ascend the Red River to seize Shreveport, Louisiana. The armies of Sigel, Banks, and Butler each suffered defeat. Only those of Meade and Sherman persisted in fighting ceaselessly. Grant attached himself to the Army of the Potomac, which Meade officially headed. Grant essentially used him as his chief of staff to implement his strategy, tactics, and other critical decisions.

Grant's campaign opened on May 5, when the 120,000-man Army of the Potomac marched into the Wilderness, a forest twenty-five miles west of Fredericksburg. Lee hurried his 60,000 troops to block Grant's advance. The fighting lasted two days, with 17,500 Union and 12,500 rebel casualties. Without a pause, Grant shifted his army southeast to get between Lee and Richmond.

To divert Lee's attention, Grant dispatched Sheridan's 10,000-man cavalry corps to arc around the rebel army's left flank and aim toward Richmond. On May 9, Custer's division spearheaded the column that stretched a dozen miles. Caught by surprise, J.E.B. Stuart raced his cavalry corps south to head off Sheridan. On May 11, Stuart massed his cavalry at Yellow Tavern just two miles north of Richmond's entrenchments. General Fitzhugh Lee's brigade charged Custer's brigade as it approached. Custer deployed his 5th and 6th Michigan regiments and artillery on the front to blunt the rebel attack while curling the 1st and 7th Michigan regiments against the enemy's flank. The rebel cavalry withdrew into Richmond.

The following day, Sheridan's troops probed Richmond's northern entrenchments defended by only a skeleton force of second-rate troops. Just then rebel cavalry attacked Sheridan's rear. Worried he might be cut off, Sheridan reluctantly ordered his men to withdraw east across the Chickahominy River and then fight their way back to the Army of the Potomac. Once again Custer's brigade led the way. His men captured a railroad bridge and laid planks across it so they could lead their horses across. Sheridan and his exhausted men and horses did not reach the Army of the Potomac near Hanover Court House until May 24. During the raid, the Union cavalry suffered 715 casualties, including 113 from Custer's brigade, but inflicted 800 casualties on the rebels, most critically J.E.B. Stuart, mortally wounded at Yellow Tavern.[416] Astonishingly, Sheridan was able to resupply and reinforce his corps within two days. On May 27, his horsemen crossed the Pamunkey River at several fords and spread out to secure them as the infantry corps followed and marched south.

Meanwhile, Lee quick-marched his troops to get ahead of Grant's advance, first at Spotsylvania. The battle raged six horrendous days starting on May 10, with 18,500 Federal and 12,500 Confederate casualties. Grant sidestepped but Lee was quicker, and their armies fought at North Anna on May 22. Grant tried again to outflank Lee only to find the rebel army entrenched at Cold Harbor. Grant ordered an assault on June 3. The Union army suffered 7,000 dead, wounded, and captured to 1,500 rebel losses.[417]

Those losses made Grant more determined than ever to prevail. Once again, he planned to curl around Lee's right flank, but first sought to divert rebel attention by sending Sheridan the opposite direction. The now 9,300-man corps would ride west to Charlottesville, rip up stretches of the Virginia Central Railroad, and then head south to destroy the locks on the James River Canal. That would sever two vital supply arteries to Richmond and clear the way for General David Hunter, who had replaced ineffectual Franz Sigel, to lead his corps in the Shenandoah Valley over the Blue Ridge Mountains and join forces with him. Then, together, they would march south against Lynchburg and capture that strategic rail junction.

Learning of Sheridan's advance, General Wade Hampton raced his 6,500 horsemen to Trevilian Station by June 11.[418] Sheridan was unaware that he faced so many rebel horsemen. He had Torbert attack Hampton's front while Custer looped along a side road and hit the enemy's right flank. General Fitzhugh Lee's division blocked the road that Custer's brigade followed. Custer led his men in a charge that routed Lee's troopers, then rode on to scatter the rebels at Trevilian Station. Custer called a halt to rest his exhausted men and horses, and await the rest of the corps. Unfortunately, many of his troops scattered to loot rebel supply wagons.

Lee rallied his men and charged Custer's rear just as rebel General Thomas Rosser attacked him from the west. The result was a seesaw battle of charge and countercharge. Men from each side were captured then liberated as their comrades rallied and rode to their rescue. The ground was strewn with dead and wounded men and horses. Colonel James Kidd, who led the 6th Michigan, recalled, "Custer never lost his nerve under any circumstances. He was however, unmistakably excited."[419] From the other side of the battlefield Rosser observed through his binoculars his old West Point friend Custer "sitting on his horse in the midst of his advance platoons" where "he encouraged and inspired his men by appeal as well as by example."[420] Astonishing, bullets literally bounced off Custer; spent bullets bruised his shoulder and arm. Rather than take cover, he raced forward to pull to safety one of his wounded troopers. When his artillery commander rode up and announced that the rebels had captured one of his guns, Custer shouted "I'll be damned if they do!"[421] He drew his sword, gathered some men, and charged. Custer and his followers killed, captured, or scattered the rebels and retook the cannon. Rosser and his staff opened fire at Custer and his men. A bullet mortally wounded the flag bearer. Custer grabbed the flag, ripped it from its pole, and stuffed it in his shirt.

Torbert meanwhile was still fighting his way south toward Trevilian Station.

Spearheading Torbert's division was General Wesley Merritt's brigade, which finally broke through, forcing the rebels to retreat. Sheridan ordered an assault the next day, June 12. That was a mistake. His men and horses were exhausted. The rebels fended off the attack. Sheridan reluctantly withdrew his battered corps to the Army of the Potomac. In all, the Union cavalry suffered 699 casualties, including 53 dead, 274 wounded, and 372 captured, while inflicting 530 rebel casualties; Custer's brigade lost 41 killed, 66 wounded, and 309 prisoners.[422]

Custer suffered a personal loss during the battle that became a public embarrassment. Some rebel cavalry rode far into the rear of the Union corps and attacked their supply train. Among the wagons they captured was Custer's with Eliza Brown at the reins. Although Eliza managed to escape, the rebels kept Custer's valise and other personal effects including his letters and his brigadier general's commission. But his troops suffered far worse. From May 4 to July 1, 1864, Custer's brigade suffered 776 casualties, the highest figure for any Union cavalry brigade during the war.[423]

In gratitude for Custer's outstanding performance, Sheridan granted him twenty days leave. Custer hurried to Libbie. Their time together was marred by rebel newspaper publication of excerpts from their letters that Hampton's horseman had captured at Trevilian Station. Readers were treated to a parade of sexual allusions of passion between them. Custer could not keep his hands off his sexy, eager wife when he was with her or his mind off her when he was away. Although the revelations rendered the Custers red-faced, their ardor for each other remained as aching as ever. After Custer returned to the army he confessed: "I frequently discover myself acting as an umpire between my patriotism and my desire to be and remain with my darling."[424] To that Libbie fired back: "I don't care if fifty rebels read this letter. I miss your kisses."[425] She tried to rein in his lust for combat with his lust for her: "Don't expose yourself so much in battle. Just do your duty, and don't rush out so daringly. Oh, Autie, we must die together. Better the humblest life together than the loftiest, divided. My hopes and ambitions are more than a hundred times already realized in you."[426]

Phil Sheridan's diversion let Grant lead the army across the James River and west to Petersburg. Although the rebels had only a skeleton force in Petersburg's defenses, the lead Union forces refused to attack when they arrived on June 15. Their reluctance is understandable. In the five weeks of nearly constant marching and fighting since the campaign began, the Army of the Potomac had suffered 65,000 casualties while inflicting only 35,000 casualties. Nonetheless, Grant later insisted "that Petersburg could have been easily captured at the time."[427] And had that happened,

Grant would have pushed Lee back into Richmond, severed the railroad, and starved him into surrender within a month. Instead, Lee and Grant massed their armies at Petersburg for what became a ten-month siege.

Grant ordered Hunter to lead his 15,000-man corps to capture Lynchburg. Lee sent General Jubal Early's 15,000-man infantry corps and Fitzhugh Lee's 2,000-man cavalry division to defend Lynchburg. Early defeated Hunter at Lynchburg on June 24, crossed into the Shenandoah Valley and marched all the way to the Potomac River. He then led his army across the river and marched toward Washington, scattered a small Union force at the Monocracy River on July 9, and approached Fort Steven, which guarded the capital's western approach, on July 11. At that point Lincoln rode out to observe the battle from the fort's ramparts. Early reckoned the fort was too strong to overrun and feared that other federal forces were converging against him. As he withdrew his army slowly back to the Shenandoah Valley, his troops looted all along the way; the worst atrocity came on July 30, when rebel cavalry burned Chambersburg, Pennsylvania, after its citizens were unable to pay the $500,000 ransom.

Grant consolidated four separate commands in northern Virginia along with the 1st and 3rd Cavalry divisions into an Army of the Shenandoah, and appointed Sheridan to lead it on July 31.[428] Sheridan and his cavalry packed on steamboats bound for Washington, which they reached on August 9. Sheridan's army then rode west. The first battle came on August 16 at Crooked Run near Front Royal, where Custer's brigade repelled attacks by two rebel cavalry brigades and then charged and captured their supply train. Over the next week, the advancing Union cavalry and retreating Confederate cavalry skirmished at Shepherdstown and Martinsburg. Early withdrew to Winchester. It took more than a month for Sheridan to bring together and supply all the disparate troops assigned to his army, while quelling General John Mosby and his "raiders" who harassed his rear.

Sheridan's 35,000 troops soundly beat Early's 17,000 troops at Winchester on September 19. While most Union troops advanced directly against the rebels, Custer's brigade hit their left flank. Three days later Sheridan defeated Early at Fisher Hill, but the victory was incomplete because cavalry generals Torbert and Averell failed to block the enemy's escape. He replaced William Averell with Custer as head of the 2nd Cavalry division. Then James Wilson resigned, and Sheridan gave Custer the 3rd division. That assignment took Custer from his beloved Michigan brigade. Meanwhile, the rebel cavalry had its own shakeup when Early replaced Fitzhugh Lee, who was wounded at Winchester, with Thomas Rosser.

Custer's division led Sheridan's advance south up the valley. On October 9, Custer and Rosser squared off at Spiker's Hill, where each swore to his staff that he was determined to capture the other. Custer outwitted his old West Point friend by curling a brigade around his flank and routing him. Although Rosser evaded capture, his supply wagon fell into Custer's hands. Custer amused himself and his men by strolling through camp clothed in Rosser's coat.

Early withdrew his army, resupplied, and reinforced it, then headed north. The attack came at Cedar Creek on October 19, and initially beat the bluecoats. Famously, Sheridan himself was not with his army but at Winchester eleven miles away. He galloped back to the sound of the guns, rallied his men, and counterattacked. Meanwhile, Custer's 3rd Division guarded the army's right flank. When Rosser appeared with his division, Custer charged, defeated them, and then angled toward the rebel rear. With Early's army decimated, Sheridan ordered his men to lay waste the Shenandoah Valley.

Throughout Sheridan's campaign, his cavalry alone captured 2,556 prisoners, 29 battle flags, 71 cannons, 52 caissons, 105 supply wagons, 2,557 horses, 1,000 horse equipages, and 7,152 cattle, and destroyed 420,742 wheat bushels and 780 barns, and captured 700,000 ammunition rounds; Custer's men accounted for the lion's share of those spoils and destruction.[429] To reward Custer, Sheridan dispatched him with ten rebel battle flags to present to Secretary of War Stanton in Washington. He also let Custer add his brother Lieutenant Thomas Custer to his staff. Finally, he recommended that Custer along with Merritt be promoted to major general.

Elsewhere, William Sherman outflanked Joe Johnston repeatedly in a campaign that began in north Georgia in early May and reached Atlanta's defenses in early July. Dissatisfied with Johnston's prudent refusal to risk his army in a major battle, President Davis replaced him with General Sam Hood, known for his aggression. Hood launched a series of attacks against Sherman's army, which repulsed each with heavy losses back into Atlanta. Sherman then curled his army south of Atlanta to cut the railroad line that supplied the city. Hood attacked and was defeated at Jonesboro on September 1, but this time he fled with his army's remnants to central Georgia to avoid getting trapped. Sherman's army triumphantly entered Atlanta on September 2.

Then the two enemy armies did something astonishing—each turned its back on the other. On November 12, Sherman marched with 62,000 troops southeast toward Savannah 285 miles away, while dispatching General George Thomas back to Tennessee to defend that state. Unable to defend Atlanta, Sherman ordered the city burned. Hood shadowed Thomas to Tennessee, gathering forces along the way. Hood defeated General John Schofield's corps at Columbia on November 26, was defeated by Schofield at Franklin on November 30, then marched his 25,000 men to besiege Nashville, which was defended by Thomas and his 50,000 men. Grant sent Thomas repeated orders to attack, which Thomas finally obeyed on

December 15. Thomas's troops decimated Hood's army. Meanwhile, after looting and burning their way across Georgia, Sherman's army captured Savannah on December 22.

Custer had mixed feelings about the nation's politics and the war. During their convention in Chicago, the Democratic Party nominated Custer's mentor and hero George McClellan the presidential candidate. Libbie expressed her mixed feelings of hope and fear that McClellan would win: "I think he will be elected and that would mean peace—perhaps dishonorable. Autie, it is treasonable and unwomanly but way down in my heart I want peace on any terms, for much as I love my country I love you more." In that, Libbie expressed the hopes of countless wives, mothers, girlfriends, fiancées, and daughters across America, both North and South. She asked who he favored. Custer replied, "my doctrine has ever been that a soldier should not meddle in politics."[430] Understandably, Custer refused publicly to reveal his views. He did, however, share his political views with McClellan: "I am a 'Peace Man' in favor of an 'armistice' and of sending 'Peace Commissioners.' I desire an honorable and lasting peace; such a peace can only be secured by the acknowledgement of one government supreme and entire; it must embrace all the states and must possess self-sustaining power; in other words, the decisions of the general government as affecting individual states must be supreme and admitting of no appeal."[431]

When the votes were counted, Lincoln received 2,203,831 and 212 electoral votes to 1,797,019 and 21 electoral votes for McClellan. Lincoln was especially gratified to receive the lion's share of votes from the troops, 119,754 to 34,291. The Republican Party also celebrated a landslide in Congress, with 42 to 10 Democrats in the Senate and 149 to 42 in the House of Representatives.[432]

Setting aside the preference of herself and her husband for McClellan, Libbie was thrilled and moved to attend Lincoln's second inauguration on March 4, 1865: "I was very near Mr. Lincoln when he delivered his greatest address on the steps of the Capitol: one line so often quoted, 'With charity to all, with malice toward none,' referring to the armies that opposed us. And I saw how quietly he received the plaudits of the people who were much more aware of his greatness than when he came from the West, almost unknown, four years before."[433]

With the rebels defeated, Custer felt it was safe enough to bring Libbie to stay at his headquarters at Long Meadow. The experience exhilarated her: "If you could only know what an exciting life I lead, hurried from one place to another.... But as these changes are to be with or near my husband I am always ready to move at a day's notice. It seemed so strange at first to sleep in a tent...almost no furniture, the free winds of heaven playing with the walls.... A soldier's life is glorious."[434] Sheridan forced all the wives to leave his army except for Libbie. In doing so he was willing to endure charges of favoritism because he esteemed Custer as his best cavalry commander and Libbie as an extraordinary woman. Libbie mostly enjoyed all the attention paid her but admitted to her parents that, "being so preoccupied with company even your chatterbox daughter sometimes gets tired of talking."[435]

As 1865 dawned, rebel resistance had pretty much collapsed. Lee's 40,000 troops stretched thin around Petersburg was the largest force and the only one that could be called an army. Scattered elsewhere were contingents that numbered mostly in the hundreds and occasionally the thousands; all they could do was raid and evade. Union troops occupied nearly all the South's key ports and inland cities, and patrolled the roads, rail lines, and navigable rivers among them. Tennessee, Louisiana, and Arkansas had already been "reconstructed" with new governments whose constitutions abolished slavery and pledged loyalty to the United States.

Lee asked Davis to enlist slaves as soldiers in return for their freedom after the war ended. Davis and his advisors rejected the notion. Freeing slaves defeated the Confederacy's reason for being. Like nearly everything else connected to the Confederacy, that decision was moot. Total defeat was just months away while, on January 31, 1865, Congress passed the Thirteenth Amendment, which abolished slavery. Lincoln signed the bill and sent it to the northern state legislatures for ratification.

Sherman's 60,000-man Army of the Tennessee headed north from Savannah on February 1, 1865. He intended to make South Carolina, the first state to rebel, "howl" even worse than Georgia. Joe Johnston commanded all rebel troops in the Carolinas, about 20,000, but was outgunned three to one. As a result, Johnston and Sherman fought the same campaign as in Georgia. Sherman's army advanced on a broad front with the wings constantly trying to swing behind Johnston, who fought delaying actions before quick-marching away. There were no pitched battles, just plenty of skirmishes in the danse macabre of the two armies northward, leaving a trail of dead and maimed men, and burnt warehouses, railroad stations, and barns behind. The rebels themselves torched Columbia, South Carolina's capital, just to deny the Yankees the pleasure.

In the Shenandoah Valley, Sheridan resumed the offensive on February 27, 1865. His orders were to march south, destroy Early's army along with the James River Canal and Virginia Central Railroad, then angle over the Blue Ridge Mountains and eventually rejoin Grant at Petersburg. Heading the army's advance,

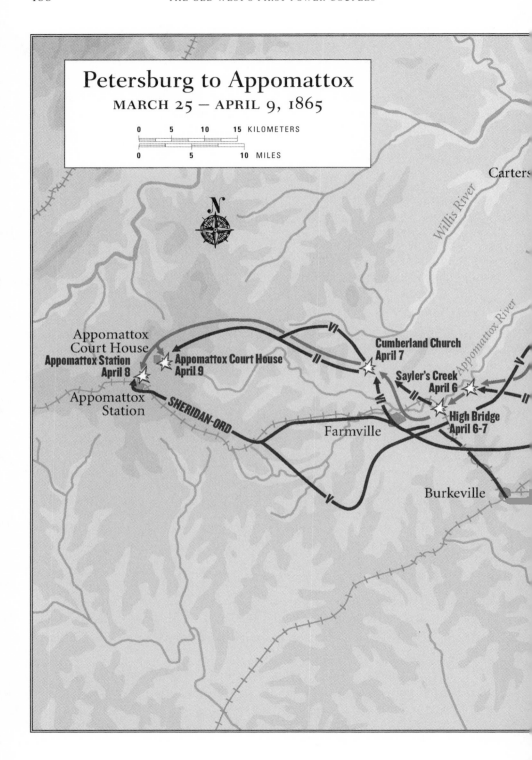

Petersburg to Appomattox

MARCH 25 — APRIL 9, 1865

0   5   10   15 KILOMETERS

0   5   10 MILES

Willis River

Carters

Appomattox River

Appomattox
Court House
Appomattox Station
April 8

Appomattox Court House
April 9

Cumberland Church
April 7

Sayler's Creek
April 6

Appomattox
Station

SHERIDAN-ORD

High Bridge
April 6-7

Farmville

Burkeville

VI

V

V

II

II

II

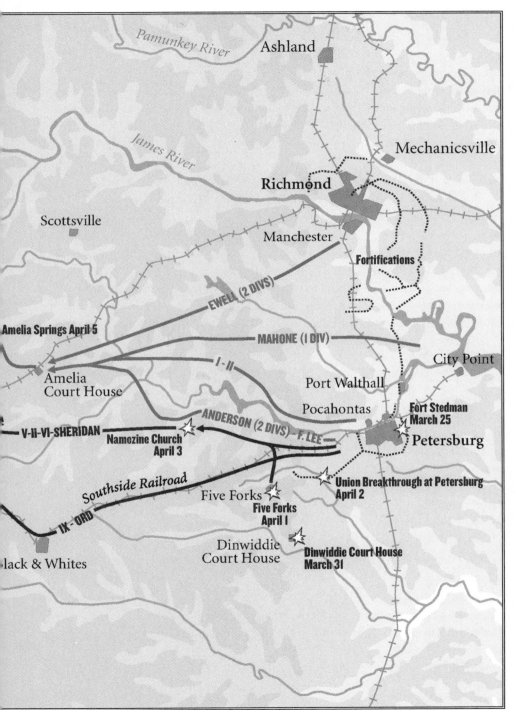

Pamunkey River

Ashland

James River

Mechanicsville

Scottsville

Richmond

Manchester

Fortifications

EWELL (2 DIVS)

Amelia Springs April 5

MAHONE (1 DIV)

City Point

I - II

Amelia
Court House

Port Walthall

Pocahontas

Fort Stedman
March 25

ANDERSON (2 DIVS) - F. LEE

V-II-VI-SHERIDAN

Namozine Church
April 3

Petersburg

Southside Railroad

Union Breakthrough at Petersburg
April 2

Five Forks

Five Forks
April 1

IX - ORD

Dinwiddie
Court House

Black & Whites

Dinwiddie Court House
March 31

Petho Cartography 2019

Custer caught up to Early at Waynesboro on March 2. With combined frontal and flank attacks, his horsemen routed Early's army, capturing 1,600 troops, eleven cannons, seventeen battle flags, and his supply wagons. Custer led his division over Rockfish Gap in the Blue Ridge Mountains and descended to occupy Charlottesville where they awaited Sheridan and the rest of the army. Grant wanted Sheridan to head south and capture Lynchburg. That proved impossible because the rebels had destroyed all the bridges and Sheridan lacked enough pontoons to cross the rain-swollen James River. Sheridan led his army east, skirted Richmond's northern defenses, arched south to cross the pontoon bridge over the James River, and reached the Army of the Potomac's rear at City Point on March 27.

Those weary cavalrymen arrived just in time. The final campaign began on March 31, when Grant sent Sheridan's corps west to curl around Petersburg and block the rebel retreat. Lee quick-marched General George Pickett's 19,000 troops to hold Five Forks, a key crossroads and rail junction. On April 1, Sheridan's troops trounced Pickett's, capturing 4,500 men, thirteen battle flags, and six cannons. That forced Lee to leave a skeleton force in Petersburg and hurry the bulk of his men westward. On April 2, Grant ordered his army to assault Petersburg, and the bluecoats swiftly overran the graycoats that Lee left behind. The two armies raced westward on parallel roads half a dozen or so miles apart.

Custer spearheaded the American army's advance. On April 6, he successfully led his division north against General Richard Ewell's corps at Sailor's Creek and captured "35 pieces of artillery, 1000 prisoners…and from 150 to 200 wagons."[436] The Custer brothers were in the thick of the fighting. A bullet killed George's horse beneath him. Tom seized a rebel flag, killed the flag bearer, who shot him in the face, and captured fourteen prisoners.[437] Custer then planted his division across the road leading westward.

When Lee halted his army around Appomattox Court House on April 7, he had only around 27,000 exhausted, starving men left. He received a letter from Grant asking him to surrender. Lee wrote Grant asking for terms. Learning of the negotiations, Custer's lust for glory and the spotlight consumed him. On April 8, without authority, he rode through the lines with a white flag to Longstreet's headquarters, where he declared: "In the name of General Sheridan I demand the unconditional surrender of this army." Custer's attitude offended Longstreet as disrespectful to Grant and Lee, who were delicately discussing how best to end the fighting. He told Custer to return to his army and let the commanders arrange terms between themselves.[438]

Despite his blatant attempt to steal the show, Custer was allowed to join the prominent generals and staff officers that accompanied Grant to the surrender at Wilmer McLean's house at Appomattox Court House on April 9. Lee arrived with just one aide. Grant grew animated chatting with Lee about their Mexican War days until Lee reminded him why they were present. Grant penned a document that paroled the rebel troops, let officers keep their pistols and swords, and anyone with a horse or mule to ride it home. He then arranged to share his army's rations with Lee's starving men. As Lee shook hands with Grant's delegation, he remarked to Captain Ely Parker, a Seneca Indian, that "I am glad to see one real American here." Parker's reply could not have been more appropriate: "We are all Americans."[439]

After the surrender, Custer issued a declaration to his men celebrating the decisive role they played in bringing it about: "The record established by your indomitable courage is unparalleled in the annals of war.... During the past six months, although in most instances confronted by superior numbers, you have captured from the enemy in open battle, one hundred and eleven pieces of field artillery, sixty-five battle flags, and upwards of ten thousand prisoners, including seven general officers.... You have never lost a gun, never lost a color, never lost a battle."[440] What Custer did not mention was that his troops would never have achieved those stunning achievements without his brilliant leadership. Sheridan so esteemed Custer's decisive role in the final defeat that he gave him the table on which Grant and Lee had negotiated and signed the surrender document. To Libbie, he explained why with these heartfelt words: "There is scarcely an individual in our service who has contributed more to bring this about than your very gallant husband."[441]

The electrifying word of Lee's surrender reached Washington early on April 10, 1865. Libbie vividly recalled that: "I was awakened to more joy than I believed I would ever know by the clang of bells, whistles, calliopes, firing of cannons, and the shouts of the newsboys. The flag at the War Department, which we weeping women all over Washington had so often looked for to announce a victory, was waving in triumph. I found that anxiety and suspense had not permanently aged me, for I jumped out of bed.... I wanted to scream and dance with joy. I had been invested with so much dignity, and so much mature and stately manner was expected me by the wives of the officers. I did not dare race and shout as my girlish intent prompted me."[442]

Libbie joined a delegation of senators, congressmen, and their wives aboard a steamboat bound for City Point, from where they would visit the victorious Army of the Potomac. Astonishingly, she thought she would find her husband in Richmond, so she not only managed to find transport there but talked Varina Davis, the wife of rebel President Davis, to let her stay at the Confederate White House. She passed two anxious days and nights in the president's bedroom afraid that the household servants might violently vent their rage on the wife of a victorious American general. Somehow Custer found out Libbie's whereabouts and hurried to be with her: "The second morning I was awakened by the sound of a sabre knocking against the stairs and sprang out of bed to look through the crack in the door. It was my husband leaping up the stairs two steps at a time. I forgot my fears. I was suffocated with delight. I cried, I laughed, and then I began to realize the war was over."[443] They did not linger in Richmond. Libbie rode beside Custer as he led the 3rd Cavalry Division back to the capital.

A national tragedy on April 14 muted much of the American celebration. That evening, John Wilkes Booth, a Confederate zealot, shot President Abraham Lincoln in the back of the head as he and his wife attended a play at Ford's Theater. Of the subsequent outpouring of elegies, perhaps none was more appropriate than Secretary of War Stanton's succinct words: "Now he belongs to the ages."[444]

CHAPTER 13

Doldrums

"I long to become wealthy, not for wealth alone, but for the power it brings."

— GEORGE CUSTER

"Everything here is so behindhand…. They need the advent of the thrifty ingenious Yankee."

— LIBBIE CUSTER

ICTORY PARADES COMMEMORATED THE WAR'S END in Washington, with General George Meade's 80,000-man Army of the Potomac marching in a grand review on May 23, and General William Sherman's 60,000-man Army of the Tennessee marching the following day. Typically, Custer stole the show although that probably was not his plan. He was riding a spirited stallion named Don Juan that he had confiscated from a Virginia plantation. His steed bolted when a woman threw a flower wreath at him, and Custer lost his hat and sword before he finally reined in the horse right before the reviewing stand where President Andrew Johnson, Grant, and their respective entourages watched in astonishment.

The American victory in the Civil War came at an enormous cost in blood and treasure. Officially, 617,528 soldiers died, 364,511 Union and 253,017 Confederate. The real number of dead soldiers and civilians exceeded 750,000 lives. Government spending from 1861 to 1865 was $3.5 billion, including $3.1 billion for military and $411.8 million for nonmilitary expenses. The national debt soared from $90.6 million in 1861 to $2.7 billion in 1865.[445]

With the war done, Washington concentrated on the policy of Reconstruction that involved purging slavery from the former rebel states and reintegrating them with the United States.[446] Although most northerners backed that policy, they differed sharply over what rights, if any, African Americans should enjoy. President Andrew Johnson was an unabashed racist who would deny blacks any civil rights: "This country is for white men and by God, as long as I am President, it shall be governed by white men."[447] Radical Republicans, who dominated both houses of Congress, insisted that blacks should exercise equal political rights, education, and economic opportunities with whites. Johnson had backed the Thirteenth Amendment that abolished slavery but opposed the proposed Fourteenth Amendment that would guarantee equal rights, suffrage, and due process for all Americans, including blacks. He also opposed the federal Freedman's Bureau, which helped blacks find food, clothing, shelter, schooling, and jobs.

Custer soon found himself embroiled in these issues in which, usually, he sided with Johnson rather than the Radical Republicans. He received orders to proceed to Texas, where he would help implement an occupation policy designed to purge rebellion and slavery from that state. The Custers booked passage on a ship to New Orleans, where they enjoyed a second honeymoon. For a week they strolled the city, ate at the best restaurants, and stayed at the luxurious St. Charles Hotel. They took a riverboat to Alexandria, Louisiana, where he assumed command over a five-regiment cavalry division that included the 1st Iowa, 5th and 12th Illinois, 2nd Wisconsin, and 7th Indiana. He was instructed to restore order to Alexandria and the surrounding region before riding to Texas.

His mission was complex. On one hand, he and his troops came to liberate slaves from their masters, and he reveled in that just cause: "Slavery was not as mild here as in States whose proximity to Free States made kindness desirable to prevent the enslaved from seeking freedom across the border. The knowledge that runaways would have to traverse thousands of miles of slave or hostile country placed slaves at the mercy of their owners.... If the War has attained nothing else it has placed America under a debt of gratitude for all time for removal of this evil."[448] Yet slavery's abolition at once liberated a people and caused economic chaos. Blacks fled their plantations for the nearest federal army camp, where they begged to be fed. That collapsed the southern economy, which depended on their labor. The worst crisis was the production of food. Crops were not planted or harvested. Mass starvation threatened black and white southerners alike. For Libbie, temporary food relief to southerners from the north would be nothing more than that—the South's economic problems were rooted in its culture: "Everything here is so behindhand.... They need the advent of the thrifty ingenious Yankee."[449]

To alleviate that crisis, Johnson issued in May and June 1865 a series of executive orders that essentially transformed slaves into serfs. He declared a blanket pardon for nearly all rebels; those with property worth $20,000 or more had to swear a loyalty oath to a federal official. He then let state officials enact what became known as the "black codes," laws that restricted the movement of blacks, forced them to labor for their former owners, and denied them such fundamental citizenship rights as testifying in court, serving on juries, voting, and running for office. Finally, he ordered federal officials and troops to enforce those measures.

So, Custer spent most of his time first in northwest Louisiana then in east Texas helping whites reassert their power over "uppity blacks." That did not trouble him. Although he favored slavery's abolition, he considered blacks mentally and morally inferior to whites, and thus undeserving of political rights and relegated forever to the most menial of jobs. In those views, he was no different from nearly all southerners and most northerners.

Custer faced enormous problems keeping his own 4,500 troops in line. With the war over, most of them wanted to be discharged and did not wait for official permission. Custer was incensed that "desertions became numerous and of daily occurrence.... As many as twelve have deserted from the same regiment in one night."[450] Atop that, some soldiers robbed, raped, and even murdered local whites and blacks. He cracked down with floggings and even executions. Unfortunately, that exacerbated rather than deterred the dismal morale that led some troops to crime or flight.

Custer's biggest personal headache was over Don Juan, the racehorse that he had confiscated. Richard Gaines, the owner, wanted either his horse back or a just price in compensation, for which he had petitioned the War Department. To Custer's embarrassment, Gaines's efforts made the newspapers. Custer insisted that he had captured Don Juan in a raid and thus neither he nor the War Department owed Gaines anything. Yet even if that were true, it did not make Custer the horse's new owner. Officially, the War Department owned that horse along with all other confiscated rebel property. The case became a rallying symbol for southerners enraged at what they called northern "aggression" and "conquest." That forced Grant to issue an order down the chain of command through Sherman and Sheridan to Custer that he return the horse to its owner. Custer was determined to keep Don Juan, whose value he privately reckoned was $10,000. He tried to resolve the matter by convening a board of officers to assess Don Juan's value, and then paid their assessed $125 to the War Department. All along Sheridan backed Custer's claim that the horse was captured rather than confiscated, and he declared the case closed as soon as the money reached the War Department's bursar.

Custer led his cavalry division on the 240-mile, nineteen-day march from Alexandria to Houston, Texas, in August 1865. The timing could not have been worse with summer at its height in that pestiferous steam bath of a region with clouds of mosquitoes day and night. Libbie sweltered in a hospital wagon converted into a bedroom. Along the way, Custer received orders from Sheridan to head to

Hempstead, Texas, a cotton production center fifty miles northwest of Houston.[451]

The vicious cycle of morale, crime, and punishment plaguing Custer's division worsened. Soldiers, including officers, wrote letters and petitions condemning Custer's tyranny to their congressional and state representatives, state governors, General Grant, and Secretary of War Stanton. Iowa's legislature passed a resolution demanding Custer's arrest and prosecution. An editorial in the *Des Moines State Register* printed these searing words about him: "His memory will be a stench in their nostrils, and that of their children's children to the remotest generation." Elihu Washburne, an Illinois congressman, wrote Grant, his friend and protégée that: "I do not know but is it necessary for Custar [sic] to do all these inhuman and barbarous things to maintain discipline, but I have observed that it was not necessary for you to do such things in any Command you ever had." Grant issued this order to Sheridan: "There is great complaint of cruelty against Gen. Custer. If there are grounds for these complaints relieve him from duty." As always, Sheridan shielded Custer, arguing that "he has not done anything that was not fully warranted by the insubordination of his command. If anything he has been too lenient."[452]

Corruption exacerbated the controversy over Custer's leadership. He invited his father, Emanuel Custer, to act as his division's purchasing agent. Although notions of conflict of interest, nepotism, and favoritism then existed, they were proscribed morally rather than legally. Libbie insisted that her husband was a model of probity: "Autie has fine opportunities for making a fortune in land or cotton or horses, or in buying government claims, but he feels that so long as the government needs his active services he should not invest."[453]

As in Alexandria, Custer deployed his troops to help Hempstead plantation and business owners reassert control over the black labor that was essential for their prosperity. The Freedman's Bureau was the newly created federal agency charged with assisting newly liberated blacks with work, food, and shelter. Custer backed those efforts: "I would like for those who say that 'the Nigger won't work,' to come here for a day or two, and I think that he would leave with the impression that Freedmen (in this neighborhood at least) were anything but lazy." He also favored whites retaining their monopoly of political power. He explained his racial outlook: "I am in favor of elevating the negro to the extent of his capability and intelligence...but in making this advancement I am opposed to doing it by correspondingly reducing or debasing any portion of the white race. And as to entrusting the negroes of the southern states with...the right of suffrage, I should as soon think of elevating an Indian chief to the popedom of Rome. All advocates of negro suffrage should visit the Southern States and see the class of people upon whom they desire to confer the privilege." Nonetheless, Custer appreciated how complex these questions were: "I regard the solution of the negro question as involving more difficulty and requiring the exercise of more real statesmanship than any political question which has been adjudicated for years." Then Custer's outlook revolutionized after the reimposition of white rule resulted in the murders of fifty blacks: "Justice to the freedman will not be granted voluntarily.... A system of oppression is being inaugurated through this state upon the part of the former owners against the Freedman."[454]

Amidst this political and moral turmoil, Custer suffered painful blows to his career. He had emerged from the Civil War as one of the most renowned combat leaders on either side. Then he received orders that relieved him of his current command and revoked his brevet or temporary rank as major general on February 1, 1866. He was to report to Washington and there await his next assignment as a captain. That demotion was certainly reasonable given that Custer was one of 135 major generals in a rapidly downsizing army for which only three were necessary. Like other demoted officers, Custer suffered a double whammy; he lost not just his lofty status, but his annual income plummeted from $8,000 to $2,000.[455]

Custer's dismissal coincided with a political crisis in Washington between the president and Congress. Johnson vetoed a bill that extended the Freedman's Bureau on February 19 and a bill that promoted civil rights on March 27, 1866. Custer was among the witnesses called by the Congressional Joint Committee on Reconstruction. Trepidation filled him when he appeared on March 10, 1866. He feared jeopardizing his army career if he said anything that offended the Radical Republicans who dominated the Committee, especially Illinois representative Washburne, who was Grant's mentor and friend. He stated that he supported civil rights, voting, running for office, and the Freedman's Bureau for blacks, and opposed conservative white efforts to suppress those rights, especially with violence.

The Custers then went in different directions, Libbie to Monroe to visit her family and Custer with some army officer buddies to New York for business and pleasure. With his headquarters at the luxurious Fifth Avenue Hotel, he met with his old mentor George McClellan and other Democratic Party powerbrokers like August Belmont, Samuel Bellow, Augustus Schell, and Horace Clark, and dined at their exclusive clubhouse, the Manhattan Club. He was introduced to such luminaries as poet and editor William Cullen Bryant, chess prodigy Paul Morphy, actress Maggie Mitchell, historian George Bancroft, and cartoonist Thomas Nast. He visited Wall Street and spoke with prominent brokers. He attended plays and concerts. He had an astonishing session with a clairvoyant who revealed many things about him that he had always kept to himself. He loved New York and wrote Libbie, "I would like to become wealthy in order to make my permanent home here."[456] But even more so, "I long to become wealthy, not for wealth alone, but for the power it brings."[457]

While Custer was burning both ends of the candle in New York, Libbie was trying to make her father's last days as comfortable as possible. Daniel Bacon died on May 18, 1866. He left his home and a monthly stipend to his wife Rhoda that would transfer to Libbie after her stepmother's death. Custer did not arrive until after his father-in-law was dead and buried. His period of mourning was brief. He entered and won the Michigan State Fair's horse race atop Don Juan. He hoped that Don Juan's fame would fetch him at least $10,000 at auction, but a heart attack killed his racehorse a few weeks later.

The uncertainty over Custer's army career eased a bit on July 28, 1866, when Congress passed a bill that established an army of 54,302 troops, including 2,835 officers and 48,081 enlisted men. Then, on August 2, Grant sent Secretary of War Stanton an officer promotion list with Custer as a lieutenant colonel assigned to the 9th Cavalry; his friend Wesley Merritt received the same rank and a 7th Cavalry post. The 9th and 10th Cavalry were "colored" regiments. Custer journeyed to Washington to thank Grant for the promotion but requested a white regiment. He made the same plea to Stanton and even President Johnson.

The president was willing to transfer Custer if first he agreed to wield his fame to help bolster the northern Democratic Party by attending a National Union convention in Philadelphia and then join him on a speaking tour of the northern states. When Custer asked his wife what she thought, Libbie warned him that he risked destroying his army career if he became too partisan at too young an age. With the same argument she also advised him to turn down an offer to run as a Democrat for a Michigan congressional seat. Custer spurned the congressional run but did attend the convention and Johnson's campaign. That provoked editorials critical of him in numerous Republican newspapers, most notably the *Washington Chronicle* and *Chicago Tribune*. But Custer got what he wanted. Johnson transferred him to the 7th Cavalry being formed at Fort Riley, Kansas. Custer needed to wrap up his affairs elsewhere before he reported for duty.[458]

Custer and Libbie arrived at Fort Riley on October 16, 1866. Accompanying them were their servant Eliza Brown and Anna Darrah, a pretty, unmarried young woman and friend of Libbie's from Monroe. Custer no sooner arrived than, on November 9, he left to spend a month in Washington. He was in the capital ostensibly to take the promotion board's oral exam for becoming lieutenant colonel. He passed easily enough and lingered before finally returning to Fort Riley on December 16. He spent much of his free time in the capital with the actress Adelaide Riston.

Like any cavalry regiment, the 7th ideally should have numbered 1,200 men in twelve companies.[459] For most of its history, the 7th varied between 900 and

1,000 men. Recruiters continually struggled to fill the ranks of the one in four men who annually deserted and the far fewer killed by disease or battle. The officers included the colonel and lieutenant colonel, three majors, and each company's captain, first lieutenant, and second lieutenant. Each major led a four-company battalion. Officially, Colonel Andrew Smith was the 7th's commander but on February 27, 1867, he was assigned to head the District of the Upper Arkansas, leaving Custer its effective commander. Stanton not only granted Custer's request that his brother Tom be transferred to his regiment, he promoted him to first lieutenant. Other key officers serving with Custer during this time included Major Joel Elliott; Captains Louis Hamilton, Myles Keogh, Robert West, and Frederick Benteen; and First Lieutenant Thomas Weir. Custer's officers would soon split sharply over whether they liked or hated him, with West and Benteen his worst enemies within the regiment.

Fort Riley was established in 1853 on the north bank just below where the Republican and Smokey Hill Rivers form the Kansas River. Fort Leavenworth is 116 miles east. Directly west along the Smokey Hill River were Forts Harker, Hays, and Wallace leading to Denver, and farther south along the Arkansas River were Forts Zarah, Larned, Dodge, and Lyon protecting that stretch of the Santa Fe Trail. During peacetime, 7th Cavalry companies garrisoned those posts usually with an infantry company; only during Indian campaigns did most 7th Cavalry companies reunite. When the Custers arrived, the Kansas Pacific Railroad had reached Fort Riley and workers daily extended it farther west. That railroad was being built alongside a stagecoach route with stations around fifteen miles apart. Farms and ranches dotted the Kansas River valley and were spreading up the Smokey Hill River and its tributaries.

Potentially threatening those spreading forts, settlements, and trails were the Cheyenne and Arapaho, mostly between the Smokey Hill and Arkansas Rivers, the Comanche and Kiowas southward, and the Sioux northward.[460] Those "wild" Indian bands and the buffalo herds that sustained them avoided the mushrooming settlements in eastern Nebraska and Kansas, and the reservations of "civilized" tribes in eastern Oklahoma. Those bands also sidestepped the high plains along the Rocky Mountains since overhunting had decimated the buffalo there. Large herds still wandered the Central Plains.

The Cheyenne had the largest population with around 3,500 people, including around 850 warriors, spread among eight bands. Of their chiefs, none was more genuinely committed to peace than Black Kettle and his band, and none was more fiercely determined to resist the invaders than Roman Nose and his Dog Soldier band.[461] Black Kettle's pledge was paradoxical, poignant, and ironic; Colorado soldiers had slaughtered more than a hundred of his people at Sand Creek on November 29, 1864, despite his well-known declaration and the American flag flying above his lodge.[462]

From his St. Louis headquarters, General Sherman commanded the Department of the Missouri that encompassed most of the central and northern plains. On March 14, 1867, he authorized General Winfield Hancock to lead an expedition that was ostensibly peaceful and diplomatic. Hancock's orders were "to go among the Cheyennes, Arapahos, and Kiowas…and notify them that if they want war they can have it now; but if they decline the offer, then impress on them that they must stop their insolence and threats."[463]

Hancock's expedition marched from Fort Riley on March 27, 1867. The 1,400 troops included eight companies of the 7th Cavalry, seven companies of the 37th Infantry, a 4th Artillery battery, and several score supply wagons, each pulled by six mules. Among the half dozen civilian scouts was James Butler "Wild Bill" Hickok. Edward Wynkoop and Jesse Leavenworth were the region's Indian agents who would translate during councils and implement any government promises.

The troops mostly came from society's dregs, men so unenterprising and unskilled that they were content to pocket $13 a month as soldiers. Many were thieves or had committed an array of other crimes. About half were foreign-born and many spoke broken English. At least they looked like soldiers when the campaign began. They wore dark blue wool jackets, white shirts, sky-blue trousers reinforced with white canvas in the seat and upper thighs, black leather boots, a black or gray broad-brimmed hat, and in winter greatcoats and fur hats. They would depend on hot lead rather than cold steel in any fight. The sabers were for parades at the fort and left behind as encumbrances when the regiment was on campaign. They were armed with seven-shot .52 caliber Spencer carbines and .44 caliber Colt or Remington percussion cap revolvers.

To Custer's credit, after reaching the plains he swiftly developed a sophisticated understanding of how to treat and fight Indians. He proved to be naturally adept at Indian diplomacy and even became versed in sign language. Libbie witnessed several of her husband's councils with the tribes: "The general's patience with Indians always surprised me. He was of such an active temperament and dispatched his own work so rapidly that I have wondered how he contained himself waiting an hour or more for them to get to the object of their visit. They took their place according to rank in a semicircle around the general. The pipe was filled and a match lighted…. It seemed to us that it went back and forth an endless number of times."[464]

Custer's views of Indians were complex. On one hand he insisted that: "It is to be regretted that the character of the Indian as described in Cooper's interesting novels is not the true one…. Stripped of the beautiful romance…the Indian forfeits his claim to the appellation of the noble red man. We see him as he is, and, so far as all knowledge goes, as he ever has been, a savage in every sense of the word." Virtually anyone who buried butchered murder victims or rescued women repeatedly gang-raped by Indian warriors shared the same harsh conclusion. Yet he found in most Indians much to admire as well as fear and scorn. Indeed he enjoyed having them around: "It is pleasant at all times…to have a village of peaceable Indians locate their lodges near our frontier posts.… The daily visits of the Indians, from the most venerable chief to the strapped papoose, their rude interchange of civilities, their barterings, races, dances, legends, strange customs, and fantastic ceremonies, all combine to render them agreeable as friendly neighbors."[465]

Custer warned his superiors "against an Indian war, depicting as strongly as I could the serious results that would follow…putting a stop to [wagon] trains on the Overland route, interfering with the work on the Pacific Railroad, all of which would be a national calamity. I regard the recent outrages as the work of small groups of irresponsible young men eager for war. The Indians stampeded…by fear of our forces." Nonetheless, he promised, "should a war be waged, none would be more determined than I to make it a war of extermination."[466]

Hancock would ignore Custer's warning and instead provoke a war that spread across the Central Plains mostly between the Platte and Red Rivers. Within that vast region, meandering eastward were the Republican, Solomon, Smoky Hill, Arkansas, Cimarron, North Canadian, South Canadian, and Washita Rivers. Scattered across that region, a dozen or so hostile bands, mostly Cheyenne, either singly or collectively followed buffalo herds, sidestepped army columns, and launched distant raids. The war began in April 1867 and persisted for several years.[467]

The expedition reached Fort Larned on April 7. Hancock had expected to convene an Indian council at Fort Larned and was angry that no bands had appeared. Scouts brought word that a large village of mostly Cheyenne but also Arapaho, Kiowa, Brule Sioux, and Oglala Sioux was a couple of score miles up Pawnee Fork which flows past Fort Larned and into the Arkansas River eight miles away. A snowstorm delayed Hancock's march to that village. Then, on April 12, a dozen chiefs arrived for a council and insisted that they were committed to peace. Hancock refused to accept their promise and informed them that he would lead his army to camp beside their village. The chiefs angrily rode away and the next morning Hancock led his army after them.

An extraordinary sight stretched before the bluecoats on April 14. Custer marveled at around several hundred mounted warriors "bedecked in their brightest colors, their heads crowned with the brilliant war-bonnet, their lances bearing the crimson pennant, bows strung, and quivers full of barbed arrows. In addition… each one was supplied with either a breech-loading rifle or revolver.… Neither side seemed to comprehend the object or intentions of the other; each was waiting for the other to deliver the first blow."[468]

Hancock halted his column, deployed his troops into battle line, and sent an interpreter forward to invite the chiefs to talk. Once they gathered he ordered the chiefs either to fight or submit. The chiefs said they wanted peace but demanded that the bluecoats stay away from their village. When Hancock asked why, Roman Nose angrily explained that the people feared another Sand Creek massacre. Hancock informed them that he intended to advance his men to camp beside their village to ensure their good behavior. The chiefs and their warriors galloped back to their village. The soldiers followed until they approached within a quarter mile. The warriors spread before their village while women and children fled in the opposite direction. Hancock ordered his men to halt and camp for the night.

That night Hancock ordered Custer to surround the village with his men and determine if anyone was still there. That order was stunningly absurd. Fulfilling it would either provoke a night battle with the likely slaughter of those who remained along with numerous deaths and wounds among the 7th Cavalry from "friendly fire," or was a fruitless exercise if they had all fled. Custer and his men discovered the village deserted except for an old woman and child. Hancock had a choice. He could treat the Indian flight as a very rational act of fear that he would try to overcome with conciliatory gestures. Or he could interpret that as an act of war and the abandoned village as that war's first spoils. He chose the latter course even though those Indians had committed no violent act. He ordered Custer to have his men destroy the village and pursue the former inhabitants. The Indians naturally viewed the army's destruction of their village as a vicious act of war. In retaliation they raided stagecoach stations and small groups of civilians and soldiers across the central plains.

Even then Custer opposed Hancock's war: "Wo be unto these Indians, if I ever overtake them! The chances are, however, that I shall not see any of them, it being next to impossible to overtake them.... I regard the outrages that have been committed lately as not the work of a tribe, but of small and irresponsible parties of young men, who are eager for war.... My opinion is that we are not yet justified in declaring war."[469] Custer was prescient. He and his men never found their prey. The Indians dispersed in small groups after agreeing where they would eventually reunite after losing their pursuers. On April 19, the 7th Cavalry rode into Fort Hays to rest and replenish supplies.

Custer's opposition to the war and failure to find any Indians only partly fueled his frustrations. He was increasingly torn between his military and marital duties. Libbie constantly filled his mind with desires and worries. Most gnawing was his guilty conscience. He hurt her deeply after she learned of some of his previous

dalliances and he agonized that she might have discovered more. He tried to reassure her: "You know I promised never to give you fresh cause for regret by attentions paid to other girls." He implored her to "read my innermost heart" and
understand that "I never thought of a single girl to whom I ever paid the slightest
attention with any feeling but that of supreme indifference, and without wishing
to see them, have cared nothing if I never met either of them again."[470] He worried
that her love for him may have diminished and she might be enticed into some
other manly officer's arms. Finally, the 38th Colored Infantry recently reached
Fort Riley and he feared for the safety of Libbie and Anna as pretty white women
with only her black cook as company. He urged her to come west either to Fort
Hays or Fort Wallace, assuring her that "at either place you will be safe and comfortable." She should "come as soon as you can.... I did not marry you for you to
live in one house, me in another. One bed shall accommodate us both." He asked
her to recall "how eager I was to have you for my little wife? I was not as impatient
then as I am now. I almost feel tempted to desert and fly to you."[471] He would soon
succumb to that temptation with disastrous results for his career.

Custer vented his frustrations on his officers and troops by inflicting harsh
punishments for the slightest infractions. In doing so, as in Alexandria and Hempstead, he exacerbated rather than alleviated a vicious cycle of worsening morale,
indiscipline, and desertion. In all, 156 of his troops fled from April 19 to July 13,
1867, apparently weighing the danger of being killed by Indians as the lesser evil
to serving under his tyranny.[472] When Captain Albert Barnitz protested Custer's
harsh measures, Custer had him arrested for insubordination. Barnitz expressed
the prevailing bitterness among most men of the 7th toward their lieutenant colonel: "Custer is very injudicious in his administration and spared no effort to render
himself generally obnoxious. I have utterly lost all the little confidence I ever had
in his ability as an officer—and all admiration for his character as a man, and to
speak the plain truth I am thoroughly disgusted with him. He is the most complete
picture of a petty tyrant I have ever seen. You would be filled with utter amazement if I were to give you a few instances of his cruelty to the men, and discourtesy
to the officers."[473]

In persecuting Barnitz, Custer engaged in a classic case of projecting his own
vilest traits on a hated scapegoat. It was Custer who had disobeyed his superior
officer. Custer ignored Colonel Smith's order on May 3 to march north to Fort
McPherson on the Platte River and then south to Fort Wallace, which would serve
as his center of operations. He was determined not to leave Fort Hays without seeing his wife, and was ecstatic when she arrived on May 17. Weeks earlier he had
shared some of his marital concerns with Sherman, who kindly escorted Libbie,
Anna, and Eliza to Fort Harker, and from there Smith brought them to Fort Hays.

There was no available housing, so Custer had a large tent erected for the ladies near Big Creek.

Custer and his troops headed north on June 1 and 229 miles later reached Fort McPherson on June 10. Along the way they only once glimpsed Indians, a hundred warriors near the Republican River, but their quarry swiftly disappeared. To his surprise, Custer found Oglala Sioux Chief Pawnee Killer and his band at Fort McPherson. Although Pawnee Killer promised Custer that he intended to keep his band at peace, he did not keep his word. After replenishing his supplies, Custer led his men back south to the Republican River's headwaters. On June 24, a raid led by Pawnee Killer failed to stampede the horses but did wound a sentry. Custer led his men in pursuit but as they neared the war party he halted his column and sent an interpreter forward to give signs for a parley. Pawnee Killer galloped away with his warriors. Custer and his men resumed their pursuit but the trail disappeared as the Indians split off in different directions. After Custer and his weary men rested, they headed back toward camp. There, Custer found that Pawnee Killer had again outwitted him by doubling back with his warriors to raid the camp.

Custer led his men to Fort Wallace. Along the way, thirty-four deserted from July 7 to 9. He ordered Major Elliott to lead a company to pursue and shoot the deserters. They caught up to five and opened fire, wounding three of them. The deserters were brought back to camp in a wagon. Custer ordered no medical care given the wounded, one of whom died. Two days later Custer and his men encountered a grisly sight—the naked, mutilated bodies of Captain Lyman Kidder and eleven of his men. Custer had them hastily buried and then pushed on to Fort Wallace where he hoped Libbie awaited him.

When Custer reached Fort Wallace on July 13, he found not Libbie but disturbing rumors about her that filled him with dread and jealousy. Lieutenant Thomas Weir had been not just Libbie's escort for the last six weeks but perhaps something much more. On June 5, Libbie and Weir nearly died together during their evening stroll when a sentry feared they were Indians and fired at them. Then during the night of June 7, a deluge flooded Fort Hays and nearly carried Libbie away. Colonel Smith and an escort conveyed the ladies to Fort Harker.

The rumors of infidelity drove Custer near crazy to be with Libbie. He assigned seventy-five of his best men to escort him the 150 miles from Fort Wallace to Fort Hays through country where hostile war parties likely lurked. He and his men left early on the morning of July 16 and arrived late on July 18. Along the way a man deserted. Custer sent six men in pursuit. Indians ambushed them, killing two while the others fled. Custer ignored his men's pleas to turn back and bury their dead comrades. When they reached Fort Hays, the men and their horses were exhausted from the grueling daily fifty-mile pace. Nonetheless, twenty men deserted that night. Custer fumed but, instead of pursuing them, headed to Fort Harker in an ambulance with half a dozen men as an escort. Along the way, a west-bound wagon train carried an order for him to stay at Fort Wallace and patrol the plains between the Arkansas and Platte Rivers. He ignored it. To his rage, Libbie was not at Fort Harker, having returned to Fort Riley, but Weir was. Custer tack-led and roughed him up until he "begged for his life" and swore he was nothing but a gentleman toward Libbie.[474] Custer took the first train to Fort Riley, where he finally had his wife firmly back in his arms. They returned to Fort Harker, where, on July 21, Smith had Custer arrested on multiple charges and sent to Fort Leavenworth to stand trial.

Custer's court martial lasted from September 15 to October 11, 1867.[475] Captain Charles Parsons served as his counsel. Ten officers would call witnesses, cross-examine them, and then judge him. Custer protested that among the court mem-bers was Colonel John Davidson, who was also a witness. The court sustained his objection and Davidson stepped down. That was Custer's only victory. The very serious charges against him spanned the time from June 1 to July 19, 1867, and included being absent without leave, disobeying orders, pursuing private business, seizing and using public property for personal gain, and conduct prejudicial to good order and discipline. Specifically, first, he abandoned two of his men who were killed by Indians; second, he ordered deserters shot dead without trial; third, he refused to administer medical aid to three wounded deserters, of whom one died; and, fourth, he abandoned his command at Fort Wallace and detached seventy-five of his troops to escort him east to be with his wife. Custer pleaded innocent to all these charges and wrote an 8,000-word defense.

The court unanimously found Custer guilty on all charges but without criminal intent or wrongdoing and sentenced him to a year's suspension from duty without pay, rank, and command. Custer was unrepentant. He insisted on his innocence and accused Hancock of scapegoating him to mask the unnecessary war that he had sparked by having the deserted Indian village burned. His enemies and many legal experts condemned the court's decision as a slap on the wrist for such serious crimes topped by murder and called for his prosecution by a civilian court.

Custer was not out of the legal woods yet. His trial intersected with national politics in which liberals and conservatives battled over the fate of black Ameri-cans. In early 1867, Congress overrode Johnson's vetoes of four bills—the Suffrage Act, for black men to vote in Washington; two Reconstruction Acts that strength-ened the federal government's powers to reform the former rebel states, and the Tenure of Office Act, which required Senate approval before a president could fire anyone that the Senate had previously approved for that office. Radical Republicans devised the Tenure of Office Act to prevent Johnson from firing Secretary of War Stanton, who backed their civil rights and reconstruction agenda. In August 1867, Johnson fired Stanton when Congress was in recess and replaced him with Grant. Politically, that act worsened Johnson's position. Like Stanton, Grant mostly supported the Radical Republicans and now Johnson had thrown down the gauntlet to Congress. Radical Republicans would soon begin an impeachment process against Johnson.

The switch from Stanton to Grant also affected Custer, who the former admired and the latter disliked. Among a secretary of war's duties is to review court martial decisions. After carefully studying Custer's case, Grant reached two conclusions: Custer should not appear on murder charges before a civilian court, but the military court's ruling was too lenient. He implied that Custer's permanent rather than temporary dismissal from the army would have been appropriate.

Having lost his legal case, Custer appealed to the court of public opinion. He wrote three articles for the magazine *Turf, Field, and Farm*, in which he defended his actions and attacked those of Hancock and other officers during the recent Indian war, and the court martial judges who presided over his case. Although the articles appeared under the pseudonym Nomad, everyone knew that Custer was the author.[476] He also wrote a letter to the *Sandusky Register* defending himself under his real name.

That enraged Custer's enemies. Captain West, Custer's most zealous critic within the 7th Cavalry, filed murder charges against him in a civilian court. On January 3, 1868, two lawmen arrested Custer as he drove a buggy with Libbie and some friends into the town adjacent to Fort Leavenworth. After paying bail, Custer walked free. During a preliminary hearing on January 18, Custer's lawyer, William Cooke, talked Judge Moses Adams into dismissing the case.

Joseph Holt was the War Department's Judge Advocate General. In February 1868, he wrote Grant that Custer had not been punished severely enough: "Genl. Custer in the manner of his thus appealing from his sentence to the public, in his misrepresentations in regard to the evidence in his case, in his attacks upon the impartiality and justice of the members of the court, in his criticisms of the course pursued by Genl. Hancock, and in the language with which he assails one of the officers who preferred charges against him, must be deemed to have been at least guilty of conduct to the prejudice of good order and military discipline."[477]

Grant briefly lost the authority to act on Custer's case. On January 13, 1868, Congress reinstated Stanton as Secretary of War and Grant as commanding general. On February 21, Johnson reacted by again firing Stanton and reinstating Grant as

Secretary of War. The House of Representatives reacted three days later by issuing articles of impeachment against Johnson. The trial opened in the Senate on March 4 and concluded on May 15 with Johnson's acquittal by one vote shy of the two-thirds needed to convict.

Meanwhile, Sheridan defended his deeply esteemed comrade in arms and friend, writing Grant: "Custer has done many things which I do not approve of—especially the letter he wrote and had published, reflecting on the court which tried him—but I would be exceedingly gratified if the General could have him pardoned.... He feels very sensibly his punishment, and I think would, if he were reinstated, make a better officer than if the sentence were carried out to its full extent. He held high command during the Rebellion and had difficulty adapting himself to his altered position. There was no one with me whom I more highly appreciated than General Custer. He never failed me, and if his late misdeeds could be forgotten…it would be…a benefit to the service."[478] In the end, Grant let his original decision stand.

The legal cloud may have dispersed from Custer, but his reputation was tarnished, and he had no immediate way of redeeming himself through war. In June 1868, the Custers returned to Monroe, Michigan, where he explored a possible political career.

Meanwhile, the Indian war on the central plains sputtered to a lull. Their chiefs claimed to want peace, but all their warriors needed to replenish their ammunition. Indian agents arranged a peace council at Medicine Lodge Creek in October 1867. The peace commission included Generals William Sherman, Alfred Terry, and William Harney; civilians Samuel Tappan and John Sanborn; and Senator John Henderson of Missouri, all presided over by Indian Commissioner Nathaniel Taylor. Several dozen chiefs represented the Southern Cheyenne, Arapaho, Comanche, and Kiowa. Under the Medicine Lodge Treaty of October 21 with the Comanche and Kiowa, and of October 28 with the Cheyenne and Arapaho, Washington granted those tribes reservations in the central plains and promised annual annuities that provided them food, blankets, ammunition, guns, and other necessities.

Another Great Plains Indian war ended half a year later. Red Cloud was the most prominent war chief among the Oglala, Brule, Miniconjou Lakota Sioux bands, Yankton Nakota Sioux, and Arapaho that from June 1866 to April 1868 fought the army to a standstill along the Bozeman Trail that linked Fort Laramie with Bozeman, the gateway to goldfields in what is now southwestern Montana.

Under the Fort Laramie Treaty, signed on April 29, 1868, Washington essentially admitted defeat and agreed to abandon the Bozeman Trail and withdraw the
troops from the forts defending it, while henceforth the lands west of the Missouri
River including the Black Hills and Powder River country would be reserved for
the Sioux peoples.[479]

Although the Fort Laramie Treaty's peace would last until 1876, the Medicine
Lodge Treaty's peace soon fell apart and as usual Washington was to blame. In
July 1868, Congress refused to appropriate the annuities promised by the Medicine Lodge Treaty. Sherman sympathized with the Indians, who faced a terrible
dilemma: "We kill them if they attempt to hunt, and if they keep within the Reservation they starve."[480]

The Cheyenne, Arapaho, and Kiowa gathered in council with Sheridan on
Pawnee Fork near Fort Larned to protest the bad faith of the Americans and their
own starving conditions. Sheridan issued them rations from army stores but that
was too little too late. Within days after the council broke up, several hundred
Cheyenne Dog Soldiers and their families left the reservation and split into separate bands led by Roman Nose and Tall Bull. War parties murdered 110 people
and gang-raped thirteen women in settlements along the Solomon and Saline River valleys, ran off sixty-five cattle from Fort Wallace, killed two army scouts, and
attacked stagecoaches and stations on the Kansas trails. Sheridan ordered two
simultaneous campaigns against those bands.

Captain George Forsyth and fifty civilian scouts headed northwest from Fort
Hays on August 29, and eighteen days later reached the Republican River's headwaters. Roman Nose and his warriors surrounded and repeatedly attacked the
scouts at Beecher Island from September 17 to 25. Colonel Benjamin Grierson's
10th Cavalry rescued them as they expended the last of their food and ammunition. The Beecher Island siege was a decisive army victory because Roman Nose
was among the score or so Indian dead.[481]

General Alfred Sully, the Upper Arkansas District commander, led the 7th
Cavalry from Fort Dodge on September 7, 1868, to search for hostile Indian
bands.[482] The column soon encountered Indians. Small war parties shadowed the
soldiers, skirmishing with them during the day and trying to stampede their horses
at night. But during an eleven-day ride, the soldiers found not a trace of a passing
village with telltale travois and pony herd tracks. They crossed a large war party
trail once, but Sully refused to follow it, citing dwindling supplies and a need to
return to Fort Dodge to replenish them. Sully's brief, failed excursion prompted
Sheridan to fire off an urgent appeal to War Secretary Grant.

A burst of bright sunshine dissipated Custer's prolonged professional fog when a telegram arrived on September 24, 1868. From Fort Hays, Sheridan wrote: "Gen Sherman, Sully, and myself and nearly all of the officers of your regiment have asked for you, and I hope the application will be successful. Can you come at once? Eleven companies of your regiment will move about the first of October against the hostile Indians from Medicine Lodge Creek toward the Wichita Mountains." The following day Custer read this message from the War Department: "The remainder of your sentence has been remitted by the Secretary of War. Report in person without delay [to] General Sheridan for duty."[483]

It was a dream come true. Custer eagerly headed west.

CHAPTER 14

High Plains

*"They were eager for revenge and could not comprehend my
conduct. They disapproved and criticized it. I paid no heed,
but followed the dictates of my own judgment.... And now my
most bitter enemies cannot say that I am either blood-thirsty or
possessed of an unworthy ambition."*
— GEORGE CUSTER

*"I was in peril from death or capture by the savages, and liable to
be killed by my own friends to prevent my capture."*
— LIBBIE CUSTER

WO DEVOTED FRIENDS and brothers in arms, Lieutenant Colonel George Custer and General Philip Sheridan, gleefully reunited at Fort Hays on October 4. Sheridan proudly gave his protégée what every aggressive, dynamic subordinate leader desires: "I rely upon you in everything and shall send you on this expedition without giving you any orders, leaving you to act entirely upon your judgment." As for how to conduct the campaign, Sheridan called for total war: "These Indians require to be soundly whipped and the ringleaders in the present trouble hung, their ponies killed, and such destruction of their property as will make them very poor."[484] To that, overall commander General William Sherman added: "if it results in the utter annihilation of these Indians, it is but the result of what they have been warned against again and again."[485] Sheridan's campaign plan involved three columns converging on the most likely refuge of the hostile tribes in the Washita River valley, with advances by varying numbers of companies from Custer's 7th Cavalry, the 3rd Infantry, and the 19th Kansas Volunteer Cavalry from Fort Dodge; Major Eugene Carr's 5th and 10th Cavalry from Fort Lyon; and Major Andrew Evans' 3rd Cavalry and 37th Infantry from Fort Bascom.

Custer rejoined the 7th Cavalry on October 10. The 7th Cavalry was south of Fort Dodge at a site Custer named Camp Forsyth after his friend who, with

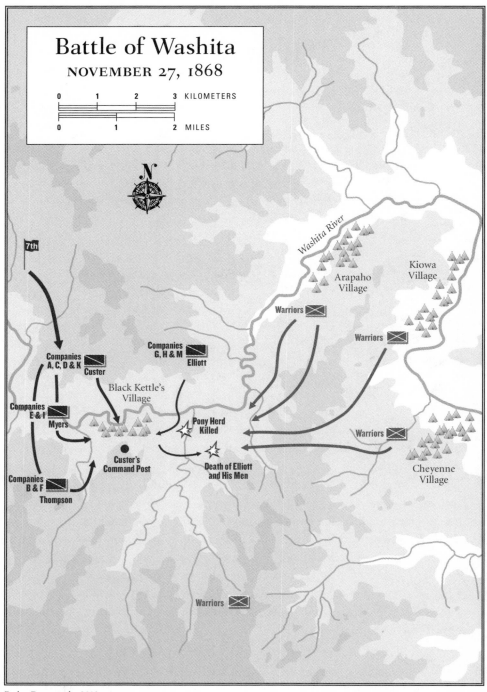

Petho Cartography 2019

most of his scouts, had survived the Beecher Island fight. He was no sooner with his men than he provoked his latest round of controversy and resentment among most of them. He ordered that each company should have the same color horses. That forced many men to trade horses that they were familiar with and fond of for new ones. Thus, did he sacrifice a portion of his regiment's morale on the altar of uniformity and style. He justified his decision on tactical grounds. In battle he could better identify a distant company if its horses looked the same. "Coloring the horses" was not his only indulgence. Accompanying him were three staghounds and two greyhounds. He justified his dogs on practical grounds as hunting aids that better let him supply his headquarter staff with meat. For scouts, he hired twelve Osage warriors and the frontiersmen Ben Clark; Jack Corbin; Ralph Romero, better known as Romeo; and Moses Milner, better known as California Joe. He originally wanted California Joe to be his head scout, but his addiction to alcohol led to his replacement by Clark. Romeo turned out to be the most effective scout, given his fluency in Cheyenne. Custer formed the forty best shots among his troops into a company of sharpshooters led by Lieutenant William Cooke.

Indian atrocities so incensed Kansas Governor Samuel Crawford that he resigned to form and lead the 19th Kansas Volunteer Cavalry. He was supposed to accompany Custer but had not yet arrived. Winter began early that year with the first snowstorm in October. Worried that blizzards would bury the plains, Sheridan ordered Custer on November 12, to march ninety miles south of Fort Dodge and establish a fort on the North Canadian River. There was a catch to Custer's freedom of action. Initially, he was under the command of General Alfred Sully, who headed the Upper Arkansas District and insisted on joining him and his 7th Cavalry. Along the way they crossed an Indian war party trail. Sully rebuffed Custer's plea to follow those warriors to their band. On November 18, they reached the North Canadian River's headwaters and established Camp Supply.[486] There, Custer pulled rank on Sully, insisting that his brevet rank was senior, and that Sully was no longer in his district. Sully angrily refused to yield. Sheridan resolved that dispute in Custer's favor after he and his escort reached Camp Supply on November 21. He ordered Sully to return to his headquarters at Fort Harker.

Sheridan was determined to inflict a severe blow against the Cheyenne and Arapaho. He had the Indian agent of their Fort Cobb reservation, Colonel William Hazen, refuse to let any bands return until they first surrendered unconditionally to Sheridan. On November 20, Hazen ordered Black Kettle's band to return to the open plains, ignoring the chief's pleas that he embraced peace and wanted to save his people from another massacre like what they had suffered at Sand Creek, just three years earlier.

Custer led his 7th Cavalry south in a blizzard on November 23.[487] Three days later, they reached the Washita River and followed it downstream. Scouts brought word of a fresh war party trail ahead. Custer detached a company to guard the supply wagons and led the rest of the regiment forward, with strict orders for silence. They plodded through knee-deep snow into the night. After scouts reported a village just ahead across the river, Custer split his command into four parts, with each to attack from a different direction at dawn the next morning, November 27. The men would fight on foot, while one of four men from each company guarded the horses in the rear. Elliott and three companies would swing wide to the left and circle around the village to cut off any retreat down the valley. Captains Edward Myers and William Thompson would each lead two companies across the river to hit the village's respective west and south sides. Custer would stay in place with Captains Louis Hamilton and Robert West, each with two companies, the sharpshooters, and the band. Custer would signal the attack by having the band play "Garryowen."

In the village was Black Kettle's Cheyenne band of around 250 men, women, and children. The war party had reached and stayed at his village as the first of four villages along an oxbow of the river. Nearly equidistant from Black Kettle's villages were Cheyenne, Arapaho, and Kiowa bands. Ironically, the 7th Cavalry was about to attack the one Indian band in the southern plains whose chief was most dedicated to peace. Nonetheless, Black Kettle had given shelter to the war party for the night.

Custer and his men had no idea what band was before them nor that three other bands were camped further down the valley. Should all warriors from all four bands swarm against them, they would be severely outnumbered, probably surrounded, and possibly overwhelmed. As the troops shivered away the long moonless night, a brilliant white light appeared in the southeastern sky and rose steadily. At first mystified, Custer soon realized that it was the planet Venus that preceded the sun by an hour or so. The Indians called it Morning Star. Custer would adopt that as his Indian name.

As the horizon lightened, Custer ordered the band to play "Garryowen." The air was so cold that the brass instruments produced little sound other than loud screeches as the musicians blew into them. A rifle shot and war cries erupted from the village. Custer shouted for his men to charge and they surged forward, firing at the Indians spilling frantically from the tepees. Warriors screamed war cries and fired back. Old men, children, and women, often cradling babies, dashed for gaps between the advancing bluecoats.

The fighting did not last long. The only soldier killed during the assault was Captain Louis Hamilton, Alexander Hamilton's grandson, while fourteen troops were wounded. As for Cheyenne losses, the official count was 103 dead warriors. Scout Ben Clark later admitted that the soldiers had killed around 150 people, roughly half men and half women and children. Black Kettle and his wife were among the dead, shot down as they tried to wade the river. Custer explained why so many women and children were killed with the men: "it is impossible at all times to discriminate, particularly when, in a hand-to-hand conflict such as the one the troops were then engaged the squaws are as dangerous…as the warriors, while Indian boys between ten and fifteen years of age were found as expert and determined in the use of the pistol and bow and arrow as the older warriors."[488]

The spoils revealed what a typical plains Indian village needed to sustain itself. They included 53 captured women and children, 52 lodges, 875 horses, 241 saddles, 573 buffalo robes, 390 buffalo skins for lodges, 100 untanned robes, 210 axes, 140 hatchets, 35 revolvers, 47 rifles, 535 pounds of power, 1,050 pounds of lead, 4,000 arrows, 12 shields, 75 spears, 90 bullet molds, 35 bows and quivers, 300 pounds of bullets, 775 lariats, 940 buckskin saddlebags, 470 blankets, 93 coats, 700 pounds of tobacco, and "all the winter supply of dried buffalo meat, all the meal, flour, and other provisions."[489] Custer ordered the lodges and the other property burned or taken as appropriate, and the horses shot.

Scouts reported other villages down the valley and more warriors massing just beyond rifle shot. A roll call revealed that Elliott and eighteen men were missing. Custer reasoned that if Elliott and his men were still alive, they would catch up; if not, then searching for them would endanger more lives. He ordered the 7th to assemble and march toward the other Indian villages. That prompted most of the lurking warriors to withdraw to defend their respective peoples. After dark, he about-faced his men toward the supply train. He explained the strategy behind these maneuvers: "To guide my command safely out of the difficulties which seemed just then to besot them I again had recourse to that maxim in war which teaches a commander to do that which his enemy neither expects nor desires him to do."[490]

The 7th Cavalry reached Sheridan's command at Camp Supply on December 2. After replenishing supplies, Custer led his regiment out again, this time accompanied by Sheridan along with the 19th Kansas Cavalry, which had arrived on November 28. They advanced down the Washita, examined Black Kettle's burned-out village and the corpses gnawed by wolves and crows. A mile beyond they found Elliott and his eighteen men, stripped and mutilated in a rough circle where they had died fighting against overwhelming numbers of warriors. Not far from there they found a captive white woman and a child that the Cheyenne had murdered as they fled their village.

The expedition marched down the Washita valley to Fort Cobb, arriving on

December 18. Colonel Hazen, Fort Cobb's commander, explained to Sheridan that the Kiowa band was a few days away and chiefs Satanta, Little Wolf, and Black Eagle had sent word that they wanted peace. What followed were two weeks of long-distance negotiations conducted by couriers before direct talks took place on January 1, 1869. The council concluded with the Kiowa chiefs promising to keep their people on a reservation in return for regular issues of food and other necessities from the government.

Meanwhile, the two other expeditions under Carr and Evans searched the plains. Carr and his men returned to Fort Lyon without finding a village. On December 25, Evans and his men attacked and routed Comanche Chief Arrow Point and his people from their village at Soldier Spring on the Red River's North Fork. The Comanche warriors rallied, bolstered by Kiowa warriors from Chief Woman Heart's nearby village, and charged. The bluecoats repelled the attack. Arrow Point was among the score of Indian killed; one soldier died. Evans had the village burned and then led his troops back toward Fort Bascom.

Custer led the 7th in pursuit of the other hostile bands on January 6, 1869. Within a few weeks he was able to entice a Cheyenne and an Arapaho band to accept the same peace terms as the Kiowa band, but Tall Bull's Dog Soldier band eluded him. For three months, Custer and his men futilely zigzagged the Texas Panhandle, periodically returning to Fort Cobb or Fort Sill to rest and resupply. Then, on March 25, the Osage scouts reported Tall Bull's village ahead on Sweetwater Creek, which flowed into the Red River. Custer knew that if he ordered an attack, the Indians would murder two white women captives. He sent ahead one of his own captive Cheyenne women with an appeal to Tall Bull for peace talks. Tall Bull sent three chiefs, Dull Knife, Big Head, and Fat Bear, to meet Custer. Tall Bull was wise to stay away. Custer had his men seize the chiefs and sent word to Tall Bull that he would trade them for the women or execute them if the women were harmed. Tall Bull freed the women and promised to return to the reservation. After the three released chiefs reached safety, Tall Bull led his people westward. He gambled that Custer would not pursue since he had the women but was nearly out of supplies. And that is what happened. Custer led his men back to Camp Supply, where they replenished and rested before heading to Fort Hays, arriving on April 18, 1869.

As usual, Custer's campaign provoked his latest batch of controversies. One was his decision to negotiate with Tall Bull rather than attack his village at Sweetwater Creek. He admitted that doing so angered his troops who, "from the highest to lowest, desired bloodshed. They were eager for revenge and could not comprehend my conduct. They disapproved and criticized it. I paid no heed, but followed the dictates of my own judgment…. And now my most bitter enemies cannot say that I am either blood-thirsty or possessed of an unworthy ambition." He was confident that he had cowed into submission the Indians even without destroying their village and slaughtering many of them: "I outmarched them, outwitted them at their own game, proved to them that they were in my power, and could and would have annihilated the entire village of over two hundred lodges but for two reasons. 1st. I desired to obtain the release of the two women held captive by them, which I could not have done had I attacked. 2d. If I had attacked them, those who escaped, and absent portions of the tribe also, would have been on the war path all summer… and now, when I can review the whole matter coolly, my better judgment and my humanity tell me I have acted wisely."[491]

Custer's humanitarian decision to prioritize the lives of those two captive women resulted in the campaign lasting another four months. Whether more people died than otherwise would have if Custer ordered an attack against Tall Bull will never be known. Regardless, he and the 7th would not win the laurels for ending the war.

Major Carr led his 5th cavalry from Fort Lyon on April 26, and, after resupplying at Fort Wallace, headed northeast. They skirmished with Tall Bull's Dog Soldiers at Elephant Rock on May 10 and Spring Creek on May 16, and then pushed on to Fort McPherson. With replenished food and munitions, Carr and the 5th departed on June 9. Over the next month they fought three skirmishes before finally catching up to Tall Bull's village at Summit Springs in Colorado on July 11. During the attack, the cavalry killed Tall Bull and fifty-two of his people and captured seventeen women and children along with 418 horses and mules. Carr had his troops burn the village after looting it. The band's remnants fled to the Northern Cheyenne. For now, no hostile Indian bands remained on the central plains. Custer warned Sheridan that: "Without delicate handling of the Indian question by persons of experience in Indian affairs, we are liable to lose all benefit of our last winter's campaign and be plunged into another war with the southern tribes. I think this can be avoided."[492]

Custer's own restraint before Tall Bull's village partly reflected a reaction against the carnage that he had ordered at the Washita and who suffered it. He had opposed the war and was disturbed to learn that the 7th Cavalry had completed the destruction of Black Kettle and his people at the Washita that began at Sand Creek three years earlier. He was hardly alone in his misgivings. Journalists then and historians since have debated two key decisions that he made, one before and the other after the assault.

The first was whether the 7th Cavalry's attack on Black Kettle's village was a battle or a massacre. What happened had elements of both. One must distinguish between Custer's intent and the result. Custer did not know what band he was attacking, only that a war party led to it. Yet the lopsided casualties in which around a hundred and fifty Indian men, women, and children were slaughtered compared to only one soldier killed and fourteen wounded during the assault certainly can be called a massacre. No men were among the 53 Cheyenne prisoners. Custer had obeyed Sheridan's order to kill any men and bring back only women and children. The dead Indian men included both those who stayed off the warpath and those who had killed, robbed, and raped American civilians, and fought American troops. Custer viewed what happened at the Washita as a battle in which, tragically, noncombatants were killed in the crossfire along with combatants. Like virtually all soldiers and most civilians, he insisted that ruthlessly destroying a village saved more lives in the long run by deterring Indian aggression. During the Fort Cobb council, he boasted in a letter to Libbie that "I wish you could see with what awe I am held by the Indians. A sound drubbing...always produces this."[493] With that done, his priority became freeing captives, which he succeeded in doing during the campaign's second phase from January to March 1868.

The second controversy involved Custer's decision not to search for Eliott and his eighteen men. Yet that controversy was unjustified. In this Custer did not face a tough moral dilemma. Indeed, the choice was clear. If he lingered and sent out search parties, warriors from the adjacent villages could gather and attack, resulting in the loss of more of his men and possibly even the entire 7th Cavalry. He and his troops were short of ammunition and were a day's ride from their supply train. There was no sound of firing in the direction where Elliott and his men likely were. Most likely they were already dead. If they were alive they would have already rejoined their comrades in the village.

A third controversy arose but was free of critical life and death decisions. Did romance blossom between Custer and a beautiful teenage Cheyenne woman named Monahsetah? She was the daughter of subchief Little Rock, who became head chief after Black Kettle's death at the Washita. Her father sold her against her will to a warrior who paid the extraordinary sum of eleven ponies for her charms. Her husband was a brute whom she shot after reaching the breaking point. The bullet crippled his body and his pride. In the divorce settlement, he got his ponies back. Unfortunately, she was pregnant and in her last two months when she was captured at the Washita. She gave birth to a boy in January as she accompanied Custer and the 7th Cavalry in the hunt for Tall Bull and his Dog Soldier band.

Most likely they were lovers. Custer certainly had an eye for pretty, sexy, passionate women like Monahsetah.[494] For months she was nearby in a tent with two other Cheyenne women whom Custer used as interpreters and whom she might have used as a babysitter while she was with him. Custer and Monahsetah would not have had to worry about a child of their own as long as she kept nursing her baby. What better way for Custer to pass the long winter nights than with Monahsetah in his arms as they cocooned in buffalo robes in his command tent. Indeed, his troops were well aware of this latest example of "Custer's luck." Captain Benteen observed: Custer "picked out a fine-looking one and had her in his tent every night."[495]

Custer wrote and spoke casually of Monahsetah to Libbie and introduced her to the ladies at Fort Hays. Libbie undoubtedly heard the rumors and suspected as much, given her husband's past flings and roving eye. Yet, in her memoir *Following the Guidon*, she describes Monahsetah without a hint of irony or jealousy. Instead she lauds her for having "made herself of service to the command. She was young and attractive, perfectly contented, and trustful of the white man's promises and the acknowledged belle among…Indian maidens…and as she was the highest in authority among the prisoners, her influence had weight with the rest of her people." She described the Madonna-like young woman: "Monahsetah let the blanket fall from her glossy hair, her white, even teeth gleamed as she smiled, and the expression transfigured her…. She was full of maternal pride." Monahsetah was keenly observant. The Custers showed her a photo of herself with her baby and were "amused and rather surprised at her quick observation, and at the perplexity in her face as she asked with signs why the papoose was on the left arm in the picture while she had held it in her right arm."[496]

Regardless of whether Custer was guilty of his latest infidelity, Libbie's faithfulness still worried him. He pretended otherwise in a letter written during the campaign: "I know you are in earnest when you say you mean never again give me an uneasy moment. I have the sublimest confidence that you never will."[497] In another letter he castigated Lieutenant Thomas Weir, whom he believed tried or succeeded in seducing his wife: "Weir I reprimanded sharply…. I think he will soon grow ashamed of his childish conduct…. The more I see of him Little One, the more I am surprised that a woman of your perceptive faculties and moral training could have entertained the opinion of him you have, but enough on this subject."[498]

At Fort Hays, Custer and Libbie resumed their life together. One huge advantage that the Custers enjoyed over other couples anywhere, but especially in dreary, hardship posts, was a lack of children to worry about. Although as newlyweds both had wanted children, they quickly came to appreciate being childless, as Custer boasted to Libbie: "I am delighted that my little darling bride is having an opportunity of really seeing…how troublesome and embarrassing babies would be to us. Our pleasure would be continually marred and circumscribed. You will not find in all our travels a married couple possessing and enjoying so many means of pleasure and mutual happiness as you and your boy. Our married life to me has been one unbroken sea of pleasure."[499]

That said, Custer suffered a deep void in his life. He was a genuinely loving man. If he could not shower affection on children, he could do so with pets. He especially adored dogs because of all animals they are the most affectionate. But he avidly collected any stray animals, including "prairie dogs, raccoons, porcupines, wildcats, badgers, young antelopes, buffalo calves, and any number of mongrel dogs."[500] Fortunately, Libbie loved animals too, although she did have a limit: "Our tents were usually a menagerie of pets: the soldiers, knowing General Custer's love for them, brought him everything they could capture. The wolf was the only one of the collection to which I objected. I was afraid of him, and, besides, he kept us, with his nightly howls."[501]

Actually, there was another animal on Libbie's no pet list. Tom Custer relished the company of creatures that even his older brother gingerly sidestepped: "Tom's next most valuable possession was a box of rattlesnakes. He was an expert in catching them. Being very agile and extremely quick, he never failed to bag his game.... The insecure cages were patched up hardtack boxes, and the snakes had to be lifted out to display them." Then one day Tom sadly announced that one of his rattlesnakes had escaped. Libbie was not pleased: "The agonizing thought was forced upon me that at that very moment a snake might be lurking under the low camp-cot, or worse still, wriggling under the blankets on which my trembling toes rested. Then, with skirts gathered about me for a sudden flight, with sudden protruding eyeballs, I shook and gasped as the box-lids were removed, and the great loathsome creatures stretched up to show their length...each one to shake his rattles in rage."[502]

Yet another timeless army pastime was devising pranks to pull on one another. A prank's victim rarely finds it as funny as the perpetrator. Custer's pranks could be cruel. One hot July day in 1870, he, Tom, and other conspirators staged an "Indian attack" to amuse a group of his officers and several of their wives, including Libbie, Annie Yates, and newly arrived Mary Reno. He led them out on the plains for a buffalo hunt after having prearranged for his Indian scouts to approach them. Custer told his group to wait while he and Tom rode to investigate. As Custer and Tom neared the "Indians," guns were pulled, and shots erupted. Libbie screamed, "Autie will be killed!" An Indian dropped from his pony and the others galloped away. The smiles on the faces of those in on the joke revealed that a play had been staged. Lieutenant Colonel Wesley Merritt was neither privy nor amused: "Yes, quit this damned nonsense—don't you see you are frightening the ladies?"[503]

Annie, the wife of Captain George Yates, left us this vivid description of then twenty-nine-year-old Custer: "I should think about 165 pounds—no spare flesh, well knit—strong muscles, lean & lithe. Eyes—A piercing blue; keen, thoughtful, observant & very quick in glancing at any object & sizing it up.... Voice—Pleasant in tone but quick & energetic with sometimes a slight hesitation if words rolled out rapidly.... A nervous forceful manner in speaking.... He was slightly moody at times & sometimes silent for hours—but usually possessed high animal spirits and was very humorous, and very appreciative of that quality in those around him."[504]

Although happy to be reunited with her husband, Libbie did not enjoy her sojourn at Fort Hays or adjacent Hays City: "The town...was a typical Western place. The railroad having but just reached there, the 'roughs,' who fly before civilization, had not taken their departure. There was hardly a building worthy of the name, except the station house. A considerable part of the place was built of rude frames covered with canvas; the shanties were made up of slabs, bits of drift-wood, and logs, and sometimes the roofs were covered with tin that had once been fruit or vegetable cans, now flattened.... The carousing and lawlessness of Hays City were incessant. Pistol shots were heard so often.... The aim of a border ruffian is so accurate that a shot was pretty certain to mean a death, or, at least a serious wound for someone.... It was at Hays City that the graveyard was begun with internments of men who had died violent deaths."[505]

The sheriff then was Wild Bill Hickok, elected in August 1869. A Hays City ordinance forbade guns in town, but some men defied that. On July 17, 1870, Hickok confronted several disorderly 7th Cavalry troops swinging guns, and shot two of them; one recovered. Like most women familiar with him, Libbie had a crush on Hickok: "Physically he was a delight to look upon. Tall, lithe, and free in every motion, he rode and walked as if every muscle was perfection, and the careless wins of his body as he moved, seemed perfectly in keeping with the man, the country, the time in which he lived.... He carried two pistols. He wore top boots, riding breeches, and dark blue flannel shirt, with scarlet set in the front. A loose neck-handkerchief left his fine throat free.... The frank, manly expression of his fearless eyes and his courteous manner gave one a feeling of confidence in his word and in his undaunted courage."[506]

Vigilante groups struggled to supplement the role of lawmen in suppressing the crime that plagued Hays City by submitting captured outlaws to "necktie parties." The trouble was that a lack of wood made it difficult to build a proper gallows. Criminals were put in a wagon and conveyed to the nearest train trestle over a ravine, hanged, and left there as a warning to others. The sight of one such dangling man haunted Libbie. Thereafter "in our hunts and pleasure rides I asked to shun the railroad track, for I never felt sure that we might not come upon a ghastly body swinging from the beams that support the bridge."[507]

Libbie loved escaping that squalid town and fort with long exhilarating horseback rides across the plains with her husband and an escort. At times she felt powerfully drawn to ride forever toward distant horizons in search of something better: "With all our experience, we, officers and all, lived day after day with the delusion that 'the top of the next divide' would reveal us some sight, and wave after wave swept on without discovering anything but the ever-deluding knoll beyond the gentle undulation into which we descended."[508]

Custer used Libbie as a diplomatic adjunct at Fort Hays. By having his wife accompany him, he at once displayed confidence in his mastery over the Indians and his dedication to peace. The Indian women were fascinated by Libbie's beauty, poise, and clothing. Libbie struggled to master her fears: "As the crowd of women and children gathered around me, I almost felt knives penetrating my dress for a deadly stab, so great was my distress." When Custer signed that Libbie was his wife, they asked if she was his only one. That further enhanced Libbie in their eyes: "The squaws came still closer, put their hands on my shoulder, smoothing and caressing me. Others took my hand in their horny old palms, the touch of which moved me to pity, as it revealed the amount and kind of work they had done....I forced a smile of feigned pleasure at all the attentions bestowed upon me, and so hid my tremors and my revulsion."[509] Custer had Libbie sit beside him during his peace council with the chiefs. While she understood that her presence may have softened the diplomacy, "in the presence of those gigantic, fierce, and gloomy chiefs, my quaking began anew."[510]

Libbie's terror to be among the Indians was certainly understandable. She had listened to the horrors that women captured by the Indians had endured, including repeated gang rapes and beatings. That "fate worse than death" prompted an unofficial but universal policy among army officers to shoot women threatened with imminent capture. That possibility magnified Libbie's dread when she was in an Indian war zone: "I was in peril from death or capture by the savages, and liable to be killed by my own friends to prevent my capture.... While I knew that I was defended by strong hands and brave hearts, the thought of the double danger always flashed into my mind when we were in jeopardy."[511]

Contributing to Libbie's discomfort was the worsening disposition of Eliza Brown, the Custer cook and laundress. Eliza was increasingly restless. She complained to Libbie that "you's always got the ginnel, but I hain't got nobody, and there ain't no picnics nor church sociables nor no buryings out her."[512] Eliza not only wanted a husband but also had to endure bleak army life on the plains and life in the Custer brothers' menagerie of wild beasts, including pet rattlesnakes. Libbie admitted that "under these circumstances it was a marvel how she kept her temper at all." Eliza had become one of those servants who morphs into a family member, and an increasingly cranky, domineering one. To assert some semblance of authority, Libbie and Custer endured what they called "black Fridays," in which "we took turns in giving our cook an order, if it was absolutely necessary to give her any. It was very odd to hear a grown person, the head of the house, perhaps say, "'You tackle Eliza this time, I did the last time.'"[513] Yet, finally the Custers reached their limit of tolerance for Eliza's arrogance. Libbie wrote that they "had to send her away as she got on a spree & was very insolent."[514] The Custers found a much more reliable black servant named Mary Adams. Officer wives preferred black women as servants because they stayed much longer than pretty white women who had their pick of the enlisted men and sometimes the officers who courted them.

The tedium of army life at a remote frontier post ate away at most people, especially those spoiled by the stimulating diversity of big cities. Annual desertion rates were as high as one of three enlisted men. Many officers and troops became addicted to alcohol, gambling, or both. Brawls, at times deadly, among the troops or with local civilians erupted over trifles. The post guardhouse was usually filled with troops punished for various offenses. Brothels provided sexual release along with various diseases.

The more confident men tried to entice the handful of married women at those posts. Sexual affairs, however, were tough to conceal in the fish-bowl environment. One's degree of privacy rose with one's rank, with the commanding officer enjoying the most opportunities to be alone with someone else behind closed doors. The trouble was that almost always someone, usually sentinels, observed who entered and left headquarters.

The Custer marriage was near the breaking point by late summer of 1870. Libbie found out about a love affair that Custer had with one of his officer's wives atop his more casual flings and his mounting gambling debts. Captain Benteen, who detested Custer, recalled that: "It was notorious that Custer was criminally intimate with a married woman, wife of an officer of the garrison, besides he was a habitué of demimonde dives, and a persistent bucker of Jayhawker Jenison's faro game. These facts all being known to Mrs. Custer rendered her—if she had any heart a broken hearted woman. From knowing her as well as I do, I only remark that she was about as cold blooded a woman as I ever knew, in which respect the pair were admirably mated."[515]

In a desperate attempt to revive their relationship, the Custers vacationed in Denver in September and St. Louis in October. In St. Louis they attended the fair and stayed at the Plantation Hotel, but a deeply wounded Libbie could only mechanically go through the motions of what should have been romantic experiences. They had a big fight and parted ways. Libbie returned to Fort Leavenworth while Custer journeyed first to Chicago to carouse with Sheridan and other army buddies, and then to New York where he prowled for ways to get rich as well as have a good time.

Custer accomplished half of his mission. He certainly indulged himself by staying at a fine hotel, eating at the best restaurants, occupying box seats at the theater and opera, and gambling and cavorting in bawdy houses. During one soiree, he sat on a sofa beside a woman with a décolletage so revealing that "I have not seen such sights since I was weaned, and yet it did not make my angry passions rise, nor nuthin else."[516] He squired the beautiful actress Clara Kellogg to the Academy of Music and visited her frequently at her home. But these decadences cost him a small fortune rather than gained him a great one. His fame and fun-loving nature let him hobnob with such financial giants as Cornelius Vanderbilt, August Belmont, Samuel Barlow, Jim Fisk, and William Aspinwall, but without money or business skills, he could only dream of partnering with them.

Custer did collaborate with Jarius Hall, the 4th Michigan's colonel during the Civil War and now a businessman. On credit and sight unseen, they bought the Stevens Lode Silver Mine from the Crescent Silver Mining Company in the mountains near Denver. They tried selling 2,000 shares for $100 each but got few takers, most notably George McClellan. The partners discounted the shares to $50 each but still sold only a handful. Then a savior appeared, John Jacob Astor Junior, who announced his intent to buy $10,000 worth. That encouraged other investors like Belmont, who said he was good for $15,000 worth. The trouble was that Astor and Belmont were just cynically trying to manipulate the price upward before dumping their shares and reaping huge profits while bankrupting the partnership as the other investors bailed out. For years Hall and Custer clung to the shell company as creditors and lawyers demanded payments for mounting bills; Libbie would inherit a portion of those and other debts that Custer had amassed.

A contrite Custer wrote Libbie a letter filled with regrets and promises. He lamented that when they were in St. Louis "the absence of the fervor that enthusiasm and joy which once characterized the manner with which you gave or accept little attentions to and from me." He begged forgiveness for his "erratic or unseemly…conduct with others." He admitted that "measured by the strict law of propriety or public opinion I was wrong." He feared that she might never again love him as she once did. He assured her that "you always have been the one great all absorbing object of my love…. My love for you is as unquenchable as my life…. No woman has nor ever can share my love with you. As there is to me but one God Supreme and alone, there is but one woman who in my heart reigns as supreme as does God over the universe."[517]

Having said all that, Custer once again resorted to trying to arouse Libby's passion through jealousy. He wrote her about how attracted women were to him, including "a beautiful girl eighteen or nineteen, blond, who has walked past the hotel several times trying to attract my attention. Twice for sport. I followed her.... She turns and looks me square in the face to give me a chance to speak to her. I have not done so, yet." Another woman "has evidently taken a strong fancy to your Bo. She makes no effort at concealment." But he insisted that Libbie had nothing to fear "because he loves only her, and her always." He assured her that: "Married life in New York does not seem married life to me.... I have yet to find husband and wife here who enjoy life as we do."[518]

While Custer was living the high life in New York, the War Department broke up the 7th Cavalry and deployed its companies to posts across nine southern states to quell the Ku Klux Klan and other white supremacist terrorist groups. The headquarters was transferred to Elizabethtown, Kentucky, where Custer and Libbie arrived on September 8, 1871. Only two companies of the 7th were present along with a 4th Infantry company. The Custers spent as little time in somnolent Elizabethtown as possible and as much time forty-five miles away in bustling Louisville, especially at the elegant Galt House Hotel.

Custer went through the motions of nearly all his duties in Elizabethtown. Only buying horses for the army brought him genuine pleasure. Chasing night riders disinterested him as much as battling rebels and Indians enthralled him. He dispatched his cavalry with deputy marshals after suspects, but rarely joined them. Indeed, he opposed the whole notion of reconstruction, of forcing white southerners to accept blacks as fellow citizens with equal civil rights, including voting and running for office.

Custer had plenty of downtime to write. He penned five articles on horses for the magazine *Turf, Field, and Farm*, and a series of articles on his experiences fighting Indians out west for the magazine *Galaxy* that would be published as *Life on the Plains* in 1874.[519] He not only enjoyed writing, but he was good at it. He was a natural storyteller, who in simple but vivid prose and a keen eye for detail displayed scenes, characters, adventures, humor, pathos, and suspense.

Libbie was delighted that one day her husband might become as famous a writer as he was a soldier. She dreamed of him being celebrated without endangering his life: "My ambition for you in the world of letters almost takes the heart out of my body.... You are going on to more honors & greatness than we dreamed of a few years ago."[520] Much later she recalled: "I think he had no idea, when it was first suggested to him, that he could write. When we were in New York...he told me how perfectly surprised he was to have one of the magazine editors seek him out and ask him to contribute articles each month.... Many times afterwards we enjoyed intensely the little pleasures and luxuries given us by what his pen added to the family exchequer." She marveled that "he had the gift of a ready writer, for though naturally reticent, he could talk remarkably well when started. I had learned to practice a little stratagem in order to draw him out. I used to begin a story and purposely bungle, so that, in despair, he would take it up, and in rapid graphic sentences place the whole before us." And that was how he wrote: "he dashed off page after page without copying or correcting."[521]

Custer received a delightful break from his tedium in January 1872. President Grant gave Sheridan a unique assignment. Grand Duke Alexis Romanov and his entourage were touring the United States. Russia was the only great power that had not recognized the rebel government during the Civil War. Grant wanted to nurture relations with St. Petersburg. Unfortunately, Secretary of State Hamilton Fish and Russian ambassador Constantin Catacazy had a falling out. Alexis wanted to see the Wild West. What better way to do so than for Sheridan and his staff to host the grand duke and his coterie on a Great Plains hunting trip? And the more colorful the frontier characters to act as guides and hunting partners, the better. Sheridan immediately thought of Custer and Buffalo Bill Cody.

Custer headed west by train to join the party at Fort McPherson. From there they journeyed sixty miles farther northwest up the North Platte River valley until they reached Spotted Tail and his band of friendly Brule Sioux. With Indians as guides, Custer, Cody, Alexis, and an escort scoured the surrounding plains in search of buffalo herds and after finding them gunned down as many of the beasts as they could. Sheridan waited for them back at camp with the rest of the American and Russian entourages. The party then journeyed to Custer's post at Elizabethtown, where Custer conveyed them to nearby Mammoth Cave. Libbie joined them for a trip to Memphis, where they stayed several days at the luxurious Overton Hotel. During a ball, she marveled at Russian-style dancing as "one gasping breathless rush around the room, dropping the speechless partner at the end of a mad whirl but leaving us only a moment to catch our breath." She noted Alexis's passion for the bevy of beautiful women in his entourage: "the Grand Duke goes in to table with whichever lady he selects and leaves first. As he changes the lady every night, we have the pleasant opportunity of being acquainted with all." She was also astonished at the ability of "these Russians to drink what seems to be a vast quantity without effect."[522] The party then journeyed by steamboat down the Mississippi River to New Orleans, for another round of sightseeing, fine dining, and dancing. Finally, they parted ways. Alexis and his entourage went to Pensacola, where the Russian fleet was visiting, while the Custers reluctantly returned to Elizabethtown.

CHAPTER 15

Last Stands

*"There are not enough Indians in the world to whip the
Seventh Cavalry."*
— GEORGE CUSTER

*"It was a splendid picture.... My husband rode to the top of a
promontory and turned around, stood up in his stirrups and
waved his hat. Then they all started forward again and in a
few seconds they had disappeared, horses, flags, men, and
ammunition, and we never saw them again."*
— LIBBIE CUSTER

GEORGE CUSTER HAD FOUGHT MOSTLY CHEYENNE on the central
plains, although their ranks were bolstered by Arapaho and Sioux.
After Custer and the 7th Cavalry were transferred to the northern
plains in 1873, Sioux became their primary enemy, along with a Cheyenne band.
The people known as Sioux did not call themselves that. Sioux is a pejorative
Chippewa name that means "Snake in the Grass." During the mid-nineteenth
century, the Sioux bands reached their height of collective power as members
of one of three alliances: The Lakota or Teton included the Hunkpapa, Oglala,
Brule, Two Kettle, Miniconjou, Sans Arcs, and Blackfeet, lived west of the middle
Missouri River; the Nakota or Yankton included the Yankton and Yanktonai, and
lived in the middle Missouri River valley; and the Dakota or Santee included the
Sissenton, Wahpekute, Wahpeton, and Mdewakanton, and lived along the Minnesota River valley.[523]

The army fought the Dakota from 1862 to 1863, and the Lakota from 1854 to
1855, from 1864 to 1865, from 1866 to 1868, from 1876 to 1881, and in 1890. Soldiers and warriors skirmished many other times during years when peace officially
reigned. Custer's expeditions into Lakota territory to search for a railroad route in
1873 and gold in 1874 were underlying causes for the war that President Ulysses
Grant's administration began waging against them in 1876.

The Northern Pacific Railroad then ran west from Duluth, Minnesota through St. Paul and as far as Bismarck on the Missouri River's east bank just across from Fort Abraham Lincoln. That stretch of track took nine years to build after Congress granted the company a charter in 1864. West beyond the Missouri River was Lakota country. Surveying parties with military escorts partly penetrated that region in 1871 and 1872 by mapping the Heart River valley from its mouth on the Missouri River above Fort Abraham Lincoln. The War Department granted the Northern Pacific Railroad's request for two military escorts to complete the survey in 1873. Survey teams would start from Forts Rice and Ellis to meet somewhere in the Yellowstone River valley. General William Sherman explained the national interests and challenges at stake: "This railroad is a national enterprise, and we are forced to protect the men during its survey and construction through, probably, the most warlike nation of Indians on this continent, who will fight for every foot of the line."[524]

Two regiments were earmarked for the westbound 1873 expedition, Colonel David Stanley's 22nd Infantry and Lieutenant Colonel Custer's 7th Cavalry.[525] The expedition would have three phases. During the first phase, those regiments would march four hundred miles up the Missouri River valley from Yankton to Fort Rice as a show of strength to Indian bands along the way. At Fort Rice, the troops would rest for a week, be resupplied, and be joined by the civilian surveying party that came by train to Bismarck. The expedition would then head west up the Heart River valley, over the low divide to the Yellowstone River valley, and then up it. The steamboat *Far West* would navigate as far as possible up the Yellowstone to distribute supplies and ferry troops back and forth across the river as was needed. After meeting the surveying party coming eastward from Fort Ellis, the expedition would return to the Missouri River, with the 22nd Infantry and three 7th Cavalry companies garrisoning Fort Rice and the rest of the 7th Cavalry garrisoning Fort Abraham Lincoln, twenty miles north.

The Custers reached Yankton on April 10, and eventually ten of the 7th's twelve companies reunited there. On May 7, the two regiments set forth from Yankton, with 810 men of the 7th, 317 men of the 22nd, 1,000 horses, and 2,500 mules.[526] As the ranking officer, Stanley was in command. Although he was a courageous officer who won a medal of honor during the Civil War, he was a poor administrator and an alcoholic. Custer was afflicted with that personality type that tends to brownnose the powerful and bully the weak. Stanley saw through him and was contemptuous of what he saw: "I have had no trouble and will try to avoid having any; but I have seen enough of him to convince me that he is a cold blooded, untruthful, and unprincipled man. He is universally despised by all the officers of his regiment except his relatives and one or two sycophants."[527] Second Lieutenant Charles Larned was also among the Custer haters: "He keeps himself aloof and spends his time in excogitating annoying, vexatious, and useless orders which visit us like the swarm of evils from Pandora's Box.... Custer is not belying his reputation—which is that of a man selfishly indifferent to others, and ruthlessly determined to make himself conspicuous at all hazards."[528]

Meanwhile, Libbie suffered her latest round of hardships and disappointments that she called "my summer of discontent." At Yankton, a thunderstorm soaked their trunks that were left sitting on the wharf. When she opened them, she found "everything mildewed and ruined.... I endured everything until my pretty wedding dress was taken out, crushed and spotted with mildew." She did not accompany Custer but instead boarded a steamboat along with the other officers' wives on what became a thirty-four-day voyage up the Missouri River. After they reached Fort Abraham Lincoln, "I was willing to live in a tent alone at the post but there were not even tents to be had." Nor were there any available rooms in nearby Bismarck. Camping out day and night, "we were devoured with mosquitoes." Upon arriving, Custer realized that Libbie and the other officer's wives were better off back east at their distant homes. That left Libbie "exhausted with weeping and too utterly overcome with the anguish of parting."[529] She returned to Monroe to await her husband's word that a proper house had been built.

When the expedition left Fort Rice on June 20, it numbered "79 officers, 1,451 men, 4 three-inch rifled artillery pieces, 353 civilian employees, 27 Indian scouts, hundreds of head of cattle, more than 2,000 horses and mules, and 275 wagons, each overburdened with 4,000 to 5,280-pound loads, including a total of sixty days' worth of rations and forty-two days' forage."[530] Custer exalted in the stunning landscapes that he traversed: "Each step was a kaleidoscopic of views, sublime beyond description.... Sometimes we found ourselves on a high summit, at others wending an uncertain way along the treacherous and craggy sides of cliffs with hardly a foothold.... What would you think of passing through acres of petrified trees, some with trunks several feet in diameter, and branches perfect?"[531]

The rising tensions between Stanley and Custer finally erupted on July 7. Custer pointedly disobeyed Stanley's order concerning a stove and refused to salute when the colonel summoned him. Stanley had Custer arrested for insubordination and humiliated him by ordering him to ride at the column's tail end. Having asserted his authority, Stanley released him the next day. In a letter to Libbie, Custer blamed the incident on Stanley's alcoholism: "In regard to my arrest...I am sorry it ever reached your ears.... I was placed in arrest for acting in strict conscientious discharge of what I knew to be my duty.... Within forty-eight hours Col. Stanley came to me, and apologized...acknowledging that he had been...wrong.... Genl. Stanley, when not possessed by the fiend of intemperance, is one of the kindest, most agreeable, and considerate officers I ever served with.... He frequently drops in my tent and adopts every suggestion I make."[532]

The expedition's first of two skirmishes occurred on August 4. Early that morning Stanley ordered Custer to lead an advanced guard of ninety troops to search for a good campsite for that evening. Around mid-afternoon, Custer halted his men at a site with enough grass and water for the entire expedition.

The expedition invaded territory where Chief Sitting Bull and his Hunkpapa Sioux band then lived.[533] His scouts had shadowed the trespassers ever since they left Fort Rice. Sitting Bull was determined to inflict a harsh blow against them whenever a chance arose. The detachment of Custer and his men was just what he had hoped for. He set up an ambush of around 250 or so warriors in a large cottonwood grove along the Yellowstone and sent half a dozen others to steal horses from Custer's camp. As the raiders approached, the sentinels opened fire. The warriors withdrew beyond rifle range and shouted taunts as Custer ordered his men to saddle up, then led twenty of them in pursuit. Suddenly Custer realized that he was being drawn into an ambush. He deployed his men in a circle, with one man holding the reins of four horses behind three comrades who stood ready with their carbines. Just then Sitting Bull and his men emerged from hiding and charged. The warriors swirled around the troops, firing with bows, rifles, and pistols, and screaming war cries. One warrior was especially bold in galloping around the perimeter as the troops fired and missed him. Custer told Bloody Knife that the next time that warrior charged past he would shoot his horse while Bloody Knife shot him. And that was exactly what happened. Sitting Bull called off his warriors, having lost two killed and several wounded. The intruders did not escape unscathed. Indians killed and mutilated three stragglers, a veterinarian, a sutler, and a private.[534] Five days later Custer and his troops fought off another charge by Sitting Bull and his warriors and then chased them for half a dozen miles. In that running fight, one soldier was killed and twenty were wounded, but Custer claimed that his troops killed or wounded forty Indians.[535] Libbie experienced mingled relief and exaltation to learn that her husband had emerged unscathed from his latest victories: "The pride and glory I feel in you is mingled with such thrills of fear and such terrified thoughts of what risks you run to achieve your victory." Yet she swelled with pride that "you are going on to more honors & greatness than we dreamed of a few years ago."[536]

The expedition lasted 66 days and traversed 935 miles altogether. Ironically, the survey results had to be shelved for several years. Not Indians but bankruptcy stopped the Northern Pacific Railroad dead in its tracks. America's economy suffered its latest "panic" collapse in September 1873, as a huge financial bubble popped after years of unbridled speculation, corruption, and fraud.[537] Although the railroad's bankruptcy removed its construction across Sioux country as cause for an Indian war, tragically, Custer's next expedition would discover something else worth fighting for.

Libbie joyfully reunited with her husband at Fort Abraham Lincoln in November 1873. She was astonished at how much the "fort" had changed in just three months.[538] In August it was nothing more than a vast squalid camp and construction site. Since then 150 or so workers had made considerable progress, most notably by erecting barracks for the troops and houses for the officers. That winter, she transformed their house into a home: "woman-like...I found a thousand things to do, and a thousand and one alternations to be made.... So for three months I kept painters and carpenters at work steadily. We curtained about twenty windows, carpeted almost all the floors, and we made a beautiful billiard-room.... This being the house of the Commanding officer it is much the largest, more entertaining being done here than in all the others put together."[539] Custer did his own decorating. For the first time, he enjoyed his own room which he transformed into his man cave filled with the stuffed heads of a buffalo, antelope, deer, and grizzly bear; fully stuffed snowy owl, eagle, and sandhill crane; Indian war shields, bows, arrows, spears, and hunting shirts; fossils, petrified wood, minerals, and feathers; rifles, pistols, and sabers; and photographs of himself and his comrades on various campaigns.

To varying degrees, every remote frontier fort was a hardship post, but Fort Abraham Lincoln was among the worst. Temperatures plummeted below zero much of each winter. Snowstorms buried them for days so that even walking from one building to another was a challenge. During the summer, clouds of mosquitoes plagued them. At first there were no wells. Each day, water was bucketed from the river into barrels and then hauled by wagon to the fort and distributed. To render the muddy water drinkable, it was poured through cloth to remove most grit, bugs, and other debris. During the winter, holes had to be chopped in the thick ice before drawing water but then it often froze solid in the barrels.

As the commander's wife, Libbie headed the little society of officer's wives. She tried to alleviate the tedium and hardships with sewing and reading circles, monthly balls, and evening serenades by the regimental band. Supply and demand helped shape relations between men and women at Fort Lincoln as elsewhere on the frontier. Being one of the few women had some advantages, as Libbie noted: "A woman...is so cherished and appreciated because she has the courage to live out there, that there is nothing that is not done for her if she is gracious and courteous. In twenty little ways, the officers spoiled us.... In our turn we watched every chance we could to anticipate their wants."[540] Once Custer intervened in one cherished activity among the ladies. To keep peace among his officers and wives, he warned them not to gossip about each other. Although Libbie was supposed to set the example, "it was a great deprivation to me occasionally;…it required great self-denial not to join in the gossip." He also insisted that she be cordial with all the wives, even those she disliked. Libbie found that challenging as well. If she lapsed in that duty during some social event, "he gave me, afterwards, in our bedroom, a burlesque imitation of my manner. I could not help but laughing."[541]

Men have their own distinct ways of blowing off tension. In addition to hunting and riding, Custer released pent up energies, anxieties, and boredom with hijinks with his brothers Tom and Boston. Libbie recalled that "the brothers played incessant jokes on each other." Custer gleefully related a prank that he and Tom pulled on Boston. They were riding through some badlands when Boston stopped to adjust his horse's saddle and told them he would catch up. Custer concocted a scheme with Tom as they spurred their horses forward. They would circle around the butte where they left Boston and spook him. Boston was alarmed to find himself suddenly alone and could not tell where his brothers had gone. Just then Custer "fired my rifle so that the bullet whizzed just over his head. I popped out of sight for a moment and when I looked again Bos' was heading his pony towards the command mile away. I fired another shot in his direction, and so did Tom, and away Bos' flew across the plains, thinking no doubt the Sioux were after him."[542] Such is the hearty way many young men express their affection for each other.

The men enjoyed privileges denied to the women. Well-armed officers were free to ride far onto the plains to explore and hunt. The ever-lurking Indian danger kept the women confined within the picket lines. That vital need became nightmarishly clear one beautiful spring day when Custer and Libbie went for a ride along the river. They pursued a deer into a cottonwood grove and, Libbie later wrote, "came to a horrible sight. The body of a white man was staked out on the ground and disemboweled. There yet remained the embers of the smoldering fire that consumed him. If the Indians are hurried for time and cannot stay to witness the prolonged torture of their victim, it is their custom to pinion the captive and place hot coals on his vitals. The horror and fright this gave us women lasted for a while."[543]

Another day Indians ran off some horses. Custer assembled his men and pursued, leaving a skeleton force to protect the fort. Libbie gathered the women together in one of the houses where they tensely awaited the regiment's return: "Each of us took turns in mounting the porch railing and, held there in place by the others, fixed the field glass on the little spot of earth through which the command had vanished." The frightening notion spread that "the running off of the herd was but a ruse to get the garrison out, in order to attack the post.... Huddled together in an inner room, we first tried to devise schemes for secreting ourselves. The hastily built quarters had then no cellars.... It would be expected that army women would know a great deal about fire-arms; I knew but few who did." The women were terrified of a fate they considered worse than death, being captured and endlessly gang-raped: "Our regiment had rescued some white women captured in Kansas, and we never forgot their stories." To their relief, the troops reappeared the next morning but were a sorry sight: "Neither men nor officers had been in the saddle during the winter. This sudden ride of so many miles, without preparations, had so bruised and stiffened their joints and flesh that they could scarcely move.... When they sat down it was with the groans of old men."[544]

Disaster struck the Custers during the frigid night of February 6, 1874, when their house caught fire and burned to the ground. Libbie vividly described how it happened: "I was awakened by a roaring sound in the chimney that had been defective;...the chimney had burst, the whole side of the room was blown out.... The gas from the petroleum paper put on between the plastering and the outer walls to keep out the cold had exploded. The roof had ignited at once and was blown off like the report of artillery." The fire destroyed nearly all their possessions. For Libbie the greatest loss was the blond wig made from her husband's hair that she liked to wear.[545]

Later that month Custer got into a literary duel with Colonel William Hazen of the 6th Infantry, which garrisoned Fort Buford at the confluence of the Missouri and Yellowstone Rivers. The *New York Tribune* published Hazen's letter, which began by exposing the corruption and lies whereby Jay Cooke promoted his Northern Pacific Railroad and ultimately bankrupted it, and then claimed that Cooke had entangled General Phil Sheridan and Custer in his venal web by routing the railroad past Fort Abraham Lincoln. This was not the first time that Custer had experienced persecution by Hazen; at West Point, Hazen had brought charges against him for allowing a fight between two lower classmen that delayed his departure for the Civil War. Now Custer replied to Hazen's letter with a 4,000-word essay in which he defended himself, Sheridan, and the Northern Pacific Railroad. The *Minneapolis Tribune* published his response on April 17, 1874, and the Northern Pacific Railroad printed it as a pamphlet. That was just the first round of their war of words. When Custer's book *My Life on the Plains* appeared later that year, Hazen countered with his pamphlet "Some Corrections to My Life on the Plains."[546]

Despite all the challenges of life at Fort Abraham Lincoln, Libbie was thrilled at their marriage's renaissance: "Of all our happy days, the happiest had now come to us at Fort Lincoln.... Life grew more enjoyable every day as we realized the blessings of our home."[547] She marveled with her husband "how we have managed

to preserve the romance…after nine year of married life and all our vicissitudes.…
But, though we have had our trials, you have the blessed faculty of looking on the
sunny side of things."[548] Just looking at her husband filled her with pride and desire:
"The general was a figure that would have fixed attention anywhere.… He wore
troop-boots reaching to his knees, buckskin breeches fringed on the sides, a dark
navy blue shirt with a broad collar, a red necktie.… On the broad felt…was fastened
a small mark of his rank. He was at this time thirty-five years of age, weighed one
hundred and seventy pounds, and was nearly six feet in height. His eyes were clear
blue and deeply set, his hair short, wavy, and golden.… His mustache was long and
tawny;…his complexion was florid.… He was the most agile, active man I ever
knew, and so very strong and in such perfect physical condition."[549]

Libbie was not alone in her adoration. William Curtis was then a precocious
twenty-four-year-old journalist for the *Chicago Inter-Ocean* newspaper. On assignment to the 7th Cavalry, he came to hero-worship Custer, reporting, "I have
heard anecdotes of his goodness and manliness from his soldiers and others." He
encountered that at Fort Abraham Lincoln when he observed Custer tutoring two
girls, one white and one black, in reading. He was just as enamored of Libbie: "His
wife, a charming lady, who has shared his marches and victories since early in the
war, is as gentle and cultivated, and yet as soldierly a woman can be."[550]

Custer received an assignment in early March 1874 that broke the winter's dol-
drums. Colonel Stanley learned that at the Standing Rock reservation a Hunkpapa
warrior named Rain in the Face had boasted of killing two of the three men slain
during the fighting on August 4, 1873. Rain in the Face was so notorious for feroc-
ity and guile that Stanley cautioned Custer to take at least 300 men to apprehend
him. Arresting Rain in the Face involved legal as well as safety issues. He had
killed those two men in battle, a legally and morally valid act unless vengeance or
"victor's justice" motivated the prosecutor.

Custer understood well both the legal and safety challenges but was mostly
concerned with the former. Although he was confident that he was legally empowered to arrest Rain in the Face, before he did so he wanted the written approval of General Alfred Terry, who headed the Dakota Department. Biographer
T. J. Stiles nicely deconstructed just how he did so. With his words dripping with
sarcasm, Custer requested permission "to arrest the Indian referred to and test
the proposition as to whether a white man has any rights which a reservation Indian is bound to respect." Stiles explained that Custer "echoed the U.S. Supreme
Court's notorious *Dred Scott* decision of 1857, in which Chief Justice Roger Taney
declared that African Americans were 'beings of an inferior order…so far inferior,

that they had no rights which the white man was found to respect.' Custer likely agreed with Taney; by reversing the formulation he expressed profound outrage at the Lakotas."[551]

Terry granted official approval. Custer dispatched his brother Captain Tom Custer, Captain George Yates, and a hundred men to the reservation store where Rain in the Face was reported to be. Hundreds of angry Indians surrounded the troops as they arrested the suspect and then rode away with him to Fort Abraham Lincoln, where he was incarcerated. Custer interrogated him at length and finally got him to confess that he had killed the two men. The question now was how to prosecute him. Four months later, military and civilian authorities were still debating the best legal way to proceed when Rain in the Face and two white outlaw cellmates broke out and escaped. Rain in the Face would reappear once more in Custer's life at the battle of the Little Big Horn. However his target there was not Custer but his brother who had incarcerated him. Libbie later revealed that Rain in the Face "cut out the brave heart of that gallant, loyal, and lovable man, our brother Tom."[552]

Sheridan gave Custer a mission for 1874. He was to lead ten 7th Cavalry companies, two infantry companies, sixty Indian scouts, three Gatling guns, and one hundred supply wagons southwest to the Black Hills to investigate rumors of gold and survey its other natural features. For that, the expedition included geologist Newton Winchell, ethnologist George Bird Grinnell, and zoologist Othniel Marsh. Atop that scientific quest, the expedition's display of military strength across Lakota territory hopefully would intimidate that tribe into staying off the warpath. Of course, doing so risked provoking what it was intended to prevent.[553]

The 1874 expedition turned out to be safer than that of the previous year. They first encountered Indians on July 13, "when about 20 were seen near the column.... They scampered off when they found they were observed.... Signal smokes were sent up around us during the afternoon.... Indians were seen watching us after we reached camp, but there were no hostile demonstrations. Some of the guides think the signals were to let their villages know where we are, and to keep out of our way." Regardless, Custer imposed strict regulations that no one stray beyond the picket line, including himself. That was a tedious burden for Custer who longed to gallop off to explore and hunt: "I feel like a young lady fond of dancing who is only allowed to sit and look on at some elegant party."[554] Even more he desired his wife: "After dinner, when we reach camp, I usually take an escort to search out a few miles of road for the following day, and when I return I am ready to hasten to my comfortable—but Oh so lonely bed." He confided to Libbie stunning news:

"The expedition has surpassed most sanguine expectations. We have found gold and probably other valuable metals."[555]

Journalist William Curtis scored the expedition's biggest scoop. He was the first to reach a telegraph office and fire off the message that gold was discovered in the Black Hills. The *Chicago Inter-Ocean* newspaper printed the story on August 17, 1874, and within days other newspapers across the nation reprinted that electrifying news. That sparked a gold rush of 18,000 prospectors, merchants, gamblers, outlaws, prostitutes, and others to the Black Hills by the year's end, with Deadwood the most notorious of the towns that mushroomed virtually overnight.

After an 883-mile round trip, Custer led his troops back into Fort Abraham Lincoln on August 30. Their arrival at once relieved, delighted, and amused the wives: "Some women did not know their husbands, and looked indignant enough when caught in an embrace by an apparent stranger. Many, like the general, had grown heavy beards. All were sun-burnt, their hair faded, and their clothes so patched that the original blue of the uniform was scarcely visible.... The boots were out at the toes.... The instruments of the band were jammed and tarnished but they still produced enough music for us to recognize the old tune of Garryowen." Her husband's homecoming transformed Libbie: "From the clouds and gloom of those summer days, I walked again into the broad blaze of sunshine which my husband's blithe spirit made. I did everything I could to put out of my mind the long, anxious, lonely months."[556]

Custer spent much of April and May 1875 in New York. As in his previous sojourns, he tried to make money with various investment schemes but ended up losing money through extravagant living. Via broker Emil Justh, he gambled with short sells and derivatives on Wall Street. At first, he scored a small profit but squandered it and descended deeper into debt. He felt doubly bad about the losses because he had promised Libbie that he had given up gambling and she had nothing to worry about. The only possibility of income came from James Bennett, the *New York Herald*'s publisher, who heard that Custer would return to the Black Hills that summer and asked him to be the journalist for his own campaign. The rumor was partly true. An expedition would set forth, but Colonel Richard Dodge would command it.

By early summer Custer was back at Fort Abraham Lincoln but was soon implicated in controversial financial schemes there. Ben Holladay and Rufus Ingalls were brilliant entrepreneurs who had gotten fabulously rich through a series of investments in transportation, first in California with a stagecoach line that they sold for $1.5 million to Wells Fargo, followed by steamship and railroad companies in Oregon. Then came the 1873 Panic that nearly ruined them. They were desperate to revive their fortune by any means. One possibility lay with rekindling their acquaintance with Custer from the Civil War. In August 1875, Custer received a letter from Ingalls asking his aid in setting up stagecoach stations and stores across the northern plains that led to the Black Hills, with one at Bismarck.

Custer agreed to help, even though the 7th Cavalry's current mission was to patrol the plains and turn back anyone heading to the Black Hills. Then in September, Secretary of War William Belknap visited Fort Abraham Lincoln, ostensibly as part of an inspection of the northern Great Plains. Belknap's tour, however, had a more nefarious motive.[557] He was an associate of Holladay, Ingalls, and a corrupt web of other businessmen, officers, and politicians. His most blatant crime was selling sutlerships at army posts and Indian reservations for large fees and then taking a cut of the profits. One of his agents was Robert Seip, who he had appointed Fort Abraham Lincoln's sutler. Seip promptly doubled prices to recoup his kickbacks to Belknap. When his troops complained, Custer gave them leave to shop in Bismarck. Seip complained to Belknap who informed Custer that his men must patronage their fort's sutler. When Custer did not back down, Belknap backed off.

That autumn, Custer returned to New York "on business" while Libbie went to Monroe. Custer immersed himself in another frenzied round of short selling and derivatives mostly enabled by Justh. The results were the same. He lost far more than he won and wallowed deeper in debt to Justh. He owed his broker $8,578, although that was a relatively minor loss for his $398,983 in total trades.[558] The only trouble, of course, was that he could not pay it off except by borrowing more money at high interest rates. Atop that, the Atlantic Publishing Company successfully sued him for pocketing an advance for his memoirs in 1867 that he had since failed to write. He granted an interview to *New York Herald* reporter Ralph Meeker, who questioned him about Indian diplomacy, military strategy, and allegations of corruption on the plains. Custer talked at length about the first two subjects but curtly denied any knowledge of graft.[559]

Libbie joined him in December but Custer's worsening money problems dampened their romance. She wrote Tom Custer that: "The holidays have been rainy, gloomy. I did not have half the fun I had anticipated, looking in at the shop windows. On Christmas morning I went to church, but came back, weary, disgruntled.... Autie always finds the day somewhat of a bore and is glad when it is over.... Autie has so many invitations, I have to drive him to accept them, as it is a privilege to meet such interesting people. One night he dined at three places."[560] Among their favorite companions were the painter Albert Bierstadt and actor Lawrence Barrett.

President Ulysses Grant had long fervently believed in peace, prosperity, and justice for the Indians. Now, as "the Great Father," he was empowered to realize his vision. What he called his "peace policy" was designed to replace corruption and violence with compassion and competence in relations with the tribes. He issued this appeal to Congress: "Cannot the Indian be made a useful and productive member of society? If the effort is made in good faith, we will stand better before the civilized nations of the earth and our own consciences for having made it."[561] As Indian Superintendent he tapped Captain Ely Parker, his long-time aide and a Seneca; in doing so Grant was the first president to appoint a non-white person to a high federal office. For peace commissioners and reservation superintendents, he chose men who were humanitarians, philanthropists, and, preferably Quakers by religion.

The gold rush to the Black Hills posed a dilemma for the Grant administration. By treaty, the Black Hills were deep within Sioux territory. Although the Sioux had themselves conquered that region from other tribes just a couple of generations earlier, they now regarded the Black Hills as a sacred part of their culture. Sioux deities dwelled there. Young men underwent vision quests there. Sioux bands frequently gathered for councils at Bear Butte just north of the Black Hills. So legally and morally, the White House was obliged to drive away the trespassers. And indeed, officially that was the policy during most of 1875, although it was not rigorously implemented. Expelling ten thousand or so enterprising Americans who staked claims to the Black Hills was infeasible on practical and political grounds. Mining, financial, mercantile, and railroad companies pressured and paid off officials and congressmen alike to seize the Black Hills from the Sioux in return for some paltry sum. And if some bands resisted, the army could simply crush them and force their surviving chiefs to submit.

The Grant administration summoned Red Cloud, Spotted Tail, and a delegation of lesser chiefs to Washington in June 1875, and asked them to surrender the Black Hills for $6 million. The chiefs agreed, but only if the government paid $70 million for that land, and not a penny less. They insisted on that sum to finesse a dilemma that trapped them. The peace chiefs were squeezed between the demands of Washington to cede and war chiefs like Sitting Bull, Crazy Horse, and Gall never to surrender the Black Hills. They reasoned that if they got the unprecedented payment of $70 million, the war chiefs might grudgingly go along. But the Grant administration rejected that figure and the chiefs rejected any counteroffers.

With negotiations dead, the political pressure by business corporations on the White House soared. Grant finally succumbed to that pressure on November 3,

1875, when he convened what became a fateful meeting with Interior Secretary Zachariah Chandler, Secretary of War Belknap, Indian Affairs Commissioner Edward Smith, General of the Army Phil Sheridan, and Department of the Platte commander George Crook. Grant did not want another Indian war, but renegade Sioux bands gave him an excuse for one; their war parties had recently raided the Crows and Arikaras. Grant and his advisors reached a consensus to issue a proclamation that all Sioux bands must return to their respective reservations by January 31, 1876, or else be considered at war against the United States.

That deadline passed. On February 1, 1876, the White House declared war against the hostile bands. Sheridan devised a plan for a three-pronged invasion of Sioux country, with Terry's column, including Custer's 7th Cavalry, advancing from Fort Abraham Lincoln, General George Crook's from Fort Fetterman, and Colonel John Gibbon's from Fort Ellis.[562]

The Custers lingered in New York until February, then headed west. They stopped in St. Paul where Custer and Terry discussed the pending campaign. On March 6, the Custers boarded the train bound for Bismarck. They almost did not make it alive. Sixty-five miles from Bismarck a blizzard buried the train for a week, and food supplies diminished to the vanishing point. The Custers finally escaped in a mule-drawn sleigh that carried them to Bismarck. There, Custer organized an expedition to rescue the rest of the stranded passengers and crew.[563]

Although President Grant was personally honest, his administration was among the most corrupt in American history. A succession of scandals engulfed his White House, including the Whiskey, Gold, Indian, Navy, and New York Custom House "Rings." Grant was not just clueless to the corruption permeating his administration but to family members whom he had tapped to be government officials. Bribes, graft, nepotism, conflicts of interest, and outright theft of public resources were rampant. For instance, the Whiskey Ring involved hundreds of bureaucrats pocketing rather than passing to the Treasury tens of millions of dollars' worth of taxes on whiskey. The latest scandal involved allegations that the Interior Department's Bureau of Indian Affairs and the War Department were larcenous from top to bottom and had siphoned off millions of dollars that were supposed to go to reservation tribes, with Secretary of War Belknap and Grant's advisor Orville Babcock the kingpins. In December 1875, the House of Representatives opened an investigation of these charges, with Heister Clymer, a Democratic Party leader, chairing the Committee on Expenditures for the War Department.

As Custer prepared his regiment for the campaign, he received a telegram from the Committee on March 15, 1876. He was immediately to hurry to Washington and testify. On April 1 and 4, he candidly answered a long series of questions concerning corruption allegations against Belknap, Babcock, Orvil Grant, the president's brother, and other leading officials. In doing so, he became a star witness for the investigation. He dined with Clymer and other Democratic Party leaders. Most likely Custer's potential political career was among the issues that they discussed. If he won glory against the Sioux during the summer he might become a leading candidate for some fall election, possibly even the presidency. On April 20, he left Washington for New York where he spent several days mingling business and pleasure. Finally, he headed west with stops to meet Sheridan in Chicago and Terry in St. Paul. A letter caught up to him from Libbie who worried that he was taking too many political risks. He reassured her that: "I seek to follow a moderate and prudent course, avoiding prominence. Nevertheless, everything I do, however simple and unimportant, is noticed and commented on. This only makes me more careful."[564] Libbie was prescient.

Grant smoldered over Custer's blatant schmoozing with his Democratic Party enemies. On April 28, he ordered Sheridan to replace him with another commander for the pending campaign. Custer was with Terry when he got the news. He hurried back to Washington and, on May 1, went to the White House to plead his case directly to the president. Grant kept him waiting most of the day before finally having an aide inform him that they would not meet. Custer headed back to St. Paul.

Meanwhile, starting with the *New York World*, Democratic Party–affiliated newspapers across the country ran front-page articles accusing Grant of punishing Custer for his critical testimony against his administration. Grant sent telegrams to Sherman and Secretary of War Alphonso Taft, asking how he should handle this latest scandal. Sherman accused Custer of engineering those newspaper stories and urged Grant to sack him for leaving Washington without permission. As Grant mulled doing so, Sherman telegraphed Sheridan what was transpiring. Sheridan promptly wired Custer, who was then in St. Paul.

Custer issued a plea to Grant through Terry, who then forwarded it up the command chain to the White House. Meanwhile, Terry and Sheridan dispatched their own arguments to Grant that Custer was essential to the campaign. On May 8, Grant finally yielded and issued permission for the plan to proceed unaltered with Custer heading the 7th Cavalry. Once again "Custer's luck" appeared to have prevailed. He had escaped being court-martialed and cashiered by the political width of a hair. As a result, the Indians would inflict its most devastating victory against the American army.[565]

General George Crook was the only commander to launch his campaign as scheduled. His nine hundred troops included five 2nd Cavalry companies, five

3rd Cavalry companies, two 4th Infantry companies, a company of Indian scouts, and drivers for wagons and pack mules. On March 1, the column marched from Fort Fetterman but proceeded slowly because a snowstorm had buried the plains the previous day. Crook sent Lieutenant Colonel Joseph Reynolds ahead with his cavalry while he stayed with the infantry guarding the supply train. On March 17, scouts brought word to Reynolds of an Indian village several miles ahead on the Powder River's west bank. The several hundred people in the village included Old Bear's Cheyenne band of fifty lodges and He Dog's Oglala band of fifteen lodges. Someone spotted the approaching cavalry and alerted the village, whose inhabitants fled. Reynolds' men overran the village, captured most of the horse herd, and burned half of the lodges. The warriors rallied and drove off the blue-coats. Casualties were light on both sides, with two Indians and four soldiers dead. Reynolds withdrew to Crook. Short of supplies, Crook led his men back to Fort Fetterman.

That setback forced Sheridan to revise the plan. After resupplying his troops, Crook would lead them against the Indians and drive them toward the Yellowstone River as Gibbon's column advanced east down the valley from Fort Ellis and Terry and Custer advanced west up the valley. On May 16, Sheridan telegraphed Terry this advice: "you must rely on the ability of your own column for your best success. I believe it to be fully equal to all the Sioux which can be brought against it, and only hope they will hold fast to meet it.... You know the impossibility of any large number of Indians keeping together as a hostile body for even one week."[566] Of this, historian T. J. Stiles offers this pithy comment: "Sheridan feared that the Lakotas would disperse before Custer reached them; it was Custer's bad luck that they did not."[567]

Terry's command might well have defeated the Sioux on its own had it re-mained united. The column that marched west on May 17 included twenty-eight officers and 747 men of the 7th Cavalry; eight officers and 135 men from two 17th Infantry companies and one 6th Infantry company; three Gatling guns and a twelve-pounder cannon manned by two officers and thirty-two men; forty-five scouts; and 179 civilian drivers for 1,694 horses and mules split among 114 six-mule wagons, thirty-seven two-horse wagons, seventy other vehicles, eighty-five pack mules; and 250 cattle.[568]

Terry, Custer, and their respective staffs led the way. As always, Custer sought to stand out by wearing fringed buckskins rather than his regulation uniform. Nearby were his brothers Tom and Boston, and nephew Autie Reed. Appropriately, Libbie's last view of Custer "was a splendid picture.... My husband rode to the top of a promontory and turned around, stood up in his stirrups and waved his hat.

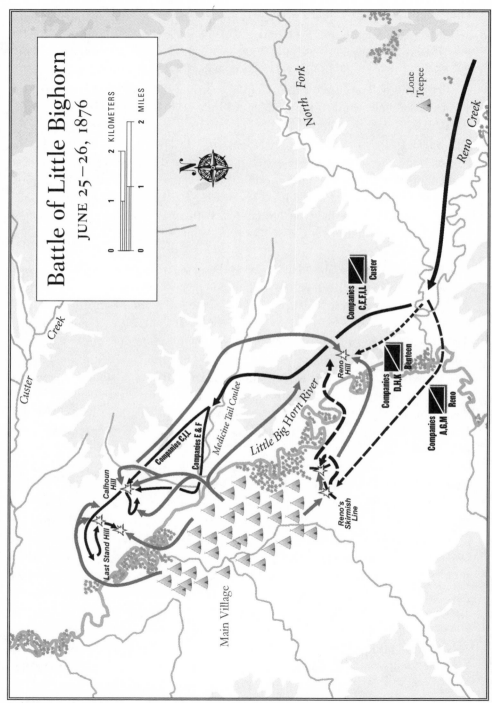

Battle of Little Bighorn
JUNE 25–26, 1876

KILOMETERS

MILES

Petho Cartography 2019

Then they all started forward again and in a few seconds they had disappeared, horses, flags, men, and ammunition, and we never saw them again."[569] She recalled: "With my husband's departure my last happy days in garrison were ended as a premonition of disaster that I had never known before weighed me down. I could not shake off the baleful influence of depressing thoughts. This presentiment and suspense, such as I had never known, made me selfish, and I shut into my heart the most uncontrollable anxiety, and could light no one else's burden."[570]

Custer's 7th Cavalry may have looked splendid but suffered fatal flaws. His two senior officers harbored deep psychic wounds and despised him. Major Marcus Reno was an alcoholic, often in his cups even on duty. The death of his wife two years earlier aggravated his addiction. Captain Frederick Benteen mourned the loss of four of his five children. Both Reno and Benteen vented their rage against Custer. The other important officer was Second Lieutenant Charles Varnum, who led the thirty-seven Arikara, six Crow, and two civilian scouts. Of the officers, although nearly all were West Point graduates and professionals, only about half had experienced an Indian campaign.[571]

Reno had commanded the regiment when Custer was away and had done little to train the men in tactics, horsemanship, and marksmanship or inure the horses to gunfire. Each soldier had a haversack, blanket, saddle, halter, lariat, and picket pin, and was armed with an 1872 model .45 caliber Colt six-shot revolver and an 1873 model .45 caliber single shot, breechloading Springfield carbine; they left their sabers behind. Their firepower had a terrible weakness. The copper casings for the bullets corroded in the leather cartridge boxes or expanded after being fired and had to be pried with a knife from the breech. In battle that squandered valuable time and distracted the soldiers from the warriors trying to kill them.

Meanwhile, Crook led 1,047 troops, a couple hundred Indian scouts, and hundreds of drivers for wagons and pack mules from Fort Fetterman on May 29. Sitting Bull presided over a swelling village on the Powder River. During a Sun Dance in mid-June, he envisioned bluecoats and their horses falling into camp on their backs while only a few Indians were on their backs. He understood that to mean that the Indians would win a great victory. Scouts brought word of Crook's approach about twenty miles away on the Rosebud River. Crazy Horse, Gall, and other war chiefs rallied around seven hundred warriors to head off the bluecoats. On June 17, the Indians attacked. Crook's troops fired 25,000 rounds but only killed thirty-six and wounded sixty-three Indians, while suffering twenty-eight dead and fifty-six wounded.[572] With his ammunition nearly exhausted, Crook had to turn back to resupply. He encamped his men at Goose Creek for six weeks as he waited for a supply train to arrive from Fort Fetterman. That let the Indians concentrate their warriors against the other two columns.

Terry ordered Custer to dispatch Reno with six companies, Indian scouts, seventy pack mules, and a Gatling gun up the Yellowstone valley to the Tongue River, up it to its headwaters, over to the Powder River headwaters, then down it to the Yellowstone, where Terry, Custer, and Gibbon would be waiting. Custer protested that reconnaissance for two reasons—it was not strong enough to defeat any village it encountered but would likely scare away any Indians. Terry overruled him, arguing that the bands were most likely much farther west but wanted Reno to confirm that. He cautioned Reno to stay away from Rosebud Creek valley, where Indians probably would be found.

Reno and his men set out on June 10. The following day the main expedition continued up the Yellowstone to the Powder River mouth where Terry had a supply base established. Custer detached his band members to help defend the post but retained their horses as remounts for his column. Reno disobeyed orders. He led his men to Rosebud Creek valley where they found several abandoned village sites and a wide trail heading west over the low Wolf Mountains to the Little Bighorn valley. Two Indian scouts brought his report to Terry on June 19. Terry was angry that Reno had blatantly defied him, but welcomed the intelligence. The following day, Reno and Gibbon appeared separately at the base camp. Gibbon's 450 troops included six 7th Infantry companies and four 2nd Cavalry companies.

Terry summoned Custer and Gibbon aboard the steamboat *Far West* on June 21. Assuming that the hostile bands were still on the Little Bighorn River, his plan was to trap the Indians in a huge pincer. Gibbon would proceed to the Big Horn River valley, ascend it to the Little Bighorn valley and then up it; while Custer ascended the Rosebud River valley to its headwaters, crossed over to the Little Bighorn's headwaters, then descended that valley. Ideally, sometime on June 26 the two columns would approach the village from opposite directions, but either column could and should attack independently if the opportunity arose.

Terry would accompany Gibbon rather than Custer, judging the latter a more capable independent commander. He issued Custer these instructions: "You will proceed up the Rosebud in pursuit of the Indians whose trail was discovered by Major Reno.... It is, of course, impossible to give you any definite instructions in regards.... [I] put too much confidence in your zeal, energy, and ability to wish to impose upon you precise orders which might hamper your action when nearly in contact with the enemy." Having said that, he suggested that Custer "proceed up the Rosebud until you ascertain definitely the direction in which the trail...leads. Should it be found (as it appears almost certain to be found) to turn toward the Little [Big] Horn...you should still proceed southward, perhaps as far as the headwaters of the Tongue [River], and then turn towards the Little [Big] Horn.... it is hoped that the Indians, if upon the Little [Big] Horn, may be so nearly inclosed by the two columns that their escape will be impossible." Finally, Custer should try to send a messenger to Gibbon as soon as he located the Indian village.[573]

Terry offered Custer reinforcements of Gibbon's four 2nd Cavalry companies and two Gatling guns. Custer politely declined. Although he did not explain why, he believed he had good reasons to do so. He was dead set that all the glory of the pending victory against the Indians would accrue solely to his 7th Cavalry; dragging along those Gatling guns would slow his march and force him to share the glory with Gibbon and possibly Crook if he appeared. Undoubtedly, the subsequent battle of the Little Bighorn would have turned out differently had Custer accepted Terry's offer.

Before leaving, Custer read a last letter from Libbie, whose premonition of disaster haunted her: "I cannot but feel the greatest apprehensions for you on this dangerous scout.... With your bright future and the knowledge that you are a positive use to your day and generation, do you not see that your life is precious on that account, and not only because an idolizing wife could not live without you?...I shall go to bed and dream of my dear."[574] She longed to reunite with her husband: "Oh Autie I feel as if it was almost impossible for me to wait your return with patience. I cannot describe my feelings. I have felt so badly for the last few days I have been perfectly unendurable to everyone. Most of the time I have spent in my room, feeling myself no addition to any one's society."[575] He then penned what turned out to be his last words to his beloved wife: "I have but a few moments to write as we start at twelve, and I have my hands full of preparations for the scout. Do not be anxious about me. You would be surprised how closely I obey your instructions about keeping with the column."[576]

Bravado naturally accompanied Custer's parting with Terry and Gibbon. Custer quipped: "There are not enough Indians in the world to whip the Seventh Cavalry." Gibbon jokingly admonished: "Now Custer, don't be greedy, but wait for us." Custer emphatically replied, "No, I will not."[577]

Custer's tone to his own officers in a meeting before they headed out was completely different and stunned them. Lieutenant Edward Godfrey recalled, "There was...something that was not Custer. His manner and tone, usually brusque and aggressive...was on this occasion conciliating and subdued." Lieutenant Wallace whispered to Godfrey, "I believed General Custer is going to be killed." When asked why, he replied: "Because I have never heard Custer talk like that before."[578]

Shorn of the band and several other contingents, Custer's immediate command now numbered around 660 men, including twenty-eight officers, 566 troops, and thirty-seven Arikara, six Crow, two civilian scouts, and a dozen or so civilians to help with the 175 mules that carried their supplies. Each man carried one hundred carbine and twenty-four pistol rounds either in his belt, cartridge box, or saddlebags. Another 26,000 rounds were packed on the mules.[579]

The troops would ride into battle highly fatigued. The three mid-summer nights that preceded the fateful day of June 25 were short to begin with, and half the men slept half the night, then stayed awake guarding the other half that tried to sleep. That last dawn they hastily ate rations, saddled up, and rode five miles to the pass across the low Wolf Mountains separating the Rosebud and Little Bighorn valleys. From that pass, dubbed the Crow's Nest, Custer spotted through his binoculars hundreds of tepees a dozen or more miles away along the Little Bighorn valley. Rather than rationally fear that he faced overwhelming odds, he instead irrationally feared that the Indians would escape if he did not attack immediately. He worried that Sioux scouts had already spotted his regiment and were racing to warn the villages. If he waited until Gibbon approached from the opposite direction, the Indians might flee and evade them both. The time to attack was now. He did not even bother sending a courier to Terry explaining what he found and intended to do.

Custer split his command into four parts. He kept four companies with 220 men, gave Reno three companies with 140 men, Benteen three companies with 125 men, and assigned Captain Thomas McDougall's 40-man company to guard the supply mules and their drivers. Custer sent Benteen to scout toward the upper Little Bighorn River and see if any Indians were there and then report back. Meanwhile, Custer and Reno trotted down either side of the creek, later called Reno Creek, which drained into the Little Bighorn; the mule train plodded farther behind them.

A mile or so above the confluence of the creek with the river, Custer ordered Reno to cross the river and charge the upper village while he rode down the valley's east side in search of a ford to cross and charge the central village. At this point he dismissed his Crow and Arikara scouts, although several chose to follow him. As for Benteen and the supply mules, he seems to have forgotten them for now.

Custer and his men faced the largest concentration of hostile Indians in American history. Of the 8,000 or so Indians, around 2,000 were warriors.[580] Nearly all were Sioux with bands of Hunkpapa, Oglala, Brule, Miniconjou, Yanktonai, Sans Arcs, Two Kettles, and Blackfeet; a Cheyenne band was also present. There were also small numbers of Arapaho, Gros Ventre, and Assiniboine. The most prominent chiefs were Sitting Bull and Gall of the Hunkpapa, and Crazy Horse of the Oglala. Sitting Bull was still recovering from the Sun Dance and would make medicine in his lodge during the battle. Crazy Horse and Gall would lead repeated attacks against the bluecoats. The Indians not only outnumbered but also outgunned the soldiers. Many carried seven-shot Spencer or Henry rifles, while Custer's men were armed with their single-shot Springfield carbines and six-shot revolvers, and unreliable ammunition. Countless warriors also fought with bows and arrows, clubs, and lances. Chief White Bull recalled the pandemonium that ensued in the village when the advancing cavalry was spotted: "All through that great camp…old men were shouting commands and advice, young men running to catch up their horses, women streaming away to the north afoot and on horseback, trying to escape the soldiers. They abandoned their tents, snatched up their babies, and called their children…young girls clutching shawls over their heads, fat matrons puffing and perspiring, and old women, shriveled as mummies, hobbling along with their sticks, trying to save themselves."[581]

Reno never assaulted the village. As the warriors surged out of their lodges and mounted their ponies, he ordered his men to halt, dismount, and form a skirmish line, with one man holding four horses and the other three men lowering their weapons and firing at the onrushing horde. As warriors galloped around his left flank, he led his men in a panicked retreat to a cottonwood grove near the river. As the Indians swelled in numbers, he led another retreat, this time across the river to the east bank where they formed a defensive circle atop a hill. Only half of Reno's men made it that far; Indians cut down most of the rest, while some hid among cottonwoods.

Soon Benteen and the mule train arrived. To escape the massing warriors, Reno and Benteen decided to withdraw to a larger hill half a mile up the valley. As the troops deployed in a circle at their new position, a courier galloped up with a message from Custer: "Benteen Come on. Big Village. Be quick. Bring pack. W.W. Cooke PS bring Pacs [sic]."[582] By that time, hundreds of Indians had followed them and were creeping all around and sniping at them. Reno and Benteen prudently disobeyed Custer's order and stayed put. They heard heavy firing to the north. When the firing died off, they assumed that Custer had retreated to safety. Reno later reported that "I could not see Custer…and at the same time the very earth seemed to grow Indians, and they were running toward me in swarms, and from all directions."[583]

About five miles north, Custer and his troops had tried crossing the river where Medicine Trail Coulee entered it, but hastily withdrew as Indians on the far side opened fire and hundreds of others splashed across the river below and above them. Inexplicably, Custer then did not race his men back to join the rest of the regiment. Instead he led his troops another mile or so north down the valley to a low ridgeline where hundreds of Indians engulfed and slaughtered them.[584]

Meanwhile, the Indian women dismantled their lodges and headed west, while hundreds of warriors crept around and sniped at the 7th Cavalry's survivors. The siege persisted the rest of that day and the next day, night, and following morning. Reno, Benteen, and their men suffered from terror, hunger, thirst, and the worsening stench of rotting dead men and horses. At one point, Reno whispered to Benteen that during the night they should abandon the wounded and escape eastward with the rest of the troops. Benteen scornfully rejected that notion.

Terry, Gibbon, and their troops appeared around midday on June 27. The warriors still besieging the 7th Cavalry's remnants galloped away. Some of the relief soldiers received the gruesome task of finding, counting, and burying the dead. Of the 647 men with whom the 7th Cavalry entered the battle, 384 survived. The Indians killed 263 and wounded fifty-two troops. The Sioux suffered thirty dead and twenty-four wounded, and six Cheyenne also died but probably twice as many died of their wounds.[585] As for Custer, historian Jeffry Wert grimly summarized the forensic report that he "had been struck with a bullet near his temple and another in his ribs below the heart. After death, his left thigh had been slashed to the bone, a finger had been severed, and an arrow shaft had been shoved into his penis." Wert cited the reaction of vehement Custer-hater Benteen on seeing his dead nemesis: "There he is, God damn him, he will never fight anymore."[586] Contrary to rumors, Custer did not save his last shot for himself; he was right-handed and the bullet left no powder marks in his left temple. He died fighting. Twenty cartridge casings were scattered around him. His brothers Tom and Boston, and nephew Autie Reed were found nearby mutilated and stripped like everyone else.

On the day of the battle, Libbie instinctively invited the officer's wives to her home: "Our little group of saddened women, borne down with one common weight of anxiety, sought solace in gathering.... We tried to find some slight surcease from trouble in the old hymns.... I remember the grief with which one fair young wife threw herself on the carpet and pillowed her head in the lap of a tender friend. Another sat dejected at the piano and struck soft cords that melted into the notes of the voices. All were absorbed in the same thoughts, and their eyes were filled with far away visions and longings."[587]

Several days later a steamboat had just docked at the landing with news of a terrible battle. "When I heard the news I wanted to die," Libbie later recalled. She had not just lost her beloved husband, but three in-laws and numerous other friends and acquaintances. She spent four weeks helping care for the wounded soldiers by day and commiserating with other widows during the evenings. On July 30, she left for her stepmother's home in Monroe, where she struggled to heal herself. A friend gave her the purpose and strength to endure: "The mantle of your heroic husband had fallen upon your shoulders. Wear it, Libbie, for his sake."[588] And Libbie devoted the rest of her long life to doing exactly that.

So, what explains the battle's outcome? Custer was solely responsible for the deaths of himself and his men. He made a series of bad strategic and tactical decisions that culminated with his devastating defeat. Terry issued Custer not orders but suggestions during their June 22 meeting. Those suggestions were sound, given that the hostile bands' whereabouts were unknown. The Indians most likely were in one of the parallel valleys running from south to north, including the eastern-most Rosebud, then the Little Bighorn, and finally the Bighorn. Custer was to ascend Rosebud valley to its watershed and, if he encountered no villages, cross over to the Little Bighorn River's headwaters and descend that valley to join forces with Gibbon's force marching up that valley. Had Custer done that, then he and Gibbon would have reached the southern and northern villages along the Little Bighorn on June 27. Struck from both sides, the warriors would have been forced desperately to fight delaying actions while the women, children, and old men abandoned their villages and fled westward. The destruction of their lodges, food, and other necessities would have struck a crippling blow to their resistance. But, of course, that did not happen. Custer discarded Terry's suggestions and instead led the 7th Cavalry along that Indian trail west over the divide into the Little Bighorn Valley and so arrived two days earlier.

Then, rather than launch an attack by all his companies except one detached to guard the supply mules, he split his attack companies into three commands. Even then, rather than have the three attack different parts of the village simultaneously, he sent Reno's three companies to attack the village alone, while he rode north with four companies along the river's east side and he did not even bother calling up Benteen's three companies that he had sent to scout further up the valley. That let hundreds of warriors rout Reno who fell back to Benteen and the mules. The Indians then surrounded them. Meanwhile, hundreds of warriors swarmed out to slaughter Custer and his men.

All that was obvious after Terry, Gibbon, and their men reached the battlefield and rescued the 7th Cavalry's remnants. Reports of the battle provoked searing criticisms of Custer. Colonel Samuel Sturgis summarized Custer as "a brave man, but also a very selfish man" who was "insanely ambitious for glory" and had launched his "attack recklessly, earlier by thirty-six hours than he should have done, and with men tired out from forced marches."[589] President Grant said as much: "I regard Custer's massacre as a sacrifice of troops brought on by Custer himself, that was wholly unnecessary.... He was not to have made the attack before effecting the junction with Terry and Gibbon."[590] An army court of inquiry on Reno's role in the Little Bighorn debacle reached the same conclusions in 1878. After twenty-six days of questioning under-oath witnesses and taking depositions, the court condemned

Custer and absolved Reno and Benteen of any wrongdoing. During the investigation, Reno was asked whether he got along with Custer and if he went "into that fight with feelings of confidence or distrust." Reno replied: "I had known General Custer a long time and I had no confidence in his ability as a soldier."[591]

Custer's succession of tactical errors determined the battle's catastrophic outcome. But his "Last Stand" was that campaign's second defeat inflicted by the Sioux on the army. Strategically, Custer's defeat would not have happened without the first Indian victory over Crook's army that forced its retreat. Sherman explained Crook's fatal mistake: "Instead of moving back to his train, he should have brought the train up to him and kept up the pressure—and had he done so, the Custer massacre was an impossibility—the moment he turned back to his train, the Indians were free to turn with their aggregate force upon each or either of the other columns."[592]

As irony would have it, news of the 7th Cavalry's devastating defeat on the Little Bighorn reached the rest of the country on July 4, 1876. At first most Americans denied the news, incredulous that any number of "savages" could defeat an entire regiment commanded by George Custer. But as the reality seeped into people's consciousness, it cast a pall over the nation's centennial celebration.

Americans had much to celebrate. Astonishing changes had transformed their nation over the preceding hundred years. The population had soared from 2.5 million to 46 million people, and the territory had tripled in size as a series of treaties stretched the western border from the Mississippi River to the Pacific Ocean. Interrelated, accelerating manufacturing, financial, commercial, and technological innovations were revolutionizing the economy. Steamboats and railroads conveyed people and goods distances in days that formerly took weeks, while telegraph lines made communication nearly instant. The country had taken giant steps toward realizing the Declaration of Independence's ideals and the Constitution's tenets, most notably with slavery's abolition, equal rights for all male citizens, and the federal government's assertion of supremacy over the states. Many of these achievements were displayed in the American halls at Philadelphia's Centennial Exhibition, a world's fair with thirty-five countries represented and attended by over 8 million visitors from May 10 to November 10, 1876.

Yet there was a dark side to these achievements. Business monopolies and oligopolies steadily strangled the economy, extracting vast profits from Americans by suppressing wages and raising prices. The rich were getting extravagantly richer while incomes for the middle class and poor stagnated or dwindled. Corruption permeated Washington, the state capitals, and cities as the rich bought the votes of politicians on laws that either expanded their wealth and power or tried to curb it. Most blacks were mired in poverty, exploitation, and discrimination despite constitutional amendments and laws that abolished slavery and upheld equal rights for all. Socialists and anarchists preached revolution and provoked riots and strikes. Millions of immigrants swelled cities beyond their capacity to supply fresh water, cart away garbage, educate children, or lock up criminals.

The army eventually avenged itself against the Indians for Custer's defeat. Buffalo Bill Cody boasted of taking the first scalp for Custer during a skirmish at War Bonnet Creek on July 17. Columns of cavalry and infantry relentlessly scoured the plains. One by one the hostile bands gave up and returned to their reservations. Starvation forced them to yield. They ran out of ammunition and could not replenish it. Even with bows and arrows, game was increasingly hard to find as white hunters decimated buffalo herds. Most notably, Crazy Horse surrendered on May 6, 1877. Sitting Bull and his band escaped to Canada but returned and surrendered on July 19, 1881. Although Sitting Bull joined Buffalo Bill Cody's Wild West Show for a season, he remained defiant, once proudly asserting: "I would rather die an Indian than live a white man."[593]

Jessie Frémont   *John Frémont*

The Legends

Libbie Custer

George Custer

CHAPTER 16
Widows

"Here on this far shore where the serene climate gentles even hard memories, I seem to look back into another life—its strifes ended—only its results in good cherished."

—JESSIE FRÉMONT

"I see my country prosperous, strong, and sure of its destiny, and I know, as the wife of every hero knows, that in some small measure my life has contributed to that."

—LIBBIE CUSTER

JESSIE BENTON FRÉMONT lived another twelve years after her husband died. She passed that time mostly happily, writing, reading, chatting with friends, tending her flower and vegetable gardens, and savoring the sweet and mulling the bitter memories. She was not forgotten. Some very prominent Californians gave her an incredible gift.

Her friend Caroline Severance led a fundraising committee that garnered $8,500 with which to purchase a lovely two-story redwood house designed by Sumner Hunt. The largest donations were $500 each from Arabella Huntington, the wife of railroad magnate Collis Huntington, and Phoebe Hearst, the wife of United States Senator George Hearst and mother of newspaper magnate William Randolph Hearst. Jessie had very mixed feelings about what Caroline had done for her. Relying on charity at once bruised her pride and swelled her heart at the outpouring of love and respect for her. With the deepest gratitude she accepted the gift, acknowledging that: "Real, heartfelt sympathy does bring healing and helps to give strength for the inevitable endurance of what seems unendurable.... I will write and have I hope good use of my life until my sun goes down."[594]

While Jessie and Lily waited for the house to be finished, they lived in a cottage overlooking the Pacific Ocean at Santa Monica. Jessie exalted in the site, offering poet John Greenleaf Whittier this rhapsodic description: "I can sit there and feel

255

the enchanting soft freshness of this blue ocean and get that stilled feeling the sea always brings me.... The broad terrace on the bluff has wide double avenues of old windswept cypress and eucalyptus trees.... And a hundred feet below the long rollers break on a firm sand beach on which one can drive many many miles."[595]

The house was ready to receive them in July 1891. Standing at the corner of Twenty-Eight and Hoover Streets, the setting was at once suburban and bucolic. A streetcar line ran along Hoover Street while the house was then set amidst twenty-eight acres of orange groves. Caroline lived just four blocks away on Adams Street.

Jessie spent much of her time writing her memoirs, aided by her son Frank, who spent half a year with her and Lily. She was determined to publish a book that asserted the Frémont version of history in the most appealing possible ways. To do that she believed she had to fine-tune expectations about her being a woman as well as the general's wife, seizing the hearts of readers before approaching their minds: "And of mine only enough to make the lighter reading for general interest. I want to make this book an entering wedge. I think I know the public. And I want it with me. I want it to find this interesting. Then, well established, I can say more sharply to facts....I must be firmly on my seat of authority before I drop them."[596] She confessed that the effort exhausted her physically and emotionally, but never dimmed her professional writing skills: "My son is a tireless worker but I have to lie by often. Still over half our writing is in the publisher's hands already. We had to examine, sift, verify, and read up masses of collateral writings and records—to condense without losing a point or becoming diffuse either."[597] She remained hopeful that future generations would revere her husband once his enemies passed from the scene: "The General's name will grow to mean much more to our people as time clears away interested writers who mystify simple facts for their own ends."[598] As always, in vindicating her husband, she vindicated herself. Her efforts to assert her last words failed, as her memoirs were never published. She attributed that failure to the zeal with which she defended the actions of her husband and herself: "The public hate a controversy. Nobody cares so much about us as we care for ourselves."[599] Nonetheless, as always for Jessie, writing was a form of meditation in every sense of the word: "And how we have outlived all of that time! Here on this far shore where the serene climate gentles even hard memories, I seem to look back into another life—its strifes ended—only its results in good cherished."[600]

Jessie became a huge fan of Theodore Roosevelt, electrified like countless other Americans by his dazzling career as a genuinely progressive politician and virile all-American man. He was now vice president of the United States, having previously served as a New York assemblyman, Dakota rancher, federal civil service commissioner, New York City police commissioner, Spanish American War hero as lieutenant colonel of the First Volunteer "Rough Rider" cavalry regiment, and New York governor. He was also a prolific and popular writer. Among his books was a fawning biography of her father, Thomas Hart Benton.[601] She gushed: "You are an inspiration. I am very, very much pleased with you, if you will allow me to say so—at seventy-six one speaks. You are my typical American on everything. With sincere respect, yours truly."[602]

Congress finally granted Jessie a $2,000 annual pension as a general's widow on September 24, 1890. That freed her from chronic anxiety for herself and her daughter: "With my pension this secures every comfort but above all independence now, and a corner stone for Lily afterward."[603] In her twilight years, Jessie finally got directly involved in promoting woman's rights. She joined Caroline Severance's Friday Morning Club, whose two hundred members dedicated themselves to bringing equality before the law and in voting booths between women and men. They hosted Susan B. Anthony in 1896. Yet, despite the efforts of the Friday Morning Club and scores of similar groups across the state, California's women did not win the right to vote until 1911. Nonetheless, that breakthrough did come nine years before the Constitution's Nineteenth Amendment granted all American women that right in 1920.

Chronic pain afflicted Jessie in the last year and a half of her life. She fell and fractured her hip and damaged her spine in June 1900. The trauma to her spinal cord left her blind for months until she gradually regained sight. The pain, however, lingered. Fortunately, Lily was her constant nurse.

Jessie Benton Frémont died on December 27, 1902. After seventy-eight years, apparently her body finally gave out. According to her wishes, she was cremated and her remains were united with those of her beloved husband at Rockland Cemetery, overlooking the Hudson River and their former Pocaho estate on the far shore.

Elizabeth Bacon Custer lived another fifty-eight years after her husband's death. She never remarried even though she was only thirty-four when Custer died, was still lovely, and undoubtedly had plenty of would-be suitors. Being childless, she devoted the same energy, creativity, and passion into promoting her husband's legacy after his death that she had poured into her marriage while he was alive.

Her toughest immediate struggle was to stave off the onslaught from creditors and lawyers for the array of unpaid and mounting bills for Custer's failed business ventures and gambling losses. She was aware of various real-estate mortgages that came to $4,372.28. She was stunned and ashamed to learn that she had inherited an additional $9,260 of debt for his stock market losses. Custer did have a $5,000

insurance policy, but the company deducted ten percent since he was killed in battle. The *Army and Navy Journal* sponsored a widow's relief fund that raised enough
money to give her several hundred dollars. Aside from that her only income for the
foreseeable future was her monthly $30 stipend as a war widow.[604]

She had to find work. She asked Frank Howe, a Pension Office official, for
a postmaster's post with its $900 annual salary. Howe forwarded that request
and it passed upward through the bureaucracy until it reached the White House.
President Grant authorized Postmaster General James Tyner to name Libbie the
postmistress of Monroe. When Libbie learned that Grant was behind the appointment, she angrily refused it because he had been among those who had publicly
condemned her husband for the Little Bighorn disaster.

Determined to start a new life, Libbie moved to New York City in 1877. Her
fame opened doors for her, most vitally to influential New York women like Candace Wheeler, Jeanette Gilder, Louisa Schuyler, Diane Lane, Caroline Belmont,
Julia Bryant, and Elizabeth Hobson, who were firmly planted in the publishing,
artistic, and high-society worlds. In varying ways, they helped find her a nice
apartment and work first as a hospital volunteer and then as a secretary for the
Decorative Arts Society. Perhaps most importantly, they provided warm friend-
ships that helped fill the emotional chasm left by the death of her husband and
other loved ones.

She found varying degrees of closure by adjusting lingering dimensions of her
husband's life. She got the War Department to transfer Custer's remains from
the Little Bighorn to West Point, along with a promise that one day she would
be buried beside him. She eventually settled her husband's debts for ten cents on
the dollar. In at least one symbolic way, she corrected the record. She objected to
a bronze statue of her husband by self-taught sculptor Wilson MacDonald that
was imbedded at West Point in 1879, condemning it as untrue to his appearance.
She protested to General William Sherman who talked Secretary of War Robert
Lincoln, the president's son, into getting that offending version warehoused in
1884. She then succeeded in lobbying for an acceptable statue designed, cast, and
erected. Libbie was financially secure enough to afford a prolonged trip to Europe
in 1883. She pursued her interest in health care by becoming a board member of
the Bellevue Training School of Nurses and a trustee for the New York Infirmary
for Women and Children.

Her literary career took off in 1885 with the publication of *Boots and Saddles*,
followed by *Tenting on the Plains* in 1887, and *Following the Guidon* in 1890.[605]
Frederick Whittaker, who wrote the first biography of Custer, gave Libbie excellent advice for her own literary career: "Don't be afraid to write of yourself. It is
through your memories that Custer's best traits will gradually and unconsciously

expand to the world…. Write away, just as you talked to me."[606] And that is exactly what Libbie did, with wonderful results. Each book received generally good reviews and sales. She wrote articles on various topics for magazines like the *New York World* and *Chicago Tribune*.

The central theme in all of Libbie's writings was what became known as "the Custer Myth," which promoted him as the all-American hero while scapegoating his subordinates for the disaster at the Little Bighorn. Biographer Shirley Leckie wondered whether Libbie's promotion of Custer's image through three books made her "a masochist, a saint, or a person who had exploited her dead husband's memory in order to sell books and derive income from speeches." She concluded "that none of these judgments, taken singly or all together, sufficed." What was certain was that Libbie "played a critical role in making and sustaining the Custer myth."[607] Leckie is correct on all counts. Libbie had unassailable financial and psychological reasons to do what she did. As for the rest of her husband's life and their marriage, Libbie's sins against history were those of omission rather than fabrication. In her memoirs she ignored or glossed over the military or sexual scandals that engulfed her husband.[608] In promoting her husband, she sought to secure her own place in history as his adoring, faithful wife. Yet at times she bore a harsh emotional burden in creating her version of the past. While writing *Following the Guidon*, she confided to a friend that: "over and over again I have had to stop writing entirely as this work has prostrated me more than I ever dreamed it would. Our life in Texas after the war went easily enough as it had no anxieties, no partings, no separations, but Kansas was so full of anguish I cannot write it without exhaustion."[609]

Libbie experienced an emotional roller coaster in 1886. She mourned the death of her stepmother, although the $5,000 inheritance eased her financial situation. Then, a decade after the Little Bighorn, she experienced the literal manifestation of the "Custer Myth" when Buffalo Bill Cody's Wild West Show came to New York. His show was called "The Drama of Civilization" and culminated with a fanciful reenactment of Custer's Last Stand." She loved the show, attended numerous performances, and enjoyed the company of Cody, Annie Oakley, and other stars. Her highly favorable portrayal of Eliza Brown in her memoir *Boots and Saddles* encouraged a visit from her old confidant and servant. Eliza had since added Davison to her name, having married Dr. Andrew Davison, a prominent Ohio attorney. Libbie and Eliza strolled through places in New York City where they shared wonderful memories.

Libbie's promotion of the "Custer Myth" literally reached a new stage in 1892. Angered at ever more history books and autobiographies critical of her husband, she embarked on a cross-country speaking tour. She swiftly overcame initial stage fright to become an articulate and well-paid lecturer. That same year she moved into an expensive house in the fashionable, wealthy enclave of Lawrence Park in New York City's Bronxville suburb. Among her neighbors was *Century Magazine* publisher Robert Underwood, with whom she frequently dined. From 1894, she spent much of each summer at the art colony her friend Candace Wheeler founded at Onteora in New York's Catskill Mountains. She loved hobnobbing with writers, artists, and other creative people there and elsewhere. She especially cherished chatting with Robert Louis Stevenson at a resort on Saranac Lake in the Adirondack wilderness. Her best male friend became John Burroughs, the naturalist. She reveled in her freedom to express herself as she wished. At one point she proudly declared to Wheeler that: "Why we are all working women; not a lady among us!"[610]

The publication in 1897 of testimony by a veteran that attacked Custer's decisions at the Little Bighorn provoked Libbie to respond with her privately printed pamphlet called "Mrs. Custer's Letter: Quoting an Unnamed Officer's Reply to Col. R.P. Hughes' Charge that Custer Disobeyed Orders." In 1900, she shifted her literary efforts with articles on topics addressed to women, such as "Where the Heart Is: A Sketch of Women's Life on the Frontier" in the February issue of *Lippincott Magazine* and "Home-making in the American Army" for the September issue of *Harper's Bazaar*. Like Jessie Frémont, Libbie tried writing children's stories but unlike her, could not master the form. Children's author Mary Burt was able to pull elements of three of her stories into *The Boy General* about Custer published in 1901.[611] The following year, Libbie joined Buffalo Bill Cody for the unveiling of a statue of her husband in the town of Custer in Custer County, Colorado.

Cyrus Brady's *Indian Fights and Fighters: The Soldier and the Sioux* became the most scholarly book on the subject to date when it appeared in 1904.[612] His systematic demolition of the "Custer Myth" enraged and depressed Libbie. This time she did not publicly respond with writings or lectures. She was just too discouraged to repeat the same carefully contrived narrative that exonerated her husband and excoriated others, especially Benteen and Reno. Instead, she diverted her energies into working with the town of Monroe to raise money to erect an equestrian statue of her husband. Sculptor Edward Potter received the commission and completed the statue in 1910. Libbie was there for the unveiling.

Throughout her last decades, Libbie remained physically and mentally spry. Fortunately, she was spared any debilitating disease. She moved into an apartment on the ninth floor of the Doral Hotel at 71st Park Avenue. She had a live-in maid to care for her and keep her company. She enjoyed spending her days chatting with friends over tea, reading, or writing letters at home, doing the same at the nearby

Cosmopolitan Club, or strolling slowly through the Metropolitan Art Museum. She initially accepted an invitation to attend the battle of the Little Bighorn's fiftieth year commemoration in 1926 but backed out when she realized she would be unable to control her emotions. Instead, she listened at home to a radio broadcast of the ceremony. During an interview by *Colliers Magazine* journalist John Kennedy, Libbie expressed her life's two greatest regrets, first the loss of her husband then the lack "of a son to bear his honored name." And yet, she took enormous pride that "I see my country prosperous, strong, and sure of its destiny, and I know, as the wife of every hero knows, that in some small measure my life has contributed to that."[613]

Elizabeth Bacon Custer's heart gave out on April 4, 1933, one month after Franklin Roosevelt took the oath as president of the United States and just four days short of her ninety-first birthday. She was buried alongside her husband at West Point. Her estate was valued at $113,581, an extraordinary sum. Libbie proved to be as adept at finance as Custer was inept. She earmarked $5,000 for the "General George Armstrong and Elizabeth Bacon Custer Scholarship Fund for Daughters of Army Officers" at Vassar College in Poughkeepsie, New York, just up the Hudson River's east bank from West Point. That scholarship still helps students today.

During her nine decades, Libbie witnessed, at times from box seats, extraordinary events convulse America, including the Civil War, slavery's abolition, the Great Plains Indian wars, the Spanish American War, World War One, the Roaring Twenties, and the Great Depression. She marveled at inventions like electric lights, flush toilets, telephones, automobiles, radio, and airplanes. She met such extraordinary leaders as Abraham Lincoln, Ulysses Grant, William Sherman, Phil Sheridan, along with infamous ones like George McClellan. And all along she proudly upheld the "Custer Myth."

CHAPTER 17

Legacies

"It is a familiar doctrine that each age studies its history anew and with interests determined by the spirit of the time."

— FREDERICK JACKSON TURNER[614]

"The American wants to persuade not only the world but himself that he is doing God's service in a peaceable spirit, even when he violently takes what he has determined to get."

— JOSIAH ROYCE[615]

AMERICAN CULTURE IS A DYNAMIC BUNDLE of celebrated ideals about the character, possibilities, aspirations, and role of its citizens and their nation in the world. Americans view history dynamically rather than fatalistically. Liberty is impossible or meaningless without "free will." Individuals acting alone or collectively to protect or enhance their respective interests shape the shifting fates of themselves and their country. The notions of "rugged individual" and "self-made man" exemplify the freedom to pursue one's happiness and achieve one's unique potential. Just as critically, Americans view their country as superior and exceptional to all others, expressed by such terms as "city on a hill," "empire of liberty," "Monroe Doctrine," "Manifest Destiny," and "American way." Yet America is also a universalistic nation in that anyone can become an American by believing and acting like one. From the beginning, the struggle of pioneers to better themselves on a frontier filled with dangers and opportunities became a key part of America's development and culture. Although the wilderness frontier disappeared by the late nineteenth century, Americans continue to express themselves on the frontiers of business, science, technology, and culture.

The ideal of Manifest Destiny is as old as America's first settlement, although the term was not coined for another two and a half centuries. Imperialism founded and developed the nation that became the United States of America. The people

263

that came to be called Americans conquered and marginalized the original peoples and took their lands and resources to enrich and empower themselves. From the beginning, Americans believed that their God and civilization were innately superior and so justified their imperialism, but it was not until December 27, 1845, that the term "Manifest Destiny" was invented to exemplify and excuse that conceit. An editorial by John O'Sullivan, the *Morning Star's* publisher and a fervent Jacksonian, insisted on "the right of our manifest destiny to overspread and to possess the whole continent which Providence has given us for the development of the great experiment of liberty and federated self-government."[616]

Such are America's core stories, beliefs, and values or mythology. Richard Slotkin defined mythology as "a complex of narratives that dramatizes the world vision and historical sense of a people or culture, reducing centuries of experience into a constellation of compelling metaphors."[617] As such, myths are glorified, idealized versions of history. Myths serve at once to celebrate a nation's past and guide the present and future. Myths help people cope with fundamental existential questions of identity, choice, meaning, and morality. A nation's myths must be believable or they would inspire few people. And for that, the myths must be rooted in the things that real people did or could have done. Those who believe and emulate national myths become intrinsic if unheralded players in it.

Heroes are integral to a nation's myths. Heroes are rare individuals who commit extraordinary feats and thereafter are celebrated as epitomizing his or her nation's loftiest values and possibilities. As such, they transcend history and become archetypes for that nation and even for humanity.[618] Paul Hutton explained the phenomenon: "Heroes are not born, they are created. Their lives so catch the imagination of their generation, and often the generations that follow, that they are repeatedly discussed and written about. The lives of heroes are a testament to the values and aspirations of those who admire them. If their images change as time passes they may act as a barometer of the fluctuating attitudes of a society."[619] Perhaps no nation has a longer or more celebrated list of heroes than the United States despite its relatively shorter history than many others.[620]

Certainly, no nation values and promotes individualism, heroic or not, more than the United States. The assumption is that each person is a unique individual with the right to develop that uniqueness. One does not have to accept fatalistically one's origins, whether they are defined by family, class, race, gender, ethnicity, or religion, to name the more prominent. One can transcend any categories that confine oneself and accentuate those that empower oneself. That assumption of uniqueness also assumes that each person has differing strengths and weaknesses, likes and dislikes, opportunities and constraints, and appealing and appalling traits. Individuals are equal only before the law. Otherwise inequality prevails.

At least that is the ideal. Just who exercised that right and how far society allowed it to be exercised has changed dramatically over four centuries. Becoming a "self-made man" was once confined solely to white men and only in recent decades has that freedom been granted to everyone. And the notion itself took a long time to take root. Communitarianism was the core value for seventeenth-century colonists. Communities scorned individuals as selfish nonconformists and often drove them away or outright persecuted them as heretics. Those who bristled under the pressure by others to conform could do what Huck Finn did and "light out for the Territory ahead of the rest."[621] With time, individualism went from America's cultural fringe on the frontier to its core.

How much can any one person affect history? That, of course, depends on the person and the level of history. On an individual level, each of us daily impacts the lives of people with whom we mingle and often countless other lives beyond our sight in minute immeasurable ways. But those interactions are rarely critical. Two people can live a lifetime together and yet rarely, if ever, decisively change the course of each other's lives. If anything, the effects of individual lives on others becomes more inconsequential as the context expands from the local to the national to the international to the global.

So, when it comes to any nation's history, only a few people change their nation's history for better or worse. People who truly shift history's course are rare, and their impacts vary enormously. One crude measure of their relative importance is the number of references to them in books or, for a select few, the number of books written about them. But that begs another question. Some people are famous for genuine achievements and others are famous merely for being famous. Yet disentangling a historic figure's substantive from symbolic importance can be a paradoxical challenge if his or her symbolic power inspired others to act in substantive ways.

One peculiar dimension of American culture is its cult of celebrity, whereby masses of people adore exceptional others for some mix of their wealth, power, intellect, personality, and appearance. Critics scorn that cult as a form of idol, or idle, worship, but that does not deter countless fans. People admire extraordinary traits in others that they wish characterized themselves. Celebrities provide ways through which far less privileged folks can live vicariously. Fans soothe pains from their own thwarted hopes by reveling in the heights of fame, wealth, and power scaled by their heroes, who are often inordinately endowed with physical strength and good looks as well.

Some celebrities are indeed merely famous for being famous and are void of any genuine feats other than self-promotion. Their fame obscures their narcissism, incompetence, venality, greed, and other pathologies. For other celebrities who did not originally seek that status, it can be a heady intoxicant that transforms once humble, down-to-earth people into caricatures of themselves. They feel they must always live up to the exaggerated expectations of their fans. Being a celebrity can be exhilarating at first, but soon becomes tiresome. All that adulation may boost the celebrant's ego at the price of the loss of privacy. Obsessive fans become infuriating as they disrupt the lives of their beloved. That is not the only drawback. Celebrities can be targets as well as models when envy turns to jealousy. People with deep unresolved inner problems can project their vilest traits onto a hated scapegoat, including a celebrity.

Which brings us to the Frémonts and Custers. John and Jessie Frémont and George and Libbie Custer epitomize or symbolize an array of American values, aspirations, and archetypes. They are complex mixes of rugged individuals, power couples, heroes, villains, celebrities, and Manifest Destiny agents. Yet, how did they understand themselves?

In his memoirs, John Frémont offered this lament: "How fate pursues a man!"[622] And yet Frémont believed in free will, not determinism; he was an existentialist, not a fatalist. He strove constantly to live life as fully as possible as was best for him. A love of nature and adventure, along with duty, ambition, and hubris, combined to inspire his five exploring expeditions. But another ingredient was even more vital. He was obsessed with breaking free of anything and anyone that held him back, including snowbound mountains in the dead of winter or American presidents and generals. For instance, during California's conquest, Commodore Robert Stockton's arrival to assume command provoked conflicting emotions in Frémont: "I was no longer burdened with responsibilities; but also I had no longer that initiative in which there is always the necessity for the thought and resource that in difficult situations gives the highest pleasure and rouses the mind into higher excitement, while it calls for the exercise of its best powers."[623] That drive for transcendence is what made his expeditions and many of his other endeavors so epic. He sought to surpass such mythical heroes as Prometheus and Sisyphus, who the Gods enslaved for challenging them. He refused metaphorically or psychologically to remain chained to a mountain or spend his life pushing a boulder up a hill.

Frémont's refusal to obey, to conform, to bow to man or nature led him on a roller coaster of dazzling achievements and devastating defeats. Alas for Frémont, history's ledger may better recall his disasters than his triumphs. His flawed character got him court-martialed on charges of mutiny and other crimes for his behavior during California's conquest, and it led to his catastrophic fourth expedition in which starvation, frostbite, or suicide killed eleven of his thirty-three men. It also led him to alienate some very powerful people, most notably President

Abraham Lincoln, General Stephen Kearny, and the entire Blair clan—Francis Preston, Frank, and Montgomery.

As the saying goes, defeat comes not from getting knocked down but afterward from failing to struggle back to one's feet. In that sense, Frémont refused to admit defeat by trying to transcend each setback with greater efforts. The trouble was that he often doubled down on bad bets and so compounded his losses in business, politics, exploration, and war. His marriage enabled him to get away with that. Having Jessie as a wife, and thus powerful Senator Thomas Benton as his father-in-law, exacerbated Frémont's hubris. Benton politically blunted most if not all obstacles impending Frémont's advancements or objections to his controversial acts, while Jessie reassured him that he could do no wrong and worked incessantly behind the scenes on his behalf.

In all, although Frémont scored some remarkable feats, none was an unqualified success. Few people, including Lewis and Clark, logged more miles across more of the West than he did in his five expeditions. Yet he and his men were rarely the first Americans to set foot anywhere. Frémont mostly mapped trails trod by countless others, not just mountain men but for long stretches hundreds of settlers heading to Oregon or California. As such he accompanied rather than initiated western emigration. Undoubtedly his reports spurred more people westward than otherwise would have hit the trail, although just how many can never be determined. The clearest and most significant example was Brigham Young, who led the Mormons to the Salt Lake Valley based on Frémont's favorable reports of its fertile soil and ample water. Even then, his expeditions had mixed records, with the first three successful and the last two disastrous. Regardless, the sobriquet "Pathfinder" is appropriate because he did find paths trod by others. However, "Mapmaker" probably better conveys the most important result of his treks.

Frémont accelerated history in only one key event, America's takeover of California. Had Frémont and his men not been there, the conquest probably would have taken longer and cost more in lives and money. But here too he provoked controversy by refusing to relinquish his roles as governor and commandant when General Stephen Kearny, his superior officer, arrived on the scene. That earned him a humiliating court-martial and disgraceful mutiny verdict.

Aside from mapmaking and California, Frémont made three other vital contributions to America's national development. Two involved what he did not do. He lost the 1856 presidential election and did not run as the Radical Republican's presidential candidate in 1864. Had Frémont won in 1856, the Civil War would have begun four years earlier and his incompetence would have led to an independent Confederate States of America. Likewise, had Frémont run in 1864, he would have been a "spoiler" that split Republican votes with Lincoln, thus letting

Democratic Party candidate George McClellan win the White House and then sign a peace treaty with the rebels that continued slavery within a confederal rather than federal United States of America. The most vital positive act of Frémont's life was to give Ulysses Grant the command of troops at Cairo, Illinois, at the juncture of the Ohio and Mississippi Rivers in August 1861. Thereafter, Grant was victorious in each of the increasingly important campaigns entrusted to him until he forced General Robert Lee to surrender his army at Appomattox.

If Frémont was a mediocre explorer, his record as a general was wretched. During his four months heading the Department of the West and three months heading the Department of the Mountains, he was as inept, timid, vainglorious, and paranoid as George McClellan was heading the Army of the Potomac. McClellan, however, inflicted far more harm to the American cause since he led the most critical front against the rebels while Frémont's fronts were secondary. Frémont's negative impact compares better to political generals like Benjamin Butler and Nathaniel Banks, who also blundered serially whenever they received independent commands. McClellan's gross incompetence prolonged the war, while that of Frémont, along with Banks and Butler, squandered blood and treasure but probably did not affect when and how the Americans finally won the war.

In sheer narcissism, Frémont ranks with McClellan and another more recent controversial general, Douglas MacArthur. All three were peacock generals who consciously played what they believed was their proper role by dressing immaculately and posing flamboyantly. Each surrounded himself with an entourage of fawning sycophants. None ever admitted when he was wrong but instead treated anyone who disagreed with him as an enemy. All three aspired to be president, with Frémont and McClellan actually running and McArthur nearly doing so. Finally, they provoked blistering criticism for holing up at their headquarters and avoiding combat. Lincoln lampooned both Frémont, for deploying three hundred cavalrymen around himself rather than against the enemy, and McClellan, for wielding the entire Army of the Potomac as his bodyguard. During the 1942 Philippines campaign, MacArthur's troops scornfully called him "Dugout Doug" for sheltering on Corregidor Island rather than commanding at the front.

Frémont was the proverbial political bull in the china shop, even when altruism and morality motivated him. Although not formally in the abolitionist movement, he reviled slavery and acted decisively when he commanded the Department of the West. On August 31, 1861, he issued a decree ordering all rebel property, including slaves, confiscated. That alarmed President Lincoln because it threatened to push the four Border States into the Confederacy. Had that happened, the slavocracy would likely have won independence and the history of America and the world would have been forever altered for the worse. Frémont grudgingly obeyed Lincoln's order to rescind his proclamation. Little more than a year later, Lincoln issued his own Emancipation Proclamation, but only when he judged that the Border States were militarily and politically secure, and, even then, it limited freedom only to slaves behind rebel lines; those elsewhere would have to await a constitutional amendment.

What explains Frémont's grandiose yet ultimately self-destructive behavior? Frémont was reserved but hardly introspective. Indeed, he sidestepped any penetrating internal examination for fear it might lead to the abyss: "Shut in on itself, the mind is driven in upon itself and loses its elasticity; but the breast expands when, upon some hill-top, the eye ranges over a broad expanse of country, or in the face of the ocean. We do not value enough the effect of space for the eye; it reacts on the mind which unconsciously expands to larger limits and freer range of thought."[624]

Had Frémont been genuinely introspective, he would have realized that he kept failing more spectacularly because his ambitions far exceeded his abilities. Instead, he focused on his initial successes as evidence that he need only redouble his efforts and he would eventually win his latest endeavor. All along he sought to capture that dynamic between material wealth and political power. He did whatever he could get away with to become fabulously rich, both as an end in itself and as a means of climbing the political ladder. He skyrocketed in both realms but then quickly burned out. He was briefly a United States senator from California, the Republican Party's first presidential candidate, and Arizona Territory's governor. For a while he was among the richest men in America but squandered that with ineptness, overconfidence, greed, and bad luck.

Twin Achilles heels explain his repeated business failures. One was that he was a reckless speculator rather than prudent investor. He poured his money into schemes whose promoters promised vast payoffs; they partly told the truth as they took the money and disappeared. If incompetence were the only charge against Frémont, that would be serious enough. Far worse, he became as unscrupulous as those who had cheated him. He bilked millions of dollars from countless victims through various fraudulent schemes. He was supposed to supply cattle to the army, but instead pocketed the fee and diverted the cattle to his own land. He submitted false claims to the government for expenses that he had never made. He reneged on repaying his creditors or paying back taxes to the government and soaring legal fees to his lawyers. He and his brother-in-law wrung huge fortunes from French investors by claiming they would upgrade an existing transcontinental railroad that did not actually exist. Eventually a French court found him guilty of fraud and sentenced him to five years in prison, but he never served a day because he was safely in America when the trial took place.

Mountain men were not easily bamboozled under any circumstances, and certainly not by poseurs or greenhorns. Two acclaimed mountain men held starkly different views of Frémont. Kit Carson was devoted to Frémont, who had plucked him from relative obscurity to guide three expeditions and share incredible adventures that made him a national hero. Carson left this tribute to his benefactor and friend: "I have heard that he is enormously rich. I wish to God that he was worth ten times as much. All that he has, or may ever receive, he deserves. I can never forget his treatment of me while I was in his employ, and how cheerfully he suffered with his men when undergoing the severest of hardships. His perseverance…[was] the main cause of his success…and…no one but he could have surmounted so many obstacles."[625] Joe Walker also rode long stretches of trail with Frémont but came away with the polar opposite view. He blistered Frémont as "morally and physically…the most complete coward I ever knew. I would say he was timid as a woman if it were not casting an unmerited reproach on that sex."[626]

Walker's smear that Frémont was a coward is unfair. Throughout his life Frémont displayed varying degrees of bravery in the face of dangers that he encountered. He was in the thick of numerous fights with Indians; during one he saved Carson's life by charging his horse over an Indian who was about to shoot him. Killing someone in self-defense is justified. Yet Frémont has been condemned for ordering or leading his men to attack not just threatening Indian warriors but also peaceful Indians. Historian Benjamin Madley estimates that "Frémont's force killed as many as 1,000 California Indian men, women, and children in what may have been one of the largest but least known massacres in American history." Atop that, Frémont ordered the murder of three innocent Mexican men in retaliation for the Mexican murder of two Americans.[627]

John Charles Frémont was a stunning failure as a politician, general, and businessman; a second-rate explorer, husband, and father; and, arguably, a mass murderer. He was a mediocrity who took advantage of some extraordinary opportunities and did some exceptional things that made him famous, and then squandered that fame and its attendant opportunities because his ambitions exceeded his abilities. Biographer Tom Chaffin summed up the charges against Frémont, condemning him as "one of the great hollow men of American history—a blowhard as an explorer, a con man as a businessman, a cipher as a politician, an abject failure as a military commander."[628]

By his own admission, George Armstrong Custer was an unabashed glory-hunter. Looking back at his younger years, he confessed to Libbie in April 1867 that: "My every thought was ambitious, not to be wealthy, not to be learned, but to be great.

I desired to link my name with acts and men, and, in such a manner as to be a mark of honor, not only to the present but to future generations."[629] In his relentless, ruthless path to that end, he provoked controversy nearly everywhere he went. People tended either to adore or despise him. He was and remains seen as reckless, callous, and reactionary, someone governed much more by his gut and heart than mind. Although that was true, Custer was much more complex than that.

Hormones, as much as ambitions, fueled Custer's alpha-male machismo and stunted his emotional development. He had enormous reserves of restless energy that he had to burn off through riding, hijinks, hunting, or sex. He was naturally inured to hardships and dangers that exhausted or demoralized lesser men. He was addicted to action and got stir-crazy when he was stuck in one routine in one place. Libbie recalled that he "celebrated every order to move with wild demonstration of joy. His exuberance of spirits always found expression in some boyish pranks, before he could set to work seriously to prepare for duty."[630] He felt most alive when his life was most imperiled. During the Civil War, he wrote these revealing lines: "You ask me if I will not be glad when the last battle is fought. So far as the country is concerned I, of course, must wish for peace…but if I answer for myself alone, I must say that I shall regret to see the war end. I would be willing, yes glad, to see a battle every day of my life…when I think of the pain & misery produced to individuals as well as the miserable sorrow caused throughout the land I cannot but earnestly hope for peace, and at an early date. Do you understand me?"[631]

He may have graduated last in his class of thirty-four cadets at West Point, but that reflected a surfeit of testosterone rather than a deficiency of brainpower. His teenage hell-raising, devil-may-care, boisterous pugnacity got him hundreds of demerits capped by a court-martial during his four years at the military academy, but those same traits made him a brilliant, fearless cavalry commander during the Civil War and against the Indians on the Great Plains.

Nonetheless, like most people, his behavior varied with his surroundings. He was outspoken among friends and reticent among strangers. With his buddies he was full of boisterous, prank-pulling, double-daring fun. With most people he was usually thoughtful, generous, and soft-spoken. When things went against him, he was a slow burn rather than a quick fuse. Broadway actor and friend Lawrence Barrett found then thirty-something Custer like a bashful schoolboy: "His voice was earnest, soft, tender, and appealing, with a quickness of utterance which became at times choked by the rapid flow of ideas, and a nervous hesitancy of speech betraying intensity of thought." He had a "chuckle of a laugh." In conversation he examined the other's face "as if each word was being measured mercilessly by the listener."[632]

Custer was a showboat and show off, constantly striving to be in the spotlight.

During the Civil War he wore a black velvet shell jacket with embroidered looping gold scrolls and a slouch hat with a gold star. On the plains, he wore buckskins with long fringes when all his troops wore regulation uniforms. No matter where he was, he sported a red bandana around his neck that was at once a style statement, beacon to his men, and taunt to his enemies, especially sharpshooters. He was as fastidious about his hygiene as he was his appearance; he washed his hands before and brushed his teeth after every meal. Even on campaign, he tried to keep his clothes clean and pressed.

He certainly looked forward rather than backward. He was no navel-gazer, not before and certainly not after he acted: "a rule which I have always laid down— never to regret anything after it is done."[633] That attitude can be considered ethical as long as he accepted responsibility for his decisions, regardless of how they turned out. The trouble was that he never admitted when he was wrong. He always defended himself by pointing to extenuating circumstances and the fog of war for shaping decisions that critics attacked.

Biographer Louise Barnett argued that Custer displayed all the characteristics of a narcissist including having a superiority complex, being super-competitive, deprecating others to elevate oneself, striving constantly to be the center of attention, and, exaggerating or manufacturing one's accomplishments and abilities.[634] Yet he could also be generous, modest, and witty, sometimes all at once, such as during this exchange with General Sherman in Washington that he related to Libbie: "I have received many compliments on my literary work. General Sherman said, 'Custer, you write so well, people think your wife does it, and you get the credit.' I said, 'Well, General, then I ought to get the credit for my selection of a wife.'"[635]

Custer had a boy's sense of fun and a ready laugh that at once let him blow off steam and be the center of attention. Libbie recalled attending a play that struck him as so comical that: "He laughed and giggled and put his…head on the seat in front of him and shook with a perfect abandonment of fun…. He was so absorbed…it made him perfectly unconscious…. The audience fixed their eyes on him instead of the actor. It was no good to try and call him to order."[636]

Custer's humor could be sadistic or sardonic depending on his mood and circumstances. He delighted in subjecting others to "practical jokes" that invariably inflicted humiliation and pain. Yet he could behold life's absurdities with wry amusement even when he was the butt. For instance, in his *Life on the Plains*, he related how his excitement at his first buffalo hunt got the best of him. He abandoned his troops to gallop after a buffalo, mile after mile before he closed to deliver the coup de grâce with his pistol. Just then the buffalo lunged at his horse, which shied. Custer "hastily brought up my pistol hand to the other. Unfortunately, as I did so my finger, on the trigger, discharged the pistol, and sent the fatal ball into the very brain of the noble animal I rode."[637] He was now afoot on the plains crisscrossed by war parties with no idea which direction his troops were. After several dismal hours a detachment of his troops found him.

He surrendered easily to gambling and sex. Like most gambling addicts, he believed that if he kept playing double or nothing he would eventually break even. Statistically that might have been true, but only if whomever he was playing with gave him unlimited credit with no interest rate. Most of the time he emptied his wallet and the other player walked off with the winnings. As for sex, he loved seducing or letting himself be seduced by beguiling woman. Somehow, he avoided getting any of his many lovers pregnant. Indeed, he and his wife Libbie never had children. While being careful might explain the lack of paternity suits from former girlfriends, what explains his childless marriage? A sexual disease may be the cause. He contracted gonorrhea during his third year at West Point. Either that or the cure could have sterilized him.

At his best, Custer represented the American ideal of the self-made man with can-do spirit. He was supremely confident in his ability to overcome all challenges, reverse any defeats, and realize his dreams. In 1873 he wrote Libbie that: "It is such a comfort to me to feel independent, much as I dote on my profession and earnestly as I am devoted to it. Yet should accident cast me adrift and I would be thrown upon my resources I have not a fear but that energy and willingness to put my shoulder to the wheel would carry me through triumphantly." But in that he realized he was hardly unique: "In this country no man of moderate education need fail if determined to succeed, so many the opportunities for honorable employment."[638]

Unlike Frémont, Custer never tried to realize whatever political ambitions he may have harbored. That might have changed dramatically in the election year of 1876 had he won rather than died at the Little Bighorn. He did have some innate political skills. As an extrovert he was a natural schmoozer. As a narcissist he naturally considered himself deserving of any promotion, award, or honor that he desired. The trouble was that his egomania could alienate as well as entice influential people. He blatantly sucked up to those in power and disdained those without it. He was usually clueless when his incessant drive to be in the spotlight made him appear vainglorious rather than heroic, boorish rather than entertaining. Many potential political allies might have genuinely admired him as a soldier, yet disdained his vanity. At least he recognized that he lacked fundamental skills for running for office: "I am not partial to speechmaking. I believe in acts not words."[639]

Custer was a fine writer with a vivid page-turning style, ear for western dialect, eye for insightful details, and flashes of sardonic humor, all traits reminiscent of Mark Twain. His *Life on the Plains* is a minor classic, but, sadly, is known only by specialists. He also had a gift for music with "so correct an ear that he often sang or whistled the airs of an opera after hearing them just once. Music so charmed him that…the general often regretted that he had not had the opportunity to learn music."[640]

Philosophically, Custer was a Social Darwinian who believed in a continual survival-of-the-fittest struggle among "races," especially between the "civilized" and the "savage." That outlook at once reflected and shaped his incessant drive to surpass all others on and off the battlefield. Although he agreed that civilized peoples should try to help savage peoples better themselves, he warned that they should be realistic about the likely results. Savages were like children who could never mature into adults: "Civilization may and should do much for him, but it can never civilize him…. Nature intended for him for a savage state; every instinct, every impulse of his soul inclines him to it. The white race might fall into a barbarous state, and after, subjected to the influence of civilization, be reclaimed and prosper. Not so the Indian. He cannot be himself and be civilized. He fades away and dies…Study him, fight him, civilize him if you can, he remains the subject of your curiosity, a type of man peculiar and undefined, subjecting himself to no known law of civilization, contending determinedly against all efforts to win him from his chosen mode of life. Cultivation such as the white man would give him deprives him of his identity. Education…seems to weaken rather than strengthen him."[641]

For Social Darwinians, war is the ultimate test that determines who is superior and inferior. As a Social Darwinian, Custer naturally glorified war in his writings, in contrast to Civil War veterans like Ambrose Bierce, Oliver Wendell Holmes, Charles Francis Adams, and Mark Twain, who either lamented or lampooned most of their experiences. Biographer T. J. Stiles found a partial explanation for their different outlooks in the nature of combat sustained by infantry and cavalry. Infantry inevitably were treated as sacrificial pawns by generals with varying degrees of incompetence who failed to understand that massed rifles and artillery had rendered mass attacks not just obsolete but self-defeating. As a psychological defense mechanism, foot soldiers must become callous and fatalistic. In contrast, the sporadic fighting, freedom of movement, and man-to-man combat that cavalrymen experienced helped them retain the more romantic outlook on warfare promoted by politicians and novelists. The infantry experiences of Bierce, Holmes, and Adams were sustained and horrific, and their writings candidly expressed their hatred of war. Twain never saw any fighting during his brief time as a rebel soldier before he deserted and headed west, so his account is sardonic. Stiles offers this insight: "As a staff officer, he had flitted in and out of combat; he was not mired in a rifle pit or firing line…. In cavalry clashes, Custer had swirled around the field on horseback instead of standing in a file of men who were gunned down in blasts of flying metal. He had led charges, galloping at the enemy and fighting with a sword, like a medieval knight."[642]

What was most vital about Custer was that he was the quintessential warrior. He personified the perfect blend of timeless fighter and modern commander. In combat he had that rare ability to size up a situation at a glance and then act decisively. Although he is best known for the defeat in which he and 262 of his men were killed at the Little Bighorn, that was an anomaly. During the Civil War, he proved to be as tactically adept as he was courageous. He was a relentless, ruthless general, like Grant, Sherman, and Sheridan, who fought total war designed to crush the enemy as thoroughly as possible. If Frémont was like Douglas McArthur in temperament, Custer resembled George Patton. Yet Custer's obsession with style over substance and appearances over depth could blind him to military genius in others. For instance, he was enamored of dapper, loquacious George McClellan, an inept general, and disdainful of disheveled, taciturn Ulysses Grant, a brilliant general.

A conundrum was imbedded in the core of Custer's military career. He was an outstanding combat leader who richly merited all the praise and promotions that he received during the Civil War. Indeed, he probably deserved at least one or two Medals of Honor for his extraordinary battle feats. Yet the skyrocketing successes and public adulation of the "boy general" at such a young age metastasized his already bloated ego. And that made him an awful commander off the battlefield.

Throughout his career Custer adhered to a double standard of behavior, one for himself, his friends, and his superiors, and another for his lessers. For instance, he insisted that his soldiers be uniform in military appearance, yet he often donned colorful civilian accessories when fighting rebels, and buckskins when fighting Indians. Far worse, he gleefully helped himself to "the spoils of war," but would have privates severely punished and even shot for doing the same. That hypocrisy ravaged the morale of his troops. The result was a vicious cycle. His regiments suffered high rates of desertion that he tried to deter with executions that provoked ever more men to seize the first chance to escape his tyranny. That vicious cycle also infected his officers, with ever more hating him. The 7th Cavalry's dismal morale did not cause its devastating defeat at the Little Bighorn, Custer's strategic and tactical errors did. But most survivors were undoubtedly glad that Custer was among the dead.

Custer was as skilled at self-promotion as he was at combat. Biographer T. J. Stiles explained how: "Custer assumed authorship over his own tale. First in letters, later in magazine articles and books, he set out to shape and reshape his life, to impose his imagined self over a reality that was remarkable enough. He would not be content until others regarded him as he wished to regard himself."[643] Stiles added this insight: "He loved the West, but he was not of the West. He projected a new image of himself through the lens of the frontier, but he cast himself as the cosmopolitan sophisticate who mastered the wilderness, inserting knowing references to New York in essays about rattlesnake broiling, buffalo hunting, and Indian fighting." Stiles contrasted Custer with an even more conscious showman: "Buffalo Bill Cody was dramatizing his own frontier image, which would lead to his famous Wild West show. Underneath the spectacle, though, Cody was an authentic child of Kansas. He went east as Custer went west and mastered the world that Barnum made."[644]

Yet Custer did not originate his own myth. That happened during the Civil War when journalists first revealed "the Boy General's" thrilling exploits to the world. Custer then swelled his own myth through his magazine articles and memoir, *A Life on the Plains*, published in 1874. Then came the stunning news of the tragedy at the Little Bighorn on June 25, 1876. In American popular culture, "Custer's Last Stand" became the nation's second Thermopylae after the Alamo and has inspired writers and artists ever since. A mere half year after the battle, dime novelist Frederick Whittaker churned out his biography, *A Complete Life of Gen. George Custer*, with overwrought elements of the Custer myth.[645] Whittaker's role in promoting the Custer myth has been compared to Parson Weems for George Washington, Henry Longfellow for Paul Revere, Timothy Flint for Daniel Boone, and Ned Buntline for Buffalo Bill Cody.[646] Poets celebrated that epic battle, including Walt Whitman's "A Death Song for Custer," Henry Longfellow's "The Revenge of Rain-in-the-Face," and John Greenleaf Whittaker's "On the Big Horn." Libbie Custer expanded the Custer myth through her three memoirs on their life together on the Great Plains. In the minds of countless Americans then and in dwindling numbers since, Custer personified the heroic, virile, dashing, adventurous image that they would like to believe about their country and themselves. With time, a counter-myth arose and slowly expanded that Custer was no hero but represented the worst of American hubris, narcissism, racism, and imperialism.[647]

No woman in nineteenth-century America was more of a political insider than Jessie Frémont. She grew up as the favored daughter of Thomas Benton, among that era's renowned senators. He treated her as his secretary and confidant. Through him she socialized with a succession of presidents, first ladies, generals, politicians, journalists, entrepreneurs, financiers, intellectuals, writers, and artists. She was more explicitly a political partner with her husband by advising him and lobbying on his behalf. Her political height was the 1856 "Frémont and Our Jessie" presidential campaign. Never before or since has any potential first lady received such explicit billing for that role. As the female half of a power couple, Jessie Frémont embodied Jackie Kennedy's sophistication and grace combined with Hillary Clinton's political savvy and toughness. Indeed, after the Frémonts, no power couple has provoked more controversy than the Clintons. In her obituary of Jessie, her friend and fellow writer Rebecca Davis succinctly explained her political persona: "She had a man's power, a man's education, and she did a man's work in the world, but her wonderful charm was purely feminine."[648]

Frémont called Jessie his "second mind." That was an apt sobriquet for their relationship, although it did not overtly acknowledge that her mind was superior in intellect, sensitivity, and creativity to his own. Jessie partnered with her father and husband to promote their common vision of Manifest Destiny: "We could count on each other—my father, Mr. Frémont, and I, as one.... I had full knowledge of the large scope and national importance of these journeys, a knowledge as yet strictly confined to the few carrying out their aim. Even to the Secretary of War and to Mr. Frémont's immediate commander, they were only geographical surveys to determine lines of travel."[649]

That dynamic among Jessie, Frémont, and Benton suffered sharp tensions from the beginning and endured for only a dozen or so years before unraveling. Like countless daughters of alpha-male fathers, Jessie found an alpha-male husband only to get caught in a tug-of-war between them for her affections and loyalties: "It is not easy to serve two masters and I would like so much to obey both of mine but if I must choose it will be for the one that I think needs & wishes me the most."[650] Her only source of power was playing them off against each other in a rivalry over who expressed the most love for her. Her father's death was at once mournful and liberating. She genuinely loved him no matter how domineering he could be, especially his rage after she eloped with Frémont. Now she just had her husband, who she adored even though "Mr. Frémont's nature demands that he be met two thirds of the way."[651]

For many progressives, the 13th Amendment, which outlawed slavery in 1865, was only one giant step in a campaign to realize for all Americans the ideals of the Declaration of Independence. The next stage was to abolish political inequality between men and women. Elizabeth Cady Stanton and Lucretia Mott organized the women's rights convention at Seneca Falls, New York, in 1848, during which a hundred people signed a declaration that began: "We hold these truths to be self-evident, that all men and women are created equal." Jessie occupied a halfway house over how far women should be free to express themselves politically. When

Stanton asked her to sign a petition championing equal rights, she replied, "Oh no. I do not believe in suffrage for women. I think women in their present position manage men better." She was even blunter in rejecting a similar appeal from Susan B. Anthony: "I cannot see the issue as you do." Nonetheless, she did open her purse and donate money to Anthony's campaign.[652]

Jessie insisted that a woman's place was behind the scenes discreetly and sweetly but persistently convincing men to do what was right. From a young age, girls were taught not to show up boys at school or sports or else they will scare them away. Wielding one's feminine charms was the best way to talk a man into doing something he would rather not do. That power was largely confined to one's family. Girls learned how to melt the hard hearts and minds of first their fathers and brothers, then their husbands, and finally their sons. Jessie feared that women would degrade their innate political and moral power if they lined up at election polls, shouted slogans at campaign rallies, or ran for public office. Her notion of a woman's proper political role was shaped by more than tradition. The wounds she had suffered during her own political battles pained her the rest of her life. Countless powerful men, including President Lincoln himself, had castigated her for meddling in politics, then exclusively a man's world. She knew well that being called "General Jessie" when her husband commanded the Department of Missouri was a double-edged sword that sliced both ways. The sobriquet at once exalted and denigrated her, but much worse, it unmanned her husband.

Jessie was an existentialist, though the term would not be coined until decades after her death. She sought meaning for her life beyond typical religious and social platitudes. She concluded that loving and helping others was the best way to justify one's existence: "Age is not the number of years one has but the number of people who love one & to whom one's death would be a horrible blank. And if one lived just to be happy and do as one pleased regardless of duties...then it would be too bitter to endure to feel that one could be dispensed with." She cited her deliberately nurturing relationships with two men, the poet Bret Harte and surveyor Edward Beale, that helped each to realize his potential: "But both of those men have had more useful lives & been more patient under trials & had more wish to do for others & put themselves aside, because of our talks together."[653]

Of the four characters, Jessie was the greatest cultural luminary; nearly every place she lived, she attracted a salon of brilliant wits, thinkers, writers, and artists. She also had the strongest character. Despite all the tragedies and setbacks that she suffered over the decades, she rarely wallowed in self-pity or sloth. Indeed, each defeat made her more determined to seize and make the most of life for herself and her loved ones. She was fifty-five years old and teaching history at remote Prescott, Arizona, where her husband served as governor, when she expressed her optimistic, activist outlook with these words: "I am just splendidly well and ready to take hold of Fortune's wheel and pull it to the place I would have it 'stick.' We shall get there." Indeed, she tried to inspire her students and anyone who would listen with her values: "You know how glad I am to join in the lifting process, and to make the dry bones of history take on flesh and color and life—and show them how after all, the conditions of humanity are all made from the same elements, and that pain and sorrow and certainly death come to all."[654]

Jessie was not just gifted with an extraordinary intelligence. She also had a sixth sense. She marveled at those times when she sensed or predicted events involving her loved ones that later proved to be true.[655] Frémont offered this explanation of her gift: "It doesn't seem strange to me. With each so much a part of the other's thoughts and feelings at all times, a crisis with either might cause these thoughts to materialize into a sense of actual physical presence."[656] As such, the Frémonts were not just a power couple, they were soul mates.

In traditional societies, women live through others. In marriage, a woman's sense of self-worth was strongly related to the success and status of her husband and her children, and she did whatever she could to enhance that. Libbie Custer lived vicariously through her husband's heroic exploits and she exalted in being married to an extraordinary man: "Autie, your career is something wonderful. Swept along as I am in the current of your eventful life I can still stop to realize that your history is simply marvelous. Every event seems to fit into every other event like the blocks in a child's puzzle.... Can you realize what wonders come constantly to you while other men lead such tame lives."[657] Libbie adored her husband: "I am prouder far to be his wife than I would be to be Mrs. Lincoln or a queen."[658] Indeed, she had a messianic view of him: "I believe if ever God sends men into the world for a special purpose Armstrong was born to be a soldier."[659]

Yet the relationship harbored some very dark sides. Being married to Custer brought Libbie intense, exhilarating periods of passion broken by prolonged stretches of mostly dull and at times acute fear, aching longing, and pangs of jealousy. Her proudest moments were riding alongside her husband at the head of his regiment on parade. Yet, looking back at their marriage, fear loomed above all: "It was a sudden plunge into a life of vicissitude and danger, and I hardly remember the time during the twelve years that followed when I was not in fear of some immediate peril, or in dread of some danger that threatened."[660] Being married to a soldier who led from the front was an enormous emotional drain. She admitted to her husband that: "It's of no use for me to try to see anything but a world of anxiety and the glory cannot cover the risks you have run."[661]

Living in a soldier's world, especially on campaign, was a grueling challenge that Libbie eventually mastered. Although raised in a genteel upper-class co-cooned lifestyle, she adapted swiftly to the physical and emotional hardships of wartime army life: "My part consisted in drilling myself to be as little trouble as I could. I had really learned, by many a self-inflicted lesson, never to be too cold or too hot, and rarely allowed a thought of hunger if we were where no supplies could be had. It was a long struggle." Overcoming a series of challenges steadily boosted a virtuous cycle of skills, confidence, and fatalism: "When a woman has come out of a danger, she is too utterly a coward by nature not to dread enduring that same thing again; but it is something to know that she is equal to it. Though she may tremble and grow faint in anticipation, having once been through it, she can count on rising to the situation when the hour actually comes."[662]

Libbie had to steel herself to gruesome sights, including mass death, that otherwise would fill her with pity and sorrow: "At first the bleaching bones of thousands of buffaloes were rather a melancholy sight to me, but I soon became as accustomed to the ghastly sockets of an unturned skull as the field mouse which ran in and out either orifice with food for her nest of little ones inside. All evidences of death are sad to a woman...and it seemed to me that the sadness of thinking of the death of these naturally peaceful creatures was softened as it is when one goes into a very old burying ground.... I suppose in a world where women reigned there would be little question that, unwilling to kill anything, in time she would be crowded out of the animal kingdom. But the buffalo were singularly pitiful prey to me."[663]

At Hays City, Custer and Libbie listened to a horrific story by a man whose wife and two children were butchered and mutilated by Indians at his home while he was tilling his cornfield. Libbie recalled that: "General Custer was so moved by this story that he could not speak, and I became so unnerved that it was many a night before I could shut my eyes without seeing the little yellow heads of those innocent children clotted with blood, and their sightless blue eyes turned to heaven as if for redress.... I was moved to deepest pity for the bereaved man, but I became so terrified that I could not even ride out of camp with an escort without inward quakings, and every strange or unaccountable speck on the horizon meant to me a lurking foe."[664]

Like her husband, Libbie favored an "eye for an eye" justice against Indian bands that warred against the United States. She defended her husband against "the current rumors that Autie and others are cruel in their treatment of the Indians. Autie and others only do what they are ordered to do. And if those who criticize these orders could only see for themselves...As we see...A woman rescued from Indian captivity who has suffered degradation unspeakable, the brutalities of the men, the venom of the women.... People in civilized conditions cannot imagine it. But we who have seen it, know."665

Like most men throughout history, Custer commanded the lion's share of physical, economic, and social power in the relationship. And, like most women, during conflicts between them Libbie wielded power indirectly through sweet reasoning and subtle manipulations rather than blunt confrontations; she gently planted and nurtured ideas in his mind that ideally blossomed with time. They settled into that division of social and economic labor in which each does what he or she does best. For instance, in socializing, "my husband...was not a voluble talker" so "most of the entertaining devolved upon me."666

Custer and Libbie had discussed him one day capitalizing on his military fame by pursuing a political career. Libbie was ambiguous over that prospect. She despised the degrading corrupt political world, while imagining the fame that her husband could win all the way to the White House. She was relieved that he had resisted the siren call of political bosses in the past. She understood that the longer he waited to enter politics, the more mature and independent he would be when he did. That time appeared to be rapidly approaching. In August 1873, she expressed her conflicting views: "Whether I can ever see you go into politics without a shudder of fear is a doubtful question.... Oh how thankful I am they did not entrap you. You would not have had the individuality of character or position you now have. I tell you Autie, I have never felt more ambitious for you nor more confident of your success than this summer. I am only a little afraid I can't keep up.... I see every day that great ambition I have for you and how I bask daily in the sunshine of your glory."667 Indeed, if given the choice, she preferred that he would win fame by mastering writing rather than politics: "my ambition for you in the world of letters almost takes the heart out of my body."668

Custer was naturally an upbeat, optimistic person. That positive outlook boosted Libbie when she was down: "I am perfectly overwhelmed with gratitude when I think what a glorious disposition yours is I am so up when I write you. So convinced that everything will turn out for the best. And so indifferent to troubling cares that I feel in your absence.... I never realized till now how dependent I am on your grand temperament for my fine spirits, good health, powers of endurance and all the bright glad hours that crowd into my days when I live with you."669

A man can extoll a woman's beauty, passion, erudition, wit, and sexiness, but often the quality that most keeps him around is when she is a "good sport." In other words, his gal is like a guy with whom he can be himself, exuberant, outspoken, and even outrageous without being judged, let alone condemned. Libbie was just such a good sport for Custer. She endured a ceaseless barrage of hardships, dangers, pranks, and even humiliations, but mostly remained loving and supportive.

Yet Libbie did have her limits. She condemned Custer's addiction to gambling and women. Each time she caught him, he begged forgiveness and promised to mend his ways, but sooner or later he was back at it. As a result, the Custers had a roller-coaster relationship of intense passionate highs and embittered lows.

Just what did John Frémont and George Custer, with their wives mostly behind and at times beside them, contribute to Manifest Destiny and the course of American history?

Frémont and Custer are famous for substantial reasons. Frémont acquired fame by leading five expeditions that mapped portions of the American West, and assuming a leading role in California's conquest. His fourth expedition ended disastrously after becoming snowbound in the San Juan Mountains, where starvation and frostbite killed eleven of his thirty-three men. Nonetheless, his fame got him nominated the Republican Party's first presidential candidate in 1856 and promotion to major general with army commands in Missouri in 1861 and Virginia in 1862, although he failed in all these endeavors. Nonetheless, Frémont is much better known for his triumphs than his defeats. In stark contrast, Custer is notorious for getting himself and 262 of his troops killed by overwhelming numbers of Indians during the battle of the Little Bighorn in 1876. Custer's tragic mistakes in that battle overshadow the reality that he was an outstanding cavalry commander during the Civil War. Unlike Frémont, who had four sometimes-overlapping careers as an explorer, soldier, businessman, and politician, Custer's career was confined to the military.

How important were the wives to their husbands' achievements? Each power couple racked up its share of career victories that might not have happened had the wives confined themselves to traditional roles or the men married different women. Each wife was adept at promoting her husband's career during his lifetime and his heroic image long after his death. In many ways, Jessie Frémont and Libbie Custer displayed more moral fiber and political savvy than their husbands. They were steel magnolias, who with grace and intelligence endured successions of scandals, dangers, and tragedies. Nonetheless, neither was a trailblazer for women's political and legal equality with men. As power couples, their respective achievements and failures varied with their differing ambitions. The Frémonts were a full-fledged power couple since John ran for the presidency and Jessie served as his effective campaign manager. The Custers never reached the overt political stage. Yet, had Custer prudently waited for the other commanders and their forces to arrive for a joint attack that defeated the Indians at the Little Bighorn, the fame that he would have won might well have propelled him into a political career that led to the White House.

Yet that begs a return to the question. What genuine impact did either man make on their nation's history? Despite all their fame, the course of the American empire would likely not have changed significantly had Frémont and Custer never existed.

The most important achievements of the Frémonts and Custers were cultural rather than practical. With heavy doses of self-promotion, the exploits of John Frémont and George Custer seized the popular imagination of nineteenth-century Americans, who elevated them into the pantheon of national folk heroes. At least, in reaching those cultural heights, they clutched résumés far weightier in concrete achievements than those of, say, Davy Crockett or Buffalo Bill Cody.

Fame, however, is ephemeral in the modern and especially postmodern world. Since the deaths of the wives, revisionist historians have systematically demolished the elaborate facades constructed by Jessie Frémont and Libbie Custer to hide their husbands and themselves. The golden sheen that once surrounded those men and their wives tarnished darker as historians exposed their myriad flaws while each subsequent generation has found its own heroes to worship.

Today, Custer is better recalled than Frémont partly because he died spectacularly, disastrously, and young, rather than obscurely and old. As important, Custer and Libbie were better self-promoters than Frémont and Jessie. So not surprisingly, Custer has provided greater inspiration for writers, painters, and movie directors. As for authors, if Frémont inspired scores of biographies and novels, hundreds have explored, celebrated, or condemned Custer. As for movies and television series, Custer has featured in scores and Frémont in dozens. Buffalo Bill Cody's Wild West Show climaxed with a reenactment of Custer's Last Stand; Frémont was ignored. No portrait of Frémont compares to "Custer's Last Fight," painted by Cassilly Adams in 1886 and turned into a lithograph by Otto Becker. The beer-brewing giant Anheuser-Busch had 150,000 prints made and distributed to saloons across the country. And those are just the most prominent representations. Paul Hutton also found Custer the inspiration for "comic book illustrations, political and humorous cartoons, posters, play money, bubblegum, greeting and post cards, record album covers, and advertisements for products ranging from whiskey to children's cereal."[670]

What has become known as the "Custer myth" will likely persist as a provocative foil for people to debate the meaning of American history.[671] What is the Custer myth? Actually, there are two. In popular culture, as opposed to academic scholarship, there is the Custer myth of the national hero and the Custer counter-myth of the Indian slaughtering narcissist whose hubris led to the slaughter of himself and 262 other troops at the Little Bighorn. Then there is the marriage of the myths. Myth implies made-up. Custer's courage was genuine, not contrived, or even exaggerated. But so too was Custer's narcissism and hubris. As such, Custer was at once a man of his time who timelessly personifies the very best and worst of his nation.

Regardless, culturally, the power seesaw between those conflicting interpretations has shifted decisively. While Americans with traditional attitudes still view Custer as a hero and martyr, most contemporary Americans have adapted either a more nuanced or outright hostile view. The dichotomy between the Custer myth and counter-myth is most glaring in Hollywood. In 1941, Errol Flynn played the myth in *They Died with Their Boots On*, directed by Raoul Walsh. In 1970, Richard Mulligan played the counter-myth in *Little Big Man*, directed by Arthur Penn. In recent decades, both the myth and counter-myth have faded into cultural obscurity as pop culture shifts to fantasy and science fiction make-believe rather than historical figures.

Elements of the counter-myth shadowed the myth from the beginning. Most officers who served beneath Custer despised him, but army culture forced them to confine their feelings to bitter mutterings among themselves. It was not until nine decades after the Little Bighorn that the cultural tide turned decisively against Custer. During the 1960s, protest movements for Civil Rights and against the Vietnam War led to critical reexaminations of all American myths. Custer has become synonymous with the traditional American attitude of contempt for and acts of conquest against the Indians. Vine Deloria asserted that view with his 1969 polemical book titled *Custer Died for Your Sins* and subtitled *An Indian Manifesto*. A year later, Dee Brown offered a broader, more scholarly interpretation with his *Bury My Heart at Wounded Knee: An Indian History of the American West.*[672] Those books helped inspire the New Western History movement that emphasized previously neglected subjects of ethnicity, gender, region, class, and ecology in explaining the past.[673]

Americans belatedly celebrated the four-hundred-year-anniversary of the European discovery of the New World during the World Columbian Exposition in Chicago held from May 1 to October 30, 1893. During that time, more than 27 million people toured exhibits from forty-six countries. Lost amidst the crush and cacophony of visitors was an academic conference during which Dr. Frederick Jackson Turner, a University of Wisconsin professor, presented his lecture, "The

Significance of the Frontier in American History."[674] Turner argued that American culture and democracy were forged by enterprising pioneers on the frontier. He pointed out that the physical frontier no longer existed, and thus the nation faced a potentially grave crisis. Where would Americans vent their energy, creativity, and individualism that made their nation great and their democracy vibrant? He called on Americans to find new frontiers of achievement while continuing to celebrate and draw inspiration from the pioneers and the western frontier that over several centuries finally receded to extinction: "The Western spirit must be invoked for new and nobler achievements."[675]

Turner is no longer fashionable among American historians and for good reasons. He rejected one single-dimensional explanation of American history to insist upon another: "The true point of view in the history of this nation is not the Atlantic coast, it is the Great West."[676] What should be obvious is that no one theory can explain any nation's past, let alone one as complex as that of the United States. Yet, the frontier as a process and place before 1890, and residually as a state of mind ever since, is critical to understanding American history.

And for that, explorations of the lives of John and Jessie Frémont, and George and Libbie Custer as extraordinary individuals, couples, and symbols, can provide fascinating, perplexing insights.

Bibliography

★

PRIMARY SOURCES

Ames, George W., ed. *A Doctor Comes to California: The Diary of John S. Griffen, Assistant Surgeon with Kearny's Dragoons, 1846–1847.* San Francisco: California Historical Society, 1943.

Barrett, Lawrence. "Personal Recollections of General Custer," in Frederick Whitaker, ed. *A Complete Life of Gen. George A. Custer.* New York: Sheldon, 1876, 629–43.

Benton, Thomas Hart. *Thirty Years' View, or A History of the Working of the American Government for Thirty Years from 1820 to 1850,* 2 vols. New York: D. Appleton, 1858, 1880.

Bigelow, John. *Memoir of the Life and Public Services of John Charles Frémont.* New York: Derby & Jackson, 1856.

Bray, Edmund C., and Martha Coleman Bray, eds. *Joseph N. Nicollet on the Plains and Prairies: The Expeditions of 1838–39.* Minneapolis: Minnesota State Historical Press, 1993.

Brininstool, E. A., ed., David L. Spotts. *Campaigning with Custer and the Nineteenth Kansas Volunteer Cavalry in the Washita Campaign, 1868-69.* Lincoln: University of Nebraska, 1988.

Burt, Mary E., ed., as told by Elizabeth B. Custer. *The Boy General: Story of the Life of Major-General George A. Custer.* New York: Charles Scribner's Sons, 1901.

Carroll, John M., ed. *The Benteen-Goldin Letters on Custer and His Last Battle.* Lincoln: University of Nebraska Press, 1991.

———. *Custer in the Civil War: His Unfinished Memoirs.* San Francisco: Presidio Press, 1977.

———. *Custer's Chief of Scouts: The Reminiscences of Charles A. Varnum.* Lincoln: University of Nebraska Press, 1987.

Carvalho, Solomon Nunes. *Incidents of Travel and Adventure in the Far West with Col. Frémont's Last Expedition.* New York: Derby and Jackson, 1859.

Crary, Catherine S., ed. *Dear Belle: Letters from a Cadet and Officer to His Sweetheart, 1858–1865.* Middletown, CT: Wesleyan University Press, 1965.

Custer, Elizabeth Bacon. *"Boots and Saddles," or Life in Dakota with General Custer.* New York: Harper and Brothers, 1885.

———. *Following the Guidon* (1890). Norman: University of Oklahoma Press, 1966.

————. *Tenting on the Plains, or General Custer in Kansas and Texas*. New York: Harper and Brothers, 1887.

Custer, George A. *My Life on the Plains*. Lincoln: University of Nebraska Press, 1968.

Custer, George Armstrong. *Wild Life on the Plains and the Horrors of Indian Warfare (1874)*. Brandon, VT: Sidney M. Southard, 1884.

Dana, Richard Henry. *"Twenty-Four Years After," Two Years Before the Mast*. Boston: Houghton Mifflin, 1887.

Dippie, Brian W., ed. *Nomad: George A. Custer in Turf, Field, and Farm*. Austin: University of Texas Press, 1980.

Ford, Worthington Chauncey, ed. *A Cycle of Adams Letters, 1861–1865*, vol. 2, Boston: Houghton Mifflin, 1920.

Frémont, Elizabeth Benton. *Recollections of Elizabeth Frémont, Daughter of the Pathfinder General John C. Frémont and Jessie Benton Frémont His Wife*. New York: Frederick H. Hitchcock, 1912.

Frémont, Jessie Benton. *Far West Sketches*. Boston: D. Lothrop, 1890.

————. *"The Origin of the Frémont Explorations," Century*, vol. 41 (March 1891), 766–71.

————. *Souvenirs of My Time*. Boston: D. Lothrop, 1887.

————. *The Story of the Guard: A Chronicle of the War*. Boston: Ticknor and Field, 1863.

————. *The Will and the Way Stories*. Boston: D. Lothrop, 1891.

————. *A Year of American Travel*. New York: Harper and Brothers, 1878.

Frémont, John Charles. *Memoirs of My Life*. Chicago: Belford, Clarke, 1887.

————. *Memoirs of My Life*. New York: Cooper Square Press, 2001.

Frost, Lawrence A., and James Calhoun. *Some Observations on the Yellowstone Expedition of 1873*. Glendale, CA: Arthur H. Clark, 1981.

Grant, Ulysses S. *The Personal Memoirs of Ulysses S. Grant (1885)*. Princeton, NJ: Great Commanders, 1998.

Greeley, Horace. *The Autobiography of Horace Greeley or Recollections of a Busy Life*. New York: E. B. Treat, 1872.

Grimsley, Mark. *And Keep Moving On: The Virginia Campaign, May–June 1864*. Lincoln: University of Nebraska Press, 2002.

Hardorff, Richard B., ed. *Washita Memoirs: Eyewitness Accounts of Custer's Attack on Black Kettle's Village*. Norman: University of Oklahoma Press, 2006.

Hay, John. *Lincoln and the Civil War in the Diaries and Letters of John Hay*, edited by Tyler Dennett. New York: Dodd, Mead, 1939.

Hazen, William B. N. *Some Corrections to "My Life on the Plains."* St. Paul, MN: Ramsley and Cunningham, 1875.

Herndon, William, and Jesse Weik. *Herndon's Lincoln: The True Story of a Great Life*, 3 vols. Chicago: Belford, Clarke, 1889.

Herr, Pamela, and Mary Lee Spence, eds. *The Letters of Jessie Benton Frémont*. Urbana: University of Illinois Press, 1993.

Jackson, Donald, and Mary Lee Spence, eds. *The Expeditions of John Charles Frémont*, 3 vols. Champlain: University of Illinois Press, 1970, 1980.

Longstreet, James. *From Manassas to Appomattox: Memoirs of the Civil War in America*. Philadelphia: J. B. Lippincott, 1908.

Lovejoy, Julia Louisa. *"Letters, 1856," Kansas Historical Society Quarterly*, vol. 15 (1947), 127–42.

McClellan, George Brinton. *McClellan's Own Story: The War for the Union*. New York: Charles Webster, 1887.

Meltzer, Melton, and Patricia G. Holland, eds. *Lydia Maria Child: Selected Letters, 1817–*

1880. Amherst: University of Massachusetts Press, 1982.

Merington, Marguerite, ed. *The Custer Story: The Life and Intimate Letters of General George A. Custer and His Wife Elizabeth*. Lincoln: University of Nebraska Press, 1987.

Nevins, Allan, ed. *Polk: The Diary of a President, 1845–1849*. New York: Capricorn Books, 1968.

Nicolay, John G., and John Hay. *Abraham Lincoln: A History*, 10 vols. New York: Century, 1890.

Onuf, Peter S. *Jefferson's Empire: The Language of American Nationhood*. Charlottesville: University of Virginia Press, 2000.

Overfield, Lloyd J., ed. *The Little Bighorn, 1876: The Official Communication: Documents and Reports*. Lincoln: University of Nebraska Press, 1990.

Pohanka, Brian C., ed. *A Summer on the Plains with Custer's 7th Cavalry: The 1870 Diary of Annie Gibson Roberts*. Lynchburg, VA: Schroeder, 2004.

Preuss, Charles. *Exploring with Frémont: The Private Diaries of Charles Preuss, Cartographer*, translated and edited by Erwin G. and Elizabeth K. Gudde. Norman: University of Oklahoma Press, 1958.

Quaife, Milo Milton, ed. *Kit Carson's Autobiography*. Lincoln: University of Nebraska Press, 1966.

Reynolds, Arlene, ed. *The Civil War Memories of Elizabeth Bacon Custer: Reconstructed from Her Diaries and Notes*. Austin: University of Texas Press, 1994.

Sheridan, Philip. *The Personal Memoirs of P. H. Sheridan*. New York: Da Capo, 1992.

Stanley, David S. *Personal Memoirs of Major General D. S. Stanley*. Cambridge, MA: Harvard University Press, 1917.

Stern, Philip Van Doren, ed. *The Life and Writings of Abraham Lincoln*. New York: Modern Library, 2000.

Tarver, M., and H. Cobb, eds. *The Western Journal*. St. Louis: M. Niedmer, 1854.

Utley, Robert M., ed. *Life in Custer's Cavalry: Diaries and Letters of Albert and Jennie Barnitz, 1865–1868*. Lincoln: University of Nebraska Press, 1987.

Wheeler, Candace. *Yesterdays in a Busy Life*. New York: Harper and Brothers, 1918.

Wilkes, Charles. *The Autobiography of Rear Admiral Charles Wilkes, United States Navy, 1798–1877*. Washington, DC: Naval History Division, 1978.

———. *Narrative of the United States Exploring Expedition During the Years 1838, 1839, 1840, 1841, 1842*. New York: Forgotten Books, 2015.

SECONDARY SOURCES

Abrams, Marc. *Sioux War Dispatches: Reports from the Field, 1876–1877*. New York: Westholme, 2012.

Alter, J. Cecil. *Jim Bridger*. Norman: University of Oklahoma Press, 1986.

Asay, Karol. *Gray Head and Long Hair: The Benteen-Custer Relationship*. New York: J. M. Carol, 1983.

Athearn, Robert G. *The Mythic West in Twentieth Century America*. Lawrence: University Press of Kansas, 1986.

Bancroft, Hubert Howe. *The History of California*, 6 vols. San Francisco: The History Company, 1884–90.

Barnett, Louise. *Touched by Fire: The Life, Death, and Mythic Afterlife of George Armstrong Custer*. Lincoln: University of Nebraska Press, 2006.

Bartlett, Ruhl J. *Frémont and the Republican Party*. Columbus: Ohio State University Press, 1930.

Bauer, K. Jack. *The Mexican War, 1846–1848.* Lincoln: University of Nebraska Press, 1992.
———. *Zachery Taylor: Soldier, Planter, Statesman of the Old Southwest.* Baton Rouge: Louisiana State University Press, 1985.
Bergamini, John D. *The Hundredth Year: The United States in 1876.* New York: G. P. Putnam's Sons, 1976.
Berthrong, Donald J. *The Southern Cheyennes.* Norman: University of Oklahoma Press, 1965.
Bicknell, John. *Lincoln's Pathfinder: John C. Frémont and the Violent Election of 1856.* Chicago: Chicago Review Press, 2017.
Blackman, Ann. *Wild Rose: The True Story of a Civil War Spy.* New York: Random House, 2006.
Borneman, Walter. *Polk: The Man Who Transformed the Presidency and America.* New York: Random House, 2009.
Brady, Cyrus T. *Indian Fights and Fighters: The Soldier and the Sioux.* New York: McClure Philips, 1904.
Brands, H. W. *The Age of Gold: The California Gold Rush and the New American Dream.* New York: Anchor, 2003.
———. *The Man Who Saved the Union: Ulysses S. Grant.* New York: Anchor, 2013.
Bray, Martha Coleman. *Joseph Nicollet and His Map: Exploring the Upper Mississippi River.* Philadelphia: American Philosophical Society, 1980.
Brown, David. *Palmerston and the Politics of Foreign Policy, 1846–54.* Manchester, UK: Manchester University Press, 2003.
Brown, Dee. *Bury My Heart at Wounded Knee: An Indian History of the American West* (1970). New York: Picador, 2007.
Bunnell, Lafayette H., and Stephen P. Medley. *The Discovery of Yosemite and the Indian War of 1850 and 1851 Which Led to that Event* (1892). New York: Endeavor, 2016.
Burnett, Peter. "Recollections and Opinions of an Old Pioneer," *Oregon Historical Quarterly,* vol. 5 (1904), 86–88.
Campbell, Joseph. *The Hero with a Thousand Faces.* New York: MJF Books, 1949.
Carroll, John M. *Custer in Texas: An Interrupted Narrative.* New York: Sol Lewis, 1975.
———. *They Rode with Custer: A Biographical Directory of the Men That Rode with General George Armstrong Custer.* Mattituck, NY: J. M. Carroll, 1993.
Caudill, Edward, and Paul Ashdown. *Inventing Custer: The Making of an American Legend.* New York: Rowman and Littlefield, 2015.
Chaffin, Tom. *Pathfinder: John Charles Frémont and the Course of American Empire.* Norman: University of Oklahoma Press, 2014.
Chalfant, William Y. *Hancock's War: Conflict on the Southern Plains.* Norman: University of Oklahoma Press, 2010.
Chamberlain, Muriel. *Pax Britannica?: British Foreign Policy, 1789–1914.* New York: Routledge, 1989.
Chambers, Lee. *Fort Abraham Lincoln: Dakota Territory.* New York: Schiffer, 2008.
Chambers, William. *Old Bullion Benton: Senator from the New West.* New York: Little, Brown, 1956.
Clarke, Dwight. *Stephen Watts Kearny: Soldier of the West.* Norman: University of Oklahoma Press, 1961.
Cognan, Gregory O. *The Culture and Customs of the Sioux Indians.* Lincoln: Bison, 2012.
Collins, Charles D. *The Cheyenne Wars Atlas.* New York: Books Express, 2012.
Connell, Evan S. *Son of Morning Star: Custer and the Little Bighorn.* San Francisco: North Point, 1984.
Cooper, Edward S. *William Babcock Hazen: The Best Hated Man.* Madison, NJ: Fairleigh

Dickinson University Press, 2005.

———. *William Worth Belknap: An American Disgrace*. Madison, NJ: Fairleigh Dickinson University Press, 2003.

Cozzens, Peter. *Shenandoah 1862: Stonewall Jackson's Valley Campaign*. Chapel Hill: University of North Carolina Press, 2008.

Crouch, Richard E. *Brandy Station: A Battle Like No Other*. New York: Willow Bend, 2002.

Darling, Roger. *Custer's Seventh Cavalry Comes to Dakota*. El Segundo, CA: Upton and Sons, 1989.

Dary, David. *The Oregon Trail: An American Saga*. New York: Alfred Knopf, 2004.

Daugherty, James Henry. *Marcus and Narcissa Whitman, Pioneers of Oregon*. New York: Viking, 1953.

Deloria, Vine. *Custer Died for Your Sins: An Indian Manifesto* (1969). New York: Macmillan, 1988.

Denton, Sally. *Passion and Principle: John and Jessie Frémont, the Couple whose Power, Politics, and Love Shaped Nineteenth Century America*. Lincoln: University of Nebraska Press, 2007.

Deverell, William, and David Igler, eds. *A Companion to California History*. New York: Wiley-Blackwell, 2014.

DeVoto, Bernard. *The Year of Decision: 1846*. Boston: Houghton Mifflin, 1943.

Dippie, Brian A. *Custer's Last Stand: The Anatomy of an American Myth*. Lincoln: University of Nebraska, 2002.

Donald, David Herbert. *Lincoln*. New York: Simon and Schuster, 1995.

Donovan, James. *A Terrible Glory: Custer and the Little Bighorn, the Last Great Battle of the American West*. New York: Little, Brown, 2008.

Donovan, Jim. *Custer and the Little Bighorn: The Man, The Mystery, The Myth*. New York: Crestline, 2001.

Drury, Bob, and Tom Clavin. *The Heart of Everything That Is: The Untold Story of Red Cloud, An American Legend*. New York: Simon and Schuster, 2014.

Dunlay, Thomas W. *Kit Carson and the Indians*. Lincoln: University of Nebraska Press, 2005.

Eells, Myron. *Marcus Whitman: Pathfinder and Patriot*. New York: Forgotten Books, 2015.

Egan, Ferol. *Frémont: Explorer for a Restless Nation*. Reno: University of Nevada Press, 1985.

Egerton, Douglas R. *Year of Meteors: Stephen Douglas, Abraham Lincoln, and the Election that Brought on the Civil War*. New York: Bloomsbury, 2010.

Eisenhower, John S. *Agent of Destiny: The Life and Times of General Winfield Scott*. New York: Free Press, 1997.

———. *So Far From God: The U.S. War with Mexico, 1846–1848*. Norman: University of Oklahoma Press, 1989.

Etulain, Richard W., ed. *Writing Western History: Essays on Major Western Historians*. Albuquerque: University of New Mexico Press, 1991.

Favour, Alpheus H. *Old Bill Williams: Mountain Man*. Norman: University of Oklahoma Press, 1981.

Fellman, Michael. *Inside War: The Guerrilla Conflict in Missouri During the Civil War*. New York: Oxford University Press, 1989.

Fishwick, Marshall W. *American Heroes: Myth and Reality*. Washington, DC: Public Affairs, 1954.

Fitzgerald, Michael W. *Splendid Failure: Postwar Reconstruction in the American South*. New York: Ivan R. Dee, 2008.

Foner, Eric. *Free Soil, Free Labor, Free Men: The Ideology of the Republican Party before the Civil War*. New York: Oxford University Press, 1995.

————. *Reconstruction: America's Unfinished Revolution, 1863–1877.* New York: Harper and Row, 1988.

Foos, Paul. *A Short, Offhand, Killing: Soldiers and Social Conflict during the Mexican-American War.* Chapel Hill: University of North Carolina Press, 2002.

Forbes, Robert Pierce. *The Missouri Compromise and Its Aftermath: Slavery and Its Meaning for America.* Chapel Hill: University of North Carolina Press, 2007.

Freeman, Douglas Southall, and Richard Harwell. *Lee.* New York: Scribner's, 1997.

Frost, Lawrence A. *The Court Martial of General George Armstrong Custer.* Norman: University of Oklahoma Press, 1968.

————. *General Custer's Libbie.* Seattle: Superior, 1976.

Fuller, James A., ed. *The Election of 1860.* Kent, OH: Kent State University Press, 2013.

Furtado, Albert. *John Sutter: A Life on the North American Frontier.* Norman: University of Oklahoma Press, 2006.

Gallagher, Gary W., ed. *The Shenandoah Valley Campaign of 1862.* Chapel Hill: University of North Carolina Press, 2003.

————. *The Shenandoah Valley Campaign of 1864.* Chapel Hill: University of North Carolina Press, 2006.

Geiger, Roger L., ed. *The American College in the Nineteenth Century.* Nashville, TN: Vanderbilt University Press, 2000.

Gienapp, William E. *The Origins of the Republican Party, 1852–1856.* New York: Oxford University Press, 1988.

Gilbert, Bil. *Westering Man: The Life of Joseph Walker.* Norman: University of Oklahoma Press, 1989.

Goetzmann, William H. *Exploration and Empire: The Explorer and the Scientist in the Winning of the American West.* New York: Alfred Knopf, 1966.

Goodwin, Doris Kearns. *Team of Rivals: The Political Genius of Abraham Lincoln.* New York: Simon and Schuster, 2006.

Graham, W. A., ed. *The Custer Myth: A Source Book of Custeriana.* Mechanicsburg, PA: Stackpole, 2000.

Gray, John S. *The Centennial Campaign: The Sioux War of 1876.* Fort Collins, CO: Old Army Press, 1976.

Greene, Jerome A. *Battles and Skirmishes of the Great Sioux War, 1876–1877.* Norman: University of Oklahoma Press, 1996.

————. *Lakota and Cheyenne: Indian Views of the Great Sioux War, 1876–1877.* Norman: University of Oklahoma Press, 2000.

————. *Stricken Field: The Little Bighorn since 1876.* Norman: University of Oklahoma Press, 2008.

————. *Washita: The U.S. Army and the Southern Cheyenne.* Norman: University of Oklahoma Press, 2008.

Greene, Theodore P. *America's Heroes: The Changing Success.* New York: Oxford University Press, 1970.

Grinnell, George Bird. *The Cheyenne Indians,* 2 vols. New Haven, CT: Yale University Press, 1923.

————. *The Fighting Cheyennes* (1915). Norman: University of Oklahoma Press, 1956.

Grossman, James R., ed. *The Frontier in American Culture.* Berkeley: University of California Press, 1994.

Guild, Thelma S., and Harvey L. Carter. *Kit Carson: A Pattern for Heroes.* Lincoln: University of Nebraska Press, 1984.

Hafen, LeRoy R. *Broken Hand: The Life of Thomas Fitzpatrick: Mountain Man, Guide, and*

Indian Agent. Lincoln: University of Nebraska Press, 1981.

Hafen, LeRoy R., and Ann Hafen. *The Old Spanish Trail*. Lincoln: University of Nebraska Press, 1993.

Hague, Harlan, and David J. Langum. *Thomas O. Larkin: A Life of Patriotism and Profit in Old California*. Norman: University of Oklahoma Press, 1990.

Harlow, Neal. *California Conquered: War and Peace on the Pacific, 1846–1850*. Berkeley: University of California Press, 1982.

Hassrick, Royal B. *The Sioux*. Norman: University of Oklahoma Press, 1964.

Hatch, Thom. *Black Kettle: The Cheyenne Chief Who Sought Peace but Found War*. New York: John Wiley and Sons, 2004.

———. *Glorious War: the Civil War Adventures of George Armstrong Custer*. New York: St. Martin's, 2014.

Hattaway, Herman, and Archer Jones. *How the North Won the Civil War: A Military History of the Civil War*. Chicago: University of Illinois Press, 1991.

Hedren, Paul, ed. *The Great Sioux War, 1876–77,* Helena: Montana Historical Society, 1991.

Herr, Pamela. *Jessie Benton Frémont*. Norman: University of Oklahoma Press, 1988.

Hofling, Charles. *Custer and the Little Big Horn: A Psychobiographical Inquiry*. Detroit: Wayne State University Press, 1981.

Hofstadter, Richard. *The Paranoid Style in American Politics*. New York: Vintage, 2008.

Hoig, Stan. *The Battle of the Washita: The Sheridan-Custer Indian Campaign of 1867–69*. Garden City, NY; Doubleday, 1979.

———. *The Sand Creek Massacre*. Norman: University of Oklahoma Press, 1974.

Holt, Michael F. *The Political Crisis of the 1850s*. New York: W.W. Norton, 1987.

———. *The Rise and Fall of the American Whig Party: Jacksonian Politics and the Origins of the Civil War*. New York: Oxford University Press, 1999.

Howe, Daniel Walker. *The Political Culture of the American Whigs*. Chicago: University of Chicago Press, 1984.

Hurtado, Albert L. *John Sutter: A Life on the American Frontier*. Norman: University of Oklahoma Press, 2006.

Hutton, Paul Andrew. *Phil Sheridan and His Army*. Norman: University of Oklahoma Press, 1999.

Hutton, Paul Andrew, ed. *The Custer Reader*. Lincoln: University of Nebraska Press, 1992.

Hyde, George E. *Red Cloud's Folk: A History of the Oglala Sioux*. Norman: University of Oklahoma Press, 1957.

Isely, Jeter Allen. *Horace Greeley and the Republican Party, 1853–1861*. Princeton, NJ: Princeton University Press, 1947.

Jackson, Donald. *Custer's Gold: The United States Cavalry Expedition of 1874*. New Haven, CT: Yale University Press, 1966.

Jackson, Helen Hunt. *A Century of Dishonor: The Classic Expose of the Plight of Native Americans* (1881). New York: Dover, 2003.

Jewett, Robert, and John Shelton Lawrence. *The Myth of the American Superhero*. Grand Rapids, MI: William Eerdman, 2002.

Johnson, Susan. *Roaring Camp: The Social World of the California Gold Rush*. New York: W.W. Norton, 2001.

Johnson, Timothy. *Winfield Scott: The Quest for Military Glory*. Topeka: University Press of Kansas, 2015.

Kammen, Michael. *Mystic Cords of Memory: The Transformation of Tradition in American Culture*. New York: Vintage, 1993.

Kelman, Ari. *A Misplaced Massacre: Struggling Over the Meaning of Sand Creek*. Cambridge,

MA: Harvard University Press, 2015.

Kidd, James H. *Personal Reminisces of a Cavalryman*. Ionia, MI: Sentinel, 1908.

Kirshner, Ralph. *The Class of 1861: Custer, Ames, and Their Classmates After West Point*. Carbondale, IL: Southern Illinois University Press, 1999.

Knight, Peter. *Conspiracy Nation: The Politics of Paranoia in Postwar America*. New York: New York University Press, 2002.

Korda, Michael. *Clouds of Glory: The Life and Legend of Robert E. Lee*. New York: Harper, 2014.

Kraft, Louis. *Custer and the Cheyenne: George Armstrong Custer's Winter Campaign on the Southern Plains*. New York: Upton and Sons, 1995.

Lavender, David. *Bent's Fort*. Lincoln: University of Nebraska Press, 1972.

Leckie, Shirley A. *Elizabeth Bacon Custer and the Making of the Myth*. Norman: University of Oklahoma Press, 1993.

Lecompte, Janet. *Pueblo, Hardscrabble, Greenhorn*. Norman: University of Oklahoma Press, 1978.

Levine, Bruce. *Half Slave and Half Free: The Roots of the Civil War*. New York: Hill and Wang, 2005.

Lewis, Ernest Allen. *The Frémont Cannon*. Glendale, CA: Arthur H. Clark, 1981.

Limerick, Patricia Nelson. *The Legacy of Conquest: The Unbroken Past of the American West*. New York: W.W. Norton, 1987.

Limerick, Patricia Nelson, Clyde A. Milner, and Charles E. Rankin, eds. *Trails: Toward a New Western History*. Lawrence: University Press of Kansas, 1991.

Linenthal, Edward Tabor. *Americans and Their Battlefields*. Urbana: University of Illinois Press, 1991.

———. *Changing Images of the Western Hero in America: A History of Popular Symbolism*. New York: Edwin Mellen, 1982.

Longacre, Edward G. *The Cavalry at Gettysburg: A Tactical Study of Mounted Operations during the Civil War's Pivotal Campaign*. Lincoln: University of Nebraska Press, 1986.

———. *Custer and His Wolverines: The Michigan Cavalry Brigade, 1861–1865*. Conshohocken, PA: Combined Publishing, 1997.

———. *The Early Morning of War: Bull Run, 1861*. Norman: University of Oklahoma Press, 2014.

———. *Lincoln's Cavalrymen: A History of the Mounted Forces of the Army of the Potomac*. Mechanicsburg, PA: Stackpole, 2000.

Lubetkin, John. *Jay Cooke's Gamble: The Northern Pacific Railroad, the Sioux, and the Panic of 1873*. Norman: University of Oklahoma Press, 2006.

Madley, Benjamin. *An American Genocide: The United States and the California Indian Catastrophe*. New Haven, CT: Yale University Press, 2016.

Marti, Werner H. *Messenger of Destiny: The California Adventures of Archibald H. Gillespie, 1846–1847*. San Francisco: John Howell, 1960.

Martin, Samuel J. *Kill-Cavalry: The Life of Union General Hugh Judson Kilpatrick*. Mechanicsburg, PA: Stackpole, 2000.

Matzke, Rebecca Berens. *Deterrence through Strength: British Naval Power and Foreign Policy under Pax Britannica*. Lincoln: University of Nebraska Press, 2001.

McKay, James. *Allan Pinkerton: The First Private Eye*. New York: Wiley, 1997.

McPherson, James M. *Battle Cry of Freedom: The Civil War Era*. New York: Oxford University Press, 1988.

———. *Tried by War: Abraham Lincoln as Commander in Chief*. New York: Penguin Press, 2008.

Merk, Frederick. *Manifest Destiny and Mission in American History: A Reinterpretation*. New York: Alfred A. Knopf, 1963.

Merry, Robert W. *A Country of Vast Designs: James K. Polk, The Mexican War, and the Conquest of the American Continent*. New York: Simon and Schuster, 2009.

Miller, David Humphreys. *Custer's Fall: The Indian Side of the Story*. Lincoln: University of Nebraska Press, 1985.

Miller, William Lee. *President Lincoln and the Duty of a Statesman*. New York: Alfred Knopf, 2008.

Mills, Charles K. *Harvest of Barren Regrets: The Army Career of Frederick William Benteen, 1834–1898*. Glendale, CA: Arthur H. Clark, 1985.

Milner, Clyde, Carol O'Connor, and Martha Sandweiss, eds. *The Oxford History of the American War*. New York: Oxford University Press, 1994.

Milner, H. Craig, and William E. Unrau. *The End of Indian Kansas: A Study of Cultural Revolution, 1854–1871*. Lawrence: Regents Press of Kansas, 1978.

Monaghan, Jay. *Civil War on the Western Border, 1854–1865*. Lincoln: University of Nebraska Press, 1955.

———. *Custer: The Life of General George Armstrong Custer*. Boston: Little, Brown, 1959.

Monnett, John H. *The Battle of Beecher Island and the Indian War of 1867–1869*. Boulder: University Press of Colorado, 1992.

Morgan, Edmund S. *American Heroes: Profiles of the Men and Women Who Shaped Early America*. New York: W.W. Norton, 2008.

Morris, Roy. *Sheridan: The Life and Wars of General Phil Sheridan*. New York: Crown, 1992.

Morrison, James L. *"The Best Little School in the World": West Point, the Pre-Civil War Years, 1833–1861*. Kent, OH: Kent State University Press, 1986.

Mueller, James E. *Shooting Arrows and Slinging Mud: Custer, the Press, and the Little Bighorn*. Norman: University of Oklahoma Press, 2013.

Mueller, Ken. *Senator Benton and the People: Master Race Democracy on the Early American Frontier*. New York: New York University Press, 2014.

Mulford, Ami Frank. *Fighting Indians in the 7th United States Cavalry: Custer's Favorite Regiment*. Corning, NY: Paul Lindsley Mulford, 1879.

Nester, William. *The Age of Jackson and the Art of American Power, 1815–1848*. Washington, DC: Potomac Books, 2013.

———. *The Age of Lincoln and the Art of American Power, 1848–1876*. Washington, DC: Potomac Books, 2013.

———. *The Hamiltonian Vision, 1789–1800: The Art of Power during the Early Republic*. Washington, DC: Potomac Books, 2012.

———. *The Jeffersonian Vision, 1801–1815: The Art of Power during the Early Republic*. Washington, DC: Potomac Books, 2013.

Nester, William R. *From Mountain Man to Millionaire: The "Bold and Dashing Life" of Robert Campbell*. Columbia: University of Missouri Press, 2011.

Nevins, Allan. *Frémont: Pathmarker of the West*. Lincoln: University of Nebraska Press, 1992.

Nevins, Allan. *Ordeal of the Union: A House Dividing, 1852–1857*. New York: Charles Scribner's Sons, 1950.

Nichols, Ronald H. *In Custer's Shadow: Major Marcus Reno*. Norman: University of Oklahoma Press, 2000.

Nobles, Gregory H. *American Frontiers: Cultural Encounters and Continental Conquests*. New York: Hill and Wang, 1997.

Olson, James V. *Red Cloud and the Sioux Problem*. Lincoln: University of Nebraska Press, 1965.

Owen, Kenneth. *Riches for All: The California Gold Rush and the World*. Lincoln: University of Nebraska Press, 2002.

Paludan, Philip Shaw. *The Presidency of Abraham Lincoln*. Topeka: University Press of Kansas, 1994.

Parker, Watson. *Gold in the Black Hills*. Lincoln: University of Nebraska Press, 1982.

Parks, Rita. *The Western Hero in Film and Television*. Ann Arbor, MI: UMI Research Press, 1982.

Parrish, William E. *Frank Blair: Lincoln's Conservative*. Columbia: University of Missouri Press, 1998,

Perkins, Bradford. *The Creation of a Republican Empire, 1776–1865*. New York: Cambridge University Press, 1993.

Perrett, Geoffrey. *Lincoln's War: The Untold Story of America's Greatest President as Commander in Chief*. New York: Random House, 2004.

Peskin, Allan. *Winfield Scott and the Profession of Arms*. Kent, OH: Kent State University Press, 2004.

Philbrick, Nathaniel. *Sea of Glory: America's Voyage of Discovery, the United States Exploring Expedition, 1838–1842*. New York: Penguin, 2004.

Phillips, Catherine Coffin. *Jessie Benton Frémont: A Woman Who Made History*. San Francisco: J. H. Nash, 1935.

Phillips, Christopher. *Damned Yankee: The Life of General Nathaniel Lyon*. Columbia: University of Missouri Press, 1990.

Pletcher, David M. *The Diplomacy of Annexation: Texas, Oregon, and the Mexican War*. Columbia: University of Missouri Press, 1973.

Potter, David M. *The Impending Crisis, 1848–1861*. New York: Harper Perennial, 2011.

Rafuse, Ethan S. *McClellan's War: The Failure of Moderation in the Struggle for the Union*. Bloomington: Indiana University Press, 2005.

Ramsay, Robin. *Politics and Paranoia*. London: Picnic Publishing, 2008.

Reedstrom, E. Lisle. *Custer's 7th Cavalry: From Fort Riley to the Little Big Horn*. New York: Sterling, 1992.

Remley, David. *Kit Carson: The Life of an American Borderman*. Norman: University of Oklahoma Press, 2012.

Richter, William L. *The Army in Texas During Reconstruction*. College Station: Texas A & M University Press, 1987.

Robbins, James S. *Last in Their Class: Custer, Pickett, and the Goats of West Point*. New York: Encounter Books, 2006.

Roberts, Brian. *American Alchemy: The California Gold Rush and Middle Class Culture*. Chapel Hill: University of North Carolina Press, 2000.

Roberts, David. *A Newer World: Kit Carson, John Charles Frémont, and the Claiming of the American West*. New York: Simon and Schuster, 2001.

Robinson, Charles. *A Good Year to Die: The Story of the Great Sioux War*. Norman: University of Oklahoma Press, 1996.

Rodman, Paul, and Elliott West. *Mining Frontiers of the Far West*. Albuquerque: University of New Mexico Press, 2001.

Rolle, Andrew. *John Charles Frémont: Character as Destiny*. Norman: University of Oklahoma Press, 1991.

Roosevelt, Theodore. *Thomas H. Benton*. Boston: Houghton Mifflin, 1889.

Rosenberg, Bruce A. *The Code of the West*. Bloomington: Indiana University Press, 1982.

———. *Custer and the Epic of Defeat*. University Park: Pennsylvania State University Press, 1974.

Royce, Josiah. *California from the Conquest in 1846 to the Second Vigilance Committee in San Francisco: A Study of American Character* (1886). Berkeley, CA: Heyday, 2002.

Sears, Stephen W. *George B. McClellan: The Young Napoleon*. New York: Da Capo, 1999.

———. *To the Gates of Richmond: The Peninsula Campaign*. New York: Houghton Mifflin, 1992.

Seiple, Samantha. *Allan Pinkerton: America's First Private Eye*. New York: Scholastic, 2015.

Sewall, Richard H. *Ballots for Freedom: Antislavery Politics in the United States, 1837–1860*. New York: Oxford University Press, 1976.

Sexton, Jay. *The Monroe Doctrine: Empire and Nation in Nineteenth Century America*. New York: Hill and Wang, 2012.

Sherwood, Glenn. *Labor of Love: The Life and Art of Vinnie Ream*. Hygiene, CO: Sunshine, 1997.

Sides, Hampton. *Blood and Thunder: The Epic Story of Kit Carson and the Conquest of the American West*. New York: Anchor, 2006.

Sklenar, Larry. *To Hell With Honor: Custer and the Little Big Horn*. Norman: University of Oklahoma Press, 2000.

Slotkin, Richard. *The Fatal Environment: The Myth of the Frontier in the Age of Industrialization, 1800–1890*. Middletown, CT: Wesleyan University Press, 1985.

———. *Gunfighter Nation: The Myth of the Frontier in Twentieth Century America*. Norman: University of Oklahoma Press, 1992.

———. *The Long Road to Antietam: How the Civil War Became a Revolution*. New York: Liveright Publishing, 2012.

———. *Regeneration through Violence: The Mythology of the American Frontier, 1600–1860*. New York: Harper, 1973.

Smith, Elbert. *Francis Preston Blair*. New York: Free Press, 1980.

———. *Magnificent Missourian: The Life of Thomas Hart Benton*. Philadelphia: J. B. Lippincott, 1958.

Smith, Henry Nash. *Virgin Lands: The American West as Symbol and Myth*. New York: Vintage, 1950.

Smith, Jean Edward. *Grant*. New York: Simon and Schuster, 2001.

Smucker, Samuel. *The Life of Col. John Charles Frémont and His Narrative of Explorations and Adventures, in Kansas, Nebraska, Oregon and California*. New York: Miller, Orton, and Mulligan, 1856.

Starr, Kevin. *Americans and the California Dream, 1850–1915*. New York: Oxford University Press, 1973.

Starr, Stephan. *The Union Cavalry in the Civil War: From Fort Sumter to Gettysburg, 1861–1863*. Baton Rouge: Louisiana State University Press, 1979.

———. *The Union Cavalry in the Civil War: The War in the East, From Gettysburg to Appomattox*. Baton Rouge: Louisiana State University Press, 1981.

Steckmesser, Kent Ladd. *The Western Hero in History and Legacy*. Norman: University of Oklahoma Press, 1965.

Stephanson, Anders. *Manifest Destiny: American Expansion and the Empire of Light*. New York: Hill and Wang, 1998.

Stiles, T. J. *Custer's Trials: A Life on the Frontier of a New America*. New York: Alfred A. Knopf, 2015.

Sully, Langdon. *No Tears for the General: The Life of Alfred Sully, 1821–1879*. Denver: Old West, 1974.

Summers, Mark Wahlgren. *The Ordeal of the Reunion: A New History of Reconstruction*. Chapel Hill: University of North Carolina Press, 2014.

————. *The Plundering Generation: Corruption and the Crisis of the Union, 1849–1861.* New York: Oxford University Press, 1987.

Tanner, Robert G. *Stonewall in the Valley: Thomas J. "Stonewall" Jackson's Shenandoah Valley Campaign, Spring 1862.* Mechanicsville, PA: Stackpole, 2002.

Trenholm, Virginia Cole. *The Arapahoes, Our People.* Norman: University of Oklahoma Press, 1973.

Turner, Frederick Jackson. *The Frontier in American History.* New York: Dover, 1996.

Twain, Mark. *Adventures of Huckleberry Finn.* New York: Random House, 1996.

Unruh, John D. *The Plains Across: The Overland Emigrants and the Trans-Mississippi West, 1840–60.* Urbana: University of Illinois Press, 1982.

Upham, Charles. *Exploration and Public Service of John Charles Frémont.* Boston: Ticknor & Field, 1856.

Urwin, Gregory J. W. *Custer Victorious: The Civil War Battles of General George Armstrong Custer.* Lincoln: University of Nebraska Press, 1983.

Utley, Robert M. *Cavalier in Buckskins: George Armstrong Custer and the Western Military Frontier.* Norman: University of Oklahoma Press, 1988.

————. *Custer and the Great Controversy: The Origin and Development of a Legend.* Pasadena, CA: Westernlore Press, 1980.

————. *Custer, the Seventh Cavalry, and the Little Big Horn: A Biography.* Norman: University of Oklahoma Press, 2012.

————. *Frontier Regulars: The United States Army and the Indian, 1866–1891.* Lincoln: University of Nebraska Press, 1973.

————. *The Lance and the Shield: The Life and Times of Sitting Bull.* New York: Henry Holt, 1993.

Van de Water, Frederick F. *Glory-Hunter: A Life of General Custer.* Indianapolis: Bobbs-Merrill, 1934.

Varon, Elizabeth. *Disunion: The Coming of the American Civil War, 1789–1859.* Chapel Hill: University of North Carolina Press, 2008.

Vestal, Stanley. *Jim Bridger: Mountain Man.* Lincoln: University of Nebraska Press, 1970.

Viola, Herman J. *Little Bighorn Remembered: The Untold Indian Story of Custer's Last Stand.* New York: Crown, 1999.

Wagoner, Jay J. *Arizona Territory, 1863–1912.* Tucson: University of Arizona Press, 1970.

Waugh, John C. *Lincoln and McClellan: The Troubled Partnership between a President and His General.* New York: Palgrave Macmillan, 2010.

————. *Reelecting Lincoln: The Battle for the 1864 Presidency.* New York: Da Capo, 2001.

Weber, David J. *The Mexican Frontier, 1821–1846: The American Southwest under Mexico.* Albuquerque: University of New Mexico Press, 1982.

Wecter, Dixon. *The Hero in America.* New York: Charles Scribner's Sons, 1941.

Weinberg, Albert K. *Manifest Destiny: A Study of Nationalist Expansion in American History.* Baltimore: Johns Hopkins Press, 1935.

Wert, Jeffrey D. *Custer: The Controversial Life of George Armstrong Custer.* New York: Simon and Schuster, 1996.

————. *From Winchester to Cedar Creek: The Shenandoah Campaign of 1864.* New York: Simon and Schuster, 1987.

West, Elliot. *The Contested Plains: Indians, Goldseekers, and the Rush to Colorado.* Lawrence: University of Kansas Press, 2005.

Wheelan, Joseph. *Invading Mexico: America's Continental Dream and the Mexican War, 1846–1848.* New York: Carol & Graf, 2007.

————. *Terrible Swift Sword: The Life of General Philip H. Sheridan.* New York: Da Capo, 2013.

White, Richard. *"It's Your Misfortune and None of My Own": A New History of the American West.* Norman: University of Oklahoma Press, 1991.

White, Robert C. *American Ulysses: A Life of Ulysses S. Grant.* New York: Random House, 2016.

Whittaker, Frederick. *The Complete Life of Gen. George A. Custer.* New York: Sheldon, 1876.

Wilentz, Sean. *The Rise of American Democracy: Jefferson to Lincoln.* New York: W.W. Norton, 2005.

Williams, T. Harry. *McClellan, Sherman, and Grant.* New Brunswick, NJ: Rutgers University Press, 1962.

Wittenberg, Eric J. *Glory Enough for All: Sheridan's Second Raid and the Battle of Trevilian Station.* Washington, DC: Brassey's Books, 2001.

————. *Little Phil: A Reassessment of the Civil War Leadership of General Philip H. Sheridan.* Washington, DC: Brassey's, 2002.

Wittenberg, Eric J., ed. *At Custer's Side: The Civil War Writings of James Harvey Kidd.* Kent, OH: Kent University Press, 2001.

Wittenberg, Eric J., and D. James Lighthizer. *The Battle of Brandy Station: North America's Largest Cavalry.* New York: History Books, 2010.

Wittenberg, Eric J., and Daniel T. Davis. *Out Flew the Sabers: The Battle of Brandy Station, June 9, 1863.* New York: Savas Beattie, 2016.

Wittenberg, Eric J., J. David Petruzzi, and Michael F. Nugent. *One Continuous Fight: The Retreat from Gettysburg and the Pursuit of Lee's Army of Northern Virginia.* New York: Savas Beattie, 2008.

CHAPTERS AND ARTICLES

Billington, Ray, "The New Western Social Order and the Synthesis of Western Scholarship," in *The American West: An Appraisal*, edited by Robert G. Ferris. Santa Fe: Museum of New Mexico Press, 1963.

Chief White Bull as told to Stanley Vestal, "The Battle of the Little Bighorn," in *The Custer Reader*, edited by Paul Andrew Hutton, 336–44. Lincoln: University of Nebraska Press, 1992.

Custer, George, "From West Point to the Battlefield," in *The Custer Reader*, edited by Paul Andrew Hutton, 33–52. Lincoln: University of Nebraska Press, 1992

Hutton, Paul A., "From Little Bighorn to Little Big Man: The Changing Image of a Western Hero in Popular Culture," in *The Custer Reader*, edited by Paul Andrew Hutton, 395–423. Lincoln: University of Nebraska Press, 1992.

Godfrey, Edward S., "Custer's Last Battle," in *The Custer Reader*, edited by Paul Andrew Hutton, 257–318. Lincoln: University of Nebraska Press, 1992.

Kate Bighead as told to Thomas Marquis, "She Watched Custer's Last Battle," in *The Custer Reader*, edited by Paul Andrew Hutton, 363–77. Lincoln: University of Nebraska Press, 1992.

Larned, Charles W., "Expedition to the Yellowstone River in 1873: Letters of a Young Lieutenant," in *The Custer Reader*, edited by Paul Andrew Hutton, 180–200. Lincoln: University of Nebraska Press, 1992.

Monaghan, Jay, "Custer's 'Last Stand': Trevilian Station," in *The Custer Reader*, edited by Paul Andrew Hutton, 53–68. Lincoln: University of Nebraska Press, 1992.

Urwin, Gregory J. W., "Custer: The Civil War Years," in *The Custer Reader*, edited by Paul Andrew Hutton, 7–32. Lincoln: University of Nebraska Press, 1992.

Abbreviations

Custer and Libbie Letters
Marguerite Merington, ed., *The Custer Story: The Life and Intimate Letters of General George A. Custer and His Wife Elizabeth* (Lincoln: University of Nebraska Press, 1987).

Frémont Expeditions
Donald Jackson and Mary Lee Spence, eds., *The Expeditions of John Charles Frémont*, 3 vols. (Champlain: University of Illinois Press, 1970, 1980).

Frémont Memoirs
John Charles Frémont, *Memoirs of My Life* (New York: Cooper Square Press, 2001).

Jessie Letters
Pamela Herr and Mary Lee Spence, eds., *The Letters of Jessie Benton Frémont* (Urbana: University of Illinois Press, 1993).

Libbie's Civil War
Libbie Custer, *The Civil War Memoirs of Elizabeth Bacon Custer, Reconstructed from her diaries and notes by Arlene Reynolds* (Austin: University of Texas Press, 1994).

Lincoln Writings
Philip Van Doren Stern, ed., *The Life and Writings of Abraham Lincoln* (New York: Modern Library, 2000).

Endnotes

1. The Oxford Dictionary defines Power Couple "as consisting of two people who are each influential or successful in their own right." To that this book would add that they are so renowned in America's national affairs that they have become celebrities.
2. For the best books on the Frémonts and Custers as couples, see: Marguerite Merington, ed., *The Custer Story: The Life and Intimate Letters of General George A. Custer and His Wife Elizabeth* (Lincoln: University of Nebraska Press, 1987); Louise Barnett, *Touched by Fire: The Life, Death, and Mythic Afterlife of George Armstrong Custer* (Lincoln: University of Nebraska Press, 2006); Sally Denton, *Passion and Principle: John and Jessie Frémont, the Couple whose Power, Politics, and Love Shaped Nineteenth Century America* (Lincoln: University of Nebraska Press, 2007).
3. George Custer to Annette Humphreys, summer [n.d.], 1863, Custer Letters, 63.
4. Pamela Herr, *Jessie Benton Frémont* (Norman: University of Oklahoma Press, 1988), 122.
5. Rolle, *Frémont*, 203.
6. Herr, *Jessie Benton Frémont*, 105.
7. Elizabeth Custer to George Custer, October [n.d.], 1864, Custer Letters, 121.
8. Donald Jackson and Mary Lee Spence, eds., *The Expeditions of John Charles Frémont*, 3 vols. (Champlain: University of Illinois Press, 1970, 1980).
9. John Charles Frémont, *Memoirs of My Life* (1887) (New York: Cooper Square, 2001).
10. George A. Custer, *My Life on the Plains* (Lincoln: University of Nebraska Press, 1968).
11. Elizabeth Bacon Custer, *"Boots and Saddles," or Life in Dakota with General Custer* (New York: Harper and Brothers, 1885); Elizabeth Bacon Custer, *Tenting on the Plains, or General Custer in Kansas and Texas* (New York: Harper and Brothers, 1887); Elizabeth Bacon Custer, *Following the Guidon* (New York: Harper and Brothers, 1890).
12. Jessie Benton Frémont, *The Story of the Guard: A Chronicle of the War* (Boston: Ticknor and Field, 1863); Jessie Benton Frémont, *A Year of American Travel* (New York: Harper and Brothers, 1878); Jessie Benton Frémont, *Souvenirs of My Time* (Boston: D. Lothrop, 1887); Jessie Benton Frémont, *Far West Sketches* (Boston: D. Lothrop, 1890); Jessie Benton Frémont, *The Will and the Way Stories* (Boston: D. Lothrop, 1891).
13. Albert K. Weinberg, *Manifest Destiny: A Study of Nationalist Expansion in American History* (Baltimore: Johns Hopkins, 1935); Henry Nash Smith, *Virgin Lands: The American West as Symbol and Myth* (New York: Vintage, 1950); Frederick Merk, *Manifest Destiny and Mission in American History: A Reinterpretation* (New York: Alfred A. Knopf, 1963); Bradford Perkins, *The Creation of a Republican Empire, 1776–1865* (New York: Cambridge University Press, 1993); Anders Stephanson, *Manifest Destiny: American Expansion and the Empire of Right* (New York: Hill and Wang, 1996); Gregory H. Nobles, *American Frontiers: Cultural Encounters and Continental Conquests* (New York: Hill and Wang, 1997); Anders Stephanson, *Manifest Destiny: American*

Expansion and the Empire of Right (New York: Hill and Wang, 1998); Peter S. Onuf, *Jefferson's Empire: The Language of American Nationhood* (Charlottesville: University of Virginia Press, 2000).

14. For the two classic books that excoriated Frémont and Custer, respectively, see: Josiah Royce, *California: A Study of American Character* (1886) (Berkeley, CA: Heyday Books, 2002); Vine Deloria, *Custer Died for Your Sins* (1969) New York: Macmillan, 1988). For broader condemnations of America's conquest and treatment of Indians see: Helen Hunt Jackson, *A Century of Dishonor: The Classic Expose of the Plight of the Native Americans* (1881) (New York: Dover, 2003); Dee Brown, *Bury My Heart at Wounded Knee: An Indian History of the American West* (1970) (New York: Picador, 2007).

    For the deepest exploration of the dynamic among American mythology, history, and identity see: Richard Slotkin, *Regeneration through Violence: The Mythology of the American Frontier, 1600–1860* (New York: Harper, 1973); Richard Slotkin, *The Fatal Environment: The Myth of the Frontier in the Age of Industrialization, 1800–1890* (Middletown, CT: Wesleyan University Press, 1985); Richard Slotkin, *Gunfighter Nation: The Myth of the Frontier in Twentieth Century America* (Norman: University of Oklahoma Press, 1992).

15. For the best Frémont biographies, see: Ferol Egan, *Frémont: Explorer for a Restless Nation* (Reno: University of Nevada Press, 1985); Andrew Rolle, *John Charles Frémont: Character as Destiny* (Norman: University of Oklahoma Press, 1991); Allan Nevins, *Frémont: Pathmarker of the West* (Lincoln: University of Nebraska Press, 1992); Tom Chaffin, *Pathfinder: John Charles Frémont and the Course of American Empire* (Norman: University of Oklahoma Press, 2014).

16. John Bigelow, *Memoir of the Life and Public Services of John Charles Frémont* (New York: Derby & Jackson, 1856), 25.

17. Allan Nevins, *Frémont: Pathmarker of the West* (New York: Longmans, Green, 1955), 16.

18. John Charles Frémont, *Memoirs of My Life* (New York: Cooper Square, 2001), 19.

19. Rolle, *Frémont*, 13.

20. Frémont, *Memoirs*, 30.

21. Martha Coleman Bray, *Joseph Nicollet and His Map: Exploring the Upper Mississippi River* (Philadelphia: American Philosophical Society, 1980); Edmund C. and Martha Coleman Bray, eds., *Joseph N. Nicollet on the Plains and Prairies: The Expeditions of 1838–39* (Minneapolis: Minnesota State Historical Press, 1993).

22. Frémont, *Memoirs*, 30.

23. John Abert to John Frémont, March 2, 1839, *Frémont Expeditions*, 1:45–46.

24. Frémont, *Memoirs*, 40.

25. Frémont, *Memoirs*, 42.

26. Frémont, *Memoirs*, 65.

27. William Chambers, *Old Bullion Benton: Senator from the New West* (New York: Little, Brown, 1956); Elbert Smith, *Magnificent Missourian: The Life of Thomas Hart Benton* (Philadelphia: J. B. Lippincott, 1958); Ken Mueller, *Senator Benton and the People: Master Race Democracy on the Early American Frontier* (New York: New York University Press, 2014).

28. Frémont, *Memoirs*, 65.

29. For the best biographies, see: Catherine Coffin Phillips, *Jessie Benton Frémont: A Woman Who Made History* (San Francisco: J. H. Nash, 1935); Pamela Herr, *Jessie Benton Frémont* (Norman: University of Oklahoma Press, 1988).

30. Sally Denton, *Passion and Principle: John and Jessie Frémont, the Couple Whose Power, Politics, and Love Shaped Nineteenth Century America* (Lincoln: University of Nebraska Press, 2007), 44.

31. Jessie Benton Frémont, *A Year of American Travel* (New York: Harper and Brothers, 1878), 44.

32. Denton, *Passion and Principle*, 47.

33. Jessie Benton Frémont, *Souvenirs of My Time* (Boston: D. Lothrop, 1887), 88.

34. William Nester, *The Hamiltonian Vision, 1789–1800: The Art of Power during the Early Republic* (Washington, DC: Potomac Books, 2012); William Nester, *The Jeffersonian Vision, 1801–1815: The Art of Power during the Early Republic* (Washington, DC: Potomac Books, 2013); William Nester, *The Age of Jackson and the Art of American Power, 1815–1848* (Washington, DC: Potomac Books, 2013).

35. For the best account, see: Robert Pierce Forbes, *The Missouri Compromise and Its Aftermath: Slavery and Its Meaning for America* (Chapel Hill: University of North Carolina Press, 2007).

36. Denton, *Passion and Principle*, xi.

37. Frémont, *Memoirs*, 66–67.

38. Frémont, *Memoirs*, 68.

39. Catharine Coffin Phillips, *Jessie Benton Frémont: A Woman Who Made History* (San Francisco: J. H. Nash, 1935), 51.

40. Both quotes from Denton, *Passion and Principle*, 70–71.

41. Both quotes from Herr, *Jessie Benton Frémont*, 65.

42. Jessie Benton Frémont, "Introduction," in Frémont, *Memoirs*, 16.

43. For the best biography, see: Hampton Sides, *Blood and Thunder: The Epic Story of Kit Carson and the Conquest of the American West* (New York: Anchor Books, 2006). See also: Thelma S. Guild and Harvey L. Carter, *Kit Carson: A Pattern for Heroes* (Lincoln: University of Nebraska Press, 1984); Thomas W. Dunlay, *Kit Carson and the Indians* (Lincoln: University of Nebraska Press, 2005); David Remley, *Kit Carson: The Life of an American Borderman* (Norman: University of Oklahoma Press, 2012).

44. Milo Milton Quaife, ed., *Kit Carson's Autobiography* (Lincoln: University of Nebraska Press, 1935), 66.

45. Frémont, *Memoirs*, 74.

46. David Roberts, *A Newer World: Kit Carson, John Charles Frémont, and the Claiming of the American West* (New York: Simon and Schuster, 2001).

47. Quaife, *Kit Carson's Autobiography*, 5, 20–21.

48. Tom Chaffin, *Pathfinder: John Charles Frémont and the Course of American Empire* (Norman: University of Oklahoma Press, 2014), 99.

49. Charles Preuss, *Exploring with Frémont: The Private Diaries of Charles Preuss, Cartographer*, translated and edited by Erwin G. and Elizabeth K. Gudde (Norman: University of Oklahoma Press, 1958).

50. Preuss, Diaries, 50, 46.

51. Stanley Vestal, *Jim Bridger: Mountain Man* (Lincoln: University of Nebraska Press, 1970); J. Cecil Alter, *Jim Bridger* (Norman: University of Oklahoma Press, 1986).

52. Frémont, *Memoirs*, 109–10.

53. Frémont, *Memoirs*, 112–13.

54. Frémont, *Memoirs*, 116.

55. Frémont, *Memoirs*, 119.

56. LeRoy R. Hafen, *Broken Hand: The Life of Thomas Fitzpatrick: Mountain Man, Guide, and Indian Agent* (Lincoln: University of Nebraska Press, 1981).

57. Frémont, *Memoirs*, 151.

58. Frémont, *Memoirs*, 157–58.

59. "Excerpt from *Memoirs*," Jessie Letters, 12.

60. Frémont, *Memoirs*, 163.

61. Charles Wilkes, *Narrative of the United States Exploring Expedition During the Years 1838, 1839, 1840, 1841, 1842* (New York: Forgotten Books, 2015); Charles Wilkes, *The Autobiography of Rear Admiral Charles Wilkes,* United States Navy, 1798–1877 (Washington, DC: Naval History Division, 1978); Nathaniel Philbrick, *Sea of Glory: America's Voyage of Discovery, the United States Exploring Expedition, 1838–1842* (New York: Penguin, 2004).

62. Ernest Allen Lewis, *The Frémont Cannon* (Glendale, CA: Arthur H. Clark, 1981).

63. Frémont, *Expeditions,* 1:346n.

64. Herr, *Jessie Benton Frémont,* 90.

65. Jessie Benton Frémont, "The Origin of the Frémont Explorations," *Century,* vol. 41 (March 1891), 766–71. For Frémont's slightly different version, see Frémont, *Memoirs,* 167–68.

66. Jessie Frémont to Adelaide Talbot, March 24, 1844, Jessie Letters, 20.

67. William R. Nester, *From Mountain Man to Millionaire: The "Bold and Dashing Life" of Robert Campbell* (Columbia: University of Missouri Press, 2011).

68. Jessie Frémont to Adelaide Talbot, February 1, 1844, Jessie Letters, 17.

69. Frémont, *Memoirs,* 205.

70. John D. Unruh, *The Plains Across: The Overland Emigrants and the Trans-Mississippi West, 1840–60* (Urbana: University of Illinois Press, 1982), 84.

71. Tom Chaffin, *Pathfinder: John Charles Frémont and the Course of American Empire* (Norman: University of Oklahoma Press, 2014), 154.

72. Frémont, *Memoirs,* 217.

73. Bil Gilbert, *Westering Man: The Life of Joseph Walker* (Norman: University of Oklahoma Press, 1989).

74. James Henry Daugherty, Marcus and Narcissa Whitman, *Pioneers of Oregon* (New York: Viking, 1953); Myron Eells, *Marcus Whitman: Pathfinder and Patriot* (New York: Forgotten Books, 2015).

75. Peter Burnett, "Recollections and Opinions of an Old Pioneer," *Oregon Historical Quarterly,* vol. 5 (1904), 86–88.

76. Frémont, *Memoirs,* 273.

77. Albert Furtado, *John Sutter: A Life on the North American Frontier* (Norman: University of Oklahoma Press, 2006).

78. Frémont, *Memoirs,* 350, 354.

79. Frémont, *Memoirs,* 364.

80. LeRoy R. Hafen and Ann Hafen, *The Old Spanish Trail* (Lincoln: University of Nebraska Press, 1993).

81. Frémont, *Memoirs,* 365.

82. Frémont, *Memoirs,* 375.

83. Frémont, *Memoirs,* 381.

84. Frémont, *Memoirs,* 345.

85. Frémont, *Memoirs,* 386.

86. Frémont, *Memoirs,* 404.

87. Janet Lecompte, *Pueblo, Hardscrabble, Greenhorn* (Norman: University of Oklahoma Press, 1978); David Lavender, *Bent's Fort* (Lincoln: University of Nebraska Press, 1972).

88. Herr, *Jessie Benton Frémont,* 99–100.

89. Frémont, *Memoirs,* 414.

90. Frémont, *Memoirs,* 414.

91. Frémont, *Memoirs,* 419.

92. For the best books on Polk's diplomacy, see: David M. Pletcher, *The Diplomacy of*

Annexation: Texas, Oregon, and the Mexican War (Columbia: University of Missouri Press, 1973); Robert W. Merry, *A Country of Vast Designs: James K. Polk, The Mexican War, and the Conquest of the American Continent* (New York: Simon and Schuster, 2009); Walter Borneman, *Polk: The Man Who Transformed the Presidency and America* (New York: Random House, 2009).

93. For interpretations of this controversy, see: Egan, *Frémont*, 274–79; Rolle, *Frémont*, 66–68, 73, 76–77, 78–79; Chaffin, *Pathfinder*, 252–53; Merry, *Country of Vast Designs*, 295; Borneman, *Polk*, 186.

94. John Abert to John Frémont, February 12, 1845, Frémont *Expeditions*, 1:395–97.

95. Frémont, *Memoirs*, 423, 536.

96. For the best overview, see: Neal Harlow, *California Conquered: War and Peace on the Pacific, 1846–1850* (Berkeley: University of California Press, 1982).

97. Milo Milton Quaife, *Kit Carson's Autobiography* (Lincoln: University of Nebraska Press, 1935), 87–88.

98. Frémont, *Memoirs*, 427.

99. Frémont, *Memoirs*, 442.

100. For the best accounts of the conquest, see: Josiah Royce, *California from the Conquest in 1846 to the Second Vigilance Committee in San Francisco: A Study of American Character* (1886) (Berkeley, CA: Heyday, 2002); Neal Harlow, *California Conquered: War and Peace on the Pacific, 1846–1850* (Berkeley: University of California Press, 1982). For broader perspectives, see: Kevin Starr, *Americans and the California Dream, 1850–1915* (New York: Oxford University Press, 1973); William Deverell and David Igler, eds., *A Companion to California History* (New York: Wiley-Blackwell, 2014).

101. David J. Weber, *The Mexican Frontier, 1821–1846: The American Southwest under Mexico* (Albuquerque: University of New Mexico Press, 1982), 206; Benjamin Madley, *An American Genocide: The United States and the California Indian Catastrophe* (New Haven, CT: Yale University Press, 2016), 1.

102. Frémont, *Memoirs*, 453.

103. Harlan Hague and David J. Langum, *Thomas O. Larkin: A Life of Patriotism and Profit in Old California* (Norman: University of Oklahoma Press, 1990).

104. Frémont, *Memoirs*, 454.

105. Frémont, *Memoirs*, 454.

106. Frémont, *Memoirs*, 463.

107. Allan Nevins, *Frémont: Pathmarker of the West* (New York: Longmans, Green, 1955), 231.

108. Madley, *American Genocide*, 42–50.

109. Milo Milton Quaife, ed., *Kit Carson's Autobiography* (Lincoln: University of Nebraska Press, 1966), 95.

110. Madley, *American Genocide*, 48.

111. Werner H. Marti, *Messenger of Destiny: The California Adventures of Archibald H. Gillespie, 1846–1847* (San Francisco: John Howell Books, 1960).

112. For interpretations of this controversy, see: Egan, *Frémont*, 327–65; Rolle, *Frémont*, 74–77, 83, 86, 88–90, 93; Borneman, *Polk*, 186, 188, 196, 269–72, 274–75; Merry, *Country of Vast Designs*, 201, 295, 296, 302, 304.

113. Frémont, *Memoirs*, 488, 490.

114. Frémont, *Memoirs*, 490–91.

115. Frémont, *Memoirs*, 407.

116. Quaife, *Carson Autobiography*, 102.

117. Frémont, *Memoirs*, 504.

118. Frémont, *Memoirs*, 517.

119. Frémont, *Memoirs*, 520.
120. For different interpretations, see: Muriel Chamberlain, *Pax Britannica?: British Foreign Policy, 1789–1914* (New York: Routledge, 1989); Anders Stephanson, *Manifest Destiny: American Expansion and the Empire of Right* (New York: Hill and Wang, 1996); Rebecca Berens Matzke, *Deterrence through Strength: British Naval Power and Foreign Policy under Pax Britannica* (Lincoln: University of Nebraska Press, 2001); David Brown, *Palmerston and the Politics of Foreign Policy, 1846–54* (Manchester, UK: Manchester University Press, 2003); Jay Sexton, *The Monroe Doctrine: Empire and Nation in Nineteenth Century America* (New York: Hill and Wang, 2012).
121. Bauer, *Mexican War*, 10.
122. K. Jack Bauer, *Zachery Taylor: Soldier, Planter, Statesman of the Old Southwest* (Baton Rouge: Louisiana State University Press, 1985).
123. For the best books on the Mexican War, see: John S. Eisenhower, *So Far From God: The U.S. War with Mexico, 1846–1848* (New York: Doubleday, 1989); K. Jack Bauer, *The Mexican War, 1846–1848* (Lincoln: University of Nebraska Press, 1992); Paul Foos, *A Short, Offhand, Killing: Soldiers and Social Conflict during the Mexican American War* (Chapel Hill: University of North Carolina Press, 2002); Joseph Wheelan, *Invading Mexico: America's Continental Dream and the Mexican War, 1846–1848* (New York: Carol & Graf, 2007).
124. Royce, *California*, 74.
125. Royce, *California*, 65.
126. Frémont, *Memoirs*, 524–25.
127. Harlow, *California Conquered*, 54, 132–35.
128. Frémont, *Memoirs*, 534.
129. For interpretations of this controversy, see: Rolle, *Frémont*, 361, 363, 364–65, 415, 441; Rolle, *Frémont*, 76–78, 85–89; Borneman, *Polk*, 271–72; Merry, *Country of Vast Designs*, 295, 303.
130. Frémont, *Memoirs*, 535–36.
131. Dwight Clarke, *Stephen Watts Kearney: Soldier of the West* (Norman: University of Oklahoma Press, 1961).
132. Frémont, *Expeditions*, 2:269.
133. George W. Ames, ed., *A Doctor Comes to California: The Diary of John S. Griffen, Assistant Surgeon with Kearny's Dragoons, 1846–1847* (San Francisco: California Historical Society, 1943), 70.
134. Tom Chaffin, *Pathfinder: John Charles Frémont and the Course of American Empire* (Norman: University of Oklahoma Press, 2014), 374–75.
135. Nevins, *Frémont*, 323.
136. Ferrol Egan, *Frémont: Explorer for a Restless Nation* (Reno: University of Nevada Press, 1985), 424.
137. Jessie Frémont to John Frémont, June 18, 1846, Jessie Letters, 24–25.
138. Allan Nevins, ed., *Polk: The Diary of a President, 1845–1849* (New York: Capricorn Books, 1968), 221, 226, 390.
139. Denton, *Passion and Principle*, 142.
140. Denton, *Passion and Principle*, 142–43.
141. Egan, *Frémont*, 431.
142. Frémont, *Expeditions*, 2:405.
143. Jessie Frémont to President James Polk, September 21, 1847, Jessie Letters, 35–36.
144. Denton, *Passion and Principle*, 146.
145. Frémont, *Expeditions*, 2:39.
146. Denton, *Passion and Principle*, 148.

147. Ann Blackman, *Wild Rose: The True Story of a Civil War Spy* (New York: Random House, 2006).
148. Frémont, *Expeditions*, 2: supplement, 197–98.
149. Frémont, *Expeditions*, 2, supplement, 326–27.
150. Frémont, *Expeditions*, 2:341.
151. Denton, *Passion and Principle*, 150
152. Denton, *Passion and Principle*, 151.
153. Frémont, *Memoirs*, 602.
154. John S. D. Eisenhower, *Agent of Destiny: The Life and Times of General Winfield Scott* (New York: Free Press, 1997); Allan Peskin, *Winfield Scott and the Profession of Arms* (Kent, OH: Kent State University Press, 2004); Timothy Johnson, *Winfield Scott: The Quest for Military Glory* (Topeka: University Press of Kansas, 2015).
155. John S. D. Eisenhower, *So Far From God: The U.S. War with Mexico, 1846–1858* (New York: Doubleday, 1989), xviii, 369–70; K. Paul Bauer, *The Mexican War, 1846–1848* (Lincoln: University of Nebraska Press, 1992), 397–98; Paul Foos, *A Short, Offhand, Killing: Soldiers and Social Conflict during the Mexican American War* (Chapel Hill: University of North Carolina Press, 2002), 85.
156. Eisenhower, *So Far From God*, 356.
157. Paul Rodman and Elliott West, *Mining Frontiers of the Far West* (Albuquerque: University of New Mexico Press, 2001), 13.
158. J. S. Holliday, *The World Rushed In: The California Gold Rush Experience: An Eyewitness Account of a Nation Heading West* (New York: Simon and Schuster, 1981); Brian Roberts, *American Alchemy: The California Gold Rush and Middle Class Culture* (Chapel Hill: University of North Carolina Press, 2000); Susan Johnson, *Roaring Camp: The Social World of the California Gold Rush* (New York: W.W. Norton, 2001); Kenneth Own, *Riches for All: The California Gold Rush and the World* (Lincoln: University of Nebraska Press, 2002); H. W. Brands, *The Age of Gold: The California Gold Rush and the New American Dream* (New York: Anchor Books, 2003).
159. Herr, *Jessie Benton Frémont*, 178.
160. Tom Chaffin, *Pathfinder: John Charles Frémont and the Course of American Empire* (Norman: University of Oklahoma Press, 2014), 395, 417.
161. Janet Lecompte, *Pueblo, Hardscrabble, Greenhorn* (Norman: University of Oklahoma Press, 1978).
162. Alpheus H. Favour, *Old Bill Williams: Mountain Man* (Norman: University of Oklahoma Press, 1981).
163. Frémont wrote extensively about the disaster in a letter to his wife dated from January 27, 29, and February 6, 1849, and included in Jessie Benton Frémont, *A Year of American Travel* (New York: Harper and Brothers, 1878), 69–81.
164. Jessie Frémont, *Year of American Travel*, 69.
165. Herr, *Jessie Benton Frémont*, 179.
166. Jessie Frémont, *Year of American Travel*, 21, 25.
167. Jessie Frémont, *Year of American Travel*, 27–29.
168. Jessie Frémont, *Year of American Travel*, 44.
169. Jessie Frémont, *Year of American Travel*, 52.
170. Jessie Frémont, *Year of American Travel*, 59.
171. Jessie Frémont, *Year of American Travel*, 81.
172. Neal Harlow, *California Conquered: War and Peace on the Pacific, 1846–1850* (Berkeley: University of California Press, 1982), 351.
173. Congressional Globe, September 13, 1850.
174. John Bigelow, *Memoir of the Life and Public Services of John Charles Frémont* (New

York: Derby and Jackson, 1856), 418–19.

175. Rolle, *Frémont*, 134–37.
176. Thomas Hart Benton, *Thirty Years' View, or A History of the Working of the American Government for Thirty Years from 1820 to 1850*, 2 vols. (New York: D. Appleton, 1858, 1880).
177. Both quotes from Herr, *Jessie Benton Frémont*, 223.
178. Rolle, *Frémont*, 147.
179. Denton, *Passion and Principle*, 199.
180. Herr, *Jessie Benton Frémont*, 228–29.
181. Andrew Rolle, *John Charles Frémont: Character as Destiny* (Norman: University of Oklahoma Press, 1991), 145.
182. William Goetzmann, *Exploration and Empire: The Explorer and the Scientist in the Winning of the American West* (New York: Vintage, 1966), 283–93.
183. Solomon Nunes Carvalho, *Incidents of Travel and Adventure in the Far West with Col. Frémont's Last Expedition* (New York: Derby and Jackson, 1859).
184. Carvalho, *Incidents of Travel and Adventure*, 132–33, 101.
185. Jessie Benton Frémont, *Far West Sketches* (Boston: D. Lothrop, 1890), 30–31.
186. M. Tarver and H. Cobb, eds., *The Western Journal* (St. Louis: M. Niedmer, 1854), 191.
187. Denton, *Passion and Principle*, 215.
188. Jessie Frémont to Elizabeth Blair Lee, April 25, 1856, Jessie Letters, 99–100.
189. For the best books on the decade leading to the Civil War, see: Allan Nevins, *Order of the Union: A House Dividing, 1852–1857* (New York: Charles Scribner's Sons, 1950); Richard H. Sewell, *Ballots for Freedom: Antislavery Politics in the United States, 1837–1860* (New York: Oxford University Press, 1976); Michael F. Holt, *The Political Crisis of the 1850s* (New York: W.W. Norton, 1987); Mark Summers, *The Plundering Generation: Corruption and the Crisis of the Union, 1849–1861* (New York: Oxford University Press, 1987); Bruce Levine, *Half Slave and Half Free: The Roots of the Civil War* (New York: Hill and Wang, 2005); Elizabeth Varon, *Disunion: The Coming of the American Civil War, 1789–1859* (Chapel Hill: University of North Carolina Press, 2008); David M. Potter, *The Impending Crisis, 1848–1861* (New York: Harper Perennial, 2011).
190. For the Republican Party's origins and early development, see: Jeter Allen Isely, *Horace Greeley and the Republican Party, 1853–1861* (Princeton, NJ: Princeton University Press, 1947); William E. Gienapp, *The Origins of the Republican Party, 1852–1856* (New York: Oxford University Press, 1988); Eric Foner, *Free Soil, Free Labor, Free Men: The Ideology of the Republican Party before the Civil War* (New York: Oxford University Press, 1995).
   For the best books on the Whig Party, see: Daniel Walker Howe, *The Political Culture of the American Whigs* (Chicago: University of Chicago Press, 1984); Michael C. Holt, *The Rise and Fall of the American Whig Party: Jacksonian Politics and the Origins of the Civil War* (New York: Oxford University Press, 1999).
191. William Nester, *The Hamiltonian Vision, 1789–1800: The Art of American Power during the Early Republic* (Washington, DC: Potomac Books, 2012).
192. William Nester, *The Jeffersonian Vision, 1801–1815: The Art of American Power during the Early Republic* (Washington, DC: Potomac Books, 2013).
193. William Nester, *The Age of Jackson and the Art of American Power, 1815–1848* (Washington, DC: Potomac Books, 2013).
194. Elbert Smith, *Francis Preston Blair* (New York: Free Press, 1980).
195. Jessie Frémont to Francis Preston Blair, August 27, 1855, Jessie Letters, 71.
196. Ruhl J. Bartlett, *Frémont and the Republican Party* (Columbus: Ohio State University Press, 1930).

197. Horace Greeley, *The Autobiography of Horace Greeley, or Recollections of a Busy Life* (New York: E. B. Treat, 1872), 354.
198. Denton, *Passion and Principle*, 239.
199. Jessie Frémont to Elizabeth Blair Lee, April 18, 1856, Jessie Letters, 98.
200. Jessie Frémont to Elizabeth Blair Lee, March 8, 1856, Jessie Letters, 94.
201. Jessie Frémont to Elizabeth Blair Lee, April 18, 1856, Jessie Letters, 97–98.
202. Jessie Frémont to Elizabeth Blair Lee, April 25, 1856, Jessie Letters, 99–100.
203. Jessie Frémont to Elizabeth Blair Lee, April 29, 1856, Jessie Letters, 99–101.
204. Jessie Frémont to Elizabeth Blair Lee, June 9, 1856, Jessie Letters, 105–06.
205. Milton Meltzer and Patricia G. Holland, eds., *Lydia Maria Child: Selected Letters, 1817–1880* (Amherst: University of Massachusetts Press, 1982), 290.
206. Julia Louisa Lovejoy, "Letters, 1856," *Kansas Historical Society Quarterly*, vol. 15 (1947), 138.
207. Herr, *Jessie Benton Frémont*, 263.
208. Charles Upham, *Exploration and Public Service of John Charles Frémont* (Boston: Ticknor & Field, 1856); Samuel Smucker, *The Life of Col. John Charles Frémont* (New York: Miller, Orton, and Mulligan, 1856).
209. Jessie Frémont to Elizabeth Blair Lee, July 2, 1856, Jessie Letters, 113.
210. Jessie Frémont to Francis Preston Blair, August 25, 1856, Jessie Letters, 133.
211. Rolle, *Frémont*, 173.
212. Jessie Frémont to Francis Preston Blair, August 25, 1856, Jessie Letters, 133.
213. Jessie Frémont to Elizabeth Blair Lee, October 20, 1856, Jessie Letters, 140.
214. Richard H. Sewell, *Ballots for Freedom: Antislavery Politics in the United States, 1837–1860* (New York: Oxford University Press, 1976), 254–91.
215. John Bicknell, *Lincoln's Pathfinder: John C. Frémont and the Violent Election of 1856* (Chicago: Chicago Review, 2017).
216. Herr, *Jessie Benton Frémont*, 277.
217. Jessie Frémont to Francis Preston Blair, January 8, 1858, Jessie Letters, 180–81.
218. Jessie Frémont to Elizabeth Blair Lee, January 31, 1857, Jessie Letters, 150.
219. Jessie Frémont to John Frémont, September 23, 1857, Jessie Letters, 171–72.
220. Jessie Frémont to Francis Preston Blair, January 8, 1858, Jessie Letters, 180.
221. Denton, *Passion and Principle*, 264.
222. Jessie Frémont to Elizabeth Blair Lee, December 15, 1857, Jessie Letters, 175.
223. Herr, *Jessie Benton Frémont*, 301.
224. Lafayette H. Bunnell and Stephen P. Medley, *The Discovery of Yosemite and the Indian War of 1850 and 1851 which Led to that Event* (1892) (New York: Endeavor, 2016); Benjamin Medley, *An American Genocide: The United States and the California Indian Catastrophe, 1846–1873* (New Haven, CT: Yale University Press, 2016).
225. For the classic account of the gold rush and California's development into a state, see: Kevin Starr, *Americans and the California Dream, 1850–1915* (New York: Oxford University Press, 1973).
226. Denton, *Passion and Principle*, 193, 264, 266, 276–77, 337.
227. Egan, *Frémont*, 483–89, 512.
228. Rolle, *Frémont*, 183, 186, 188–89, 236–37.
229. Egan, *Frémont*, 510.
230. Jessie Frémont to Francis Preston Blair, July 16, 1858, Jessie Letters, 205–06.
231. Jessie Frémont to Francis Preston Blair, July 16, 1858, Jessie Letters, 206.
232. Denton, *Passion and Principle*, 275.
233. Richard Henry Dana, *"Twenty-Four Years After," Two Years Before the Mast* (Boston: Houghton Mifflin, 1887), 453.

234. Jessie Frémont to Elizabeth Blair Lee, June 14, 1860, Jessie Letters, 230.
235. Jessie Frémont to Elizabeth Blair Lee, June 2, 1860, Jessie Letters, 227–28.
236. Herr, *Jessie Benton Frémont*, 312.
237. Herr, *Jessie Benton Frémont*, 313.
238. Jessie Frémont to Editors of the Alta California, February 26, 1861, Jessie Letters, 235–37.
239. Denton, *Passion and Principle*, 285,
240. Douglas R. Egerton, *Year of Meteors: Stephen Douglas, Abraham Lincoln, and the Election that Brought on the Civil War* (New York: Bloomsbury, 2010); James A. Fuller, ed., *The Election of 1860* (Kent, OH: Kent State University Press, 2013).
241. First Inaugural Address, March 4, 1861, *Lincoln Writings*, 646–57.
242. For the classic unsurpassed overview of the Civil War, see: James McPherson, *Battle Cry of Freedom: The Civil War Era* (New York: Oxford University Press, 1988). For the best military account, see Herman Hattaway and Archer Jones, *How the North Won: A Military History of the Civil War* (Chicago: University of Illinois Press, 1991).
243. For the best books on Lincoln and his presidency, see: Philip Shaw Paludan, *The Presidency of Abraham Lincoln* (Topeka: University Press of Kansas, 1994); David Herbert Donald, *Lincoln* (New York: Simon and Schuster, 1995); Doris Kearns Goodwin, *Team of Rivals: The Political Genius of Abraham Lincoln* (New York: Simon and Schuster, 2006); William Lee Miller, *President Lincoln and the Duty of a Statesman* (New York: Alfred Knopf, 2008); James M. McPherson, *Tried by War: Abraham Lincoln as Commander in Chief* (New York: Penguin, 2008). For Lincoln's place in the era named after him, see: William Nester, *The Age of Lincoln and the Art of American Power, 1848–1876* (Washington, DC: Potomac Books, 2013).
244. William Herndon and Jesse Weik, *Herndon's Lincoln: The True Story of a Great Life*, 3 vols. (Chicago: Belford, Clarke, 1889), 2:334.
245. Paludan, *Lincoln*, 35–36.
246. Hattaway and Jones, *How the North Won*, 9–10, 18–19.
247. Chaffin, *Frémont*, 456.
248. Andrew Rolle, *John Charles Frémont: Character as Destiny* (Norman: University of California, 1991), 190.
249. John S. D. Eisenhower, *Agent of Destiny: The Life and Times of General Winfield Scott* (New York: Free Press, 1997).
250. James M. McPherson, *Tried by War: Abraham Lincoln as Commander in Chief* (New York: Penguin, 2008), 39.
251. Edward G. Longacre, *The Early Morning of War: Bull Run, 1861* (Norman: University of Oklahoma Press, 2014).
252. For Missouri during the Civil War, see: Jay Monaghan, *Civil War on the Western Border, 1854–1865* (Lincoln: University of Nebraska Press, 1955); Michael Fellman, *Inside War: The Guerrilla Conflict in Missouri during the Civil War* (New York: Oxford University Press, 1989).
253. William E. Parrish, *Frank Blair: Lincoln's Conservative* (Columbia: University of Missouri Press, 1998); Christopher Phillips, *Damned Yankee: The Life of General Nathaniel Lyon* (Columbia: University of Missouri Press, 1990).
254. Denton, *Passion and Principle*, 293–94.
255. Herr, *Jessie Benton Frémont*, 327–28.
256. Jessie Frémont to Elizabeth Blair Lee, July 27, 1861, Jessie Letters, 255.
257. Jean Edward Smith, *Grant* (New York: Simon and Shuster, 2001), 117.
258. Smith, *Grant*, 645.
259. Herr, *Jessie Benton Frémont*, 332.

260. Abraham Lincoln to John Frémont, September 2, 1861, *The Life and Writings of Abraham Lincoln*, edited by Philip Van Doren Stern (New York: Modern Library, 2000), 679. Lincoln Letters, 679.

261. Denton, *Passion and Principle*, 316.

262. For the message, see: Jesse Frémont to Abraham Lincoln, September 10, 1861, Jessie Letters, 262. For her account of her meeting with the president, see: The Lincoln Interview: Excerpt from "Great Events," Jessie Letters, 264–69.

263. The Lincoln Interview: Excerpt from "Great Events," Jessie Letters, 266.

264. John Hay, *Lincoln and the Civil War in the Diaries and Letters of John Hay*, edited by Tyler Dennett (New York: Dodd, Mead, 1939), 133.

265. Abraham Lincoln to John Frémont, September 11, 1861, *Lincoln Life and Writings*, 680.

266. The Lincoln Interview: Excerpt from "Great Events," Jessie Letters, 267.

267. Jessie Frémont to Abraham Lincoln, September 12, 1861 (1st letter), Jessie Letters, 270.

268. Jessie Frémont to Abraham Lincoln, September 12, 1861 (2nd letter), Jessie Letters, 271.

269. Abraham Lincoln to Jessie Frémont, September 12, 1861, Jessie Letters, 271.

270. Chaffin, *Frémont*, 466.

271. Nevins, *Frémont*, 520.

272. Allan Nevins, *Frémont: Pathmarker of the West* (Lincoln: University of Nebraska Press, 1992), 513.

273. Denton, *Passion and Principle*, 326.

274. John Greenleaf Whittier, *Antislavery Poems: Songs of Labor and Reform* (Boston: Houghton Mifflin, 1892), 222.

275. Robert G. Tanner, *Stonewall in the Valley: Thomas J. "Stonewall" Jackson's Shenandoah Valley Campaign, Spring 1862* (Mechanicsville, PA: Stackpole Books, 2002); Gary Gallagher, *The Shenandoah Valley Campaign of 1862* (Chapel Hill: University of North Carolina Press, 2003); Peter Cozzens, *Shenandoah 1862: Stonewall Jackson's Valley Campaign* (Chapel Hill: University of North Carolina Press, 2008).

276. Jessie Frémont, Sydney Howard Gay, June 21, 1862, Jessie Letters, 329.

277. Jessie Frémont to George Julian, January 16, 1864, Jessie Letters, 362.

278. Jessie Benton Frémont, *The Story of the Guard: A Chronicle of the War* (Boston: Ticknor and Field, 1863), 222–23.

279. Rolle, *Frémont*, 188–89, 236–37.

280. Chaffin, *Frémont*, 480.

281. John Waugh, *Reelecting Lincoln: The Battle for the 1864 Election* (New York: Da Capo, 2001).

282. Denton, *Passion and Principle*, 345.

283. Jessie Frémont to Nelly Haskell, November 1, 1864, Jessie Letters, 383.

284. Jessie Frémont to John Greenleaf Whittier, January 20–21, 1880, Jessie Letters, 480.

285. Jessie Frémont to William Sherman, August 10, 1871, Jessie Letters, 402–03.

286. Jessie Frémont to Jeremiah Black, February 21, 1875, Jessie Letters, 427.

287. Rolle, *Frémont*, 238–39.

288. Glenn Sherwood, *Labor of Love: The Life and Art of Vinnie Ream* (Hygiene, CO: Sunshine, 1997).

289. Jessie Frémont to Jeremiah Black, Christmas Night, 1874, Jessie Letters, 424.

290. Jessie Frémont to Nathaniel Banks, January 30, 1877, Jessie Letters, 391.

291. Rolle, *Frémont*, 246–48.

292. Jessie Frémont to William Morton, November 23, 1878, Jessie Letters, 458.

293. Jessie Benton Frémont, *Souvenirs of My Time* (Boston: D. Lothrop, 1887); *Far West Sketches* (Boston: D. Lothrop, 1890); *The Will and the Way Stories* (Boston: D. Lothrop, 1891).

294. Tom Chaffin, *Pathfinder: John Charles Frémont and the Course of American Empire* (Norman: University of Oklahoma Press, 2014), 487.

295. Rolle, *Frémont*, 260–61.

296. Josiah Royce, *California from the Conquest in 1846 to the Second Vigilance Committee in San Francisco: A Study of American Character* (1886) (Berkeley, CA: Heyday, 2002), 88–89.

297. John Charles Frémont, *Memoirs of My Life* (Chicago: Belford, Clarke, 1887).

298. Chaffin, *Frémont*, 4.

299. Rolle, *Frémont*, 267.

300. For the best biographies, see: Frederick F. Van de Water, *Glory-Hunter: A Life of General Custer* (Indianapolis: Bobbs-Merrill, 1934); Jay Monaghan, *Custer: The Life of General George Armstrong Custer* (Boston: Little, Brown, 1959); Jeffrey D. Wert, *Custer: The Controversial Life of George Armstrong Custer* (New York: Simon and Schuster, 1996); Robert M. Utley, *Custer: Cavalier in Buckskin* (Norman: University of Oklahoma Press, 2001); Louise Barnett, *Touched by Fire: The Life, Death, and Mythic Afterlife of George Armstrong Custer* (Lincoln: University of Nebraska Press, 2006); T. J. Stiles, *Custer's Trials: A Life on the Frontier of a New America* (New York: Alfred Knopf, 2016).

301. Custer, Letters, 4.

302. George Custer to his parents, [n.d.], Maria Custer to George Custer, [n.d.], Custer Letters, 6.

303. Elizabeth B. Custer, *"Boots and Saddles," or Life in Dakota with General Custer* (New York: Harper and Brothers, 1885), 94.

304. James L. Morrison, *"The Best Little School in the World": West Point, the Pre-Civil War Years, 1833–1861* (Kent, Ohio: Kent State University Press, 1986).

305. Libbie's Civil War, 11.

306. Custer's Letters, 7–8.

307. Stiles, *Custer's Trials*, 10.

308. Roger L. Geiger, ed., *The American College in the Nineteenth Century* (Nashville, TN: Vanderbilt University Press, 2000).

309. Stiles, *Custer's Trials*, 7.

310. George Custer, "From West Point to the Battlefield," *The Custer Reader*, ed. Paul Andrew Hutton (Lincoln: University of Nebraska Press, 1992), 42.

311. Catherine S. Crary, ed., *Dear Belle: Letters from a Cadet and Officer to His Sweetheart, 1858–1865* (Middletown, CT: Wesleyan University Press, 1965), 42, 239.

312. Crary, *Dear Belle*, 42–44.

313. Stiles, *Custer's Trials*, 17.

314. Crary, *Dear Belle*, 215.

315. Stiles, *Custer's Trials*, 17–18.

316. Wert, *Custer*, 34.

317. Stiles, *Custer's Trials*, 12.

318. Custer, "From West Point to the Battlefield," 44.

319. Ralph Kirshner, *The Class of 1861: Custer, Ames, and Their Classmates After West Point* (Carbondale, IL: Southern Illinois University Press, 1999); James S. Robbins, *Last in Their Class: Custer, Pickett, and the Goats of West Point* (New York: Encounter Books, 2006).

320. For the best biographies, see: Lawrence A. Frost, *General Custer's Libbie* (Seattle: Superior, 1976); Shirley A. Leckie, *Elizabeth Bacon Custer and the Making of a Myth* (Norman: University of Oklahoma Press, 1993).

321. Leckie, *Elizabeth Bacon Custer*, 7, 12–13.

322. Leckie, *Elizabeth Bacon Custer*, 9–10.

323. Leckie, *Elizabeth Bacon Custer*, 15–16.

324. Daniel Bacon to the Richmonds, June [n.d.], 1862, Custer Letters, 43.

325. Elizabeth Bacon (Custer) to Aunt Eliza Sabin, spring [n.d.], 1862, Custer Letters, 43.

326. For the best books on Custer's Civil War years, see: Gregory Urwin, *Custer Victorious: The Civil War Battles of General George Armstrong Custer* (Lincoln: University of Nebraska Press, 1983); Edward G. Longacre, *Custer and His Wolverines: The Michigan Cavalry Brigade, 1861–1865* (Conshohocken, PA: Combined, 1997); Eric J. Wittenberg, ed., *At Custer's Side: The Civil War Writings of James Harvey Kidd* (Kent, Ohio: Kent University Press, 2001); Thom Hatch, *Glorious War: The Civil War Adventures of George Armstrong Custer* (New York: St. Martin's, 2014).

327. George Custer, "From West Point to the Battlefield," *The Custer Reader*, ed. Paul Andrew Hutton (Lincoln: University of Nebraska Press, 1992), 48.

328. John M. Carroll, ed., *Custer in the Civil War: His Unfinished Memoirs* (San Francisco: Presidio, 1977), 101–02.

329. Catherine S. Crary, ed., *Dear Belle: Letters from a Cadet and Officer to His Sweetheart, 1858–1865* (Middletown, CT: Wesleyan University Press, 1965), 105.

330. For the best books on Union cavalry, see: Stephen Starr, *The Union Cavalry in the Civil War: From Fort Sumter to Gettysburg, 1861–1863* (Baton Rouge: Louisiana State University Press, 1979); Stephen Starr, *The Union Cavalry in the Civil War: The War in the East, From Gettysburg to Appomattox* (Baton Rouge: Louisiana State University Press, 1981); Edward G. Longacre, *Lincoln's Cavalrymen: A History of the Mounted Forces of the Army of the Potomac* (Mechanicsburg, PA: Stackpole, 2000).

331. Stephen W. Sears, *George B. McClellan: The Young Napoleon* (New York: Da Capo, 1999); Ethan S. Rafuse, *McClellan's War: The Failure of Moderation in the Struggle for the Union* (Bloomington: Indiana University Press, 2005); John C. Waugh, *Lincoln and McClellan: The Troubled Partnership between a President and His General* (New York: Palgrave Macmillan, 2010).

332. Sears, *McClellan*, 137.

333. Doris Kearns Goodwin, *Team of Rivals: The Political Genius of Abraham Lincoln* (New York: Simon and Schuster, 2006), 379–81, 383.

334. Richard Slotkin, *The Long Road to Antietam: How the Civil War Became a Revolution* (New York: Liveright, 2012), 45–46.

335. George Custer to his parents, March 17, 1862, Custer Letters, 27–28.

336. Slotkin, *Antietam*, 100.

337. James McKay, *Allan Pinkerton: The First Private Eye* (New York: Wiley, 1997); Samantha Seiple, *Allan Pinkerton: America's First Private Eye* (New York: Scholastic, 2015).

338. George Custer to his parents, March 17, 1862, Custer Letters, 27.

339. For the best account, see: Stephen W. Sears, *To the Gates of Richmond: The Peninsula Campaign* (New York: Houghton Mifflin, 1992).

340. George Custer to Ann Reed, May 15, 1862, Custer Letters, 30.

341. George Custer to Ann Reed, March 11, 1862, Custer Letters, 27.

342. George Custer to Ann Reed, April 20, 1862, Custer Letters, 29.

343. Stiles, *Custer's Trials*, 41.

344. Barnett, *Touched by Fire*, 29.

345. Stiles, *Custer's Trials*, 49–50.

346. George Brinton McClellan, *McClellan's Own Story: The War for the Union* (New York: Charles Webster, 1887), 365.

347. Douglas Southall Freeman and Richard Harwell, *Lee* (New York: Scribner's, 1997); Michael Korda, *Clouds of Glory: The Life and Legend of Robert E. Lee* (New York: Harper, 2014).

348. George Custer to the Reeds, August [n.d.], 1862, Custer Letters, 33.

349. McPherson, *Tried by War*, 66, 138.

350. Slotkin, *Long Road to Antietam*, 274.

351. Slotkin, *Long Road to Antietam*, 383.

352. Stiles, *Custer's Trials*, 73.

353. Herman Hattaway and Archer Jones, *How the North Won the Civil War: A Military History of the Civil War* (Chicago: University of Illinois Press, 1991), 266.

354. Peter Knight, *Conspiracy Nation: The Politics of Paranoia in Postwar America* (New York: New York University Press, 2002); Robin Ramsay, *Politics and Paranoia* (London: Picnic, 2008); Richard Hofstadter, *The Paranoid Style in American Politics* (New York: Vintage, 2008).

355. Philip Shaw Paludan, *The Presidency of Abraham Lincoln* (Topeka: University Press of Kansas, 1994), 155.

356. Slotkin, *Long Road to Antietam*, 371.

357. Smith, *Grant*, 162.

358. Ulysses S. Grant, *Personal Memoirs of Ulysses S. Grant* (New York: The Great Commanders, 1998), 174.

359. Libbie's Civil War, 6.

360. Elizabeth Bacon (Custer) to Daniel Bacon, [n.d.], 1862, Custer Letters, 50–51.

361. George Custer to Ann Reed, May [n.d.], 1863, Custer Letters, 53.

362. George Custer to Annette Humphreys, summer [n.d.], 1863, Custer Letters, 63.

363. Stiles, *Custer's Trials*, 86.

364. Stiles, *Custer's Trials*, 88.

365. Richard E. Crouch, *Brandy Station: A Battle Like No Other* (New York: Willow Bend Books, 2002); Eric J. Wittenberg and D. James Lighthizer, *The Battle of Brandy Station: North America's Largest Cavalry* (New York: History Books, 2010); Eric Wittenberg and Daniel T. Davis, *Out Flew the Sabers: The Battle of Brandy Station, June 9, 1863* (New York: Savas Beattie, 2016).

366. Stiles, *Custer's Trials*, 93, 94.

367. Samuel J. Martin, *Kill-Cavalry: The Life of Union General Hugh Judson Kilpatrick* (Mechanicsburg, PA: Stackpole, 2000).

368. Edward G. Longacre, *The Cavalry at Gettysburg: A Tactical Study of Mounted Operations during the Civil War's Pivotal Campaign* (Lincoln: University of Nebraska Press, 1986).

369. Jeffrey D. Wert, *Custer: The Controversial Life of George Armstrong Custer* (New York: Simon and Schuster, 1996), 95.

370. Eric J. Wittenberg, J. David Petruzzi, and Michael F. Nugent, *One Continuous Fight: The Retreat from Gettysburg and the Pursuit of Lee's Army of Northern Virginia* (New York: Savas Beattie, 2008).

371. George Custer to Annette Humphreys, July 19, 1863, Custer Letters, 52.

372. Abraham Lincoln to James Conkling, August 26, 1863, Lincoln Writings, 777–78.

373. Libbie's Civil War, 45.

374. Stiles, *Custer's Trials*, 145–46.

375. Leckie, *Elizabeth Bacon Custer*, 34.

376. George Custer to Daniel Bacon, October [n.d.], 1863, Custer Letters, 67.

377. Elizabeth Bacon (Custer) to Rebecca Richmond, fall [n.d.], 1863, Custer Letters, 64.
378. Leckie, *Elizabeth Bacon Custer*, 33.
379. Elizabeth Bacon (Custer) to George Custer, October [n.d.], 1863, Custer Letters, 74, 80.
380. Elizabeth Bacon (Custer) to George Custer, December 26, 1863, Custer Letters, 77.
381. Elizabeth Bacon (Custer) to George Custer, January [n.d.], 1864, Custer Letters, 78.
382. Elizabeth Bacon (Custer) to George Custer, December 27, 1863, Custer Letters, 75.
383. Stiles, *Custer's Trials*, 115.
384. Elizabeth Bacon (Custer) to George Custer, December 23, 1863, Custer Letters, 76.
385. Wert, *Custer*, 129.
386. Stiles, *Custer's Trials*, 142.
387. Elizabeth Bacon (Custer) to Rebecca Richmond, January [n.d.], 1864, Custer Letters, 79.
388. Elizabeth Bacon (Custer) to George Custer, January [n.d.], 1864, Custer Letters, 79.
389. Leckie, *Elizabeth Bacon Custer*, 37.
390. Stiles, *Custer's Trials*, 150.
391. Stiles, *Custer's Trials*, 153.
392. Leckie, *Elizabeth Bacon Custer*, 40.
393. Libbie's Civil War, 45.
394. Elizabeth Custer to George Custer, April [n.d.], 1864, Custer Letters, 89.
395. George Custer to Elizabeth Custer, April 23, 1864, Custer Letters, 92.
396. Elizabeth Custer to George Custer, June 10, 1964, Custer Letters, 102.
397. Elizabeth Custer to her parents, June [n.d.], 1864, Custer Letters, 106.
398. Elizabeth Custer to her parents, March 28, 1864, Custer Letters, 88–89.
399. Elizabeth Custer to her parents, June [n.d.], 1864, Custer Letters, 108–09.
400. Elizabeth Custer to her parents, April [n.d.], 1864, Custer Letters, 90–91.
401. Elizabeth Custer to her parents, April [n.d.], 1864, Custer Letters, 90–91.
402. George Custer to Elizabeth Custer, May 1, 1864, Custer Letters, 95.
403. Elizabeth Custer to George Custer, June [n.d.], 1864, Custer Letters, 101.
404. George Custer to Elizabeth Custer, June [n.d.], 1864, Custer Letters, 101–02.
405. Elizabeth Custer to George Custer, October [n.d.], 1864, Custer Letters, 129.
406. Edward Caudill and Paul Ashdown, *Inventing Custer: The Making of an American Legend* (New York: Rowman and Littlefield, 2015), 99–103.
407. Stiles, *Custer's Trials*, 155.
408. Wert, *Custer*, 142–44.
409. Ulysses S. Grant, *The Personal Memoirs of Ulysses S. Grant* (Princeton, NJ: Great Commanders, 1998); Jean Edward Smith, Grant (New York: Simon and Schuster, 2001);
     H. W. Brands, *The Man Who Saved the Union: Ulysses S. Grant* (New York: Anchor, 2013); Robert C. White, *American Ulysses: A Life of Ulysses S. Grant* (New York: Random House, 2016).
410. T. Harry Williams, *McClellan, Sherman, and Grant* (New Brunswick, NJ: Rutgers University Press, 1962), 105.
411. Smith, *Grant*, 15.
412. Charles Francis Adams Jr. to Charles Francis Adams, May 29, 1864, Worthington Chauncey Ford, ed., *A Cycle of Adams Letters, 1861–1865*, vol. 2 (Boston: Houghton Mifflin, 1920), 131–34.
413. Libbie Custer to her parents, March 28, 1864, Custer Letters, 87–88.
414. George Custer to Elizabeth Custer, May 16, 1864, Custer Letters, 97.
415. Phil Sheridan, *The Personal Memoirs of P. H. Sheridan* (New York: Da Capo, 1992); Roy Morris, *Sheridan: The Life and Wars of General Phil Sheridan* (New York: Crown,

1992); Paul Hutton, *Phil Sheridan and His Army* (Norman: University of Oklahoma Press, 1999); Eric J. Wittenberg, *Little Phil: A Reassessment of the Civil War Leadership of General Philip H. Sheridan* (Washington, DC: Brassey's, 2002); Joseph Wheelan, *Terrible Swift Sword: The Life of General Philip H. Sheridan* (New York: Da Capo, 2013).

416. Caudill, *Inventing Custer*, 108–12.

417. Mark Grimsley, *And Keep Moving On: The Virginia Campaign, May–June 1864* (Lincoln: University of Nebraska Press, 2002).

418. Eric J. Wittenberg, *Glory Enough for All: Sheridan's Second Raid and the Battle of Trevilian Station* (Washington DC: Brassey's Books, 2001).

419. James H. Kidd, *Personal Reminisces of a Cavalryman* (Ionia, MI: Sentinel, 1908), 353.

420. Wittenberg, *Glory Enough*, 123–24.

421. Jay Monaghan, "Custer's 'Last Stand': Trevilian Station," *The Custer Reader*, ed. Paul Andrew Hutton (Lincoln: University of Nebraska Press, 1992), 61.

422. Wittenberg, *Glory Enough*, 156–58.

423. Gregory J. W. Urwin, "Custer: The Civil War Years," *The Custer Reader*, ed. Paul Andrew Hutton (Lincoln: University of Nebraska Press, 1992), 7.

424. George Custer to Elizabeth Custer, July 1, 1864, Custer Letters, 111.

425. Elizabeth Custer to George Custer, October [n.d.], 1864, Custer Letters, 124.

426. Elizabeth Custer to George Custer, March [n.d.], 1865, Custer Letters, 144.

427. Grant, *Memoirs*, 441.

428. Jeffrey D. Wert, *From Winchester to Cedar Creek: The Shenandoah Campaign of 1864* (New York: Simon and Schuster, 1987); Gary W. Gallagher, ed., *The Shenandoah Valley Campaign of 1864* (Chapel Hill: University of North Carolina Press, 2006).

429. Barnett, *Touched by Fire*, 123.

430. Elizabeth Custer to George Custer, fall [n.d.], 1864; George Custer to Elizabeth Custer, fall [n.d.], 1864, Custer Letters, 118–19.

431. Wert, *Custer*, 178–79.

432. John Waugh, *Reelecting Lincoln: The Battle for the 1864 Presidency* (New York: Da Capo, 2001).

433. Libbie's Civil War, 181.

434. Elizabeth Custer to Rebecca Richmond, November 15, 1864, Custer Letters, 132.

435. Elizabeth Custer to her parents, December 25, 1865, Custer Letters, 135.

436. Phil Sheridan to Ulysses Grant, April 6, 1865, Custer Letters, 150.

437. George Custer to Daniel Bacon, April [n.d.], 1865, Custer Letters, 150–51.

438. James Longstreet, *From Manassas to Appomattox: Memoirs of the Civil War in America* (Philadelphia: J. B. Lippincott, 1908), 627.

439. James M. McPherson, *Battle Cry of Freedom: The Civil War Era* (New York: Oxford University Press, 1988), 849.

440. George Custer to 3rd Cavalry Division, April 9, 1865, Custer Letters, 161.

441. Phil Sheridan to Elizabeth Custer, April 10, 1865, Custer Letters, 159.

442. Libbie's Civil War, 146.

443. Libbie's Civil War, 149–50.

444. David Herbert Donald, *Lincoln* (New York: Simon and Schuster, 1995), 599.

445. William Nester, *The Age of Lincoln and the Art of American Power, 1848–1876* (Washington, DC: Potomac, 2–13), 226–27.

446. For the best books, see: Eric Foner, *Reconstruction: America's Unfinished Revolution, 1863–1877* (New York: Harper and Row, 1988); Michael W. Fitzgerald, *Splendid Failure: Postwar Reconstruction in the American South* (New York: Ivan R. Dee, 2008); Mark Wahlgren Summers, *The Ordeal of the Reunion: A New History of Reconstruction*

(Chapel Hill: University of North Carolina Press, 2014).

447. Jean Edward Smith, *Grant* (New York: Simon and Schuster, 2001), 422.

448. George Custer to Daniel Bacon, July [n.d.], 1865, Custer Letters, 166.

449. Elizabeth Custer to her parents, July [n.d.], 1865, Custer Letters, 269.

450. Stiles, *Custer's Trials*, 224.

451. For Libbie's account of their time in Louisiana and Texas, see: Elizabeth Bacon Custer, *Tenting on the Plains, or General Custer in Kansas and Texas* (New York: Harper and Brothers, 1887). See also John M. Carroll, *Custer in Texas: An Interrupted Narrative* (New York: Sol Lewis, 1975).

452. Stiles, *Custer's Trials*, 227.

453. Elizabeth Custer to her parents, October 22, 1865, Custer Letters, 170.

454. Stiles, *Custer's Trials*, 132–35.

455. John D. Bergamini, *The Hundredth Year: The United States in 1876* (New York: G.P. Putnam's Sons, 1976), 57.

456. George Custer to Elizabeth Custer, April 2, 3, 18, 1866, Custer Letters, 180–82.

457. Leckie, *Elizabeth Bacon Custer*, 85.

458. Stiles, *Custer's Trials*, 245–52.

459. For the best overview, see: E. Lisle Reedstrom, *Custer's 7th Cavalry: From Fort Riley to the Little Big Horn* (New York: Sterling, 1992). See also: Robert M. Utley, ed., *Life in Custer's Cavalry: Diaries and Letters of Albert and Jennie Barnitz, 1865–1868* (Lincoln: University of Nebraska Press, 1987); John M. Carroll, *They Rode with Custer: A Biographical Directory of the Men That Rode with General George Armstrong Custer* (Mattituck, NY: J. M. Carroll, 1993).

460. For an overview of the tribes and warfare on the central plains, see: H. Craig Miner and William E. Unrau, *The End of Indian Kansas: A Study of Cultural Revolution, 1854–1871* (Lawrence: Regents Press of Kansas, 1978).

461. For the Cheyenne and their close ally the Arapaho, see: George Bird Grinnell, *The Cheyenne Indians*, 2 vols. (New Haven, CT: Yale University Press, 1923); George Bird Grinnell, *The Fighting Cheyennes* (1915) (Norman: University of Oklahoma Press, 1956); Donald J. Berthron, *The Southern Cheyennes* (Norman: University of Oklahoma Press, 1965); Virginia Cole Trenholm, *The Arapahoes, Our People* (Norman: University of Oklahoma Press, 1973); Thom Hatch, *Black Kettle: The Cheyenne Chief Who Sought Peace but Found War* (New York: John Wiley and Sons, 2004).

462. Stan Hoig, *The Sand Creek Massacre* (Norman: University of Oklahoma Press, 1974); Ari Kelman, *A Misplaced Massacre: Struggling Over the Meaning of Sand Creek* (Cambridge: Harvard University Press, 2015).

463. William Y. Chalfant, *Hancock's War: Conflict on the Southern Plains* (Norman: University of Oklahoma Press, 2010).

464. Elizabeth Custer, *Boots and Saddles*, 212.

465. Custer, *Life on the Plains*, 20–21, 29.

466. George Custer to Elizabeth Custer, May 2, 1867, Custer Letters, 199.

467. For the best scholarly overviews, see: Elliot West, *The Contested Plains: Indians, Goldseekers, and the Rush to Colorado* (Lawrence: University of Kansas Press, 2005); Jerome A. Green, *Washita: The U.S. Army and the Southern Cheyenne* (Norman: University of Oklahoma Press, 2008); William Y. Chalfant, *Hancock's War: Conflict on the Southern Plains* (Norman: University of Oklahoma Press, 2010); Charles D. Collins, *The Cheyenne Wars Atlas* (New York: Books Express, 2012). Then there is Custer's vivid, entertaining version: George Armstrong Custer, *Wild Life on the Plains and the Horrors of Indian Warfare* (1874) (Brandon, VT: Sidney M. Southard, 1884).

468. George A. Custer, *My Life on the Plains* (1874) (Lincoln: University of Nebraska Press,

1968), 44–45, 47.
469. George Custer to Elizabeth Custer, May 2, 1867, Custer Letters, 199.
470. Shirley A. Leckie, *Elizabeth Bacon Custer and the Making of the Myth* (Norman: University of Oklahoma Press, 1993), 96–97.
471. George Custer to Elizabeth Custer, May 1, 2, 6, 1867, Custer Letters, 197–200, 202.
472. Leckie, *Elizabeth Bacon Custer*, 107.
473. Stiles, *Custer*, 281.
474. Leckie, *Elizabeth Bacon Custer*, 105.
475. Lawrence A. Frost, *The Court Martial of General George Armstrong Custer* (Norman: University of Oklahoma Press, 1968).
476. Brian W. Dippie, ed., *Nomad: George A. Custer in Turf, Field, and Farm* (Austin: University of Texas Press, 1980).
477. Stiles, *Custer*, 300–01.
478. Wert, *Custer*, 265.
479. George E. Hyde, *Red Cloud's Folk: A History of the Oglala Sioux* (Norman: University of Oklahoma Press, 1957); James V. Olson, *Red Cloud and the Sioux Problem* (Lincoln: University of Nebraska Press, 1965); Bob Drury and Tom Clavin, *The Heart of Everything That Is: The Untold Story of Red Cloud, An American Legend* (New York: Simon and Schuster, 2014).
480. Stiles, *Custer*, 307.
481. John H. Monnett, *The Battle of Beecher Island and the Indian War of 1867–1869* (Boulder: University Press of Colorado, 1992).
482. Langdon Sully, *No Tears for the General: The Life of Alfred Sully, 1821–1879* (Denver: Old West, 1974).
483. Wert, *Custer*, 267–68.
484. Elizabeth Custer, *Following the Guidon*, 11–12.
485. Wert, *Custer*, 270.
486. Robert C. Carriker, *Fort Supply, Indian Territory: Frontier Outpost on the Plains* (Norman: University of Oklahoma Press, 1970).
487. For the Washita campaign, for scholarly accounts see: Stan Hoig, *The Battle of the Washita: The Sheridan-Custer Indian Campaign of 1867–69* (Garden City, NY; Doubleday, 1979); Louis Kraft, *Custer and the Cheyenne: George Armstrong Custer's Winter Campaign on the Southern Plains* (New York: Upon and Sons, 1995). For first person accounts, see: E. A. Brininstool, ed., David L. Spotts, *Campaigning with Custer and the Nineteenth Kansas Volunteer Cavalry in the Washita Campaign, 1868–60* (Lincoln: University of Nebraska, 1988); Richard B. Hardorff, ed., *Washita Memoirs: Eyewitness Accounts of Custer's Attack on Black Kettle's Village* (Norman: University of Oklahoma Press, 2006).
488 George Custer, *Life on the Plains* (1874) (Lincoln: University of Nebraska Press, 1968), 336.
489. Elizabeth Custer, *Following the Guidon*, 40.
490. Custer, *Life on the Plains*, 352.
491. Elizabeth Custer, *Following the Guidon*, 56–57.
492. Elizabeth Custer, *Following the Guidon*, 214–15.
493. Elizabeth Custer, *Following the Guidon*, 51.
494. Barnett, *Touched by Fire*, 157, 194-97, 321.
495. Barnett, *Touched by Fire*, 196.
496. Elizabeth Custer, *Following the Guidon*, 90–97.
497. Lawrence A. Frost, *General Custer's Libbie* (Seattle: Superior, 1976), 178.
498. Leckie, *Elizabeth Bacon Custer*, 116.

499. Frost, *Custer's Libbie*, 178.
500. Elizabeth Custer, *Following the Guidon*, 120.
501. Elizabeth Custer, *Following the Guidon*, 122.
502. Elizabeth Custer, *Following the Guidon*, 114–15.
503. Brian C. Pohanka, ed., *A Summer on the Plains with Custer's 7th Cavalry: The 1870 Diary of Annie Gibson Roberts* (Lynchburg, VA: Schroeder, 2004), 66–67.
504. Pohanka, *Summer on the Plains*, 8–17, 150–51.
505. Elizabeth Custer, *Following the Guidon*, 153–54.
506. Elizabeth Custer, *Following the Guidon*, 161.
507. Elizabeth Custer, *Following the Guidon*, 158.
508. Elizabeth Custer, *Following the Guidon*, 192.
509. Elizabeth Custer, *Following the Guidon*, 85–87.
510. Elizabeth Custer, *Following the Guidon*, 100.
511. Elizabeth Custer, *Boots and Saddles*, 56–57.
512. Elizabeth Custer, *Following the Guidon*, 238.
513. Elizabeth Custer, *Following the Guidon*, 231, 12–13.
514. Leckie, *Elizabeth Bacon Custer*, 122.
515. Frederick Benteen to Theodore Goldin, February 17, 1896, John M. Carroll, ed., *The Benteen-Goldin Letters on Custer and His Last Battle* (New York: Liveright, 1974), 262.
516. Frost, *Custer's Libbie*, 147.
517. Leckie, *Elizabeth Bacon Custer*, 126.
518. George Custer to Elizabeth Custer, [n.d.], 1871 (3 letters), Custer Letters, 233–34, 237.
519. There are two versions, the original complete George Armstrong Custer, *Wild Life on the Plains and the Horrors of Indian Warfare* (1874) (Brandon, VT: Sidney M. Southard, 1884), and the abridged George A. Custer, *My Life on the Plains* (Lincoln: University of Nebraska Press, 1968).
520. Leckie, *Elizabeth Bacon Custer*, 159.
521. Elizabeth Custer, *Boots and Saddles*, 149–51.
522. Elizabeth Custer's diary, February 5, 1873, Custer Letters, 246–47.
523. Royal B. Hassrick, *The Sioux* (Norman: University of Oklahoma Press, 1964); Gregory O. Cognan, *The Culture and Customs of the Sioux Indians* (Lincoln: Bison, 2012).
524. Stiles, *Custer's Trials*, 387.
525. James Calhoun, *Some Observations on the Yellowstone Expedition of 1873*, ed. Lawrence A. Frost (Glendale, CA: Arthur H. Clark, 1981); Roger Darling, *Custer's Seventh Cavalry Comes to Dakota* (El Segundo, CA: Upton and Sons, 1989).
526. Lawrence A. Frost, *Custer's 7th Cavalry and the Campaign of 1873* (El Segundo, CA: Upton and Sons, 1986), 26.
527. David S. Stanley, *Personal Memoirs of Major General D. S. Stanley* (Cambridge, MA: Harvard University Press, 1917), 239–40.
528. Charles W. Larned, "Expedition to the Yellowstone River in 1873: Letters of a Young Lieutenant," *The Custer Reader*, ed. Paul Andrew Hutton (Lincoln: University of Nebraska Press, 1992), 184, 185.
529. Elizabeth Custer, *Boots and Saddles*, 87–89.
530. Stiles, *Custer's Trials*, 386.
531. George Custer to Elizabeth Custer, July [n.d.], 1873, Custer Letters, 254–55.
532. George Custer to Libbie Custer, September [n.d.], 1873, Custer Letters, 265–66.
533. Robert M. Utley, *The Lance and the Shield: The Life and Times of Sitting Bull* (New York: Henry Holt, 1993).
534. Ami Frank Mulford, *Fighting Indians in the 7th United States Cavalry: Custer's Favorite*

Regiment (Corning, NY: Paul Lindsley Mulford, 1879), 134–44.

535. E. Lisle Reedstrom, *Custer's 7th Cavalry: From Fort Riley to the Little Big Horn* (New York: Sterling, 1992), 79–90.
536. Leckie, *Elizabeth Bacon Custer*, 158.
537. John Lubetkin, *Jay Cooke's Gamble: The Northern Pacific Railroad, the Sioux, and the Panic of 1873* (Norman: University of Oklahoma Press, 2006).
538. Lee Chambers, *Fort Abraham Lincoln: Dakota Territory* (New York: Schiffer, 2008).
539. Elizabeth Custer, to Eliza Sabin, March [n.d.], 1874, Custer's Letters, 269.
540. Elizabeth Custer, *Boots and Saddles*, 126.
541. Elizabeth Custer, *Boots and Saddles*, 138–40.
542. Elizabeth Custer, *Boots and Saddles*, 233, 307–08.
543. Elizabeth Custer, *Boots and Saddles*, 155.
544. Elizabeth Custer, *Boots and Saddles*, 159–66.
545. Elizabeth Custer, *Boots and Saddles*, 115–17.
546. Edward S. Cooper, *William Babcock Hazen: The Best Hated Man* (Madison, NJ: Fairleigh Dickinson University Press, 2005), 239–41; William B. Hazen, *Some Corrections to "My Life on the Plains,"* (St. Paul, MN: Ramsley and Cunningham, 1875); Watson Parker, *Gold in the Black Hills* (Lincoln: University of Nebraska Press, 1982).
547. Elizabeth Custer, *Boots and Saddles*, 231–32.
548. Elizabeth Custer to George Custer, July [n.d.], 1873, Custer Letters, 250.
549. Elizabeth Custer, *Boots and Saddles*, 107–08.
550. *Chicago Inter-Ocean*, July 9, 1874.
551. Stiles, *Custer's Trials*, 417.
552. Elizabeth Custer, *Boots and Saddles*, 204–09, 215.
553. Donald Jackson, *Custer's Gold: The United States Cavalry Expedition of 1874* (New Haven, CT: Yale University Press, 1966).
554. George Custer to Elizabeth Custer, July 15, 1874, Custer Letters, 273.
555. George Custer to Elizabeth Custer, July 2, 1874, Custer Letters, 272.
556. Elizabeth Custer, *Boots and Saddles*, 192–94.
557. Edward S. Cooper, *William Worth Belknap: An American Disgrace* (Madison, NJ: Fairleigh Dickinson University Press, 2003).
558. Stiles, *Custer's Trials*, 427.
559. *New York Herald*, October 2, 1875.
560. Elizabeth Custer to Tom Custer, December [n.d.], 1875, Custer Letters, 276.
561. Jean Edward Smith, *Grant* (New York: Simon and Schuster, 2001), 523.
562. For the Sioux War of 1876 and beyond, see: Jerome A. Greene, *Battles and Skirmishes of the Great Sioux War, 1876–1877* (Norman: University of Oklahoma Press, 1996); Charles Robinson, *A Good Year to Die: The Story of the Great Sioux War* (Norman: University of Oklahoma Press, 1996); Jerome A. Greene, *Lakota and Cheyenne: Indian Views of the Great Sioux War, 1876–1877* (Norman: University of Oklahoma Press, 2000); Marc H. Abrams, *Sioux War Dispatches: Reports from the Field, 1876–1877* (New York: Westholme, 2012).
563. Elizabeth Custer, *Boots and Saddles*, 253–60.
564. George Custer to Elizabeth Custer, April 28, 1876, Custer Letters, 293.
565. For the best overviews of Custer's last campaign, see: Bruce A. Rosenberg, *Custer and the Epic of Defeat* (University Park: Pennsylvania State University Press, 1974); Brian W. Dippie, *Custer's Last Stand: The Anatomy of an American Myth* (Missoula: University of Montana Press, 1976); John S. Gray, *The Centennial Campaign: The Sioux War of 1876* (Fort Collins, CO: Old Army Press, 1976); Charles Hofling, *Custer and the Little Big Horn: A Psychobiographical Inquiry* (Detroit: Wayne State University Press, 1981);

Evan S. Connell, *Son of Morning Star: Custer and the Little Bighorn* (San Francisco: North Point, 1984); David Humphreys Miller, *Custer's Fall: The Indian Side of the Story* (Lincoln: University of Nebraska Press, 1985); Lloyd J. Overfield, ed., *The Little Bighorn, 1876: The Official Communication: Documents and Reports* (Lincoln: University of Nebraska Press, 1990); E. Lisle Reedstrom, *Custer's 7th Cavalry: From Fort Riley to the Little Big Horn* (New York: Sterling Publishing, 1992); James Donovan, *A Terrible Glory: Custer and the Little Bighorn, the Last Great Battle of the American West* (New York: Little, Brown, 2008).

566. Stiles, *Custer's Trials*, 440.

567. Stiles, *Custer's Trials*, 456.

568. Connell, *Morning Star*, 101–02; Reedstrom, *Custer's 7th Cavalry*, 111.

569. Leckie, *Elizabeth Bacon Custer*, 182.

570. Elizabeth Custer, *Boots and Saddles*, 265.

571. Ronald H. Nichols, *In Custer's Shadow: Major Marcus Reno* (Norman: University of Oklahoma Press, 2000); Charles K. Mills, *Harvest of Barren Regrets: The Army Career of Frederick William Benteen, 1834–1898* (Glendale, CA: Arthur H. Clark, 1985); John M. Carroll, ed., *The Benteen-Goldin Letters on Custer and His Last Battle* (Lincoln: University of Nebraska Press, 1991); Karol Asay, *Gray Head and Long Hair: The Benteen-Custer Relationship* (New York: J. M. Carroll, 1983); John M. Carroll, ed., *Custer's Chief of Scouts: The Reminiscences of Charles A. Varnum* (Lincoln: University of Nebraska Press, 1987).

572. Utley, *Frontier Regulars*, 256.

573. Alfred Terry to George Custer, June 22, 1876, Custer Letters, 308–09.

574. Elizabeth Custer to George Custer, June [n.d.], 1876, Custer Letters, 304.

575. Leckie, *Elizabeth Bacon Custer*, 185.

576. George Custer to Elizabeth, June 22, 1876, Custer Letters, 307.

577. Jeffrey Wert, *Custer: The Controversial Life of George Armstrong Custer* (New York: Simon and Schuster, 1996), 336.

578. Edward S. Godfrey, "Custer's Last Battle," *The Custer Reader*, ed. Paul Andrew Hutton (Lincoln: University of Nebraska Press, 1992), 277.

579. Donovan, *Terrible Glory*, 190–91.

580. Robert Utley, *Frontier Regulars: The United States Army and the Indian, 1866–1891* (Lincoln: University of Nebraska Press, 1973), 259; Paul Hedren, ed., *The Great Sioux War, 1876–77* (Helena: Montana Historical Society, 1991), 13.

581. Chief White Bull as told to Stanley Vestal, "The Battle of the Little Bighorn," *The Custer Reader*, ed. Paul Andrew Hutton (Lincoln: University of Nebraska Press, 1992), 337.

582. Donovan, *Terrible Glory*, 257.

583. Reedstrom, *Custer's 7th Cavalry*, 135.

584. For recent interpretations, see: Larry Sklenar, *To Hell With Honor: Custer and the Little Big Horn* (Norman: University of Oklahoma Press, 2000); Robert Utley, *Custer, the Seventh Cavalry, and the Little Big Horn: A Biography* (Norman: University of Oklahoma Press, 2012).

585. Godfrey, "Custer's Last Battle," 310; Kate Bighead as told to Thomas Marquis, "She Watched Custer's Last Battle," *The Custer Reader*, ed. Paul Andrew Hutton (Lincoln: University of Nebraska Press, 1992), 372–73.

586. Wert, *Custer*, 355.

587. Elizabeth Custer, *Boots and Saddles*, 267–68.

588. Leckie, *Elizabeth Bacon Custer*, 199.

589. Robert M. Utley, *Custer and the Great Controversy: The Origin and Development of a*

Legend (Pasadena, CA: Westernlore, 1980), 45–46.

590. Utley, *Custer and the Great Controversy*, 44.

591. Connell, *Morning Star*, 11.

592. Barnett, *Touched by Fire*, 282.

593. Robert M. Utley, *The Lance and the Shield: The Life and Times of Sitting Bull* (New York: Henry Holt, 1993), 269.

594. Jessie Benton to John Greenleaf Whittier, February 8, 1891, Jessie Letters, 540.

595. Jessie Benton to John Greenleaf Whittier, February 8, 1891, Jessie Letters, 540.

596. Jessie Benton to William Carey Jones, October 28, 1890, Jessie Letters, 536–37.

597. Herr, *Jessie Benton Frémont*, 443.

598. Jessie Benton to Samuel Pickard, May 28, 1893, Jessie Letters, 550.

599. Herr, *Jessie Benton Frémont*, 443.

600. Jessie Benton to John Greenleaf Whittier, November 19, 1889, Jessie Letters, 530.

601. Theodore Roosevelt, *Thomas H. Benton* (Boston: Houghton Mifflin, 1889).

602. Jessie Benton to Theodore Roosevelt, August 21, 1899, Jessie Letters, 552–53.

603. Jessie Benton to William Carey Jones, October 28, 1890, Jessie Letters, 536.

604. Stiles, *Custer's Trials*, 457–58.

605. Elizabeth Bacon Custer, *"Boots and Saddles," or Life in Dakota with General Custer* (New York: Harper and Brothers, 1885); Elizabeth Bacon Custer, *Tenting on the Plains, or General Custer in Kansas and Texas* (New York: Harper and Brothers, 1887); Elizabeth Bacon Custer, *Following the Guidon* (1890) (Norman: University of Oklahoma Press, 1966).

606. Barnett, *Touched by Fire*, 365.

607. Leckie, *Elizabeth Bacon Custer*, xiii, xiv.

608. Elizabeth Bacon Custer, *"Boots and Saddles," or Life in Dakota with General Custer* (New York: Harper and Brothers, 1885); Elizabeth Bacon Custer, *Tenting on the Plains, or General Custer in Kansas and Texas* (New York: Harper and Brothers, 1887); Elizabeth Bacon Custer, *Following the Guidon* (1890) (Norman: University of Oklahoma Press, 1966).

609. Libbie's Civil War, xii.

610. Candace Wheeler, *Yesterdays in a Busy Life* (New York: Harper and Brothers, 1918), 422.

611. Mary E. Burt, ed., as told by Elizabeth B. Custer, *The Boy General: Story of the Life of Major-General George A. Custer* (New York: Charles Scribner's Sons, 1901).

612. Cyrus Brady, *Indian Fights and Fighters: The Soldier and the Sioux* (New York: McClure Philips, 1904).

613. John B. Kennedy, "A Soldier's Widow," *Colliers*, January 29, 1927, 10, 41.

614. Frederick Jackson Turner, *The Frontier in American History* (New York: Dover, 1996), 323.

615. Josiah Royce, *California From the Conquest in 1846 to the Second Vigilance Committee in San Francisco: A Study in American Character* (1886) (Berkeley, CA: Heyday, 2002), 110.

616. Frederick Merk, *Manifest Destiny and Mission in American History* (Cambridge, MA: Harvard University Press, 1963), 32.

617. Richard Slotkin, *Regeneration Through Violence: The Mythology of the American Frontier, 1600–1860* (New York: Harper Perennial, 1973), 6.

618. For the classic study, see: Joseph Campbell, *The Hero with a Thousand Faces* (New York: MJF Books, 1949).

619. Paul A. Hutton, "From Little Bighorn to Little Big Man: The Changing Image of a Western Hero in Popular Culture," *The Custer Reader*, ed. Paul Andrew Hutton (Lin-

coln: University of Nebraska Press, 1992), 395.

620. For overviews of the hero and American culture, see: Dixon Wecter, *The Hero in America* (New York: Charles Scribner's Sons, 1941); Marshall W. Fishwick, *American Heroes: Myth and Reality* (Washington, DC: Public Affairs, 1954); Theodore P. Greene, *America's Heroes: The Changing Success* (New York: Oxford University Press, 1970); Edward Tabor Linenthal, *Americans and Their Battlefields* (Urbana: University of Illinois Press, 1991); Michael Kammen, *Mystic Cords of Memory: The Transformation of Tradition in American Culture* (New York: Vintage, 1993); Robert Jewett and John Shelton Lawrence, *The Myth of the American Superhero* (Grand Rapids, MI: William Eerdman, 2002); Edmund S. Morgan, *American Heroes: Profiles of the Men and Women Who Shaped Early America* (New York: W.W. Norton, 2008).

    For the role of the frontier, the West, and heroes in American culture, see: Henry Nash Smith, *Virgin Land: The American West as Symbol and Myth* (Cambridge, MA: Harvard University Press, 1950); Kent Ladd Steckmesser, *The Western Hero in History and Legacy* (Norman: University of Oklahoma Press, 1965); Bruce A. Rosenburg, *The Code of the West* (Bloomington: Indiana University Press, 1982); Edward Tabor Linenthal, *Changing Images of the Western Hero in America: A History of Popular Symbolism* (New York: Edwin Mellen, 1982); Rita Parks, *The Western Hero in Film and Television* (Ann Harbor, MI: UMI Research, 1982); Robert G. Athearn, *The Mythic West in Twentieth Century America* (Lawrence: University Press of Kansas 1986); James R. Grossman, ed., *The Frontier in American Culture* (Berkeley: University of California Press, 1994).

621. Mark Twain, *Adventures of Huckleberry Finn* (New York: Random House, 1996), 363.

622. Frémont, *Memoirs*, 486.

623. Frémont *Memoirs*, 561.

624. Frémont *Memoirs*, 30.

625. Milo Milton Quaife, *Kit Carson's Autobiography* (Lincoln: University of Nebraska Press, 1966), 126–27.

626. Bil Gilbert, *Westering Man: The Life of Joseph Walker* (Norman: University of Oklahoma Press, 1989), 215–16.

627. Benjamin Madley, *An American Genocide: The United States and the California Indian Catastrophe* (New Haven, CT: Yale University Press, 2016), 48.

628. Chaffin, *Frémont*, xix.

629. Stiles, *Custer's Trial*, 236.

630. Elizabeth Custer, *Boots and Saddles*, 11.

631. Barnett, *Touched by Fire*, 53.

632. Lawrence Barrett, "Personal Recollections of General Custer," in Frederick Whitaker, ed., *A Complete Life of Gen. George A. Custer* (New York: Sheldon, 1876), 629–43.

633. Stiles, *Custer's Trials*, 89.

634. Louise Barnett, *Touched by Fire: The Life, Death, and Mythic Afterlife of George Armstrong Custer* (Lincoln: University of Nebraska Press, 2006), vi–ix.

635. George Custer to Elizabeth Custer, April 17, 1876, Custer Letters, 290.

636. Libbie's Civil War, 43.

637. George Custer, *My Life on the Plains* (1874) (Lincoln: University of Nebraska Press, 1968), 82.

638. George Custer to Elizabeth Custer, July [n.d.], 1873, Custer Letters, 257.

639. George Custer to Elizabeth Custer, March 18, 1866, Custer's Letters, 179.

640. Elizabeth Custer, *Boots and Saddles*, 216–17.

641. Custer, *Wild Life on the Plains*, 28, 31.

642. Stiles, *Custer's Trials*, 374, 369–75.

643. Stiles, *Custer's Trials*, 34.

644. Stiles, *Custer's Trials*, 377.

645. Frederick Whittaker, *The Complete Life of Gen. George A. Custer* (New York: Sheldon, 1876).

646. Hutton, "From the Little Bighorn to Little Big Man," 399.

647. For fascinating explorations of the Custer Myth's political and cultural causes and effects, see: Brian A. Dippie, *Custer's Last Stand: The Anatomy of an American Myth* (Missoula: University of Montana Press, 1976); Robert M. Utley, *Custer and the Great Controversy: The Origin and Development of a Legend* (Pasadena, CA: Westernlore, 1980); W. A. Graham, ed., *The Custer Myth: A Source Book of Custeriana* (Mechanicsburg, PA: Stackpole, 2000); Louise Barnett, *Touched by Fire: The Life, Death, and Mythic Afterlife of George Armstrong Custer* (Lincoln: University of Nebraska Press, 2006); Edward Caudill and Paul Ashdown, *Investing Custer: The Making of an American Legend* (New York: Rowman and Littlefield, 2015).

648. Rebecca Harding Davis, "In Remembrance," *The Independent*, (New York: The Independent, 1903), 239.

649. Jessie Benton Frémont, "The Origin of the Frémont Explorations," *Century*, vol. 41 (March 1891), 768.

650. Jessie Frémont to Elizabeth Blair Lee, February 1, 1858, Jessie Letters, 185.

651. Jessie Frémont to Elizabeth Blair Lee, August 17, 1858, Jessie Letters, 211.

652. Both quotes from Herr, *Jessie Benton Frémont*, 381.

653. Jessie Frémont to Nelly Haskell, November 1, 1864, Jessie Letters, 383–84.

654. Jessie Frémont to William Morton, November 23, 1878, Jessie Letters, 458.

655. Jessie Benton Frémont, *Far West Sketches*, 31–35; Denton, *Passion and Principle*, 175–76, 210–11.

656. Catherine Coffin Phillips, *Jessie Benton Frémont: A Woman Who Made History* (San Francisco: J. H. Nash, 1935), 193.

657. Leckie, *Elizabeth Bacon Custer*, 158.

658. Elizabeth Custer to her parents, April [n.d.], 1864, Custer Letters, 90.

659. Stiles, *Custer's Trials*, 171.

660. Elizabeth Custer, *Boots and Saddles*, 10.

661. Leckie, *Elizabeth Bacon Custer*, 158.

662. Elizabeth Custer, *Boots and Saddles*, 48, 78.

663. Elizabeth Custer, *Following the Guidon*, 186–87.

664. Elizabeth Custer, *Following the Guidon*, 225.

665. Elizabeth Custer to Eliza Sabin, [n.d.], 1868? Fort Hays, Custer Letters, 284.

666. Elizabeth Custer, *Boots and Saddles*, 153.

667. Leckie, *Elizabeth Bacon Custer*, 158–59.

668. Leckie, *Elizabeth Bacon Custer*, 159.

669. Leckie, *Elizabeth Bacon Custer*, 159.

670. Hutton, "From Little Bighorn to Little Big Man," 406.

671. For the best overviews of the Custer Myth, see: Bruce A. Rosenberg, *Custer and the Epic of Defeat* (University Park: Pennsylvania State University Press, 1974); Robert M. Utley, *Custer and the Great Controversy: The Origin and Development of a Legend* (Pasadena, CA: Westernlore, 1980); Louise Barnett, *Touched by Fire: The Life, Death, and Mythic Afterlife of George Armstrong Custer* (Lincoln: University of Nebraska Press, 2006); Edward Caudill and Paul Ashdown, *Inventing Custer: The Making of an American Legend* (New York: Rowman and Littlefield, 2015).

For the cultural meaning of Custer's Last Stand, see: Brian W. Dippie, *Custer's Last Stand: The Anatomy of an American Myth* (Lincoln: University of Nebraska, 2002); Herman Viola, *Little Bighorn Remembered: The Untold Indian Story of Custer's Last Stand* (New York: Times, 1999); Larry Sklenar, *To Hell With Honor: Custer and the Little Bighorn* (Norman: University of Oklahoma Press, 2000); James Donovan, *Custer and the Little Bighorn: The Man, The Mystery, The Myth* (New York: Crestline, 2001); Jerome Green, *A Stricken Field: The Little Bighorn since 1876* (Norman: University of Oklahoma Press, 2008); James E. Mueller, *Shooting Arrows and Slinging Mud: Custer, the Press, and the Little Bighorn* (Norman: University of Oklahoma Press, 2013).

672. Vine Deloria, *Custer Died For Your Sins: An Indian Manifesto* (New York: Macmillan, 1969); Dee Brown, *Bury My Heart at Wounded Knee: An Indian History of the American West* (1970) (New York: Picador, 2007).

673. For leading New Western History writings, see: Patricia Nelson Limerick, *The Legacy of Conquest: The Unbroken Past of the American West* (New York: W.W. Norton, 1987); Richard White, *"It's Your Misfortune and None of My Own": A New History of the American West* (Norman: University of Oklahoma Press, 1991); Richard W. Etulain, ed., *Writing Western History: Essays on Major Western Historians* (Albuquerque: University of New Mexico Press, 1991); Patricia Limerick, Clyde Milner, and Charles Rankin, eds., *Trails: Toward a New Western History* (Lawrence: University Press of Kansas, 1991); Clyde Milner, Carol O'Connor, and Martha Sandweiss, eds., *The Oxford History of the American War* (New York: Oxford University Press, 1994).

674. Frederick Jackson Turner, *The Frontier in American History* (New York: Dover, 1996).

675. Turner, *Frontier*, 310.

676. Turner, *Frontier*, 3.

Acknowledgments

OF ALL THOSE I WANT TO THANK for producing such a beguiling version of my book, Aaron Downey comes first. Aaron is an outstanding editor—farsighted, meticulous, creative, flexible, and witty. I also extend my deep gratitude to publishers Ross and Susan Humphreys, David Jenney for his beautiful book design, Jason Petho for his excellent maps, and Jim Turner for his careful text review.

Index

About the Author

WILLIAM NESTER is the award-winning author of numerous books on American national security, global politics, military history, and the nature of power. He is a professor at St. John's University in New York.